D1611721

BOSTON STUDIES IN THE PHILOSOPHY OF SCIENCE

VOLUME LVII

PERSONS AND MINDS

SYNTHESE LIBRARY

MONOGRAPHS ON EPISTEMOLOGY,

LOGIC, METHODOLOGY, PHILOSOPHY OF SCIENCE,

SOCIOLOGY OF SCIENCE AND OF KNOWLEDGE,

AND ON THE MATHEMATICAL METHODS OF

SOCIAL AND BEHAVIORAL SCIENCES

Managing Editor:

JAAKKO HINTIKKA, *Academy of Finland and Stanford University*

Editors:

ROBERT S. COHEN, *Boston University*

DONALD DAVIDSON, *University of Chicago*

GABRIËL NUCHELMANS, *University of Leyden*

WESLEY C. SALMON, *University of Arizona*

VOLUME 121

BOSTON STUDIES IN THE PHILOSOPHY OF SCIENCE

EDITED BY ROBERT S. COHEN AND MARX W. WARTOFSKY

VOLUME LVII

JOSEPH MARGOLIS

PERSONS AND MINDS

The Prospects of Nonreductive Materialism

D. REIDEL PUBLISHING COMPANY

DORDRECHT-HOLLAND / BOSTON-U.S.A.

Library of Congress Cataloging in Publication Data

Margolis, Joseph Zalman, 1924—
    Persons and minds.

    (Boston studies in the philosophy of science ; v. 57)
(Synthese library ; v. 121)
    Bibliography: p.
    Includes index.
    1.   Psychology.   2.   Materialism.   I.   Title.
II.   Series.
Q174.B67 vol. 57 [BF41]   501s   [128'.2]   77—16498
ISBN 90—277—0854—1
ISBN 90—277—0863—0 pbk.

Published by D. Reidel Publishing Company,
P.O. Box 17, Dordrecht, Holland

Sold and distributed in the U.S.A., Canada and Mexico
by D. Reidel Publishing Company, Inc.,
Lincoln Building, 160 Old Derby Street, Hingham,
Mass. 02043, U.S.A.

Printed in The Netherlands

For Herbert Feigl,
hospitable antagonist

Persons and Minds is an inquiry into the possibilities of materialism. Professor Margolis starts his investigation, however, with a critique of the range of contemporary materialist theories, and does not find them viable. None of them, he argues, "can accommodate in a convincing way the most distinctive features of the mental life of men and of lower creatures and the imaginative possibilities of discovery and technology" (p. 8). In an extraordinarily rich analysis, Margolis carefully considers and criticizes mind-body identity theories, physicalism, eliminative materialism, behaviorism, as inadequate precisely in that they are reductive. He argues, then, for ramified concepts of emergence, and embodiment which will sustain a philosophically coherent account both of the distinctive non-natural character of persons and of their being naturally embodied. But Margolis provokes us to ask, what is an embodied mind? The crucial context for him is not the plain physical body as such, but culture. "Persons", he writes, "are in a sense not natural entities: they exist only in cultural contexts and are identifiable as such only by reference to their mastery of language and of whatever further abilities presuppose such mastery" (p. 245). The hallmark of persons, in Margolis's account, is their capacity for freedom, as well as their physical endowment. Thus he writes, ". . . their characteristic powers − in effect, their freedom − must inform the order of purely physical causes in a distinctive way" (p. 246).

This is a work that refuses to compromise such distinctive properties of persons by reduction or elimination; and yet holds fast to (non-reductive) materialism. At the same time, Margolis's argument develops a running commentary on contemporary attempts either to bridge this gap, or to deny it. Starting from Feigl's classic formulation (in *The 'Mental' and the 'Physical'*), Margolis proceeds to an informed discussion of the relevant views of Quine, Goodman, Sellars, Putnam, Strawson, Feyerabend, Chisholm, Rorty, Davidson, Fodor, Cornman, David Lewis, and others; of behaviorist and cognitivist approaches to language, mind and action; to a close consideration of physiological and experimental psychology; to reflections on animal psychology; to considerations of the nature of cultural entities; of sensations and intentional states; of the question of the compatibility of freedom with causality.

In short, Margolis's work proposes both a sustained critique of contemporary Anglo-American philosophies of mind and of action; and of the philosophies of science which are correlated with them; as well as the detailed construction of a major alternative to reductive materialism. We think this is an important book — rigorously analytic and deeply humanistic — a vigorous contribution to modern philosophy.

Center for Philosophy and History of Science,   ROBERT S. COHEN
Boston University   MARX W. WARTOFSKY
May 1977

TABLE OF CONTENTS

EDITORIAL PREFACE   VII

PREFACE   XI

ACKNOWLEDGEMENTS   XIII

INTRODUCTION

General Introduction   3

Chapter 1. The Theory of Persons Sketched   11

PART ONE. Mind/Body Identity

Chapter 2. The Relation of Mind and Body   28

Chapter 3. The Identity Theory   34

Chapter 4. Radical Materialism   45

Chapter 5. Materialism without Identity   60

PART TWO. Toward a Theory of Persons

Chapter 6. Problems Regarding Persons   81

Chapter 7. Language Acquisition I: Rationalists vs. Empiricists   97

Chapter 8. Language Acquisition II: First and Second Languages
             and the Theory of Thought and Perception   118

Chapter 9. Propositional Content and the Beliefs of Animals   146

Chapter 10. Mental States and Sentience   171

PART THREE. Sentience and Culture

Chapter 11. Psychophysical Interaction   199

Chapter 12.   The Nature and Identity of Cultural Entities   225

Chapter 13.   Action and Ideology   243

REFERENCES   263

GENERAL INDEX   279

INDEX OF REFERENCES   293

PREFACE

The beginnings of this book go back a long way. As far as I remember my earliest efforts concerned the reconciliation of the ontological and scientific issues laid out so honestly by Herbert Feigl, in his original essay *The 'Mental' and the 'Physical'*, and the then new currents bearing on the asymmetry of first- and third-person accounts of mental states introduced by Ludwig Wittgenstein. What has happened since those early days, frankly, is that, apart from my own growing appreciation of the complexity of the conceptual issues involved, I came to rely on sources not prominently represented in the philosophical traditions associated with my first orientation. These had to do, principally, with my continuing concern with the conceptual puzzles regarding the fine arts, culture, and the acquisition of language and with my developing conviction that no theory of mind and persons was worth its salt without being oriented in terms of biological survival and evolution. The happy result is that I have been forced to read widely in a literature not strictly confined to professional philosophy. I would like to think, therefore, that this book will signify a fresh conceptual vision, of interest to all those who touch, however variously, on the nature of the minds of animals and men and on the cultural distinction of human persons.

I owe a particular debt to Grace Stuart, who, as so many times before, has put the manuscript in final and readable form. And I must thank Donald Callen, a student of mine at Temple University, for spotting both typographical errors and stylistic infelicities.

Philadelphia, Pennsylvania.   J. M.
February 1977.

ACKNOWLEDGEMENTS

Portions of a number of papers that have appeared elsewhere have been incorporated, with alterations, into various chapters. The original papers include: "Proposals Toward a Theory of Persons", in Raphael Stern and Louis Horowitz (eds.), *Ethics, Science and Psychotherapy* (New York: Haven, 1977); "Countering Physicalistic Reduction", *Journal for the Theory of Social Behavior*, VI (1976); "On the Ontology of Persons", *New Scholasticism*, L (1976); "Puccetti on Brains, Minds, and Persons", *Philosophy of Science*, XLII (1975); "Mastering a Natural Language", *Diogenes*, No. 84 (1973); "First- and Second-Language Acquisition and the Theory of Thought and Perception", *Studies in Language*, I (1977); "Behaviorism and Alien Languages", *Philosophia*, III (1973); "The Perils of Physicalism", *Mind*, LXXII (1973).

INTRODUCTION

GENERAL INTRODUCTION

Candor and strategy endorse an explicit argument. The account that follows is committed to a novel and resiliant materialism for the entire range of phenomena said, informally, to be mental or psychological or to concern the distinctive attributes of sentient beings and persons. The novelty lies primarily in resisting reductive tendencies, consistently with a materialist commitment, by way of exploiting a relationship hardly ever mentioned in the literature of what has come to be called the philosophy of mind or philosophical psychology. Standard discussions of the materialist cast characteristically interpret relevant mental and physical predications in terms of an identity relationship between the mental and the physical (or, more recently, allegedly responding to the exigencies of "normal science" or of an impending "scientific revolution" (Kuhn [1970]; Feyerabend [1975]), by eliminating the mental altogether as a *façon de parler*). Assuming the inadequacy of mind/body identity theories and so-called eliminative materialism (R. Rorty [1970]) and assuming the appeal of materialism itself, there appear to be surprisingly congenial and ready ways of accommodating mental phenomena, sentient beings, and persons, if we allow ourselves the advantage of interpreting what confronts us, in terms of the relationship of embodiment and of a correspondingly reasonable constraint on the relationship of composition. Composition is familiar in physical theory, particularly where the relationship between macroscopic bodies like trees and stones and microtheoretical entities like protons and electrons is at stake; but it is rarely considered in the context of analyzing the mental or psychological. And embodiment, though (actually) intuitively and informally appealed to in much of our discourse about cultural phenomena, as for instance in distinguishing between Michelangelo's *David* and the block of marble "in which" it is to be found, is almost never mentioned — let alone used in an explicit and systematic way — in providing an account of the nature of minds and persons. 'Embodiment', we may suppose, is a term of art designed to codify and regularize a distinction that has some inexplicit currency in our ordinary discourse. Strictly speaking, what is required is a distinction between alternative senses of the verb 'is' and its cognates; for we say, casually enough, that A is B, in linguistic contexts where either identity or composition or embodiment (none being equivalent to any of the others) is intended or, of course, where altogether different considerations obtain, predication or spatio-temporal continuity or equivalence or class membership, for instance. These distinctions, fairly characterized as logical or conceptual, may also be construed as ontological inasmuch as they bear in a decisive way on the viability of a materialist account of minds and persons.

About materialism itself, it should be said that, in the sense relevant to the analysis intended though not perhaps in that of other settings, the term must be somewhat generously construed, without risking its traditional force. To characterize a theory as materialistic, in the sense here intended, is not to disallow its making provision for adjustments of at least three distinct sorts: first, for formal or logical or functional states of systems (Putnam [1960]; Fodor [1968]) composed only of physical parts, states defined (though not realized or instantiated) without regard to the physical systems with respect to which they are in some sense associated and without regard to the fact that they may be associated with physical systems of distinctly different sorts, biological organisms or electronic equipment, for instance; second, for changing characterizations of the ultimate "substance" of which gross physical matter is composed, or to which it is related by some suitable alternative principle (Hanson [1963]; Sellars [1963a]); third, for the possibility that we may, elsewhere, need to make ontological concessions favoring nonmaterial abstract entities (numbers, classes, universals, abstract particulars, for instance) that do not entail any (relevant) form of dualism (Quine [1960]; Goodman [1966]). Strategies favoring or disfavoring any or all of these sorts of adjustment are admittedly complex but, by and large, adjustments only of the first sort seem to bear narrowly on the circumscribed issues of philosophical psychology, for instance, on the materialistic interpretation of consciousness. The second seems directed to global theories of matter at a level of discourse far more fundamental than what appears to be required in speaking of sentience, intelligence, intention, and the like: this may not actually be true, of course, in which case the formulation of an adequate materialism will have to wait for a satisfactory characterization of "matter" and "energy". But the third seems to be decidedly indifferent to familiar disputes about dualistic tendencies in accounting for mind/body phenomena.

The details of the materialist theory intended will be supplied in their proper place. But two of its general features should be noted straight off. First of all, though it is compatible with the admission, required by the analysis that follows, that whatever there is or exists is composed only of matter or is suitably related to what is composed only of matter, the theory is not, and is not intended to be, compatible with the strong thesis that all mental and psychological attributes are reducible to physical or material attributes, explainable or analyzable without remainder in terms of such attributes (E. Nagel [1961]). There are several different forms of reductionism relevant here: one, that whatever exists is material in nature, that is, is or is composed of matter alone — what, minimally, in the traditional ontological sense, is treated as materialism; another, that persons and sentient creatures (to narrow the scope of the thesis in the relevant way) are nothing but bodies having nothing but physical attributes — what has come to be called physicalism, the view prominently associated with Hobbes. Physicalism, of course, entails a third, at least partial theory, namely, that all mental and psychological attributes are physical or material attributes even if (as, for instance, in the view of Smart [1962]) mental and psychological predicates are not synonymous with physical or material predicates; those predicates are, on the thesis, thought to be extensionally equivalent (though not, necessarily, always testably so) and, for reasons of theoretical economy, the attributes designated are said to be one and the same. Perhaps the latter theory, which seems to lack a name, may be termed attribute materialism and the traditional theory mentioned above, ontic materialism. In any case, the theory to be proposed is compatible with ontic materialism but not with attribute materialism. Often, since dualism is opposed to materialism, it is claimed that the rejection of attribute materialism is tantamount to the adoption of dualism. If so, so be it. But it ought to be noticed that the reasons for rejecting attribute materialism are utterly different from those urged against ontic materialism, do not commit us to any dualism of *substance*, and are noncommittal, so far forth, about the variety of attributes that may actually be ascribed to anything. On the opposing view, functional materialism would, anomalously, be construed as a form of dualism. The reasons for the contrast will be clearer, later, but we may fix our intuitions at least by remarking that, since chess may be played in all sorts of ingenious and unforeseen ways, there is no equivalence between ascribing a chess move and ascribing any (even a large, determinate disjunction of) physical movements; *a fortiori*, the attributes cannot be identical (Putnam [1960]; Taylor [1964]). In fact, this single instance suggests as well the advantages of a materialism that allows for embodied phenomena. Also, it is sometimes maintained that theories are dualistic if they fail to provide a semantic rule in terms of which all mental and psychological predicates may be shown to be translatable by physical predicates. If this constraint is preferred, then the account that follows is admittedly dualistic; though, if so, then, anomalously once again, explicitly materialistic, even radically reductionistic, accounts like that of

J. J. C. Smart or explicitly anti-dualistic accounts (Ryle [1949]) would also count as forms of dualism. Wilfrid Sellars [1963a], for example, and other reductive materialists openly admit that intentional discourse cannot be reduced to discourse about purely physical phenomena. Such philosophers are sanguine about reductionism because they feel that there are strategies available for neutralizing the effect of the admission. But, for one thing, they have in effect admitted a dualism of attributes — even if in a thin sense of 'attribute'; and for another, if their strategies go awry — which will be shown in due course — then their admission will require a more robust sense of 'attribute' and will undermine their own reductionism. The linguistic abilities of human persons threaten just such a consequence. Again, though ontic dualism preserves a mystery, attribute dualism need not: there may well be quite intelligible conceptual connections between distinct predicative categories even though there be no intelligible ontic connections between radically different substances.

It should be said at once, however, that this talk of ontic and attribute materialism is not meant to give assurance that we have a settled way of deciding either ontic commitment or the nature of what there is (Quine [1953]). On the contrary, there is good reason to believe that we lack a perspicuous way of settling either question (Margolis [1977a]). For instance, on W. V. Quine's view regarding the radical indeterminacy of translation (Quine [1960]), it is possible to construct two incompatible ontologies each fitting a native speaker's utterance under stimulation conditions, without being able to decide conclusively which ontology is the correct one. (A parallel problem arises for the characterization of sets.) If so, we cannot say precisely what any speaker is committed to in speaking as he normally does: he cannot be committed to the entities of all such incompatible ontologies; and we cannot say which set of entities he is committed to. Similar problems arise regarding speakers' intentions, the putative commitments of a theory, alleged ontic commitments at stages in the development of science at which we are reasonably sure our canonical formulations cannot be close to some final explanatory account. Related problems arise as well for the so-called Axiom of Existence (Searle [1969]), the thesis that "whatever is referred to must exist", since, on the argument, we may then not be able (anomalously) to determine what it is we actually *are* referring to, whatever our intentions may be. There appears to be a *reductio ad absurdum* confronting every formulation of John Searle's or Quine's sort.

A second feature of the materialism to be advanced is this: not only is it opposed to the reduction of attributes in the manner sketched, it is also hospitable to the postulation of emergent entities (hence, to the postulation of emergent attributes) that, though linked to entities that are materially composed (that is, the entities, not the attributes), cannot themselves be characterized solely in terms of composition or material attributes. In particular, the theory is hospitable to postulating culturally emergent entities, the existence of which and the intelligibility of the existence of which depend on the admission of a cultural context where the relevant productive forces obtain. The kinds of entities encompassed by the notion of a cultural entity, at least provisionally so classified, include persons, works of art, artifacts, words and sentences, and machines. According to the argument to be provided, such entities are to be treated as both culturally emergent and materially embodied. Persons, for instance, may be roughly distinguished as sentient beings capable of the use of language and of self-reference; they are normally embodied in specimens of *Homo sapiens* but may, in principle, be embodied in electronic gear or, as Martians or dolphins or chimpanzees, the evidence permitting, in other biological forms; and their actually existing depends on culturally qualified causal forces that explain how they come to emerge from the physical bodies in which they are embodied. Possible economies regarding one kind of cultural entity (machines, for instance) cannot be counted on to insure reductive economies regarding other kinds of cultural entity: in particular, there is good reason to think that the analysis of persons is crucial to any wholesale reductionism; after all, all other cultural phenomena are due to the activity of persons.

The coherence of such a way of speaking needs, of course, to be articulated. But it would permit us, within certain constraints, to speak, for instance, of both a certain block of marble and Michelangelo's *David* occupying the same space — or, a person and his body — where, of course (as the example of the *David* economically confirms precisely because it "has no mind"), no dualism is intended. As may be clear already, the scope of the cultural is larger than that of the personal and merely overlaps that of the mental; alternatively put, embodiment and emergence are not restricted to the mental or psychological. Needless to say, it is just the reality of cultural phenomena that is so characteristically ignored or slighted in the great bulk of the literature on the mind/body problem and the problem of the analysis of persons. Notoriously, for example, P. F. Strawson [1959] fails to provide, in his analysis of persons, for the genuinely distinctive cultural import of man's linguistic capacity; his persons turn out to be hardly more than sentient (though intelligent) animals. One may almost say that the bare admission of cultural phenomena shows at a stroke the inadequacy of all forms of radical or reductive materialism. The argument needs to be supplied, of course. But one has only to consider that the complex phenomena of the cultural world depend on intensional distinctions, and that no known strategy for eliminating or neutralizing the intensional – notably, Quine's [1960] effort to sketch a global extensional program for eliminating the opacity of belief contexts – shows the least prospect of success. (We shall return to the issue.)

The assumption underlying this account is, quite simply, that there are no viable forms of materialism that have yet been advanced that accommodate in a convincing way the most distinctive features of the mental life of men and of lower creatures and the imaginative possibilities of discovery and technology; and, that there is no likelihood of formulating an adequate materialism that fails to account for the central mental and psychological phenomena in terms of the concepts of emergence and embodiment. The argument, therefore, seeks to show that an emergentist materialism – if a term is wanted – is internally coherent, viable with respect to the central problems of philosophical psychology, and rather more reasonable than any alternative form of materialism so far developed could claim to be. Materialism itself, as will be seen, obliges us to distinguish among the relationships of identity, composition, and the spatio-temporal continuity of bodies through their changing phases. The cultural emergence of entities entails, as will be seen, embodiment: its admission, therefore, obliges us to sort out the relationship of embodiment from the others mentioned, as well as the distinguishing properties of embodying and embodied entities and the conceptual conditions under which embodied entities are also emergent entities (what, to suggest a useful application, may resolve an unexplained puzzle in Strawson's treatment [1959] of both persons and physical bodies as basic particulars). But it needs also to be noted that mental and psychological phenomena, as in bodily sensation, perception, emotion, and action, which may all be ascribed to animals and infants as well as to full-fledged human persons, do not presuppose cultural emergence, even if their explicit ascription does, that is, the speech act of making ascriptions. The difference between a merely sentient creature and a person, therefore, is of crucial importance, for the former as well as the latter are said, in some sense, to "have a mind". Consequently, it cannot be maintained that all mental and psychological phenomena are culturally emergent; it is possible that all such phenomena should, in some sense, be construed as emergent relative to an inanimate physical world and that, in that regard, further complications will arise regarding composition, continuity, and embodiment. These matters will have to be examined in their place.

Nevertheless, though minds may not be culturally emergent phenomena, even if they be emergent, persons must be culturally emergent — even cyborgs and androids — and the admission of minds may be shown to preclude what has been termed attribute materialism. This is an extremely powerful double point that bears on the range of discovery accessible to neural physiology and, in particular, brain physiology — *a fortiori*, to animal and human behavioral psychology and the social sciences that build upon them. To explore the implications of these conceptual matters should suggest in the most instructive way the bearing of philosophy on the work of the empirical sciences as well as the need for philosophy to respond to the conceptual puzzles that the sciences themselves set. Two central problems may, by their obvious importance, suggest the tactical advantages of the thesis mentioned: one, that of the individuation of persons relative to the data on split-brain phenomena; and two, that of the tenability of attribute materialism relative to "many—many" correlations of the neurological/psychological sort. Both of these issues will be pursued.

The nature of persons and minds is a staggering question. It haunts absolutely every philosophical issue, for the utterly simple reason that every compelling conception about any matter whatsoever is addressed to the minds of human persons. Whatever we take to be *true, we take* to be true. Every philosophical theory is peculiarly incomplete, therefore, if it lacks an explicit account of the nature of minds and persons or at least an account of how determinate claims of a restricted scope are or may be affected by findings of this large sort. For example, the general distinction between so-called rationalist and empiricist theories of language acquisition, prominently associated in various ways with the work of Noam Chomsky [1972] and his opponents, is unintelligible — certainly without any prospect of solution — without a clear analysis of what a rationalist or empiricist theory of the mind might be like or how either might be confirmed or disconfirmed. A general theory of persons, it will be seen, illuminates this troublesome puzzle in a decisive way.

The argument proposed, therefore, is designed to show the viability and relative force of what has here been termed an emergentist materialism. It proceeds in a dual way, by considering the weakness of standard theories — the identity theory, physicalism, eliminative materialism, behaviorism, and the like; and by way of explicating, dialectically, the principal features of mental life that bear on providing a comprehensive account of such phenomena and on appraising the adequacy of competing theories regarding those phenomena — consciousness, sentience, intention, thought, desire, emotion, action, and speech. Finally, the conceptual connection between the philosophy of mind and moral philosophy is sketched, in order to exhibit both how a theory of the nature of persons substantively affects the prospects of the behavioral and historical disciplines and how antecedent convictions regarding the objectivity with which assessments of human behavior are made must be made to cohere with defensible views about the nature of minds and persons. But we must be careful here. It has been neatly put that a fair sense of 'impossible' — regarding efforts to show that a certain philosophical undertaking is an impossible one — is afforded by Gödel's Proof. It can hardly be supposed that, for the most interesting mind/body theories — for instance, versions of the identity theory — one could show that the usual accounts advanced are flatly impossible, in the sense there intended. But we may provide plausible grounds for thinking that such theories are impossible or cannot be possible unless this or that condition is met (which, dialectically considered, may be shown not to have been met, or even noticed, or may be shown not to be clearly manageable on any known strategy). Philosophical arguments normally have that sort of weakness; but in the press of exchange, rather more decisive epithets of approval and rejection are more often than not employed. We shall proceed, first, after sketching the theory here favored, by discounting the identity theory and other forms of radical or reductive materialism. As will be obvious, however, a good many disputes will remain conditional, in that context, simply because there may not be an absolutely knockdown basis on which to show such views to be "impossible" and because the entire argument ultimately takes the form of a plausible and reasoned proposal.

What remains, of course, is the argument.

CHAPTER 1

THE THEORY OF PERSONS SKETCHED

We may begin at the end, so that the intended force of intervening and inevitably piecemeal arguments will be entirely clear. But in doing so, we initially risk, of course, the full detail of those arguments themselves. What is wanted is a fair sketch of a theory of persons, sufficiently focussed to inform and collect the developing argument, sufficiently explicit to suggest what is required in the way of further support, and sufficiently fresh to be worth the effort. Otherwise, though given arguments may be forceful enough, we should miss their larger motivation.

It is notoriously easy to give a provisionally sensible account of what a person is, without being able to manage, in the terms of such an account, all the strenuous issues traditionally associated with mind/body theories and with theories of the individuation and identity of persons. Still, odd as it may seem, there is, among some of the most debated theories of persons, not even an inkling of that distinction. For example, P. F. Strawson [1959] offers a theory of persons, for purposes of sorting the viability of alternative ontologies, in which it is reasonably clear that he provides no distinctions that a higher sentient animal would not meet. And Bernard Williams, who explicitly notes this failure in Strawson (Williams [1973b]), himself pursues the question of the necessary and sufficient conditions for identifying and reidentifying persons without any attention at all to the distinguishing marks of persons *qua* persons — regardless of his sanguine view that persons are identified by means of identifying their bodies (or, certain bodies).

It may be that persons are nothing but physical bodies of a certain sort or sentient creatures of a certain sort; but in order to decide the matter one ought first to provide some of the distinctive features of persons, particularly those that are bound to afford the best test of either of the doctrines mentioned or of others that are similarly engaged. Here, then, two preliminary distinctions may provide an economy: we shall want to be precise about whether (i) we are speaking of persons, sentient organisms, physical bodies or of their parts, whatever their parts may be taken to be; and about whether (ii) we are speaking of persons or of sentient organisms or of physical bodies, whatever may be claimed to be their difference or lack of difference.

The issue may be made instructive by considering an illustration. Robert

Solomon [1974], for instance, in a compelling account of Freud's so-called *Scientific Project*, argues the following: "What persists throughout Freud's work is a neurophysiological model of mind with its neuroanatomical commitments suspended. This is not to say, of course, that there could be neurophysiological processes without a brain and nervous system. It is rather to admit ignorance — along with Freud — of the exact localizability of those physiological processes in the brain and nervous system. What can be maintained with some certainty is that psychological processes are functionally equivalent to some physiological processes without assuming that the arrangement of such processes corresponds in any specifiable way to the anatomical structure of the central nervous system." Further, Solomon says, developing at once both Freud's early conjecture and his own preference: "But now the identity thesis is not the identity of sensations and brain processes any longer, but the identity of the psychic apparatus and the nervous system and their respective functions. This is, of course, exactly what Freud had argued. But what sort of identity is this? At first, we might say that both the psychic apparatus and the nervous system are nothing less than a *person*, that persons are the particulars that have both minds and nervous systems, sensations and brain processes. But this will not quite do. A nervous system is not a person, nor is a psyche a person. We need something less than a person for our locus of identity ... the unspecified organism which is the subject of Freud's *Project*. It is at once the subject of both neurological and psychological predicates. In other words, it is both a nervous system and the psychic apparatus."

Here, a number of things may be noted. First of all, Solomon's account (and Solomon's view of Freud's account) is, at least initially, rather like Strawson's: the subject of both physical and psychological predications is a sentient organism of some sort — explicitly not a person. Hence, on this view, the nature of a person remains unclear. Secondly, Solomon's thesis presupposes that a so-called "psychic apparatus" as well as a "nervous system" may be individuated in a way that is independent, epistemically, of one another, in virtue of which, on the evidence, the ontological identity of what is thus dually designated may be confirmed (cf. Penelhum [1970]). Solomon expressly denies that such an identity, an identity of systems as well as of functions, entails an identity of precisely localizable parts. How this identity is to be established or whether it can really be established, he does not say, though it is clear that numerically distinct systems may have the same (kind of) function. The reason his claim is problematic is simply that it has been thought by both reductive and non-reductive theorists about persons (Williams and Strawson, for instance) that the individuation of persons as well as of minds (if the notion be allowed at all) cannot be achieved without some dependence on the individuation of physical bodies. Solomon's intention to support an identity theory at all costs leads him – accommodating Freud's fertile imagination – to neglect to tell us how first, precisely, to individuate a "psychic apparatus" in order to determine whether it is the same as, or different from, a "nervous system". Thirdly, in arguing for the identity of certain psychic and nervous systems, Solomon must hold – since he expressly denies (given the empirical evidence) that the "parts" of those psychic and nervous systems are or need be identical (whatever we may mean in speaking of psychic "parts") – that both psychic and nervous systems may be assigned functions and, at times, assigned the same function. But it is a fair question to ask, apart from whether such systems may be assigned functions at all, whether they may, coherently, be assigned the same kind of function. For example, it is characteristically maintained – notably, by Freud's own teacher, Franz Brentano [1973] – that mental phenomena are distinguished from physical phenomena in exhibiting the property of intentionality; Brentano in fact considered other putative distinctions between the two, on which he held somewhat varying opinions. But he maintains explicitly that "we ... found *intentional in-existence*, the reference to something as an object, [to be] a distinguishing feature of all mental phenomena. No physical phenomenon exhibits anything similar." There is, therefore, an unexpressed premiss in Solomon's account – to the effect that the apparently essential or characteristic distinction of intentionality can be dismissed or overtaken; for if that were not so, the relevant forms of the identity thesis would be threatened. It would be impossible to assign functions involving intentionality to both psychic and nervous systems; *a fortiori*, it would be impossible to assign the same function (of such a sort). Notably, for example, Brentano does not take "external" perception, the perception of external or public objects to exhibit, as such, intentionality.

Here, the argument may be permitted to take a dialectical form. The identity thesis, read in the most inclusive sense, faces two conceptual barriers at the very least. Granting, provisionally, that persons are not merely sentient organisms – in the straightforward sense in which, for instance, the great apes are not persons – identity theorists must show that sentient organisms are rightly construed as physical bodies of a certain sort *and* that persons are rightly construed as physical bodies of a certain sort or as sentient organisms that themselves are rightly construed as physical bodies of a certain sort. It is an extraordinary fact that Herbert Feigl, who canvassed the mind/body problem as painstakingly as any, has no entry for "persons" in the Index to his important essay, *The "Mental" and the "Physical"* [1967] ; and indeed, he offers no discussion of the distinctive properties of persons in the original *Essay*. In fact, in the Postscript to the *Essay*, Feigl remarks: "Some philosophers feel that the central issue of the mind-body problems is that of intentionality (sapience); others see it in the problem of sentience; and still others in the puzzles of selfhood. Although I have focused my attention primarily on the sentience problem, I regard the others as equally important. But I must confess that . . . the sapience and selfhood issues have always vexed me less severely than those of sentience." In effect, therefore, Feigl confines his reductive enterprise to the first of the two barriers mentioned. His physicalist program is distinguished by the effort to account for (what he terms) "physical$_2$" phenomena. By "physical", he means "the type of concepts and laws which suffice in principle for the explanation and prediction of inorganic processes"; and by "physical$_2$", he means, the extension of "physical" to "the phenomena of organic life". The point of the exercise is to eliminate so-called "nomological danglers", and the admission of biological emergence would have entailed just such danglers relative to the program of physicalism.

Now, even at the first barrier against the identity theory, Feigl concedes (with Wilfrid Sellars) that "*intentional* (in Brentano's sense) features [are] irreducible to a physicalistic description . . . [though] this [he adds] does not seem to me a serious flaw in physicalism." His reason, dependent on Sellars' analysis, is that "this irreducibility is on a par with (if not a special case of) the irreducibility of logical categories to psychological or physiological ones" (cf. Sellars [1965]; [1964]). The trouble is that, though the irreducibility of intentionality may be benign enough, construed as a logical or semantical category, it does not follow that the *intentional properties of sentience or of sentient organisms* can be physicalistically construed *if* such properties are, in some fair sense, essential properties of a range of biological organisms *and if* the logical category of intentionality is admittedly irreducible. It is either irrelevant or unfavorable to the reductive analysis of admittedly psychological properties to note that the logical category of intentionality cannot be reduced psychologically or physiologically. But if this much is so at the first barrier, how much more decisive will it be at the second? On any plausible view of the nature of a person, linguistic ability will have to be marked as as central or as essential as any property that we might assign. In that event, it is not enough to observe that the semantic and syntactic properties of a *language* cannot be reduced psychologically or physiologically; what is at stake, precisely, is *the psychological ability of certain entities to speak*. It looks very much as if, *if* language is irreducible in the manner conceded, then linguistic ability (which is a property of persons) is similarly irreducible. But if that is so, then the identity theory must be conceded to have been dealt a fatal blow.

The fact is that Sellars, on whom Feigl relies, appears to offer a patently inadequate theory of persons (or sketch of such a theory). Here is one formulation of Sellars' [1963a] view: "A person can almost be defined as a being that has intentions. Thus the conceptual framework of persons is not something that needs to be *reconciled with* the scientific image [that is, an advanced materialistic schema], but rather something to be *joined* to it. Thus, to complete the scientific image we need to enrich it *not* with more ways of saying what is the case, but with the language of community and individual intentions, so that by construing the actions we intend to do and the circumstances in which we intend to do them in scientific terms, we *directly* relate the world as conceived by scientific theory to our purposes, and make it our world and no longer an alien appendage to the world in which we do our living." This would be plausible only if (what is contrary to fact) the agents who make intentional ascriptions make them only for an observed and independent population and never (or never need to) make them for themselves. The intentionality of the scientific endeavor itself must be a further instance of "what is the case", of what one's activity can be factually "described" as exhibiting. Contrary to Sellars, then, the puzzle is, precisely, to "reconcile" intentionality with the scientific image, not to "add" or "join" the one to the other, because the adding or joining is itself to be explained. And although Feigl does observe that Stephan Körner and Roderick Chisholm both press the irreducibility of the intentional, Körner [1966] expressly opposes the reduction of intentional phenomena at the same time that he urges that "the very nature of the natural sciences is to ignore intentionality and thus human nature in so far as it is mental and not only physical." If so, his view threatens the scope of science. And Chisholm's [1967] discussion of intentionality tends at the very least to reinforce the barrier.

But all of these views skirt the distinction between sentient organisms and persons. There are a great many candidate distinctions regarding persons. Intentionality is, in fact, somewhat ambiguous. For if consciousness, sentience, desire, belief, and intention are ascribable to some sub-set of biological organisms other than man, then intentionality is not a distinguishing feature of persons as such but obtains already on the level of sentient organisms. In Sellars' account, however, it is reasonably clear that the "irreducibility of the personal is [approximately] the irreducibility of the 'ought' to the 'is' ";

Sellars also says, along the same lines, that "the fundamental principles of a community, which define what is 'correct' or 'incorrect', 'right' or 'wrong', 'done' or 'not done', are the most general intentions of that community with respect to the behavior of members of the group". So it is clear that Sellars means to consider that range of intentional phenomena that is restricted to entities that may be called persons, roughly, to beings (i) that can understand and follow rules, (ii) that are capable of using language, (iii) that can make intensional distinctions, (iv) that can impose normative constraints upon themselves, (v) that can judge reflexively, (vi) that are capable of choice and of assuming responsibility. These need not (and undoubtedly are not) altogether independent distinctions. But they are certainly among the most usual distinctions drawn, and they oblige us to consider that the term 'intentional' may be used equivocally in speaking of sentient and of linguistic abilities. In a fair sense, linguistic capacity is the most fundamental — assuming, that is, that the intensional is linguistic, that rule-governed distinctions are both intentional and intensional, that the normative is also intensional, that reflexive judgment presupposes linguistic ability, and that choice and responsibility presuppose reflexive judgment and the capacity to follow rules. The irony is that, so seen, Sellars's and Feigl's admission of the irreducibility of language may well be viewed as an unintended concession to the untenability of the identity thesis regarding persons and bodies or persons and sentient creatures. That is, on the argument, their own reductionism is defeated out of their own mouths.

There is a further advantage to our account. For, Sellars's theory may be characterized as a *forensic* theory of persons, in the sense John Locke first advanced — except that (a most important consideration) Sellars, but not Locke, construes persons solely as forensic entities. Locke [1894], that is, construes the term 'person' as a forensic term, "appropriating actions and their merit; and so belongs only to intelligent agents capable of a law, and happiness, and misery. This personality extends itself beyond present existence to what is past, only by consciousness — whereby it becomes concerned and accountable; owns and imputes to itself past actions, just upon the same ground and for the same reason that it does the present." Locke's view, then, is that persons are constituted as such precisely in virtue of first forming a "self", by means of "identity of consciousness". Whatever difficulties this may have generated for Locke, that Joseph Butler was so quick to expose, the fact remains that Locke's intuition treats the forensic import of being a person as a consequence of its other properties, whereas Sellars seems to regard persons as the result of no more than christening or treating things as responsible members of a community. This is the essential significance of Sellars' distinction between "reconciling" persons with the scientific image and merely "joining" them to it. Were his theory more full-blooded, Sellars (and Feigl with him) could not have dismissed the problem of persons so readily. It would have obliged both to consider alternatives to the identity theory. In effect, Sellars concedes that the intentional is physicalistically irreducible. But it is unresponsive of Sellars to take the irreducibility of the category of the intentional to be no threat to physicalism if what is at stake is the irreducibility of the inherently intentional (intentionally characterized) *abilities* and *attributes* of persons. A parallel argument may be constructed for the intentional properties of sentience or of sentient organisms — which is not to say that the sense in which sentience is intentional is the same as the sense in which linguistic ability is intentional. (Let us concede, at this point, that the term 'intentional' is equivocal. But, although the intentionality of the linguistic cannot be construed as the same as the intentionality of the sentient, it is the first that is of decisive importance here.)

If, then, it is, on the preceding sketch, a fair theory of persons to treat them essentially as linguistically competent beings, the question immediately arises as to whether persons are natural entities. The sense of the question is important. If we regard the "natural" as that which can be explained in Feigl's sense of the "physical" or of whatever can be explained in Feigl's sense of the "physical$_2$", then there is some reason for thinking that persons are not as such natural entities. The reason is this: there appears to be no physical or physical$_2$ account of language and linguistic competence, and we have just seen that Feigl, Sellars, Körner, and Chisholm acknowledge a certain critical irreducibility. The principal line of argument against the conclusion that persons, primarily human persons, by default — not members of *Homo sapiens* — are not natural entities is the one developed by Noam Chomsky. In reviewing his theory of linguistic universals, that man's mind by nature is so structured that all so-called natural languages are determinate articulations of an innate or native set of invariant rules, Chomsky [1972] reflects: "I have been using mentalistic terminology quite freely, but entirely without prejudice as to the question of what may be the physical realization of the abstract mechanisms postulated to account for the phenomena of behavior or the acquisition of knowledge [in particular, the acquisition of language]. We are not constrained, as was Descartes, to postulate a second substance when we deal with phenomena that are not expressible in terms of matter in motion, in his sense. Nor is there much point in pursuing the question of psychophysical parallelism, in this connection. It is an interesting question whether the functioning and evolution of human mentality can be accommodated within the framework of physical explanation, as presently conceived, or whether there are new principles, now unknown, that must be invoked, perhaps principles that emerge only at higher levels of organization than can now be submitted to physical investigation. We can, however, be fairly sure that there will be a physical explanation for the phenomena in question, if they can be explained at all, for an uninteresting terminological reason, namely that the concept of 'physical explanation' will no doubt be extended to incorporate whatever is discovered in this domain, exactly as it was extended to accommodate gravitational and electromagnetic force, massless particles, and numerous other entities and processes that would have offended the common sense of earlier generations." The point may be conceded — but only up to a point. It is not in the least obvious that "*whatever* is discovered in this domain" can be counted on to enlarge the concept of "physical explanation". In particular, Chomsky's linguistic universals are rules and not laws of nature, not only in the sense that they may be violated and conformed to — and therefore behave intensionally — but also in the sense that, in principle, on Chomsky's own view, alternative and nonequivalent rules could, contingently, have replaced the putative rules Chomsky claims to have approximated. Chomsky holds, then, that "deep structures of the sort postulated in transformational-generative grammar are real mental structures"; but he also maintains that "the person who has acquired knowledge of a language has internalized a system of rules that relate sound and meaning in a particular way". The trouble is that, *if* intentionality and, in particular, the intensionality of language and of rules are irreducible, *then there can be no purely physical explanation of the psychological capacity of human beings to behave linguistically.* This is the essential issue between so-called rationalists and empiricists (cf. Margolis [1973c]). Dialectically, then, if the puzzles of intentionality can not be overtaken, we must look to alternative theories of the relationship between persons and physical bodies or between persons and sentient organisms. But to concede this much, we may observe very briefly, is to begin to take a radically different view from the one that appeals to reductionists, regarding the relationship between the physical and cultural sciences. The unity of science may still be a viable objective, but its nature would have to be strikingly different from the thesis favored by its early advocates (Neurath *et al.* [1955]). In particular, all those disciplines that depend on admitting the linguistic abilities of human persons would not be reducible (in the sense favored by Feigl) to the terms of the principal physical sciences.

A promising "empiricist" suggestion is this. Assuming that persons are distinguished by their linguistic competence and that such competence is culturally acquired, regardless of whatever *innate lawlike* regularities may facilitate such acquisition, then persons are culturally emergent entities that are, to be sure, physically embodied — that is, embodied in physical bodies or in sentient organisms. These proposals call out for clarification, of course, but the strategy intended deserves to be reviewed. The argument is, first of all, dialectically linked to the admission of the irreducibility of the intentional, once it is clear that that admission infects the explanation of intentionally qualified psychological phenomena — in particular, the phenomena of linguistic and other rulelike behavior. The concession is granted by some of the most strenuous advocates of the identity thesis; but, on the foregoing argument, it clearly threatens that thesis. Hence, secondly, the present proposal rejects the identity thesis. But it does not and need not reject materialism, if we understand by materialism the theory that whatever exists (or at least whatever exists for the range of putative entities including persons, sentient organisms, plants, physical bodies, subatomic particles, machines, works of art, and the like) is *composed of* matter (cf. Wiggins [1967]) or of whatever matter itself can be reduced to (recalling Chomsky's warning about massless particles) or is suitably linked to whatever is composed of matter (as by embodiment). So the admission of persons as culturally emergent does not in the least entail the admission of a substance other than matter out of which, dualistically, persons are composed. Thirdly, then, the recommended thesis, though entirely hospitable to materialism, is opposed to reductive materialism, in the precise sense intended by Feigl's program. In that sense, persons are emergent entities; and in that sense also, the explanation of the competence and behavior of persons introduces "nomological danglers". The justification for this, however, is that just these very danglers were already inadvertently admitted by the advocates of reductionism insofar as they acknowledged the irreducibility of intentionality. Fourthly, the theory of persons mentioned is not intended to be restricted to human persons only. On the theory, it is entirely possible, as with feral children, that some human animals never yield human persons; and that other creatures — chimpanzees, dolphins, Martians — may be persons or incipient persons or that some advanced machines may come to exhibit the competence of persons. In all of these cases, we would have to postulate a context of culture in which the entities in question were trained or groomed or perhaps even constructed. Finally, it should be clear that a theory of persons is, in effect, a sketch of a theory of culture. For, on the thesis proposed, it is only by training certain biologically gifted animals in culturally significant ways – in particular, training such animals in a cultural context in which they can learn to speak (however they do that), that the only persons that we are presently aware of actual emerge. We can guess, therefore, that there must be some relatively congruent account of whatever culturally significant products, arrangements, activities result from the life of a community of persons. What this suggests is that any proposal regarding the unity of science, admitting the concessions of Feigl and Sellars, must be clearly separated from proposals regarding the relevant forms of reductionism (cf. Neurath *et al.* [1955]). The venture, therefore, suggests a comparatively large landscape. But it is just for the sake of systematically large advantages of such sorts that one is willing to tinker with innovative forms of materialism.

A brief aside may afford a feeling of the plausibility and range of our suggestion. Works of art are among the most distinctive products of human culture. But it is very clear, admitting the irreducibility of the intentional, that poems for instance exhibit certain inherent intentional properties as of the significance of the words of which they are composed, their historically qualified style, and their inherent purposiveness. No purely physical account of language can be supported; and words and sentences themselves cannot be reduced to mere physical marks or sounds. It seems reasonable to consider, therefore, that words and sentences are embodied in physical sounds and physical marks and are culturally emergent items of some sort; and that, correspondingly, poems are culturally emergent items of some sort embodied in some admittedly complex way in arrangements of sound or physical marks (Margolis [1977c]). The details that need to be worked out here would take us too far afield. But what we can see is that the cultural domain includes persons as principal agents and whatever persons may produce: works of art, linguistic episodes, *certain* kinds of organization (political states, for instance). A good approximation to the similarity between persons and what they produce or do may be fixed by characterizing persons as entities capable of following rules – hence, of recognizing, inventing, revising, violating, conforming to rules (Schwayder [1965]; Lewis [1969]); and by characterizing the products, arrangements, actions of persons as that which is rule-governed or rulelike – hence, as calling for interpretation in accord with the rulelike regularities by which communities of persons are guided (traditions, customs, institutions, practices and the like). The upshot is that just as it is the inherent intentionality of psychological phenomena and, in particular, of the linguistic competence of persons that threatens to undermine the prospects of reductive materialism, so too, the inherent intentionality of language, art, cultural behavior and organization produces a comparable difficulty. Roughly then, intentionality of the cultural sort may be said to be bifocal, exhibited both in the rule-following capacities of persons and in the rule-governed or rulelike properties of what persons produce or do. Furthermore, to emphasize the need for a unified theory of culture — linking persons and what persons produce — dramatizes what is characteristically neglected in familiar reductionistic programs (cf. Smart [1962]) as well as the potential economy of replacing identity versions of materialism with other varieties. Certainly, the distinctive features of medicine, psychotherapy, the law, ethics, politics, art, history, and religion seem thereby initially more open to accommodation.

As far as materialism is concerned, it seems, now, entirely fair to view all culturally distinctive properties as functional properties (Putnam [1960]; Fodor [1968]) ascribed to suitable entities. *If*, that is, intentionality is irreducible and *if* the rule-governed and rule-following forms of intentionality can only be ascribed to suitable culturally emergent entities, then, clearly, the admission of persons, works of art, and the like cannot possibly threaten materialism as such. The rubric for speaking of persons and their activities may, then, be instanced in the following way: when a person P speaks, the linguistic utterance U produced is assigned to P; P is embodied in a certain physical body and, derivatively, P's linguistic utterance U is embodied in a certain physical event; P is characterized in terms of certain functional competences and their exercise, and U is characterized in terms of certain functional properties dependent on P's competence. Hence, no dualistic intrusions are required, and the original concession of Feigl and Sellars is suitably incorporated into a more fine-grained theory. The functional properties of, say, utterances U and U' need not, in principle, vary with the embodiments of U and U' — which is a neglected part of what we mean in speaking of two statements conveying the same proposition or of two performances being of the same piece of music (cf. Margolis [1977b], [1977c]). It is, also, of course, entirely possible to speak of functional (and of intentional) properties below the level of culture — that is, not genuinely rule-following or rule-governed properties — and to assign such properties, for example purposive or informational properties, to natural sentient systems of some sort. But what we have been drawing attention to, here, is the need a certain subset of intentional or functional properties imposes upon us to explore the prospects of a non-reductive materialism. So that if, by some strategy, the biological could, in Feigl's sense, be reduced to the physical, it would by no means follow that culturally emergent phenomena — persons, in particular — could also be thus reduced.

What, then, of persons and their properties? Persons are emergent entities in the benign sense that, possessing the properties of linguistic competence, other rule-following abilities, and other attributes presupposing such abilities, they possess properties essentially lacking in purely physical bodies and in mere biological organisms. Furthermore, on the assumption of the irreducibility of the rulelike, the culturally significant capacities and behavior of persons are emergent in the more important systematic respect that they cannot be explained in physical or physical$_2$ terms, in Feigl's sense (Meehl and Sellars [1956]). They may be explained, however, on the assumption that the initial conditions under which they emerge and the effective causal forces adduced are themselves so qualified that elements functionally informed in the appropriate rulelike ways are admitted into the explanans. Alternatively put, only the necessary physical or physical$_2$ conditions of cultural events may be specified. For example, a speaker of English may, under favorable conditions, bring it about that a languageless child gradually masters English. Hence, the causal explanation of culturally emergent phenomena may be said to depend on the admission of embodied cultural phenomena (or on some equally adequate alternative), relative to which the appropriate functionally qualified forces may be specified. Furthermore, since the emergent entities are physically or biologically embodied and distinguished only functionally, the relevant laws of cultural explanation (whatever they may be) will be congruent with (though not reducible to) the physical or biological laws governing their embodying entities. A child must learn language, then, in some way that is congruent with the way in which physical forces operate on the neurophysiological organization of his body and brain. The admission of cultural emergence harbors no mysteries except empirically contingent ones – for instance, regarding the physical gifts on which our linguistic abilities critically depend. Once again, then, there is no question that these admissions fundamentally affect the prospects of the unity of science. It is not so much that there is no methodological unity to the sciences – the behavioral and social sciences as well as physics, chemistry, and astronomy (and, controversially, biology) – as that we are unclear how to formulate the nature of that unity. On the argument, whatever it may be, it cannot be captured in terms adequate to the purely physical sciences themselves, cannot be captured in terms of the extremes supported by reductive materialism.

The quarrelsome and explicitly novel notion, then, is that of embodiment. But whatever may be made of that notion, it must be stressed that the concept of a person cannot, as Sellars' view seems to imply, be introduced as a merely theoretical concept, this is, as a concept introduced in order to explain what is directly observed or reportable *or* merely to "add" some theoretically defined role to what is observable or reportable. The reason is not merely that "it is characteristic of *bona fide* theoretical entities that statements asserting that they *are* theoretical entities must invariably be contingent," that "claims about *inferences* to *T* [a theoretical entity] can be true only where talk about *observations* of *T* makes sense" (Fodor [1968]); it is rather that the concept of a person cannot be introduced at all if not reflexively, that is, to fix our own agency in reporting, experiencing, and performing in whatever way we do. We may be uncertain about the nature of what a person is, but at all costs our theory must accommodate the full range of our first-person encounters (cf. Cornman [1968a]). Hence, the effort either to "reconcile" persons with the scientific image or to "join" them to it must count as such an encounter. Sellars, it must be remembered, maintains, in his well-known summary of "Empiricism and the Philosophy of Mind" (Feigl and Scriven [1956]) preceding his correspondence on intentionality, with Chisholm (Sellars and Chisholm [1958]), that in that paper he argued "for the legitimacy of theoretical concepts in *behavioristic psychology*, and then . . . suggested that our pre-scientific or common sense concepts of 'inner' (mental) episodes began as something analogous to theoretical concepts introduced to explain certain forms of observable behavior." It does not help matters that Sellars adds, there, that he had also argued "that though the framework of thoughts began as a 'theory' and was used as theories are used, it subsequently acquired, in a manner the general principle of which is readily understood, a reporting role". For the issue at stake calls directly for a reporting or describing role that cannot be postponed any later than the introduction of theoretical concepts themselves. This, it may fairly be claimed, is closely connected with Chisholm's objection to Sellars's account of the connection between language and thought; and this is precisely what, assuming the irreducibility of intentionality (Chisholm [1955–56]; Sellars and Chisholm [1958]), invites us to investigate forms of materialism that eschew identity. One of the by-benefits, of course, on which Sellars and Chisholm appear to agree, is that the admission of intentional concepts precludes the adequacy of logical behaviorism with respect to the analysis of mind (Fodor [1968]; Chomsky [1959]; Margolis [1973b]).

Consider, now, embodiment. The thesis at stake is that one particular, a person, is embodied in another particular, a physical body or sentient organism. Since persons are said to be culturally emergent entities, their characteristic functional distinctions — rule-following attributes — are ascribed to entities (persons) adequate to such predication, in the sense that their very existence is and can be explained only in terms of cultural training or the like and not in physical or physical$_2$ terms. To say that a person is embodied in a physical body or sentient organism is to gain all the advantages of identification afforded by the extensional treatment of bodies and organisms. But if persons are distinguished in terms of culturally functional attributes — fundamentally, linguistic ability — then it is clear that persons cannot as such be composed of material parts, though being embodied in physical bodies or sentient organisms, they are embodied in what is thus composed and in *that* sense are composed of nothing but matter. So seen, embodiment provides a resolution of Strawson's well-known puzzle regarding the relationship of physical bodies and persons. For Strawson [1959] insisted, but utterly without clarification, that persons were "primitive" entities or "basic particulars", not to be understood as analyzable for instance as "a secondary kind of entity" joining "a particular consciousness and a particular human body" — in effect, dualistic, unanalyzable entities. Since, however, physical bodies are also primitives for Strawson, the threat of dualism remains regardless of what he says; or, alternatively, the threat of reductionism. The embodiment thesis admits of a *relationship* between persons and their bodies, precisely because persons like bodies are particulars. Strawson rightly opposed construing a person as "an animated body or . . . an embodied anima". But it is possible to view persons as primitive or basic particulars and at the same time to concede a relationship between persons and bodies. The clue lies in the fact (i) that persons are emergent entities; and (ii) distinguished only in functional terms. For actual functions must be linked with actual physical bodies. One cannot, for example, speak without actually uttering sounds or the like. The functional distinction of persons cannot actually obtain, therefore, except insofar as persons are physically embodied. Dualism, which haunts Strawson's account, presupposes the independence of two substances; but the embodiment thesis makes the primitive status of persons ontologically dependent (though not reducible). What we may say, heuristically, if the analogy is not too distracting, is that Sellars's theory of persons is that they are *modal entities*, in a sense loosely like that in which modal operators, though not sentences themselves, produce, when simply added to well-formed sentences, new and distinctive well-formed sentences. And Strawson's theory is that they are *atomic entities*, in a sense loosely like that in which atomic sentences are neither truth-functional compounds nor (perhaps less conventionally) modal sentences. But, on the foregoing argument, persons cannot be either "modal" or "atomic", since they are complex entities that *emerge* from a certain cultural process. Persons and all the other cultural entities are functionally emergent entities that cannot exist except embodied in physical bodies or sentient organisms. Hence, embodiment both favors materialism and precludes a dualism of substances; but once emergent, persons exhibit relationships with their own bodies and may even causally produce (as in neurosis and depression) changes in their bodies.

The embodiment relation is, therefore, *sui generis*: signifies a use of 'is' distinct from that of identity and composition. It is nonsymmetrical and irreflexive; and questions of transitivity seem not to arise. So embodied and embodying entities are (i) numerically distinct though (ii) not (both) ontologically independent of one another. Granting (ii), it follows (iii) that embodied entities have at least some of the attributes of their embodying entities. This of course corresponds completely with Strawson's distinction (1959) between P-predicates and M-predicates; it also explains the benign sense in which a person and his body may occupy the same space and in which a person and his body may have the very same property (not merely the same kind of property). Nevertheless, if the force of (i) and (ii) be granted, then (iv) embodied particulars must possess properties of a kind that embodying particulars cannot possess. So embodiment accommodates cultural emergence.

These, then, seem to form a coherent and distinctive set of features. They are preeminently exhibited by persons and other culturally emergent entities — works of art, words and sentences, artificial persons. But whether there is a use for the embodiment relationship where other than culturally functional attributes are concerned may be duly noted as a fair question. Once again, the principal advantage of our scheme is that it forces us to attend, in the face of reductionistic temptations, to the most distinctive aspects of human existence. Symptomatically, Strawson, who falls just short of the conception, emphasizes that consciousness and corporeal characteristics may jointly be ascribed to persons; Strawson adds that they may and must be able to be self-ascribed in the same sense in which they are ascribed to others. But his reason for so saying concerns the rejection of a private language rather than the clarification of the nature of a person. In this sense, his account is defective in a way that is remarkably like that of Sellars's. The point is that, insofar as science is itself a cultural enterprise, its very admission constitutes a barrier against reductive materialism — which is characteristically ignored simply because the resultant propositions of science, and not the human effort in affirming them, commands our attention.

This, then, may serve as the sketch of a new theory of persons.

PART ONE

MIND/BODY IDENTITY

CHAPTER 2

THE RELATION OF MIND AND BODY

The point of raising the identity theory is, frankly, to dismiss it. But it remains the most convenient way to board the central controversies regarding the nature of minds and persons. If we ask ourselves how mind and body are related, we come at once to see not only the potential bias of the question but also its complexity. For one thing, the terms 'mind' and 'body' seem to designate particular things that exist or kinds of existing things; and it has not always been thought obvious that this use is justified. For example, one need not, in admitting that Peter has a pain, be obliged to admit that there are such things as pains, that pains are actual entities of some sort. One might well argue that our English idiom misleads us and that, in a language in which, say, we could characterize what is true of Peter by saying "Peter pained" or "Peter sensed painly" (Cornman [1971]), the temptation to speak of pains as actual entities will have been weakened or even eliminated. Motivation here may be both ontological and epistemological: ontological, because the admission of pains as actual entities drives us, on the face of it, to a dualism of substances or to some form of idealism — since felt sensations (perhaps, more strongly, sensations that exist only in that they are felt: *esse est sentiri*) are thought to be particularly difficult to characterize as material entities (R. Rorty [1965]); epistemological, because admitting the peculiar interior status of sensations or replacing that idiom with the verbal or adverbial idiom suggested may force or encourage us to adopt or to reinforce certain favored views of sentient knowledge (the view that we have indubitable private knowledge of our "immediate" sensations, for instance Baier [1962], or even a solipsistic view) that might well be quarrelsome in other ways.

The problem, however, is decidedly more complex. For it is a fact that we cannot, in ordinary English (and in as neutral a metaphysical spirit as we can command), qualify someone's having a pain, the pain that he has, or the experience of having a pain, in a way that perspicuously allows us to match the ordinary entailments we should concede with what could be straightforwardly deduced in accord with our elementary logical canons. For example, if "having a pain" and "having a sharp pain" were predicated of Peter, we should, as we now understand the matter, have to regard each predicate expression as indissoluble or monadic; but in that case, we should not be able to deduce from 'Peter has a sharp pain', the sentence 'Peter has a pain' — which seems minimally required by our logical intuitions and which we should (still conventionally) expect our canonical paraphrases to preserve. No, the grammatical convenience of referring to pains as "entities" is also a logical convenience: if we predicate of a pain that it is sharp and of long duration, we can straightforwardly infer that it is sharp. *If* we wish to permit the grammatical and logical convenience sketched, to save the range of things we are prepared to say (Kenny [1963]; Davidson [1969b], [1967b]), then we should treat reference or denotation (in the sense that we designate what we are speaking about, what it is we are making predications of) as a purely grammatical activity (Margolis [1973a], [1977a]), utterly neutral to the question of the existence of entities or of ontic import or commitment (*contra* Searle [1969] and Quine [1960]). The complications are not negligible but they can be managed. For our present purpose, we should merely allow that to speak of pains does not as such entail a threat to materialism, because it does not as such convey any ontological preference at all. The logical peculiarity noted suggests, rather, that certain constructions of natural languages are generated for the sake of economies internal to their flexible use rather than for the sake of simply picturing the ontological commitments of those who use them (Alston [1958]).

A similar, though also somewhat different, challenge may be made about the use of 'body' alleged to designate particular physical objects. It has sometimes been held that so-called physical objects, gross or macroscopic physical objects like trees and dogs and stones and planets, are not themselves entities that actually exist but convenient fictions that facilitate our reference to what really exists: on prominent alternative views, our reference to whatever is discriminated in primitive or direct or fundamental perception (so-called sense data, as in the view of Russell [1918] and Ayer [1940]) or to whatever is most fundamental to the explanatory theories of the physical sciences (so-called micro-theoretical entities, as in the view of Sellars [1963a]). Questions about the existence of mental entities and gross physical entities are not entirely parallel, simply because doubts about the very existence of mental entities are generated with relatively full confidence in the existence of physical entities and because doubts about macroscopic physical objects are generated with a view to providing the most economically reductive and comprehensive theory of the nature of physical objects and physical phenomena themselves.

The chief sense in which we are puzzled about the mind is the sense in which the admission of mental phenomena may be systematically related to

our relatively settled theories of physical phenomena; and the sense in which
an adequate theory of matter and energy still eludes us (along the lines
suggested earlier on, regarding a generous reading of 'materialism') is emphatically not one in which the complications posed by the nature of mind
may be expected to alter the impact of the challenges compared. At least the
argument is wanting. In this context, the admission of indeterminism in
physics is sometimes taken, quite misleadingly, as a basis for human freedom,
and the admission of the equations bearing on the transformability of matter
and energy, as a basis for some form of ultimate idealism, perhaps even
conventional theologies. Materialism holds sway in the domain of the physical
sciences, even if in the generous sense identified; but what the proper account
of mental and psychological phenomena may be and how such an account
may be coherently linked to the materialism prevailing elsewhere are just the
questions that must be confronted. Nothing else could possibly explain the
variety of ontological speculation about the mind.

But our original question also suggests that the terms 'mind' and 'body'
range over relatively homogeneous phenomena, and this is by no means
obvious. For instance, mental phenomena include dreams, pains, emotions,
moods, intentions, mental calculations, thoughts, beliefs; also, other phenomena, not easily called mental but certainly psychologically qualified − such as
actions, behavior, perception − invite characterization in mental terms. In
fact, the single most suggestive demarcation among mental phenomena
concerns intentionality (Brentano [1973]). On Descartes's view, for instance,
both sensations and beliefs were counted equally as forms of thinking. But
belief necessarily takes an intentional object ('S believes that . . .') whereas
sensation (in the non-perceptual sense) does not ('S felt pain' or 'S pained' or
'S sensed painly'). It is instructive to note as well that, on Brentano's view,
what we ordinarily call perception, that is, the perception of an external
public object (of some suitable sort) does not exhibit the intentionality of
mental phenomena; "Strictly speaking", he maintains, "external perception is
not perception"; "inner perception [*Wahrnehmung*] is . . . the only kind of
perception which is immediately evident." So it is not clear that even *if* there
were entities of the mental or psychological sort, such entities would, or
would have to, be related to physical entities in a uniform way; a corresponding caution, of course, obtains even if we deny that there are mental entities
and even if we have some uncertainty about what, precisely, may be said to
exist with regard to our talk of physical objects. Clarity about our provisional
commitments is surely required, but if science and philosophical progress
depended on settling with certainty the nature of what there is, there would,

quite frankly, be very little prospect of even modest gains. In any case, assuming the ontic neutrality of mere grammatical reference, materialism requires that seeming mental entities be reinterpreted somehow, predicatively, in terms of physical bodies or of entities composed of matter or of entities at least suitably related to entities composed of matter. The constraint threatens to become vacuous.

Here, then, we must proceed dialectically. If it were provisionally held that there are mental and physical entities or that mental and physical states are real states, we should quite naturally — for instance, following Smart [1962] — inquire whether and in what sense they could be said to be identical. (We shall continue to speak of whatever may be said to exhibit the relation of self-identity as "entities", though, as has been suggested, so speaking is intended to be ontologically neutral: we may, for instance, wish to speak of properties and states as self-identical.) But even to allow this much draws us at once to admit the heterogeneity of what may qualify as an entity of the physical or material sort. For, Smart's solution requires an identity of *states*; and states (and processes and events, for that matter), though they may be material entities of some sort, cannot be classified as physical objects — as, stones, planets, trees, and dogs. The upshot is that even if an identity theory were vindicated (or, as with R. Rorty [1965], a form of eliminative materialism, that is, an identity theory *manqué*), we should still have to ask ourselves the nature of what it is that is thus identified. Are we speaking of bodies, states, processes, events, compositional parts, substances, or attributes as self-identical? Clearly, the scope of any would-be reductive program is at stake. Nevertheless, if we admit mental and psychological "entities" (in the sense given), we are bound to consider whether they are or are not identical with physical or material entities.

This shows at a stroke how much there is in common among dualists like Descartes and contemporary metaphysical monists like Smart and Armstrong [1968]. For, philosophers of both sorts are convinced that there are actual mental and physical entities and wish only to sort the evidence to decide whether given mental entities are one and the same as given physical entities or whether they are not. Thus, Hobbes, still in the spirit of Descartes's philosophical orientation but irresistibly attracted by the need for conceptual economy, insists that the mind is nothing but matter in motion; and, in the *same* spirit, Berkeley provides, against Locke, an idealist reduction of physical objects to "ideas". So, materialism and idealism are simply alternative forms of monism that concede basic entities of some favored sort; other possibilities, neutral monism, say, suggest the limits of the endeavor (Vesey [1964] ;

Spicker [1970]).

But there are other eligible maneuvers. For example, granting the heterogeneity of mental and psychological phenomena, it is quite conceivable that
persons should be entertained as independent entities (inviting, therefore, the
appraisal of straightforward versions of the identity theory or of eliminative
materialism) and that pains should be treated only predicatively. Or, the distinction between the mental and the physical might well be construed in
terms of relatively closed and exclusive modes or domains of discourse (as for
instance, in rather different ways, seems to be endorsed by Ryle [1949],
Bergmann [1962], Brodbeck [1963], [1966], and even Spinoza). The difficulty of the latter maneuver is, however, just that it characteristically avoids
or rejects discourse in which reference to the mental and the physical are
mingled, as in psychophysical causal claims (Broad [1925]) or as in the
analysis of persons, that appear to require the joint admission of physical and
psychological attributes (Strawson [1959]); in short, though its sponsors are
not, strictly speaking, ontic dualists, they do nevertheless fail to satisfy us in
just the area of inquiry in which traditional dualists have so notoriously
failed.

What needs to be stressed, principally, is that the appeal of ontological
economy does not, on the face of it, drive us to prefer a version of the
identity theory or of eliminative materialism. It leads us, first, to prefer
monism to dualism in order to avoid mystification regarding relationships
between distinct substances: ontic dualism, in this sense, is invariably an
admission of failure. And it leads us, secondly, to prefer materialism to
idealism (or, neutral monism) because the motivation of a monistic account
cannot reasonably exclude an interest in unifying our theory of the mind
with the strong achievements of the physical sciences. Needless to say, to the
extent that the sciences are alleged to be compatible with non-materialistic
accounts (Cornman [1962]), the preference of materialism is conditional; but
that issue is a separate one. It is simply a mistake — or rather, a weakness of
imagination — to suppose that there are no viable forms of materialism other
than that of the identity theory or, more radically, of eliminative materialism.
Merely to have introduced relationships other than identity in order to
facilitate our analysis of the mental and the psychological, in particular, the
relations of composition, embodiment, and emergence, fixes the gap in the
argument — offered by Smart [1963], for instance — that effectively equates
ontological economy with the confirmation of the identity theory. The
admission of *alternative* forms of coherent materialism simply draws us on to
the complexity of sorting the decisive considerations.

In our own time, then, materialism has proved to be the most fashionable of the alternative monistic accounts. The reasons are not hard to provide. Idealism holds, traditionally, either that the public physical world we know is a system of ideas in God's mind, which insures its stability and public availability, or else a construction, heuristic or fictional or instrumental, from the private ideas or sensations of a particular mind or particular minds. The first alternative, usually assigned to Berkeley, exhausts itself in specifying God's function and is, in every other respect, not necessarily opposed to the views of its apparent antagonists, including materialists. The second alternative, sometimes called subjective idealism, which threatens Berkeley's own theory — since, on his view, God plays no determinate epistemic role in human cognition (think of the gulf between God's ideas and human ideas) — generates the seemingly insoluble problem of communication between independent minds and the recovery of a publicly shared world. Hence, idealism seems to be a philosophical extravagance rather as dualism is: one needs a sustaining God or a pre-established Harmony among minds or independent spiritual entities (Leibniz) or a Deity coordinating events in the separate mental and physical domains (Malebranche) in order to insure anything like the familiar public world. Ontic dualism, of course, merely celebrates the mystery. Materialism, on the other hand, has in its favor the stunning achievement and promise of the physical sciences as well as the detailed evidence of the late planetary appearance of sentience and intelligence. It may be that malicious interests opposing, say, the immortality and sanctity of the soul are directing the philosophical prospects of materialism; but, if so, theirs is only a by-benefit. It is the vision of the unity of science — or, better, the vision of the unity of the world (that science wishes to reflect), of a single, comprehensive conceptual system adequate to the whole of intelligible discourse — that spurs us on. It is a foregone conclusion that the accomplishments of the physical sciences will have to be counted as occupying a central role in the formulation and testing of such a vision. Hence, materialism, if viable, will suit us best.

CHAPTER 3

THE IDENTITY THEORY

It could not be convincingly maintained that the mind is the brain, because a dead or inert brain (or a dead or inert body, for that matter) would exhibit no properties on the admission of which the ascription of mental properties could be justified at all. It is surely only when the brain or body is functioning in some appropriate way, that is, in a way suitably linked to the behavior of a sentient or intelligent creature, that we can speak of the mind. The concession draws attention at once to the problem of avoiding a circular account of the mind, which, because it touches on the ascription of *any* mental attribute, is even more profound than the so-called problem of other minds (Wisdom [1952]). It also suggests the impossibility of ascribing mental attributes without trading on the conceptual linkages between one kind of mental attribute and another (say, between intentions and beliefs or beliefs and desires). But, resisting that issue for the time being, the best that we can expect, in attempting to view the mind as part of the body, is to determine that mental *states* (or processes or events) will prove to be brain states or neural states (or processes or events). What are the realistic prospects of such a theory? The quick answer must be: nil.

We must consider, first, what it means to speak of identity. Everything, we suppose, is identical with itself: the denial is self-contradictory. In that sense, there can be no "contingent" identities, logically contingent identities, although there may be identities that only empirically contingent data can confirm — that, for instance, the Morning Star and the Evening Star are one and the same planet. Also, the necessity of self-identity extends to whatever we may wish, however provisionally, to treat as a "thing" about which we speak and make predications; for, to speak thus is only to make grammatical reference — in an ontologically neutral manner, as has already been suggested. Objects, states, processes, conditions, events, and attributes may, in this sense, be admitted to be self-identical (entities); and, of everything that is self-identical, what is true of a thing is, on pain of contradiction, true of it.

These seem to be trivial comments but they are actually remarkably important, since, as we ordinarily speak, we simply cannot say the same things about brain states and mental states. For example, if Peter's dream (being in a state of dreaming) frightened Peter, it cannot ordinarily be said that Peter's neural state N, alleged to be identical with the dream state, frightened him. We have, at the present time, no linguistic practice that would permit such a predication of a neural state straightforwardly, and its provision may fairly be said to depend on vindicating some well-developed form of the identity thesis itself (or some suitable surrogate). It would hardly be enough to show that such a predicational extension need not be incoherent; we should require as well that some theory be specified in terms of which the actual extension be justified and the adjusted claims independently confirmed. In any case, as far as the identity theory is concerned, *if* what is identified under two distinct designations *is identical only if* what may be said of what is identified under one designation must, preserving truth, be able to be said of what is identified under the other, and so said on epistemically independent grounds, then the identity theory is quite easily refuted. On the other hand, *if* neural state N is admitted to be identical with the dream state in question, then, even though we have no previously established practice in accord with which we would affirm that Peter's neural state (N) frightened Peter, we may, trivially – or, on pain of contradiction – affirm as well, since the dream state frightened Peter, that state N frightened Peter. But this is another way of saying that, in order to make an empirically contingent claim that is relevant, we must either be able to show that epistemically independent predications confirm an actual identity or that, confirming an identity on some empirical grounds, we are thereupon justified in construing certain other paired predications as designating one and the same attribute without further evidence.

The trouble is that it is extremely difficult to say *what* the identity theory requires, in a way that would enable us to decide that it was true or false. It certainly does not require, in the opinion of its proponents, the synonymy of matched mental and physical predicates or even the substitutivity (preserving linguistic coherence in relevant sentential contexts) of mental and physical predicates (Smart [1962]). It is more than doubtful, for instance, that the expression 'dreaming' could mean whatever *any* expression designating a purely neural state could *mean*; and it is fairly obvious that if 'the onset of brain state B occurred *k* units from the *corpus callosum*' makes sense, it need not (supposing brain state B to be identical with a state of dreaming) be necessary to construe 'the onset of dream state D occurred *k* units from the *corpus callosum*' as equally intelligible. There are deep problems here that need still to be sorted. We need only note, for the moment, that the identity theory is designed to survive the constraints mentioned.

Self-identity requires that what is true of something is true of it. It does not, and cannot usefully be made to, require that whatever may be truly *said* of something, in one linguistic context, must be capable of being said truly of that same thing in every conceivable linguistic context. That constraint is much too stringent, for it would oblige us to deny identity in the most elementary cases; and if it were claimed that this was indeed how we construe all identity claims, often and loosely characterized as Leibniz's law, then it is simply a false claim (and the law is invalid). Even outside the context of the mind/body problem, as is well known, co-designative terms are not always substitutable, *salve veritate*. For example, although Samuel Clemens and Mark Twain are one and the same man, not realizing this, you may well believe, reading *A Connecticut Yankee in King Arthur's Court*, that you are reading Mark Twain's novel and yet not believe (without contradiction) that you are reading Samuel Clemens' novel. We explain the discrepancy, of course, not by denying the identity of Mark Twain and Samuel Clemens but by explicating the logical peculiarities of certain kinds of sentences and idioms (those, particularly, that involve propositional attitudes) that disallow exhibiting identity in a perspicuous way. But, in that case, obviously, appeal to Leibniz's law — or, at least, appeal to Leibniz's law in testing the sentences of natural languages that have not yet been canonically paraphrased in order, precisely, to eliminate the anomaly (supposing, for the sake of the argument, that that is possible) — is indecisive (Cartwright [1971]). And, if the problem is as general as it seems reasonable to suppose, the proponents of the identity theory could hardly be expected to rest their case on the substitutivity criterion.

Of course, there *is* a sense in which Leibniz's law must be true, namely, just the sense in which, since whatever there is is necessarily identical with itself, necessarily what is true of it is true of it — and necessarily what may be truly said of it (in that sense) may be truly said of it (Chisholm [1973]). But what this comes to is simply that there must, in principle, be a way of saying that what is true of a thing is true of it, not that all linguistic contexts permit the substitutivity of co-designative terms, *salve veritate*. So it is true of the man (call him Samuel Clemens or Mark Twain) that he wrote the novel *A Connecticut Yankee*; and it is true that, believing what you do, you must believe *of that man* that you are reading his novel. But it does not follow from this that if 'S believes that Mark Twain wrote *A Connecticut Yankee*' is true and 'Mark Twain = Samuel Clemens' is true, then 'S believes that Samuel Clemens wrote *A Connecticut Yankee*' is also true: an equivocation remains between an intentional and a non-intentional reading of the conclusion, corresponding to the equivocation on 'say' just noted (Quine [1960]). More-over, it is a critical weakness of familiar paraphrastic programs regarding belief contexts (notably, Quine's [1960]) that the extensionally perspicuous specification of that about which S has a belief depends, for logical reasons, on our being able to specify the referent in question *in the original intentional context* — precisely where, as Quine holds, reference is opaque (Margolis [1977e]). Schematically, if S believes that *p*, where, on the hypothesis, whatever referent, somehow specified in the context 'that *p*', S has a belief about, there will be no way to specify that referent (call it R) relevantly and in an extensionally accessible way without denying that that can already be done in the context 'that *p*'. Grant that Tom believes that Cicero denounced Cataline. If 'Cicero denounced Cataline' is, in context, referentially opaque, then how can we extract the truth, 'Tom believes-true, of Cicero and Cataline [now transparently identified] the sentence "the first denounced the second?" '

Obviously, the substitutivity criterion can only operate successfully when an independent and adequate conception of identity has been supplied in terms of which the relevant equivocation on 'say' can be favorably resolved. Also, it should be noted, even if $x=y$ and if 'Fx' makes sense, it does not follow that 'Fy' makes sense; *or*, that, if it does not, then it must be false that $x=y$. If, for instance, Smith's wishes are said to be identical with the firing of neuron N (a preposterous hypothesis, it may be admitted), it does not follow that if it makes sense to say that the firing occurred three inches from the base of Smith's skull, then it must make sense to say that the wish occurred three inches from the base of Smith's skull. That is, even if Leibniz's law must be satisfied in identity claims, it does not follow that (what may be termed) the Law of Transferable Epithets (Fodor [1968]) must be satisfied as well. In general, it is neither clear when relevant predications violate a rule of language nor when innovations in linguistic use are inadmissible (R. Rorty [1965]). But in any case, admitting, say, that 'Fy' *does not make sense* where 'Fx' does does *not* entail any violation of Leibniz's law, since the law is then, simply inapplicable. Hence, as we shall see, certain versions of the identity thesis are somewhat more resiliant than might otherwise be supposed.

Difficulties, however, threaten to mushroom. It is one thing to confront sentential patterns in which reference is obscured by introducing so-called intentional considerations of belief (Chisholm [1957]). It is quite another where properties thought to be essential or strongly characteristic of mental states are not even attributable to physical states supposed to be identical with them, or *vice versa*. For example, mental states are just the sort of thing that people are "directly" aware of (Brentano [1973]; Chisholm [1966]); but if neural states are thought to be identical with such states, then it is more then awkward to admit that they are never the sort of thing that we are aware of — in the intentionally relevant sense. (The objection, as stated, is not intented to be decisive.) Hence, even if we relax the conditions of identity below the (apparent) strictness of Leibniz's law, we must draw the line somewhere; we must decide *what* range of predications would be decisive in testing for the presence of an actual identity. The trouble is that there is *no* plausible and general concession regarding the relaxed matching of mental and physical predication that would support the identity claim, because none of the most distinctive ways of qualifying mental states are eligible for qualifying physical states and none of the most distinctive ways of qualifying physical states are eligible for mental states (Cornman [1968a]). Some qualifications are noticeably neutral and jointly admissible, for instance, that a particular state, mental or physical, persists for a given time. So either the identity theory is flatly false or else it must be supported by an altogether different strategy from that of an appeal to a straightforward application of Leibniz's law.

The only conceivable strategy is to search for theoretical grounds for affirming an identity rather than to collect a decisive set of equivalent sentences matched for mental and physical states in such a way that what is predicated of what is identified as a mental state may be independently predicated, *salve veritate*, of what is identified as a physical state (and thought, for that reason, to be one and the same). If physical location, for instance, cannot, on our idiom, be assigned to mental states (unless some form of the identity theory is independently confirmed) and if mental states but not physical states (in the same respect) are what we are said to be directly or introspectively aware of, then the substitution test must fail to vindicate the identity theory. Unfortunately, there is no clear prospect of proving the theory by appeal even to the first alternative — by which certain favored correlations are construed as supporting a theoretical identity. An idiom thus developed would not generate contradictions, but others could always say — preserving whatever information is already accessible to us — that the putative identity was no more than a certain correlation between mental and physical states (Brandt and Kim [1967] ; Kim [1966]).

The ulterior reason for resisting is, quite simply (apart from the distinction between correlation and identity), just that the substitutivity discrepancies that would be noted bear directly on confirming *any* theory about mind/body identities. A decisive consideration, for instance, is this: we may, if we wish, *assign* the (intentional) content of a thought to some particular neural state and *then* speak of the thought and neural state as identical; but we *could never independently discover*, by any physical means whatsoever, that a given neural state actually had that (intentional) content or was satisfactorily correlated with it (whatever that might mean) (*contra* Dennett [1969]). The relevant characterization does not even fit our talk of physical states and can only be defended by some appropriate "assignment", that is, by reference to some already accepted theory of the relationship between mental and physical states. But that is precisely what needs to be established. If Paul is in the state of thinking that pheasant would be good for dinner, how could we determine which state, to be matched with that mental state, *had that same content*? The project is either impossible or the reason the objection is said to be inconclusive needs still to be explained. There is, in the entire literature, no clear resolution of the issue. Consequently, at least conditionally, the identity theory will have to be rejected if, in so doing, we are not committed to a dualism of entities; otherwise, we need merely observe that the theory is not demonstrably more compelling than other, non-equivalent views, and that we cannot yet prove that the theory is correct. (There are issues suggested here, obviously, that will need to be explored.)

The principal trouble in speaking of the identity of mental and physical states is that either we lack a clear sense of the *kind* of thing of which a given mental state and a given physical state are said to be one and the same instance (what kind of *thing* are mental and physical states instances of?) or of the kind of thing to which, as one and the same, they may be attributed (of *what* are they the same state?), or else the putative kind in question itself generates our puzzles of identity (what is it to be a *state*?). In speaking of the identity of Mark Twain and Samuel Clemens, for instance, we were able to say that they are one and the same *man*: we were able to say that we could refer to the same man by using either of two names. But if we held that a *person* was identical with a certain *body*, *what* thing — what thing of what *kind* — would it be that was identified under the designations 'person' and 'body'? If one answers, why it is the same *entity*, then the claim has been rounded out by employing a noticeably vacuous term, the most abstract kind-term possible, for which no clear criteria of individuation and reidentification are available. And if it is said that they are one and the same *body* (Williams [1970]), then the argument clearly requires a demonstration of *how* to reduce persons to bodies (physicalism). The first reply is no reply at all; the second, a genuine reply, fails to wear its supporting argument on its sleeve.

There are no formulable grounds for individuating and reidentifying *entities* as such, in any natural language, though there are such grounds for

men and persons, that is, for the usual species of things (Wiggins [1967];
Hirsch [1977]). Similarly, if one says that a pain is identical with a neural
state, if one holds that they are one and the same *state*, then the kind-term
involved is, though perhaps less vacuous, equally unequipped with criteria for
the individuation and reidentification of instances. (Also, there is noticeably
less precision in individuating mental states of particular kinds [pains, for
instance] than there is in individuating physical states of particular kinds
[losses of determinate amounts of weight, for instance].)

We have very definite theories, admittedly open to adjustment in anomalous circumstances, about which equivalences would have to hold if a man,
putatively the same in two different contexts of reference, were to be shown
to be one and the same. But we have absolutely no clues for showing, in
general, that what are claimed to be two *entities* or two *states* or two *processes*
or two *events* or two *conditions* or two *things* or two *attributes* are, as such,
really one and the same. Our sortals must be more restrictive than these and
must be linked to workable criteria for deciding relevant cases.

Characteristically, then, identity claims are made with respect to well-
entrenched sortals (Strawson [1959]; Wiggins [1967]), for a well-entrenched
sortal is simply a kind-term with respect to which established usage provides
ready criteria for individuating and reidentifying instances (without, necessarily, precluding anomalous cases or the need for revisions in theory and
without denying that there are grounds for affirming the persistence of a wide
range of objects more fundamental than the criteria of any particular sortal
collecting subjects of such objects [Hirsch (1977)]). There are, therefore, two
sorts of difficult cases to be noted, either of which may be involved in the
defense of the identity theory: one, where the alleged identity concerns
entities corresponding to vacuous or nearly vacuous sortals for which we have
no developed individuating criteria (mental and physical states viewed as the
same *states*, for instance); the other, where the alleged identity concerns
entities individuated in accord with different sortals (*mental states* viewed as
physical states, for instance).

The two sorts of strategy are very similar: for, with regard to the first,
wherever linguistic constraints in accord with Leibniz's law affect the use of
provisionally distinct sortals (mental states and physical states, for instance),
it is supposed that reference to the same sortal (vacuous or nearly vacuous —
states *tout court*, for instance) will obviate those constraints or expose them
as benign and with regard to the second, it is supposed that, in spite of such
constraints, certain entities sorted in accord with different sortals are really
one and the same instances of *some* sortal. The first strategy (T. Nagel [1965]

possibly) employs Leibniz's law in the manner already sketched; the second defends what has come to be called cross-category identities, that is, identities holding of things sorted in accord with different sortals (Cornman [1962]). The latter cannot, therefore, appeal to Leibniz's law except in the sense already noted, that whatever is true of a thing is true of it (and may be said to be), not in the sense in which substitutivity of co-designative terms preserves truth in all or all relevant linguistic contexts. The defense of cross-category identities is quite strenuous, obviously, though not, it must be admitted, impossible so far forth.

Smart [1962] had offered as an instance of a cross-category identity (without naming it such) the identity of lightning and an electrical discharge of a certain sort; and Cornman had offered as an explicit instance the identity of the temperature of a gas and the mean kinetic energy of the gas molecules. It is important to notice, in this connection, that no one has as yet formulated a satisfactory general strategy for proving cross-category identities; that the strongest (though not exclusive) instances admitted (Feigl [1967]) involve highly developed physical theories about the micro-theoretical *composition* of selected macroscopic physical or material entities; and that *no* comparable theory is available regarding mental phenomena or persons. Again, as Cornman rightly insists, identity theories are not, as such, materialistic theories: he also mentions "double aspect" and idealistic theories — which he regards as compatible with "the requirements of science".

The critical consideration, however, is this: cross-category identity is inherently opposed to the translation of predicates, in the sense that, though (on Smart's or Cornman's view) mental processes are identical with physical processes, mental attributes are ascribable to processes characterized as mental that are not also ascribable to those same processes characterized as physical, and *vice versa*. Cornman, for example, regards it as a "category mistake" to speak of "a fading or dim brain process", whereas more radical reductionists (mentioned in Shaffer [1961]) would not, in principle, admit cross-category constraints on predication. The advantage of the cross-category view, whether materialistic or "double aspect" or idealistic, is, precisely, its compatibility with the prevailing features of actual discourse about the mind and body; but its disadvantage lies in its dependence on an (as yet) unformulated commitment to qualifications more detailed than those of Leibniz's law. In fact, on Cornman's account, the very strength of cross-category identity theories is its apparent weakness, viz. that since cross-category predications involve a category mistake (Ryle [1949]), such predications lack truth-values — hence, fail even to call into play the Leibnizian principle of the identity of indiscernibles. The trouble is, it is not clear *what* justifying principle the identity thesis does call into play, since, on the face of it, it seems intended to overtake the cross-category problem itself.

There is at least one other fundamental difficulty with identity theories of every sort. Cornman puts the issue in terms of formulating the difference between identity and psychophysical parallelism: both theories, he claims, admit as a necessary condition some "one-to-one simultaneity-correspondence". This alone precludes defining mental predicates in terms of just those physical predicates answering to a favorable correlation, for the correlation is supposed to be empirically contingent. But, whereas Cornman is concerned to show that the correlation itself may be interpreted quite differently in terms of identity and parallelism (with respect to the latter, the phenomena are distinct and causally independent of one another; with respect to the former, they are not), the question remains *whether* a one-one correspondence of *any* pertinent sort can be provided for identity theories — *a fortiori*, for parallelist theories. In a sense, the question is an empirical one. Nevertheless, it is quite easy to show that *no* satisfactory one-one correspondence is empirically available and none may be possible. Consider that, assuming some neural process and some thought provisionally linked in a particular identity claim, the kind of process in question may actually be empirically correlated with thoughts having an indefinitely varied intentional content and the kind of thought in question may be empirically correlated with indefinitely many different neural processes. There is good reason to believe that such a situation actually obtains, both because of the functionally specified role of physiological processes correlated with thought (Putnam [1967a]) and because of the conceptual need to *assign* (if we wish) the intentional content of a given thought *to* a given neural process with which it is associated; such a content cannot be *detected* in the process itself. In short, instead of a one-one correlation (or a one-many correlation, which is merely a liberalized instance of a one-one correlation) we seem to have a many-many correlation (*contra* Feigl [1967]). A many-many correlation is a correlation in terms of indeterminately many alternatives, whereas a one-many (or one-one) correlation is a correlation in terms of *determinately* many alternatives. A fuller account of ascriptions of intentional content remains to be provided; but on the condition that it can be supplied, assuming, with Feigl and Cornman (and Parfit [1971]), that a one-one correlation is a necessary condition, the identity theory may well fall. Alternatively put, to confirm a one-one correlation for sentient creatures and for persons would be tantamount to the discovery of a finite machine program for the entire set of mental states of such creatures. We cannot, therefore, hold that the identity theory is conceptually incoherent; but there is good reason to believe that it is untenable in the context of persons and extremely unlikely in the context of the higher animals.

These considerations lead us to another that is often obscured. Would-be entities like states and events are characteristically dependent on the admission of entities that appear to occupy a more fundamental position in ordinary discourse, entities like persons and physical bodies. For, events befall creatures and physical objects, and states are the states *of* creatures and physical objects. (More radical ontologies may well be possible, but that is not the issue here [Strawson (1959)]. It is certainly not in terms of such ontologies that familiar identity claims have been advanced.) It is true, of course, that a person cannot exist without being in some state or other or without having some event or other befall him. In that sense, persons are as much dependent on events and states as states and events, on persons and bodies. But there is a difference. One may identify a person without regard to any particular event or state and, in fact, say, *of that person*, that he is in this or that state or that this or that event has befallen him. But we cannot normally identify events or states (there are some exceptions) except *as* the events or states of this or that person of body. (Here, we must admit an asymmetry between "sortal" and "characterizing universals" [Strawson (1959)].) For instance, the event of Caesar's death presupposes the identifiability of Caesar and its being true, of Caesar, that he died. Hence, given the existence of Caesar (the existence of a certain man) and given what may be truly predicated of Caesar (that he died), we may, by a purely grammatical nominalization — for all sorts of conveniences, including logical conveniences regarding polyadic predicates — speak of the *event*, Caesar's death. The event will then be taken (in relevant contexts) as an "indissoluble" entity, replacing Caesar-and-certain-predications-of-him, about which we may speak further. But then whether the entity, Caesar, can be said to be *related* to the would-be entity, Caesar's-death, will depend on what has been predicated of Caesar, with respect to which, thus qualified, the would-be entity (Caesar's death) is said to be related. For instance (*contra* Davidson [1970]), Caesar cannot have died Caesar's-death, since admitting Caesar's death as an entity already depends on its being true of Caesar that he died. Any attempt to claim that the usual sort of relationship that holds between independent entities holds also between a thing to which something has occurred and the corresponding event (or state) will always produce a certain redundancy, will always multiple entities, will threaten an infinite regress, and will defeat the very point of the original maneuver. For instance, we should then have to speak of Caesar's having died Caesar's dying Caesar's-death. We may, therefore, speak of such entities as "subaltern particulars" (Margolis [1973a]), treating them only as nominalized surrogates for certain predications.

The reason for drawing attention to the distinction is that it illuminates a further weakness of certain would-be cross-category identities. For, if we claim the identity of pains and neural states, we cannot satisfactorily appraise the force of the claim unless we consider what may be predicated of more fundamental entities. To speak of the identity of subaltern particulars, precisely because they are treated, however provisionally, as entities, often obscures essential discrepancies between what may be predicated of *persons* and *sentient creatures* and what may be predicated of mere *physical bodies*. If, for instance, Peter *has* a pain (or thought), it may well make no sense (may be a category mistake) to say that a certain physical body *has* a pain (or thought). But if we consider only the (indissoluble) states of having-a-pain and having-a-neural-discharge-of-such-and-such-a-sort, we may be led to suppose that they may be taken as one and the same, without regard to the potential discrepancy noted. That threat will merely appear to have been eliminated or neutralized. The point remains that, since states and events are subaltern particulars, nothing can be said about their identity without consulting what may be said about entities more fundamental to our conceptual scheme. In short, mental states and brain states could not be said to be identical unless it were first shown that what is predicated of sentient creatures and physical bodies is itself demonstrably identical, which returns us to the puzzle regarding Leibniz's law and cross-category identities. Alternatively put, such states may be treated as identical only within a theory in which persons or sentient creatures and their properties are nothing but physical bodies and their physical properties. This position, usually called physicalism, is the most uncompromising version of the identity theory. But it faces its own special difficulties.

CHAPTER 4

RADICAL MATERIALISM

Before turning to physicalism, we may round out our account conveniently by considering what has come to be called eliminative materialism: the physicalist and the eliminative materialist both claim to provide extreme reductionist interpretations of the identity claim. Feyerabend [1963a], for instance, rejects the identity thesis, from the vantage of materialism, because, in being committed to empirical statements of the form

> X is a mental process of kind A $\equiv$ X is a central process of kind α

the thesis implies that "mental events have physical features" and that "some physical events, viz. central processes, have non-physical features". In that sense, the intended monism is thought to constitute "a dualism of features". R. Rorty [1965], on the other hand, embraces the "disappearance form" of the identity theory rather than the "translation form", precisely because, following Cornman [1962], if identity signifies a relation such that

$$(x)\,(y)\,[(x = y) \supset (F)\,(Fx \equiv Fy)],$$

what may be called "strict identity", then the identity thesis produces meaningless expressions, expressions that commit a category or conceptual mistake. Rorty's theory is really an identity theory *manqué*, since the intended relation between physical and mental entities is one that holds between "existent entities and non-existent entities when reference to the latter once served (some of) the purposes presently served by reference to the former" [*sic*]. The views of Feyerabend and Rorty on identity, therefore, are surprisingly similar, though one raises questions of meaningfulness where the other does not and though the other takes himself to embrace a ("disappearance") version of the identity theory where the first does not.

These eliminative theories are difficult to assess for the simple reason that they never actually show *why*, plausibly, we should construe reference to the mental as reference to something fictional, mythical, non-existent, or something (the physical itself) only poorly, improperly, dimly understood. Noticeably, both Feyerabend [1963b] and Rorty only press the legitimacy and eligibility of (eliminative) materialism — its "right" to be heard. This may be

conceded straight off, *if* all that is meant is that there is no evident incoherence in the thesis itself. But that would hardly do. For one thing, it is not
equally clear that the grounds for advancing the thesis on Feyerabend's view,
for instance, are capable of being coherently formulated; for another, the
coherence of the thesis, on either Feyerabend's or Rorty's view, goes no
distance at all toward confirming it. The strategy of appealing to the revolu-
tionary possibilities of science (Kuhn [1970]; Feyerabend [1975]) offers
nothing specifically relevant to the particular eliminative proposals advanced —
whatever the validity of the general strategy (Lakatos and Musgrave [1970]).

There are more specific complaints. For one thing, Feyerabend freely
admits that "experiences, thoughts, etc. are not material processes", given
ordinary English or other natural languages; that is, they cannot be adequately
"analyzed in a materialistic fashion". But if we ask what the materialistic
replacement ought to be — since identity is denied and the ordinary idiom,
taken to be a distorted language for making reference to "atoms, aggregates
of atoms and . . . the properties of, and the relations between such aggregates", which alone are said to exist — we are told that it is simply premature
to ask, that "the materialistic philosopher must be given *at least* as much
time" to develop his account as the theory embedded in ordinary English
took to form. For a second, Feyerabend admits that there are "observational
facts" now favoring the anti-materialist, as that men have experiences,
thoughts, and the like. But if we ask whether these are not decisive we are
told that the "common idiom" is not really adapted to *facts* but only to
beliefs; that the putative facts are formulated in terms of the common idiom
and therefore "already prejudiced in its favor"; that observational evidence is
inherently indecisive. For a third, Feyerabend insists that the force of the
identification of mental phenomena as distinct from material phenomena, as
in "ordinary English", can only be appraised "*after* it has been shown that
the new language [materialese] is *inferior* to ordinary English". But if we ask
for the confirming grounds for such appraisals of superiority and inferiority,
we are told that, for instance, "a new theory of pains . . . *will* change the
meaning of 'I am in pain' "; that (Feyerabend [1962]) the meanings of terms
occurring in different theories must be different or that the meaning of a
term is a theory; that all observational language is in need of interpretation by
way of the theory — hence, is non-convergent where ordinary English and
"materialese" are opposed to one another; that, in effect, there is no formulable basis on which to *test* such competing theories, since the tests themselves
must be captured by the idiom of one theory or the other. But this is to
confuse theory and meaning (Putnam [1965]). Assuming that Feyerabend

acknowledges that appraisals of the "inferiority" of ordinary English or materialese are intelligible (which, after all, is the point of his own complaint), what he says is tantamount to advancing an incoherent thesis, a thesis that cannot make literal sense of the comparative explanatory power of competing theories (Margolis [1970a]); for that would require that the sense of critical terms, terms designating the phenomena to be explained, be essentially unchanging relative to competing theories *about the same phenomena* – whatever other forces may affect a change in sense. As Hilary Putnam trimly puts the point, Feyerabend's thesis would require that, as we have abandoned Galileo's theory of temperature, Galileo would not have *understood* the denial of the statement (said to be "constitutive of the Galilean concept") that "the temperature shown by a thermometer is not dependent upon the chemical composition of the fluid used". But that is simply preposterous.

To hold, fairly, that observational language is theory-laden is not equivalent to holding that the meaning of observational terms is a theory, *and* to be able to specify alternative theories or to specify alternative theories or to specify alternative interpretations of some observational data entails possession of a language that is relatively theory-free. The mere fact that ordinary language may change diachronically, so that current distinctions regarding mental events *may* be eliminated or replaced in *some* way favoring the eliminative materialist's convictions has the effect, ironically, of preserving the very distinctions in question, simply because whatever can be said can be said. Also, if distinctions currently embedded in ordinary language call for defense, so, too, will the (favorably) altered idiom, which, then, presupposes the possibility of a comparison of explanatory power. In any case, once certain distinctions are confirmable in accord with a given natural language, we require a determinate defense for the revision or elimination of the categories affected: from this point of view, eliminative materialism is an objective only, not a philosophical program of any testable sort.

Further problems arise for eliminative materialism because Richard Rorty [1970], while refraining from claiming that the ordinary way of reporting introspective experience is wrong, wishes to claim that sentences formulated in "the neurological vocabulary" are as legitimately used to convey "a report of experience", even though "there is nothing in common between the two experiences" [thus reported] save that they are had under the same conditions – viz., "the manipulation of the body in certain specified ways". But this, in itself, hardly bears on the elimination of the mental, may merely provide for reporting of a *new* kind; and *whether* it might justify eliminating reference to the mental would at least depend on a comparison of the properties of putatively introspective reports of both kinds, which happens not to have been provided at all. Rorty also fails to explain how we may determine that the experiences said to be had are had "under the same conditions" − in such a way that the eliminative program goes through. Unlike Feyerabend, Rorty restricts his attention to discourse about sensations (as opposed to thoughts). If so, it is doubtful that he envisages an eliminative program for all mental discourse, or at least an eliminative program based on uniform grounds; also, there are good reasons for thinking that first-person reports about sensations and first-person reports about the "experience" of neurological processes (provisionally, perceptual reports) are of such different sorts (Margolis [1973a]) that the prospect of *replacing* one with the other cannot be encouraged without a rather strenuous argument. For instance, perceptions are "transitive", in the sense that what one actually perceives must exist independently of its being perceived, whereas sensations (as of pain) are "intransitive", in lacking such objects. (We shall return to this issue, later.) In fact, Rorty's chief argument is that his own view is not vulnerable to the charge that sentences in the one idiom "entail" (*contra* Cornman [1968a]) what is stated in the other or "express" (*contra* Bernstein [1968]) what the other express. In this, he seems to be justified, precisely on the grounds of cross-category mistakes. But then, he has failed to provide any connection at all between the two idioms such that *replacement* of the one by the other can be defended and confirmed; and if the argument is made to depend solely on the avoidance of category mistakes, then, on Rorty's own view, it may be quite impossible to supply any defense at all for such a replacement. There must be *some* conceptual relationship between the two idioms, in virtue of which eliminative materialism might be thought defensible; but if there is, then *something* like entailment or theoretical connection must obtain between matched sentences of each sort − proof against the category-mistake complaint. Also, as Rorty's critics have fairly observed, we now possess a "theoretico-reporting" term, 'sensation' (Cornman [1968b]), which, though open to diachronic changes in its use, cannot be systematically eliminated (*contra* Quine [1966]) without a suitable defense. Rorty thinks the criticism is wedded to the Myth of the Given (Sellars [1963b]) but his charge is a *non sequitur*: the criticism is simply that a reporting use of language is not an explanatory use and can be eliminated or altered (if at all) only on distinctive grounds, in spite of the fact that both uses are theory-laden. Even if explanation is thought to be or to entail description, *that* the competing descriptions are equivalent or related in whatever corresponding way the eliminative materialist claims still needs to be assessed.

Arguments against Rorty's position may, perhaps, be collected in the following way: (i) the reporting role of sensation terms cannot be replaced by any idiom insofar as it merely provides for the scientific explanation of whatever is reported (Cornman [1971]); (ii) it is possible to deny that there are mental entities, in the ontologically relevant sense, without denying that sensation terms have a reporting use, a use in reporting phenomenal experience; (iii) a putatively physical idiom, introduced to replace or eliminate our mental idiom, will acquire the reporting role of our mental idiom, unless that reporting role can be independently eliminated; (iv) there is no clear prospect of, and no formulable sense in anticipating, eliminating the use of our mental idiom in reporting phenomenal experience. (Notice, incidentally, that these objections outflank Rorty's attempt to disqualify the mental distinguished by its alleged incorrigibility. To reject incorrigibility as the distinguishing mark of the mental is not to reject the mental; in fact, it is not even to suppose that what is distinguished as the mental is uniform in any determinate way whatsoever [(cf. Rosenthal [1977])].) This is not to deny that it is logically possible that, for some utterly unspecified reason, the reporting use of sensation terms may be eliminated; but that hardly gives the eliminative materialist a positive argument. *If*, then, the cross-category constraint is conceded, there cannot but be descriptive distinctions provided by our reporting idiom that *cannot* be replaced by any purely physical idiom. To admit a reporting idiom is, trivially, to admit an idiom that is theory-laden, but it is not to admit an idiom that is first introduced to serve a merely explanatory role. Cornman [1971], who pursues all of these lines of objection, advocates his own "adverbial materialism" as proof against the objections of eliminative materialism and of reductive materialism in general. Its strength lies in replacing sensa with "objectless sensing events" (*à la* Chisholm [1966]) and then identifying such (mental) events with physical events: the identification of sensa with "brain parts" proves to be "cross-category" but that of sensing events with physical events does not. Since, on Cornman's view, the identity statement intended contains "one pure theoretical term and one term that is both phenomenal and theoretico-reporting", nothing is lost (as with eliminative and reductive materialism) regarding the phenomenal aspect of mental life. These are substantial gains that show the identity theory in its best light — and as a clear option. But though Cornman has ingeniously accommodated certain of the principal conceptual difficulties, his theory — on his own view — presupposes "a one-to-one correspondence" between "correlated" phenomena, and we have already seen that there is good reason to believe that no such correlations are empirically forthcoming (that only "many-many" correlations seem likely). This appears to be as true of non-intentional phenomena like pains as it is of intentional phenomena like beliefs — that is, speaking "with the vulgar while thinking adverbially", as Cornman suggests. The problem of the identity theory remains at bottom the empirically unpromising one of establishing the requisite correlations, even after conceptually untenable versions have been eliminated. What are we to make of D. M. Armstrong's problem [1973] regarding whether the belief that *a & b* is or is not the same belief as the belief that *b & a*? And how shall we understand Daniel Dennett's problem [1969] generated by the fact that the intentional content of a belief can only be assigned to a neural process? In fact, Cornman does not consider at all that there are functional or intentional attributes associated with the use of language and intelligence that depend on the cultural context of behavior and that cannot, though they require suitable central nervous states, reasonably be thought, by any correlative means, to be identical with such states. The issue will require considerable elaboration. When we turn to pains, the picture is, almost surprisingly, as difficult. For, though pains are often correlated with C-fibers, they are also correlated with A-fibers — the thesis being that pains of different sorts are associated with each (White and Sweet [1955]). But also, pains may be blocked (that is, do not occur when anticipated because of the stimulation of given fibers); the neural connections are largely unclear "as soon as the fibers enter the spinal cord" (Cassinari and Pagni [1969]); indeed, "virtually the whole brain [must be] considered to be the pain centre" (Melzack [1973]); and, with anomalies like the pain of the *couvade* and others, it is virtually impossible to draw a correlated neural process for the pain reported and obviously experienced. Cornman rightly stresses that the ultimate solution of the mind/body problem is, in his sense, an "external" issue (Cornman [1966]), but the empirical question (which provides an "internal" clue about the plausibility of alternative theories) remains.

The opposite extreme of the eliminative view is that of the physicalist, who (T. Nagel [1965]) holds (usually restricting the scope of his theory) "that a person, with all his psychological attributes, is nothing over and above his body, with all its physical attributes". Apart from the question of whether it is true, it is not really clear what would be sufficient to establish the truth of the thesis. It is obviously tempting to think of persons as mere physical bodies (Williams [1970]), of whatever complex and interesting sort they may be; so properties normally attributed to persons are, on the thesis, analyzable without remainder in purely physical terms. If, for instance, John writes Arthur a letter about the glories of Venice, we are to suppose that an adequate account of what happened could be given in terms of the motions of John's arm and pen, his brain states and the like, *and some device for ascribing the significance or meaning or content* of the letter (itself reduced in purely physical terms) to some set of purely physically identifiable and analyzable elements. Unless such a device were available, no version of physicalism would be remotely plausible. It will not do, as we have already seen (*contra* Sellars [1963a] and Feigl [1967]), to regard the intentional as not betraying a "flaw" in physicalism, on the grounds that roles involving intentionality can simply be "added" to an otherwise adequate physicalism; what is at stake is, precisely, the analysis of the distinctive *attributes* of persons and sentient organisms, attributes as essential to their nature as any purely physical attributes could be. This is the reason, perhaps, that, in spite of the embarrassment of a dualism of entities, Descartes was unable to subscribe to any form of metaphysical monism − just as contemporary dualists (Polten [1973]; Eccles [1965] and, adjusted, [1970]), find a ramified monism impossible to accept.

Human persons, Descartes realized, have dreams, thoughts, intentions, and the like; these conditions and the capacity to grasp their significance cannot, in any obvious way, be reduced to merely physical attributes or be ascribed to mere extended matter. Consequently, though Descartes was unable to say what the nature of a human being's unity is, he believed that it must, in some sense, be a unity of matter and mind. There is, also, evidence that, in recognizing these complications, Descartes himself may not have been entirely committed to Cartesian dualism (Spicker [1970]), even though his latter-day disciples are so committed (Shaffer [1966]). In our own time, persons are said, most notably by P. F. Strawson [1959], to be entities of such a kind that, unlike purely physical bodies, both mental or psychological predicates and physical predicates may and must be used in ascribing properties to them − so-call M-predicates and P-predicates. So, for instance, a person but not a stone may be depressed or have a pain and yet a person as well as a stone may fill a certain volume of space. Nevertheless, though he is right in claiming that much, Strawson never says *what* the nature of the distinctive entity is (person or sentient creature), in virtue of which we may understand *why* both M-attributes and P-attributes are ascribable to it but not to such equally distinctive entities as stones. In this sense, though he is not a dualist, Strawson fails to provide a foundation for distinguishing his own view from that of the dualists: persons occupy a special place in his ontology, but he never explains why they are capable of possessing the properties they have or what the relationship is between a person and a body. The puzzle has exercised the phenomenologists as well (Spicker [1970]; Engelhardt [1973]).

The intended benefit of physicalism is that, if true, it would obviate an entire set of difficulties said to bear on the application of Leibniz's law, concerning what is attributable to mental states and physical states, to pains and brain states, for instance, or to persons and bodies. For, what has regularly been noted (Smart [1962] ; Nagel; Fodor [1968]) is that, at the very least, we cannot independently ascribe physical location to pains (the supporting arguments tend to vary somewhat), whereas we seem able to locate physical states straightforwardly. Thomas Nagel proposes, as a pilot endeavor, that "instead of identifying thoughts, sensations, after-images, and so forth with brain processes . . . a person's having the sensation [may be identified] with his body's being in a physical state or undergoing a physical process." In this way, both terms of the identity are "of the same logical type", namely, that of "a subject's possessing a certain attribute". The proposal is not designed to provide a detailed basis for supporting the cross-category identity of persons and bodies, but only to eliminate an essential blockage *and* to facilitate thereby the identity of the *having* of mental and physical states. The maneuver involves shifting from entities to attributes, that is, shifting, in grammatical terms, from subjects to predicates, with the apparent advantage of eliminating predicative asymmetries respecting what may be said of mental states and physical states. If, for instance, it is supposed that the difficulty of locating sensations, in the same sense in which the occurrence of bodily states may be located, counts against the identity thesis, then the needed symmetry is apparently restored by the independently plausible shift to speaking of the "having" of sensations and bodily states: "both going on in the same place — namely, wherever I (and my body) happen to be" (Nagel).

Not quite restored, however, or at least not obviously restored by the maneuver in question. For one thing, *some* asymmetry remains even regarding location. Psychological states occur "in the same place" in which "I (and my body) happen to be", in the sense in which the location of a person is assigned the location of a certain body (that person's body); the psychological state is not, and cannot be, first located in the body and *then* assigned to the person, and the assignment does not presuppose that persons are identical with bodies. Contrariwise, physical states are always, in principle, locatable in some portion of the body. It was perhaps in the spirit of overtaking this difference that Feigl [1967], converting a metaphor into literal location, once held that "my feelings or sentiments of elation, depression, delight, disgust, enthusiasm, indignation, admiration, contempt, etc. seem to me to be spread roughly through the upper half or two-thirds of my body". Psychological and mental states are always "located in the mind", which is itself not (yet) clearly located in some part of the body, or else *ascribed to* or *predicated of* — not located in — some person or sentient organism; whereas physical states are located in some part of the body or ascribed to some part of the body that can be located with respect to the whole body. So, if the original asymmetry were a difficulty that told against the identity thesis, it could not be said to be entirely eliminated by the maneuver given; and if construing mental and physical states predicatively obviates the question of their location (as opposed to that of the ascribability of spatially qualified attributes), the gain cannot be characterized appropriately in terms of restoring spatial symmetry. For, then, the issue would depend on whether the adjusted predicative expressions were indissolubly simple or not, that is, on whether Nagel's proposal had merit. Alternatively, if *having* mental states and physical states poses the question of their spatial location, then additional difficulties are bound to arise. For, if they are assigned to persons, *their* spatial location will, trivially, always be the same ("wherever I [and my body] happen to be") and would be the same even for different physical states otherwise said to occur in different parts of the body. Also, *whether mental states may be assigned to the body* — predicated *of* the body — is just the problem of the identity thesis and of physicalism. Hence, if the asymmetry respecting the physical location of mental and physical states constitutes a genuine problem to be resolved, it cannot be said to be resolved merely by ascribing *having* mental states to the body; for *that*, so to say, is the genus of the difficulty of which the asymmetry of spatial location is a familiar species. Also, it is not clear that providing a symmetrical account of location in terms of having mental and physical states precludes an asymmetrical account of the location of mental and physical states themselves. This, of course, bears, on the analysis of the adjusted predicative expressions.

A second difficulty follows closely on the first. For, if we grant that the adjustment recommended restores the symmetry of spatial location with respect to the having of mental and physical states, we are encouraged to consider whether or not there are other asymmetries respecting *having* mental and physical states and whether and how we might characterize alternative or additional qualifications of mental and physical states as opposed to qualifications of having such states. For instance, a person might *savor* having a certain sensation, but it makes no sense to say that his *body* savors being in a certain physical state. Here, the problems multiply.

Consider, for instance, that there may be asymmetries respecting non-spatial qualifications of mental and physical states. For instance, to remind ourselves of familiar cases, we may speak of a searing or throbbing or burning pain — whether literally or metaphorically intended is not important — where 'searing,' 'throbbing,' 'burning' are not univocally applicable in characterizing the physical state allegedly identical with the mental state in question (Cornman [1968a]). This is not yet to say that states so characterized could not be identical. But the strategy required under such circumstances would call for cross-category identities; the physicalist, precisely in attempting to *restore* the symmetry of predication for mental and physical states, has declined that advantage. But if such discrepancies persist, then the general strategy of shifting from speaking of mental and physical states to the *having* of mental and physical states neither bears pertinently on asymmetries of the original sort (of which the spatial asymmetries are simply important specimens) nor on the prospect that additional asymmetries may arise for the adjusted idiom as well.

Consider, then, the adjustment recommended. Can we treat *having* mental and physical states symmetrically? Well, what is crucial here is simply that to take note of the (univocal) *predicative* use of 'have' and of cognate expressions, as in attributing mental and physical states to some entity, does not really bear on the issue. The matter is not, however, entirely obvious. *If* mental and physical states are to be construed predicatively, then, necessarily, 'have' and its cognates will be used univocally to express the relevant predications. It does not follow from this that the state of having a certain pain and the state of having a certain neural discharge — significantly correlated, say — are one and the same state; nor does it follow that, even if it is maintained that they are one and the same state, there may not be formulable differences in the sense in which that to which the mental state is attributed has or possesses that state and in which that to which the physical state is attributed has or possesses that state. Such differences are, in fact, precisely what is accommodated by the notion of cross-category identities. In any event, insisting on the univocity of 'have' in the predicative sense, that is, in a purely syntactical sense, does not contribute to the confirmation of the identity thesis or physicalism. The univocity of the predicative sense is trival and entirely compatible with both symmetries and asymmetries of the substantive sort instanced; also, on the cross-category theory of identity, familiar asymmetries (not further specified) are taken to be compatible with the identity thesis, though, presumably, they are not compatible with physicalism. This is the reason Nagel goes astray when, collecting the benefit of shifting to the identity of attributes, he says that "my having a certain sensation or thought is of the same logical type as [my] body's being in a [certain] physical state or undergoing a [certain] physical processes", namely, that of 'a subject's possessing a certain attribute' ".

All subjects, we may concede, possess attributes, in the same sense of "possessing attributes" — for any attributes possessed — in that sentences of a (syntactically) predicative form convey statements making such attributions. Saying this does not oblige us to suppose, for example, that there are not other senses in which an eye has a certain color, a sense distinct from that in which an eye has a certain disease or in which an eye has a certain association for me or in which an eye has a certain similarity to an almond or the like; that is, it does not oblige us to suppose that there are not other significant, relevant, and alternative senses of 'have' (or of cognate expressions) in which such expressions are used whenever they are *also* used in the purely predicative sense. For, consider that the purely syntactical sense in which some *F* is predicated of some *a* presupposes, wherever *a* and *F* are selected from a range of identifiable subjects and attributes, that the *conceptual appropriateness* (a kind of adequation) of linking such subjects and such predicates can be independently defended. Thus, for instance, it is arguably inappropriate to predicate of John's cutting his steak that it was *garish* or *meteorological* or *morphemic* or the like — not merely false but inappropriate in terms of the relations between categories. In fact, the very eligibility of the cross-category identity thesis entails there being formulable constraints of a conceptual sort on predication itself, and the attempt of physicalists to resolve predicative asymmetries argues a similar commitment. In just that spirit, Nagel says "being offensive" cannot properly be ascribed to a collection of molecules as such. But then, *in the same sense*, one wonders whether "having a pain" properly conveys a predication that *can* be made of *bodies*. The short answer is No, for the extraordinarily simple (provisional) reason that having pain can only be predicated of *sentient entities* (animals or persons): only a creature of a kind capable of feeling pain can actually have pain. This is, the physicalist is debarred, on his own assumption, from predicating having pain of bodies *until* he has demonstrated that the predication *is* conceptually (and not merely syntactically) appropriate: hence, it is indecisive, for trivial reasons, that the intended identity is formulable in terms of "the same [syntactical] type", viz., predicates. The issue has simply not been joined. The point of interest here is, precisely, that the purely syntactical feature of predication — or, what passes for a purely syntactical consideration, doubtless already informed by a grasp of the relations between categories — cannot decide the substantive issue of the conceptual appropriateness of such predicative linking. But if so, then, it contributes nothing to the issue of physicalism to shift from subjects to attributes, as in speaking of having certain mental and physical states.

There is more to the quarrel. A man may have a balloon, in the same

predicative sense of 'have' as, but in some relevantly different sense of possessing from, that in which a man may have a certain height; and yet, saying
so does not as such disqualify (or favor) the identity thesis or physicalism.
Merely noting that there are alternative modes of possessing, in which
attributes of a given complexity, appropriately (univocally) predicated of
certain subjects, are said to be possessed by those subjects, does not decisively
bear on the issue at stake. The question regarding the conceptual appropriateness of predicating pains and other mental states of bodies does not preclude
the appropriateness of predicating attributes of different kinds of suitable
subjects, does not preclude occasions on which predications may convey
various senses in which subjects *possess* whatever attributes they may be said
to possess. No, the essential question is whether there is any sense of possession, not restricted to merely syntactical or formal uses, in which bodies may
be said to have mental states or selected mental states. Broadly speaking, the
question is a conceptual or metaphysical question, not a syntactical one.

Events and states may indeed be admitted as particulars, in a way that
preserves whatever putative advantage is said to hold in shifting from subjects
to attributes, as in shifting from pains to having pains and from neural discharges to undergoing neural discharges. In order to capture the improvement
intended, one merely needs to speak of the event of the onset of (having)
pain or the state of (having) pain and the event of the onset of (undergoing)
neural discharges. What this maneuver promises to insure is that the variability
of the sense of 'have' and its cognates may be admitted without disadvantage
to the identity thesis or to physicalism, at the same time that the putatively
restored symmetry regarding spatial location and the like is not lost. (Also, of
course, the maneuver permits the informal entailments of natural languages to
be captured canonically, posing on the conventional view, a question of ontic
commitment.) But then, the identity thesis must be construed in terms, once
again, of cross-category identity and cannot rest entirely on the symmetrical
use of selected predicative expressions. Hence, the strategy of defense must
be entirely different.

On the other hand, the ontic admission of events and states raises distinct
difficulties, both with and without reference to the identity thesis or to
physicalism. We sense this if we consider that we normally wish to predicate
relevant events and states *of* such substantives as bodies and persons and, on
the strong hypothesis, we can no longer do this. It is also to the point to
notice that, at least sometimes, we wish to qualify the pains and the event of
the onset of a pain or the state of being in pain in different ways; if events
and states are admitted as indissoluble particulars, otherwise admissible

qualifications of pains (as opposed to qualifications of the onset of pain) would appear to be precluded or, if admitted, would return us to the asymmetries earlier construed as posing a difficulty for physicalism. Only if we treat the "entities" in question as subaltern particulars — thus, only to facilitate certain grammatical maneuvers — can we at one and the same time preserve the flexibility of reference required and remain neutral as to ontic commitment.

The difficulties posed by events and states are of a bivocal nature, for events and states seem to lend themselves to being treated, in grammatical terms, both predicatively and substantively. Predicatively, we find ourselves at a stalemate if, say, the extension of would-be mental predicates excludes physical bodies as appropriate values. The identity of attributes can, then, only be attempted by developing a theory about cross-category identities and not by "restoring" predicative symmetries through an adjustment of grammar alone. It seems, therefore, not unfair to say, where cross-category identities are involved, that that the term 'have' and cognate expressions are used predicatively is quite inconclusive for the validity of the identity thesis or physicalism. For, where it is a syntactical sign of predication, the formal symmetry that obtains will not resolve the question of the conceptual appropriateness of linking certain subjects and certain attributes; and where it appears to be a syncategorematic element internal to the (indissoluble) characterization of some substantive (events or states) — for instance, the state-of-*having*-a-pain and the state-of-*being*-in-neural-condition-N — it ceases to bear on the eligibility of the physicalist thesis itself. But this is emphatically *not* to say that the asymmetries noted regarding the use of 'have' and cognate expressions, or the asymmetries regarding spatial and non-spatial attributes, do not themselves bear on the prospects of physicalism. On the contrary, it is the mark of the force of cross-category theories that they demonstrate how such asymmetries need to be supplied. In short, where 'have' and its cognates function predicatively, they do so compatibly with just the asymmetries acknowledged by cross-category identity theorists (and their opponents); and where 'have' and its cognates function syncategorematically, relevant asymmetries are merely obscured. Identity theories formulated in terms of events or states tend, therefore, to mask and not to resolve antecedent difficulties.

Admittedly, the foregoing arguments fail to disprove the identity theory: they do show, however, that the strategies thought to strengthen the thesis are hopelessly weak and that the questions it must answer remain almost untouched (Margolis [1971a]). It is useful to emphasize, therefore, that a repudiation of identity theories, more particularly, a repudiation of physicalism, does not as such entail a repudiation of materialism. It has often been argued (Smart [1963]) that, since the reasonableness of materialism is so greatly enhanced by considerations of ontological economy (as against dualism), identity theories are correspondingly rendered more reasonable as well; hence, too, dualists (Polten [1973]) are inclined to think that a rejection of physicalism or the identity theory somehow entails dualism. Neither view is tenable. All one need consider is the possibility of a coherent materialism distinct from the identity thesis. One such form of materialism might claim, for instance, that the *composition* of everything that exists, that of which everything that exists is composed, is matter, but that not everything that exists *is* a physical or material object and/or that not all the attributes of what exists are physical or material attributes. The argument may be put quite trimly. Distinguish, as we have, between ontic dualism and attribute dualism. The rejection of ontic dualism (Cartesianism) leads not to the identity thesis but to ontic monism. Concede, as we have, that materialism is the most plausible form of ontic monism. In effect, that is to concede a compositional thesis (Wiggins [1967]) rather than an identity thesis. So it does not follow at all from the admission that whatever there is is composed of matter that whatever there is has only physical or material properties. That is just the challenge that confronts physicalism − which we may now say appears either in the form of the identity thesis or in the form of eliminative materialism. The weakness of the latter lies largely in its having to construe sensations, images, thoughts and the like as unreal; the weakness of the former, in its being unable to establish that such phenomena, real enough, are nothing but purely physical phenomena. Nothing (ontologically significant) hangs, as we have seen on the grammatical use of such phenomena as the peoper subjects of predication, so dualists cannot be encouraged by that convenience; on the other hand, its admission does count heavily against a quantificational criterion of ontic commitment (*contra* Quine [1953]). Most positively, what the argument shows is the initial viability of a nonreductive materialism. The mere intelligibility of this alternative − one among a number of options − serves to challenge the automatic conclusions just sketched. In particular, if what has been earlier termed emergentist materialism is viable, then challenges against physicalism and other versions of the identity thesis need not be resisted just because materialism would then seem to be threatened.

We shall, in due course, explore the prospects of a materialism not committed to the identity theory, physicalism, eliminative materialism, or the like. But for the moment, we need only acknowledge − in the company, let it be said, of dualists, epiphenomenalists, parallelists, so far forth − that there is as yet no version of the identity theory that has provided a detailed strategy for confirming, on either scientific or philosophical grounds (should these be thought to diverge), *any* putative identities of the mind/body sort. Once the arguments favoring monism and, in particular, materialism are explicitly separated from the support of the identity theory, we are inexorably led to consider more flexible versions of materialism. But to do that we need to make a fresh start.

CHAPTER 5

MATERIALISM WITHOUT IDENTITY

Broadly speaking, dualist theories are of three sorts, the elements of which may well overlap in any particular account: first, classic ontological theories (Descartes', most prominently) that hold to a fundamental difference of substance between mind and body; second, semantic theories (Polten [1973]) that hold that because they differ in sense from physical expressions, mental expressions must, somehow, refer to (denote) something other than what physical expressions refer to, thus defeating monism as well as the identity theory; and third, accounts that, on either empirical or conceptual grounds, find it impossible to confirm what has earlier been termed attribute materialism, that is, the reduction of mental attributes to physical attributes. Among empirical scientists of the last persuasion may be mentioned Eccles [1970], Sherrington [1951], Penfield [1965], and, equivocally, Sperry [1969]. Eccles' [1970] statement may be taken as a paradigm: "When thought leads to action, I am constrained, as a neuroscientist, to postulate that in some way, completely beyond my understanding, my thinking changes the operative patterns of neuronal activities in my brain. Thinking thus comes to control the discharges of impulses from the pyramidal cells of my motor cortex and so eventually the contractions of my muscles and the behavioral patterns stemming therefrom."

The Cartesian view, it must be said straight off, is a philosophical scandal, in that it requires, precisely, a form of interaction between mind and body but, by the substantive exclusion of mind from body (*res cogitans* and *res extensa*), it makes an utter mystery of interaction itself. Since it is the relationship between the mind and body that is the very "world-knot" that needs to be explicated, the most charitable interpretation of the Cartesian view is that it is a dramatization of our ignorance. Semantic theories of the sort mentioned are, at best, unnecessary and, at worst, untenable. For, identity theorists like Smart [1962] cannot be said to be holding an incoherent thesis in subscribing to the cross-category identity theory; and the claim that differences in sense entail differences in reference (or denotation) is simply false. It is not irrelevant, it may be added, that Smart believes that expressions about mental phenomena can be replaced (non-synonymously) by "topic-neutral" expressions. Here, he means of course to overtake the semantic problem of cross-category identity. But the principal difficulty of Smart's proposal is simply that it is not clearly topic-neutral. Thus he holds that "When a person says, 'I see a yellowish-orange after-image', he is saying something like this:*'There is something going on which is like what is going on* when I have my eyes open, am awake, and there is an orange illuminated in good light in front of me, that is, when I really see an orange' ". One objection is that Smart has not demonstrated that, in the perceptual paradigm (which the after-image is suitably linked to), mental distinctions are not entailed. Smart attempts a purely behavioral account of normal perception, but this will not do: his view requires (unjustifiably) a correlation between, say, simple colors and other properties that can be discriminated: otherwise the behavioral reading will not work. But then, if what is going on in an after-image is like what is going on 'in perception, we have yet to eliminate mental or phenomenal elements. On the other hand, ignoring that question, Smart has failed to be explicit about the respect in which what is going on in the after-image is like what goes on in perception: he has not shown us, therefore, that the comment in question is actually topic-neutral; only if he could specify the respect in which the one is like the other, in topic-neutral terms, would his claim stand. But it is difficult to see, particularly if a behavioral reading is rejected, how the needed qualification could be supplied. Eric Polten rejects what he dubs the Fregean thesis (Frege [1960]), holding instead that "different senses [*sic*] *never* refer to the same referent". Here, Polten confuses 'sense', in the sense of the intension or connotation of general terms, with the sense in which Frege was prepared to concede that different definite descriptions (and even different proper names) might, in a natural language, denote one and the same individual thing. (The theory that that mental predicates cannot be translated into physical predicates constitutes a form of dualism we have already acknowledged and discounted.)

Clearly, possibilities of both sorts (bearing on Polten's thesis) abound: regarding predicative expressions, it is quite likely that, say, 'featherless biped' and 'creature capable of speech' should have the same extension (which is not to say, be it noted, that intensions "refer" to extensions); and regarding definite descriptions and proper names, it seems clear that, in normal use, the following would be taken to refer to one and the same thing: 'Cicero' and 'Tully', 'the most famous student of Plato's' and 'the teacher of Alexander the Great', 'Aristotle' and 'the teacher of Alexander the Great'. The point is that to deny such extensional or denotative equivalences would be to wreak general havoc upon theories of natural language: valid assertions of identity do not depend exclusively on synonymy. It is simply an empirical question whether predicative expressions differing in intension but not incompatible, have or have not the same extension; and it is simply a fact of ordinary usage that one and the same thing may, effectively, be denoted by different proper names or different definite (attributive) descriptions (Donnellan [1966]). So it is false to hold that expressions differing in sense cannot have the same reference because such expressions "refer [*sic*] to *different* properties of [a given] individual" (Polten). And it is misleading to hold that expressions (now, disambiguating the remark in favor of indefinite descriptions or general predicative expressions rather than proper names or definite descriptions) refer to properties, in particular, to mental and physical properties, without an explicit account of the ontological import of reference or of the reality of universals (Quine [1957]). In the present context, arguments of these sorts may be taken, fairly, to be confused versions of the third sort of dualism.

The third sort of dualism is, in spite of its critics (Smart; Feyerabend [1963b], arguing in different ways) entirely benign. The reason, quite simply, is that if we admit attributes that are not physical attributes or not reducible to physical attributes, we are not bound, by that admission alone, to a Cartesian dualism. The thesis that we are is a *non sequitur*. In fact, the admission entails no claim at all about *substantive* differences between mind and body or between mental and physical attributes: it need not even restrict itself to such attributes or theorize about the kinds of attributes there are. For example, consider the property of being "equivalent to the sum of 3 and 4". Here, we admit a property that is neither of the mental nor physical sort and that cannot be reduced in any conceivable way to any recognizably physical property. Yet, the admission of this property does not in the least affect, so far forth, the prospects of materialism or Cartesian dualism. We may well admit that the number of oranges in this grocery sack has the property of being "equivalent to the sum of 3 and 4". The property will be definable without regard to questions about the mind or body but will also, suitable criteria of application provided, be used in ascriptions involving physical objects. It may seem that the mention of numerical properties fails to come to grips with the issue regarding the reduction of mental properties but it is readily shown that this is not the case.

Consider, for instance, that a Turing machine may be completely described by its machine table; that is, that a "logical description" may be given that includes the finite set of states ("logical states") that a Turing machine (an "abstract machine") may have, without "any specification of the *physical nature* of these 'states' or, indeed, of the physical nature of the whole machine" (Putnam [1960]; Turing [1950]). "Physically realized," the machine may be said to have, "from the engineer's point of view an almost infinite number of additional 'states' (though not in the same sense of 'state,' . . . [so-called] *structural states*)" (Putnam). For instance, a cardboard Turing machine may buckle. Hilary Putnam ingeniously develops an analogy between the logical states of Turing machines and mental states of human beings and the structural states of Turing machines and physical states of human beings. The analogy generates its own problems, as we shall soon see. Nevertheless, what Putnam nicely shows are (1) that logical attributes may be defined independently of any physical realization, but may be ascribed to given physical systems (and, in principle, to non-physical systems, if otherwise intelligible); (2) that such attributes and the abstract machines of which they are the properties "may be physically realized in an almost infinite number of different ways"; (3) that logical attributes and, by analogy, mental attributes may always be discriminated as distinct from the physical attributes (structural attributes) in which they are "realized" or instantiated, whether or not an identity holds between "logical" or "functional" states and "mental" states.

The force of these considerations confirms the relative neutrality of the third sort of dualism: unless we have more telling distinctions between mental and physical attributes, we could not, by reference to distinctions analogous to that of logical and structural states, expect to support Cartesian (or ontic) dualism. Nevertheless, to favor materialism is not, as has been said, tantamount to favoring the identity theory: there are other alternatives, and there are difficulties confronting standard theories.

Consider some representative positions. Fodor [1968], reviewing cross-category identities, stresses that, on an empiricist view, "a concept is specified, in part, by reference to the kinds of *evidence* [italics added] that are typically employed in justifying claims that something falls under that concept", and that the concept of a mental state may be construed as a "theoretical concept" only if that classification is understood in the following way: (1) as not providing an ontological classification but only a classification with regard to how the "existence claims about that entity [that is, a theoretical entity] are justified"; (2) as classifying a mental state as an "inferred entity" just *"where it is logically possible to observe* (makes sense to speak of observing) *that something is [such a mental state]* ". There are, however, at least two decisive difficulties in Fodor's argument about the status of mental states. For one thing, the theoretical/observational distinction, fair as it is, sheds no light at all on the implications of the direct, introspective reporting role of first-person discourse about mental states. Fodor's argument concerns only

second- and third-person discourse of an observational sort — more, as he
reasonably explains, having to do with the *justification* of claims about others'
mental states than about their *discovery* (thus by-passing the puzzles of
solipsism); also, on Fodor's view, concepts of mental and psychological states
are "functionally" connected with hypotheses about "the etiology of
behavior" precisely when they are introduced, in *explanatory* contexts, as
theoretical states for which suitable behavioral evidence is accessible. For a
second, Fodor confuses the need for "noninferential verifications of second-
person mental ascriptions" with the defense of some form of psychophysical
identity: he cannot, he admits, see, "if one assumes that no psychophysical
identity statements are true, . . . what other candidates for observational
verifications of second-person mental ascriptions the inferred-entity view
could possibly offer." But he himself acknowledges, against behaviorism, that
"existential statements about theoretical entities are *always* logically independent of statements about the observational data" and that some theory must
be invoked in virtue of which the observational data constitute "the best
possible *prima facie evidence*" for mental ascriptions. Fodor, therefore, fails
to come to terms (i) with the fact that the definition of functional properties
is independent of the conditions of their realization or instantiation (whether
physically or otherwise); (ii) with the fact that, even if materialism is favored,
the realization or instantiation of functional properties does not as such entail
any version of the identity theory; (iii) with the fact that, since we lack a
Turing machine program for human beings, we cannot, even on his own
favored view, formulate a finite disjunction of physical states of which some
determinate disjunct may be specified as identical with the mental (functional)
state in question.

Fodor's argument attempts to persuade us that *if*, on empirical grounds,
the need for relying on observationality is granted and *if* discourse about
theoretical entities must be suitably linked, in an evidentiary way, with
discourse about observational entities (where the demarcation line, of course,
is diachronically variable), then materialism cannot but be supported — *a
fortiori*, *some* form of psychophysical identity. The argument is very close to
Smart's, though with differences to be detailed, and fails for the same reason.
Alternative forms of materialism are available that need not and do not subscribe to the identity thesis (but that allow for observationality). What is
important to note in the present context is that Fodor's argument does not
depend at all on the conceptual peculiarities of experienced mental states, or
on what sorts of entities they may be ascribed to, or on what asymmetries
there may be regarding first- and third-person reports of mental states

(versions of "observationality", if you like). Consequently, since the argument supporting the identity thesis is a *non sequitur*, we may fairly conclude that the most plausible materialist alternative will depend at least on a detailed account of mental states themselves. In any case, if relationships other than identity be admitted that preserve second- and third-person observationality (emergence and embodiment, for instance), if we distinguish between the theory-laden nature of observation itself and inference from observation (implicit in admitting perceptual reports), and if we admit that perceptual judgments may be drawn (as Fodor himself says) in accord with criteria that, though veridically satisfied, do not entail that the mental states and episodes judged to obtain obtain, then it is impossible, merely conceding second- and third-person observationality of mental states and the definition of what it is to be a theoretical concept, to deduce straight off that some form of psychophysical identity must be true. (We shall return to the question of criteria at a later point.)

Both Fodor and Putnam, in fact, restrict themselves largely to noting only the viability of theoretical identities just where the analogy regarding the difference between logical and structural states is admitted. In so doing, however, both oppose reductive identities, essentially for two reasons: for one, because mental states are to be defined functionally by analogy with logical states or in terms of the functional connection of such states with the behavior of organisms rather than in terms of their microtheoretical components (Place [1956]; Oppenheim and Putnam [1958]); for another, because functional states are thought to be functionally similar or identical with one another, without necessarily being similar or identical in their material realization. Fodor emphasizes, for instance, that pains cannot be said to have any parts or any microtheoretical parts; but he does not satisfactorily explain the sense in which pains may or must be functional states (even if second- and third-person observations of another's pain entail reference to functional or behavioral criteria). If pains neither have parts nor are functional states but are actually and directly experienced in a familiar phenomenological sense, then neither reductive nor eliminative identities nor identities of the functional sort could be confirmed — at least uniformily for all mental phenomena. The question is whether materialism can still be sustained. We may notice, also, that we are forced here once again to consider the difference between at least two kinds of mental phenomena — of which beliefs and intentions serve as instances of the intentional kind and pains, of the non-intentional kind. It may be promising to construe intentional mental states as functional or even, relative to behavior, as dispositional (dispositional, on the assumption at least of the

rational organization of the beliefs, intentions, desires, and the like of creatures of different sorts [Frankfort (1971)]). But it is not at all clear that
pains can be plausibly construed either as functional or as dispositional. Pains
have an undeniable phenomenal quality, the proper materialist interpretation
of which constitutes a serious puzzle. Images, of course, have both a distinct
phenomenal quality and an intentional nature; but pains lack an intentional
nature, in the sense of their not being "directed upon an object". The point
is seriously missed by G. E. M. Anscombe [1963], who, insisting on the
"intentionality of sensation", has perceptual images and perception-like
"sensation" chiefly in mind. She may have shown that there is a fair sense in
which the perceptual verbs function intransitively — therefore, intentionally
— though the account of the relationship of such cases to a full theory of
perception is lacking (her instances do not yield a uniform array: e.g., "I hear
a ringing in my ears", "I see the print very blurred: is it blurred, or is it my
eyes?"). In any event, she offers, to support the extension of her account to
pain, the single instance of "phantom limb" pain. However difficult the case
may be, it turns entirely on the analysis of the "location" of pain. If, however, locational remarks about pain (whether the phantom limb variety or any
other) are taken to be descriptive of the felt quality of a pain ("where it is
felt to be at") rather than an attempt to determine the actual location of a
pain, the entire interpretation collapses. The decisive reason for this is simply
that Anscombe is not prepared to view the location of an actual pain in an
actual limb as intentional in the same sense. The point is that it is not intentional at all, not even in the phantom limb case.

Actually, to construe pains functionally, in terms of hypotheses about
"the etiology of behavior", has to do more with the conditions of public
discourse about pain than with whatever may distinguish such mental states
in first-person contexts (cf. Dennett [1969]). Pain states — doubtless, the
other bodily sensations to some extent — are extremely varied and complex.
Melzack [1973], for instance, suggests that "pain may be defined in terms of
a multidimensional space comprising several sensory and affective dimensions.
The space comprises those subjective experiences which have both somatosensory and negative-affective components and that elicit behavior aimed at
stopping the conditions that produce them." But, though he acknowledges
the "diversity of pain experience" and the difficulty of achieving a "satisfactory definition", Melzack insists that "if injury or any other noxious input
fails to evoke negative affect and aversive drive ... the experience cannot
be called pain. Conversely, anxiety or anguish without concomitant activity
in the somatic afferent system is not pain." It is not clear, in the face of

empirical evidence regarding the discrimination of "subjective experiences" of the relevant "somatosensory" sort, in which aversive dispositions are absent, as in cases of asymbolia for pain or certain leucotomies, or even in taking pleasure in low-level pain (Sternbach [1968]; Trigg [1970]), how Melzack can justifiably preclude such experiences from counting as experiences of pain. Alternatively put, it seems quite reasonable to distinguish the "sensory" from the "interpretive" component that links the first with "negative affect and aversive drive". Even if the linkage is "normal", it appears not to be necessary: the very concept of pain as a form *of sensory* — or, perhaps better, sentient — discrimination provides for such demarcation. Also, the distinction does not in any way violate Melzack's intended warning, implicit in the remark that pain is "a perceptual experience whose quality and intensity are influenced by the unique past history of the individual, by the meaning he gives to the pain-producing situation and by his 'state of mind' at the moment". In fact, he himself notes that, as in describing a "splitting headache", we employ a descriptive vocabulary characteristically favoring figurative, "as if" predicates: "A splitting headache, then, does not mean that the head is being split open. It obviously represents a figure of speech, meant to convey some property of the total pain experience — that the pain feels *as if* the head were being split open." But *if* such sensory discriminations, *characteristically* linked to certain affective and aversive responses, may be marked off, then Melzack's insistence on the joint satisfaction of sensory and affective conditions is implausible. Furthermore, if pain were construed, as with Pitcher [1970], as a mode of perception and if, as such, so-called pain receptors were construed as "nociceptors" (Sauerbruch and Wenke [1963]), that is, as adjusted to discriminate what is "potentially or actually productive of tissue damage" (Sweet [1959]), then it would, by analogy with other sensory modes, be gratuitous to add contingent, even if "normal", affective and aversive elements to the definition of pain (*contra* Armstrong [1962]). This is not, it may be said, to endorse a perceptual theory of pain but only to show that a functional view is likely to be untenable. The perceptual model of pain, however attractive and convenient it may appear to be, is ultimately untenable as well (Margolis [1977d]). It fails to come to terms with such anomalous phenomena as the *couvade*, in which tissue damage or potential damage is simply irrelevant, or with the non-noxious stimulation of causalgic pain after complete healing, or with apparent central nervous system abnormalities that produce *tic douloureux* in the absence of nerve damage and in spite of fine-grained surgery on putatively offending nerves, or with post-traumatic pain, or psychogenic pain (Melzack [1973]). But if a perceptual model of pain is untenable and an intentional and dispositional account of pain is also untenable, then the usual functional accounts of mental states (Putnam's and Fodor's, for instance) have simply failed to address themselves to a quite distinctive range of phenomena.

On the other hand, where a functional view of mental states is reasonable, as with thought and emotion, then precisely because of their intentional content (a matter to which we shall return), Fodor's [1968] "two-phase" defense of psychophysical identities is rendered doubtful again. Fodor sorts out, in the context of psychological explanation, those "phase-one psychological theories [that] postulate functionally equivalent mechanisms when and only when they postulate constructs [mental states] of which the behavioral consequences are, in theoretically relevant respects, identical". But, as he says, "the second phase of psychological explanation has to do with the specification of those biochemical systems that do, in fact, *exhibit* the functional characteristics enumerated by phase-one theories" [italics added]. We need only remark, here, the problem of "many-many" correlations, in virtue of which given "biochemical systems" can, where suitably "correlated", only be *assigned* the functional characteristics in question. We shall return to the issue.

In Putnam's case, some further details about the nature of mental states are supplied, that show even more clearly the need to explore alternative forms of materialism. In particular, Putnam treats the following two statements as suitably similar, in the context of comparing logical or mental and structural or physical states:

(a)   The machine ascertained that it was in state A,
(b)   Jones knew that he had a pain.

But, in a physically realized (or physically instantiated) system, (a) would convey the machine analogue of *perception*; that is, in principle, "state A" would either be suitably inferred by way of observational evidence (*à la* Fodor) or else it would itself be observed (perceived). In this sense, state A must be observationally accessible, publicly accessible, accessible symmetrically for first-, second-, and third-person discourse. But the precise question to be asked about (b) is whether "ascertaining" (a significantly ambiguous term now) that one is in pain *is* a matter of public perception, symmetrically for first-, second-, and third-person discourse, is spite of the fact that, on the hypothesis advanced by Fodor, if mental states are theoretical entities, there must, in principle, be a basis merely for collecting observational *evidence* about such states.

So Putnam's case for theoretical identity depends either on conflating perception and sensation or, at the very least, on a failure to explore their similarities and differences. It needs to be noted that the privacy of sensation, if admitted, is quite different from the privacy of, say, proprioception and interoception: the first has to do with the putative intransitivity of sensation, that is, that sensations do not exist independently of having sensations; and the second has to do, admitting the transitivity of perception, with certain forms of privileged access to *what, in principle, is publicly accessible through other perceptual modes* (Margolis [1973a]). Perception is transitive in the sense that what is actually perceived must exist independently of perception or be an actual independent property of what exists.

Secondly, in supposing that "the functional organization (problem solving, thinking) of the human being or machine" can be described in terms of logical states without regard to "physical realization", Putnam inadvertently implies that *all* mental states may be uniformly so construed. Nevertheless, it is open to serious dispute, as we have seen, whether a functional account (Putnam [1967a]; Chihara and Fodor [1965]) can be provided uniformly for sensation and thought. It is even possible that a theoretical identity may be defended for some sorts of mental states and not for others – or, on different grounds for different kinds of mental states – if it should prove to be the case that sensations, as opposed to thoughts, cannot be functionally interpreted. This is the force, for instance, of insisting on a reporting role with regard to sensations, where it is understood that the experiential aspect of sensation cannot be captured by eliminative maneuvers or analogues of perceptual reporting (Cornman [1968a]; Feigl [1967]). Incidentally, an economical way of seeing the required distinction between sensation and perception is afforded by merely considering that, according to the perceptual interpretation of pain sketched above (Pitcher [1970]; Sweet [1959]), we are said to perceive not only that a part of one's body is actually in a "damaged, bruised, irritated, or pathological state" but also that one's body is *potentially* in such a state. Where the verb 'feel' or its cognates is assigned a non-propositional accusative (Chisholm [1966]), it would be questionbegging, in context, to assume a specifiably *independent* object; and where the verb is assigned a propositional accusative *only*, it is impossible to hold that the verb has a perceptual sense or (at least) to hold that it does so for that reason alone. Sentences like 'I see that you are right' or 'I hear what you say' (even sentences with apparently non-propositional accusatives, for instance, 'I see your point') are not normally used to state anything about sensory perception. Verbs of sensory perception, suitably used in epistemic contexts, may be said, in effect, to take

both propositional and non-propositional accusatives (Chisholm [1966];
Sibley [1971]; Margolis [1973a]). Of a man who has some perceptual
(visual) belief of the appropriately epistemic sort, we must be able to say
both (i) that he sees P (an independent, existent object, state of affairs, or the
like suitably accessible to his sense of sight) and (ii) that he sees that *p* (a
relevant proposition about P). (The formula is sufficiently flexible to accommodate visual error, visual illusion, and the like; the full details do not concern
us here.) But it is doubtful that, in speaking of the cognitive awareness of
sensations (as of pain), we are speaking of a fully perceptual phenomenon
(*contra* Armstrong [1962] and Pitcher [1970]), that is, one in which what is
being relevantly discriminated is an independent object (or state of affairs or
the like) publicly accessible to others by other perceptual modes.

This suggests certain further difficulties in Putnam's account. For one
thing, returning to Putnam's specimen sentences (a) and (b), the selection
of the verb 'ascertain', in (a), is, really, devilishly equivocal. For it is quite
possible, where machines are concerned, that 'ascertain' *not* be used in any
epistemically developed sense. One might say (extravagantly) that the
thermostat "ascertained" that the room's temperature had fallen below the
temperature set and, as a consequence, it "turned on" the blower. Where
'ascertain' is intended in a non-epistemic sense (or, is used as a *façon de
parler*), *no* appropriate analogue holds between (a) and (b), for in (b), 'know'
is unequivocally used in an epistemic sense. But where 'ascertain' is used
epistemically, we lack altogether, as yet, an account of precisely how a
machine can be said to *know* that it is in state A. This is not to deny (or to
affirm) that machines are capable of knowledge. It is only to remind us that
we normally admit direct knowledge and experience of certain mental states
(notably, pains), but it is an open question what we intend by saying that a
machine has knowledge of its own internal states. The problem is compounded
because, having specified the *kind* of sensation Jones knows he has, we know
we have at least the beginning of a theory of how *he* may come to know it.
But, precisely, in (a), no specification is provided of the *kind* of state state A
is; hence, we have no idea at all of the relevant sensory or sentient mechanisms
by which the machine may come to know that it is in state A. Again, the
verbs 'ascertain' and 'know' do not by themselves, as do the verbs 'see,' 'hear,'
'smell' and the like, convey anything about the relevant sensory or sentient
mechanisms by which given (non-propositional) objects may be appropriately
discriminated. The use of propositional objects appears to confirm Putnam's
intention to use 'ascertain' in the epistemic sense; but the normal way in
which the requisite account is provided involves specifying the appropriate

non-propositional objects (of whatever sort) accessible to this or that mode of perception (or other mode of sentience) (Margolis [1962]). Furthermore, the usual theories of knowledge entail the ascribability of belief (and other mental states) (Chisholm [1966] ; Margolis [1973a] ; Lehrer [1974]).

These considerations argue that Putnam is at least premature in holding that "every philosophic argument that has ever been employed in connection with the mind-body problem, from the oldest and most naive (e.g., 'states of consciousness can just be *seen* to be different from physical states') to the most sophisticated, has its *exact* [italics added] counterpart in the case of the 'problem' of logical states and structural states in Turing machines". One further consideration may be mentioned. An actual (not an abstract) Turing machine is made and is programmed to do what we call "ascertaining that it is in state A". It is, on the story, in virtue of *that* that the epistemically relevant idiom is employed at all. It is, in short, because it has a finite and assigned program, in terms of which its functional states can be said to be detected at all, that we are prepared to make cognitive ascriptions to the machine. In that case, the ascription is conceptually parasitic on our being able to make such ascriptions of ourselves, under conditions that are either utterly different from those under which the machine functions or else are at least not known to be similar. But if that is the case, then it must be concluded that Putnam's charge is entirely questionbegging — which is not, of course, to deny that machine-like creatures may someday appear in outer space, regarding "whom" it may well be preposterous to deny that "they" are capable of knowledge. In that event, however, we should probably find ourselves in the same predicament as before; that is, we should lack the finite machine program (as we do with ourselves) in virtue of which Putnam's original analogy was advanced. Hence, Putnam's alternatives simply miss the mark: "if the mind-body problem is identified with any problem of more than purely conceptual interest (e.g., with the question of whether or not human beings have 'souls') then *either* it must be that (a) no argument *ever* used by a philosopher sheds the *slightest* light on it (and this independently of the way the argument tends), or (b) that some philosophic argument for mechanism is correct, or (c) that some dualistic argument does show that *both* human beings *and* Turing machines have souls!" Putnam has yet to explain the sense in which machines may be said to have cognitive states: to the extent that he does, he will be obliged to exceed his own alternatives. Not every functional state is a cognitive state (as the "behavior" of the thermostat and of plants makes clear) and what the precise analogy is between the functional states of machines and the *cognitively* functional states of men needs still to be speficied. Presumably, for instance, this distinction reflects consideration in virtue of which Noam Chomsky [1972], though committed to the thesis that persons are preset for language, resist the views of those who would reduce persons to finite-state automata. We shall return to the issue.

The argument thus far pursued has the advantage of proceeding with as little detailed commitment as possible to the peculiarities of discourse about mental and psychological phenomena. All that has been presumed is that a viable materialism is not exhausted by versions of the identity theory, that the connection between observationality and materialism bears on evidentiary requirements rather than on identity as such, that mental and psychological concepts may not be open to a uniform analysis, and, finally, that special attention must be paid to the distinctive features of first-person reports of mental states. In this sense, the introduction of such distinctions as that between logical and structural states (and mental and physical states) shows the benign nature of the third sort of dualism. In fact, Putnam [1967a] specifically acknowledges that "the functional-state hypothesis is not incompatible with dualism"; and he takes it that mental states are *not* brain states, physico-chemical states of the brain or of the whole nervous system, but are, rather, functional states of the sort he has specified. He holds, against Smart, that the hypothesis that pain is a brain state is most unlikely, since to support it one would have "to specify a physical-chemical state such that any organism (not just a mammal) is in pain if and only if (a) it possesses a brain of a suitable physical-chemical structure; and (b) its brain is in that physical-chemical state"; it is unlikely, that is, that "parallel evolution, all over the universe, might *always* lead to *one and the same* physical 'correlate' of pain". Its weakness lies, however, in construing the reporting use of first-person discourse about mental states in terms of the theoretical status of mental states themselves. That maneuver cannot be adequate because, whatever other difficulties may arise (the threat of solipsism, for instance, or the need to exclude the *qualia* of mental experience from the domain of science (Brodbeck [1963], [1966]), first-person reports or first-person knowledge of mental states need not be, and are often characteristically not qualified as, functionally linked to the etiology of behavior (to use Fodor's phrase). Obviously, the problems involved here present us with the possibility of forcing a retreat to a dualism or an epiphenomenalism of a sort that leaves us with "nomological danglers" (Feigl [1967]) or, even more disappointingly, with a full Cartesian dualism. The question remains how this may be forestalled. Still, it cannot be forestalled by the strategy of so-called functional materialism. At any rate, the force of that theory cannot be fully assessed without a close analysis of mental and psychological states, cannot be assessed without determining whether they are or are not conceptually homogeneous with respect to the functionalist thesis or whether there are other materialist alternatives that may accommodate them. This, however, is precisely what is missing.

This identifies as well the incompleteness of David Lewis's recent challenge [1966], that "we who accept the materialistic working hypothesis that physical phenomena have none but purely physical explanations must accept the identity theory [reverting to Smart's thesis, that] as a matter of fact − every experience is identical with some physical state". Lewis formulates his argument thus: "The definitive characteristic of any (sort of) experience as such is its causal role, its syndrome of most typical causes and effects. But we materialists believe that these causal roles which belong by analytic necessity to experiences belong in fact to certain physical states. Since those physical states possess the definite characteristics of experience, they must be the experience." But there are problems to be met. For one thing, *if* experiences, mental phenomena, have as their definitive characteristic, some "typical" causal role, that causal role may include or incorporate the causal role assigned to "certain physical states" without being identical with that (sort of) role: unless reductionism were independently confirmed, it would not be possible, on Lewis's proposal, to explain how experience causes such intentional states as fright to occur. We might well have to fall back to psychophysical laws, without yet violating materialism. It would still be possible to admit the "definitive" *causal* role of experience, provided that some relationship other than identity, but compatible with materialism (embodiment, for instance), were advanced and defended.

Doubtless, such psychophysical laws could be no more than probabilistic and constrained within quite restricted contexts, but that fact would merely set constraints on the program of the unity of science. Secondly, *if* experiences were related to physical states by some relation other than identity, even if "purely physical explanations" could be provided for physical states (somehow, in an as yet unexplained way) related to experiences, the causal role of physical states would not, for trivial reasons, provide us with an explanation of experiences. Lewis is quite right, however, in holding that *if* a causal role is definitive of experience, epiphenomenalism and parallelism are ruled out "because they deny the efficacy of experience"; he is also right in holding that a radical behaviorism is ruled out because it denies "the reality and *a fortiori* the efficacy of experiences" (since "a pure disposition is a fictitious entity"). Thirdly, it is not clear whether, or what is meant by saying that, the definitive causal roles of experiences "belong by analytic necessity" to them. Certainly, if they are so defined, then the role belongs by analytic necessity to them. It is entirely possible, however, to concede or deny, as has already been said, that experiences possess certain causal roles, without holding that such causal roles are definitive of experiences as such. It seems open to dispute, for instance, that what is definitive of pains, mental images, and after-images *is* the possession of certain causal roles, *even though* public discourse about mental phenomena presupposes suitable causal linkages and even though the efficacy of experiences may be a matter of considerable interest in the relevant sciences. It may, for instance, be that the *qualia* or intentional content of such mental phenomena, introspectively accessible, are what is distinctive of them. In that case, even (a restricted form of) epiphenomenalism is not quite as easy to dismiss as Lewis seems to believe. Suppose that what is "distinctive" of a thought is that, in Brentano's sense [1973] it is "directed upon an object", exhibits "intentional in-existence". It would then be possible to hold *both* that thoughts are causally effective (though their actual effects, not issuing in recognizable behavior, are often negligible and, conceivably, impossible to specify) *and* that epiphenomenalism is benign, since (and in the sense that) the mere intentional *content* of a thought cannot itself have a causal role. Lewis seems to have nothing to say about this possibility.

We may, furthermore, very briefly trace those empirical and conceptual considerations that tend to keep alive what has been termed the third sort of dualism — the benign sort — regardless of the deeper ontological convictions discussants may harbor. The points required are easily collected. On the conceptual side, we have already noted, *via* functional materialism, the difference between functional and physical states. Systems that are "functionally equivalent" need not be anatomically or physically similar (Fodor [1968]), simply because functional states are defined without regard to physical realization and are even compatible, so far forth, with non-physical realization. But if that is so, then "we have no right to assume *a priori* that the nervous system may not sometimes produce indistinguishable psychological effects by *radically* different physiological means. How much redundancy there may be in the nervous system is surely an open empirical question" (Fodor). Not only is it an open question, but we cannot even formulate *determinately* many alternative physical states appropriately associated with a given psychological effect (of the functional sort). To be able to do so would, in effect, be to possess the finite machine program of human mental states. Hence, here, we have a "one-many" relationship in which the "many" cannot, by some disjunctive connection, facilitate *any* identity claims. (As Lewis [1966] aptly observes, in the context of the identity thesis, states "are to be taken in general as universals".) On the empirical side, we must concede (Eccles [1965]) the implication of the fact that "indubitable evidence of the convergence of sensory information in the cortex is provided by those experiments in which a single cortical neuron is shown to be activated from several different sensory inputs", that "there are now hundreds of examples of multisensory convergence on single cortical neurons in all parts of the cerebral cortex, as well as in all the subcortical centers".

Considerations of this sort, adumbrated by Putnam [1967a], show decisively that mind/body identity involving simple physico-chemical states without reference to functional states must be a false thesis. Smart [1962] had inclined to such a thesis, though his conception of "topic-neutral" causal accounts of mental phenomena or experiences lends itself very nicely to a functional interpretation as well (Lewis [1966]). On a functional reading, there seems to be a general postulate adopted in neurophysiological studies (Fessard [1961]; Mountcastle [1965]), "that for every perception there is a specific spatio-temporal pattern of neuronal activity in the neuronal networks of the cerebral cortex and the related subcortical ganglia" (Eccles).

Unfortunately, no such isomorphism has ever been empirically established even though significant correlations have been. Also, as we shall see, the manner in which a *correlation* is established in psychoneurological contexts may well favor a relationship other than identity. In fact, the relationship intended seems to involve a "material counterpart" rather than a "correlation" (Eccles [1970]). Lewis, combining a functional account with Smart's theory, has spoken of "causal isomorphs". But then, the causal characterization of experiences may very easily lead to identifying *different* kinds of experiences in virtue of counterpart causal isomorphs — if we qualify (as already suggested) the thesis that the causal roles of experiences belong "by analytic necessity" to them; and, Lewis himself takes the causal role to be merely "typical", so that "experience has some characteristics or other besides its definitive causal role [that] confer a sense upon ascriptions of it in some exceptional cases [*sic*] for which its definitive typical causes and effects are absent (and likewise upon denials of it in some cases for which they are present)".

The neurophysiological postulate is itself open to dispute in a number of ways. For one thing, as in memory studies (Hydén [1967]), the DNA of nerve cells is thought to produce, in response to certain frequency patterns, "uniquely specific RNA". Whether or not detailed theories about the chemical role of RNA in memory are correct (Eccles admits that "there is evidence that RNA is concerned in learning", though not, he says, "in the specific manner that Hydén postulated"), the general argument seriously affects *all* functionalist theories, simply because even mental states like memory states — that ought to lend themselves best to a purely functional account — may not be characterizable exclusively in functional terms. Imagine for instance that the concept of a "memory trace" requires not merely a specific spatio-temporal neuronal pattern but also, in general but variably, for entities of different kinds, the production of "uniquely specific RNA". We still lack, for all possible systems, a sense of anatomical or physiological constraints on the realizability of *functional* states; and we may be unable, for human beings and animals, to characterize mental states solely in either functional or physical terms.

More than this, there is a serious prospect that the required neuronal pattern is itself circularly stipulated by reference to the very mental phenomena that, on the functional thesis (as interpreted by Lewis), it would be identified with or (as interpreted by Eccles), it would be dependent on. That is, *how* could Hydén show that specific memory phenomena, intensionally sorted, are associated with "uniquely specific RNA"? The thesis seems obviously questionbegging. Even Eccles, adhering to the postulate mentioned, admits that, although the "memory of any particular event is dependent on a specific reorganization of neuronal associations (the engram)", any engram (Lashley [1950]) "has multiple representation in the cortex" and "is not just some particular fixed wiring diagram, but . . . a tremendous complex of pathways, so that any one memory is actually laid down in many places" [*sic*]. But this suggests that an engram cannot be identified with a specific neuronal pattern but is itself functionally associated with alternative neuronal patterns. But then, we are unable, at the present time (and, conceivably, on the evidence, unable in principle) to specify determinately many alternative neuronal patterns correlated with given mental phenomena. It looks very much as if, on empirical grounds, indeterminately many single neurons may be associated with the same or different mental phenomena; and *even indeterminately many alternative neuronal patterns* may be associated with any given mental phenomenon. The matter is uncertain at the moment, which is simply to say that the third sort of dualism has rather strong empirical and conceptual credentials. Taken all in all, the difficulty inherent in overcoming (indeterminately) many-many correlations of the mind/body sort suggests once again the advantage of exploring a materialism uncommitted to the identity thesis. For, although there would normally be an advantage to insist on theoretical identity rather than mere correlation (Putnam [1967a]), there is no advantage to be had where one-one, or one-(determinately) many, or (determinately) many-one correlations are lacking. Congruently with these concessions, we may simply observe that lawlike regularities of a functional sort are entirely eligible that (i) are logically distinct from structural (or physical) regularities and that (ii) are, lacking a finite machine program, neither reducible to nor replaceable by lawlike regularities of the structural sort. There would in fact, lacking a machine program, be no antecedent reason for supposing that the regularities coordinated with given functional laws would themselves conform with the normal constraints on physical laws — even though sub-sets of such regularities might so conform (Fodor [1975]).

A final consideration may be briefly mentioned. If S remembers p, though p be logically equivalent to q, it is quite possible that S will not (in the sense relevant to reporting mental phenomena — in the sense Eccles calls "psychic memory") — remember q (Armstrong [1973]). But then, there is absolutely no purely physical means and no means associated with alternative neuronal patterns by which to distinguish the memory that p and the memory that q. The issue requires much closer inspection. Nevertheless, every mental phenomenon possessing intentional content, like memory and belief but *not* like bodily sensation, is subject to the paradoxes of intensional characterization. (It is, ironically, part of Descartes's heritage that the scope of the mental, which Descartes recognizes as "thought", is taken to include both mental phenomena like sensations, that are not intentional in at least the sense of not being "directed upon an object", and phenomena like beliefs, that are [Descartes (1931); Geach (1957)] — without carefully sorting the difference.) Hence, for conceptual reasons, there is hardly any prospect that any form of the identity theory may be sustained: for, if remembering that p and remembering that q are taken as the same neural state, we make a mystery of the failure to remember the one where we remember the other; and if remembering that p is identical with some neural state, it seems impossible to specify properties of that state answering to the intensional characterization of the memory state, in virtue of which the failure to remember q *could be explained*.

This last point has been mentioned merely to strengthen the sense of the reasonableness of investigating alternative versions of materialism not committed to the identity theory. In itself, it raises problems of the most strenuous sort; but those require a new frame of reference.

PART TWO

TOWARD A THEORY OF PERSONS

CHAPTER 6

PROBLEMS REGARDING PERSONS

The question of the nature of persons obviously lies behind a good many disputes regarding the relationship of mind and body. There is, in fact, something utterly fatuous about the persistent quarrels of the various forms of reductive materialism if it is true that the ascriptions in question are primarily intended to be made of persons and sentient creatures and if the nature of those entities is generally ignored. It may not unfairly be supposed that the various stalemates, the implausibility, the lack of compelling force of the alternatives we have canvassed are in large measure due to the almost total absence of a sustained analysis of persons. In fact, Wilfrid Sellars [1963a] may very nearly be alone among the strongest proponents of reductive materialism in attending to the nature of persons; and what he says is more problematic than sufficiently developed to assure us that a straightforward materialism can accommodate the concept. His general formula, not unreasonable termed "forensic", runs as follows: "to recognize a featherless biped or dolphin or Martian as a person requires that one think thoughts of the form, 'We (one) shall do (or abstain from doing) actions of kind A in circumstances of kind C.' To think thoughts of this kind is not to *classify* or *explain*, but to *rehearse an intention*." He goes on, as we have already had occasion to note, "thus the conceptual framework of persons is not something that needs to be *reconciled with* the scientific image [Sellars' version of reductive materialism], but rather something to be *joined* to it. Thus, to complete the scientific image we need to enrich it not with more ways of saying what is the case, but with the language of community and individual intentions . . . ." The implication seems to be that an adequate account of persons (i) will not disturb the kind of physicalism sufficient to describe and explain the inanimate world, and (ii) will require an idiom not primarily adjusted to *further* veridical descriptions, descriptions beyond whatever is accessible to the reductionist, but adjusted rather to the assignment of what may be satisfactorily expressed in prescriptivist terms. This is the reason that Sellars maintains that "the *irreducibility* [italics added] of the personal is the irreducibility of the 'ought' to the 'is' ". But he fails to account for the fact that both speech and sentience — and, derivatively, the capacity to report the phenomenal content of our experience — *does* require an enriched language for saying what is the case, or else a demonstration that what Sellars himself takes to be irreducible is actually reducible. In theorizing about persons, we are tempted to sort systematically all familiar solutions until it dawns on us that we lack a fully adequate and compelling theory and that, very likely, a really promising solution will elude our more conventional habits of mind. Still, we are bound to consider: the dualist solution or the more extreme idealist solution of disembodied souls or persons; the reductive solution that persons are nothing more than complex bodies; the solution that persons are ontologically as primitive as bodies but not reducible to them; and the solution that persons are forensically specified in terms of the special status or rights and responsibilities assigned to selected bodies or sentient creatures or the like, that may be independently individuated and identified. Here, philosophical prejudice serves as an economy. The dualist and the idealist solutions, however temptingly formulated, say, by Cartesians and Christians, simply fail to come to terms with the fact that what we want is an account that fits the life and behavior of the members of *Homo sapiens*. The forensic solution suffers the distinct disadvantage that it fails to accommodate the reflexive nature of the relevant attributions. It would be fine to suppose that bodies or sentient creatures were persons only insofar as we treated them as entitled to a certain status or as capable of intentions and behavior requisite to that status, but the theory fails to note that *we*, after all, actually make the ascriptions of one another; hence, nothing like the notion of a legal fiction could possibly account for the initial assignment of such status, whatever advantages there might be in construing human persons, once identified, as legal or legal-like persons.

The temper of our time, therefore, is not unreasonably impatient with these possibilities and has, for all intents and purposes, pondered the choice between a reductive account of persons (generally, that persons are simply complex bodies) and an account that persons are ontologically primitive (generally, that persons have both physical and "personal" attributes and are not, as such, analyzable as a merely complex organization of bodies — which, in their own right, are said to be ontologically primitive). Clearly, both the reductive and the nonreductive endeavors are provisional, in the sense that both bodies and persons may be replaced, in some ingenious ontology, by "successor" entities that might serve our metaphysical appetites better if only we could see that far ahead.

These two possibilities, however, prove quite inconclusive, as may readily be shown by a brief scan of the respective views of Bernard Williams and P. F. Strawson. Williams [1973b] is an advocate of the thesis that persons are simply complex bodies and Strawson [1959], of the thesis that persons are non-reducible and primitive entities. This is not to say, of course, that all reductive and all nonreductive theorists would be willing to subscribe to their arguments. Nevertheless, the difficulties facing these obviously informed views draw us on to considerations affecting the prospects of all familiar accounts of either sort. Consequently, our argument, here, is primarily negative and critical. Strawson's view requires some care. As he puts it: "the concept of a person is to be understood as the concept of a type of entity such that both predicates ascribing states of consciousness *and* predicates ascribing corporeal characteristics, a physical situation etc., are equally applicable to an individual entity of that type." Here, he says only that predicates (what he calls "P-predicates") ascribing states of consciousness or conditions that entail consciousness and predicates ascribing corporeal characteristics ("M-predicates") are both applicable to persons. He does not, therefore, insist, here, that persons are "primitive": in this respect, what he says may be admitted equally by reductive and nonreductive theorists — except for eliminative materialists (Feyerabend [1963a], [1963b]), who are quite opposed to admitting any entities but material entities or to ascribing to such entities any mental attributes. In fact, what Strawson says here is, at least provisionally, acceptable to Cartesian dualists, though not to out-and-out idealists.

Strawson also says that "the concept of a person is logically prior to that of an individual consciousness. The concept of a person is not to be analyzed as that of an animated body or of an embodied anima." The reason, consistent with the foregoing, is that, *if* material bodies lack P-attributes (as Strawson clearly believes), then the priority of persons to consciousness or conscious states secures the systematic advantages regarding individuation, identification, and reidentification that accrues to any network of particulars. Strawson says explicitly that "states of consciousness could not be ascribed at all, *unless* they were ascribed to persons, in the sense I have claimed for this word". But of course, *if*, following some ingenious reduction, persons were bodies, then even though states of consciousness had to be identified as part of the history of particular persons (that is, even though, as Strawson points out, we must speak of contingent experiences as, non-contingently, *my* experiences and *your* experiences), we could in principle do so consistently with a reductive account. Strawson does not actually appear to demonstrate that persons cannot be reduced to bodies; what he attempts to show is only that both persons and bodies must be admitted as "basic particulars" in his ontology — which of course (trivially) need not be denied by the reductionist. It is true that he resists the reduction and affirms the primitiveness of the concept of a person, but there is not even the sketch of a compelling argument to be found on either issue. Speaking of M- and P-attributes, he says, notoriously, that "among the things we ascribe to ourselves are things of a kind that we also ascribe to material bodies to which we should not dream of ascribing others of the things that we ascribe to ourselves" (" . . . material bodies to which we would not dream of applying predicates ascribing states of consciousness"). But this merely indicates his opposition to reductionism. And speaking of concepts that are primitive, he says, by way of his fullest explication, that "All I have said about the meaning of saying that this concept [the concept of a person] is primitive is that it is not to be analyzed in a certain way or ways. We are not, for example, to think of it as a secondary kind of entity in relation to two primary kinds, viz., a particular consciousness and a particular human body." The reason for *that* policy is simply that Strawson has shown that the concept of "a pure individual consciousness" could only have at best "a logically secondary existence, if one thinks, or finds, it desirable". But that goes no distance at all to showing that the concept of a person could not be analyzed reductively in terms of the concept of a material body: reductionists who view material bodies as primitive, in the sense Strawson intends, could consistently argue that persons are merely complex bodies.

The strange thing is that Strawson actually fails to give us a plausible sketch of what a person is. His concept of a person is the concept of an entity to which P- and M-predicates are equally applicable. But those predicates do not presuppose *persons*, on any familiar view of what distinguishes persons. In fact, what Strawson is speaking about are better characterized as *sentient creatures* or *animals*, as Williams [1973] rightly suggests. Ironically, what misleads (or may have misled) Strawson is his careful contrast between P-predicates and M-predicates. For, he claims (intending to avoid problems of solipsism and skepticism) that "it is a necessary condition of one's ascribing states of consciousness, experiences, to oneself, in the way one does, that one should also ascribe them, or be prepared to ascribe them, to others who are not oneself, . . . that the ascribing phrases are used in just the same sense when the subject is another as when the subject is oneself." P-predicates are distinguished from M-predicates in at least this respect, that "they are both self-ascribable otherwise than on the basis of observation of the behavior of the subject of them, and other-ascribable on the basis of behavior criteria". There is an asymmetry, therefore, in the conditions for the self-ascription and other-ascription of P-attributes; whereas M-attributes are ascribable only on public grounds — observational grounds, for instance. Material bodies, *if* persons are not material bodies, are incapable of making any ascriptions at all. Obviously, Strawson is speaking about the ascrib*ability* of P- and M-attributes, about the use of P- and M-*predicates*. But he fails to notice that what distinguishes persons from merely sentient creatures, as well as from material bodies, surely includes at least the capacity to *make ascriptions* in the first place. Oddly, he is guilty of much the same omission as those who hold a forensic conception of persons, for instance, Sellars. It is easy to suppose that Strawson regards it as essential to persons that they be capable of self-ascription. But the truth of the matter is that he maintains only that ascribing states of consciousness to oneself entails one's being prepared to ascribe such states to others. Solipsism is thereby avoided. The implications of being the kind of entity that *can* ascribe attributes Strawson does not discuss; and the condition under which P- and M-attributes are distinctively ascribed presupposes that unexplained capacity. In fact, it is just such a capacity that is ordinarily thought to be sufficient to distinguish persons from merely sentient creatures.

The upshot, therefore, is decisively unfavorable to Strawson. Strawson insists that the concept of a person is primitive; but, given his convictions, he does not show either why this must be so or why the claim must be satisfied nonreductively rather than reductively. And though he insists that the concept of a person is presupposed by the concept of a P-predicate, his "persons" prove to be no more than sentient creatures or animals; hence, for all we know, true persons – distinguished at least by the capacity to make (linguistic) ascriptions – are such that we may not need to claim that the concept of a person is primitive. This is not to deny that it is entirely possible to maintain that physical bodies are primitive, that persons are primitive and possess attributes ascribed to physical bodies, *and* that persons are not physical bodies. But it is impossible to defend the view without explaining how persons can be entities at all and, under the conditions given, primitive as well.

In a curious sense, the weakness of Bernard Williams' account of persons [1973b] is just the reverse of Strawson's; but a fair assessment of his view is complicated by his having recently collected his papers without reconciling what he has said in different places [1973b]. Thus, for example, in "The Self and the Future" [1970], Williams admits into his discussion of a certain issue that " 'mentalistic' considerations (as we may vaguely call them) and considerations of bodily continuity are involved in questions of personal identity (which is not to say that there are mentalistic and bodily criteria of personal identity)". The point of this provision is to leave as an open question the question whether bodily continuity and "mentalistic considerations" are criteria or necessary conditions of personal identity. Williams, of course, had canvassed in a number of places particular puzzles about the conditions of personal identity; and he had concluded, notably in "Personal Identity and Individuation" (1956–57), that "bodily identity is always a necessary condition of personal identity where 'bodily identity' includes the notion of spatio-temporal continuity".

Now, it is quite clear that the strong thesis regarding bodily identity is Williams's favored position. But the question remains whether and how Williams demonstrates that the thesis is the correct one. The puzzles that he considered in "Personal Identity and Individuation", the earliest of his published accounts on the general topic of personal identity, all have to do with change of personal identity without change of body, bodily interchange among distinct persons, and the intelligibility of the concept of a particular personality without reference to a body. Apart from the prospects of ingenious counterinstances – for instance, regarding brain surgery, brain transplants, and the like – there are at least two considerations that Williams has not met at all. One is that, assuming only that the question of the conditions of personal identity is an open question in the sense already indicated, that is, that we grant that bodily continuity and identity are "considerations" *involved* in questions of personal identity (in arguably different ways), we could not possibly draw Williams' conclusion of the 1956–57 paper. We could not possibly draw the conclusion from the cases there canvassed unless we supposed not only that the argument was decisive but also that the cases canvassed *exhausted* all the relevant ways in which anyone might otherwise challenge Williams' conclusion. The other consideration is that the conditions for the individuation and reidentification of particulars could only be specified if the particulars in question were properly identified as particulars of this or that *sort* and what it was to be *of that sort* were itself specified.

Williams certainly never shows that his cases are exhaustive: in fact, they are not. Nor does he say what it is to be a person. Furthermore, in his own arguments, he characteristically conflates the concession about what may be *involved* in the question of personal identity and his insistence on his own favored thesis. Thus, for instance, after surveying the complicated case in which a certain Charles is said, on the basis of extraordinary memory claims, to be the same person as Guy Fawkes, Williams declares: "The only case in which identity and exact similarity could be distinguished, as we have just seen, is that of the body – 'same body' and 'exactly similar body' really do mark a difference. Thus I should claim that the omission of the body takes away all content from the idea of personal *identity*." What Williams obviously means is that, in the context of the Charles/Guy Fawkes case, it is not enough to show that Charles has the same character and the same supposed past as Fawkes (Charles' brother Robert, it turns out, may make similar claims, though Charles and Robert are clearly not identical): that shows only that, in the respects given, they are "exactly similar". Only reference to the same body, *in the context supplied*, could satisfy the question of identity. Note, therefore, that the conclusion ("the omission of the body takes away all content from the idea of personal *identity*") favors the weaker concession and does not lead to the originally intended thesis ("bodily identity is always a necessary condition of personal identity").

The equivocation is essential to Williams' argument. Thus, again regarding the Charles/Guy Fawkes case, he says: "Hence it is a necessary condition of making the supposed identification on non-bodily grounds that at some stage identifications should be made on bodily grounds. Hence any claim that bodily considerations can be absolutely omitted from the criteria of personal identity must fail; these facts do rule out the stronger thesis [that there is no conceivable situation in which bodily identity would be necessary, some other conditions being always both necessary and sufficient − Locke's theory, for instance] ." But, even if there were "bodily grounds" *involved* in confirming personal identity, that would not show that bodily identity was a necessary condition of personal identity. Nor, does insisting that "bodily considerations" cannot "be absolutely omitted from the criteria of personal identity" show that bodily identity is a necessary condition of personal identity. It is only because Williams thinks that the case he has drawn permits no other conclusion *and* because he wrongly supposes that, as it permits no other conclusion, all other relevant puzzle cases regarding personal identity are bound to lead to the very same conclusion, that he takes the one doctrine to be tantamount to the other.

The reason it is both important and entirely fair to press the difference is simply that Williams never actually says *what it is to be a person* (except in the quarrelsome sense that, whatever it may be said to be, it is nothing but a complex body). Had he specified the nature of a person, we might have been able to decide whether a part of the argument not actually provided but plausibly supplied would force us to the conclusion Williams wants. After all, it does seem odd to believe that if there are considerations of bodily continuity or bodily identity which are involved in deciding personal identity, that − quite apart from any disputes about the *nature* of persons − it must be the case that bodily continuity or bodily identity "is always a necessary condition of personal identity".

If, of course, persons are nothing but bodies, then, on pain of contradiction, bodily identity must always be a necessary condition of personal identity. In fact, at the same time he makes the concession about what is "involved" in the question of personal identity, Williams [1970] argues that persons are nothing but bodies. If he had been able to demonstrate that persons were bodies, he would not have needed to consider independently the bodily exchange cases and the like. But a careful reading of the "Are Persons Bodies?" paper will show that Williams (rightly) does not take himself to have demonstrated that persons are bodies. After exploring certain difficulties in Strawson's account, he says that he will close his own with "four leading objections to the view that persons are material bodies, and say something against them" – possibly not decisive but at least "discouraging ... to the objections". The objections concern the conceivability of disembodied persons; the nonsubstitutability *salve veritate* of 'Jones' (taken as referring to a person) and 'Jones's body'; the false conditional that if persons are material bodies, then all properties of persons are material properties; and the essential issue of whether the identity of persons is the same as the identity of bodies.

Williams sees that the objection linked to the last issue is bound to be "the most forceful one", but in meeting it he considers only the sort of case suggested by Sydney Shoemaker [1963] and Wiggins [1967], the exchange of brains rather than the exchange of bodies – because it "avoids the *reduplication problem*" (as in the Charles/Guy Fawkes case). Here, accepting Shoemaker's case (about which he has misgivings), Williams draws our attention to the fact that a problem very much like that which dogs Strawson's account will arise: it will "at any rate leave us with a job still to do, namely to make clear how the ascription of bodily properties to persons is not the ascription of anything to bodies ... ". But that is simply to testify to an unresolved problem. Williams moves on then to consider the case of "the transfer of information between brains" as opposed to "the physical transfer of brains", but this he thinks will generate the reduplication problem. The upshot is that, though he strongly believes that persons are bodies, he has no decisive argument to show that it must be so. Hence, the weakness of Williams' entire argument may be put in the following way. If he could have shown that persons were bodies, then it would have followed at once (trivially) that bodily identity was a necessary condition of personal identity; but he has not shown that persons are bodies. And if he had shown that, for certain specimen cases, personal identity could not be established without establishing bodily identity, he could have concluded that bodily identity was a necessary condition of personal identity only if he could also have shown that his specimen cases exhausted all the relevant possibilities regarding the relationship between bodily and personal identity; but he has not shown that his cases exhaust all the possibilities or capture what is essential to every such possibility. It is entirely possible that, in *some* contexts, reference to bodily identity is taken to decide the question of personal identity precisely because (whatever might have been) countervailing considerations did not obtain. Hence, he has not shown that bodily identity *is* a necessary condition of personal identity but only, perhaps, that (as might have been conceded at the outset) bodily continuity and identity are considerations *involved* in the question of personal identity.

Our strategy has, of course, been dialectical and entirely destructive, but it is almost never noticed how extraordinarily thin the reductionist view of persons tends to be. If there are kinds of cases that Williams has not canvassed, which are coherent and would entail the denial of the bodily identity condition, then Williams's arguments must be strongly inconclusive. And if there may be relations between persons and bodies other than that of identity, then once again Williams's arguments must be strongly inconclusive. But those conditions are readily satisfied. For one thing, Strawson, in holding that the concept of a person is primitive, must be denying that persons are identical with bodies; and since he opposes Cartesian dualism, Strawson must be committed to there being some significant relationship other than identity between persons and bodies. Williams never attempts to show that it is impossible or incoherent to maintain such a view — only that Strawson's position is open to serious difficulty having to do with the ascription of M- and P-attributes. But *anyone who held that persons are emergent or emergent entities with respect to bodies* — for instance, with respect to the use of language or the capacity to ascribe attributes to things or to exhibit certain distinctive cultural properties — would be advancing a theory not obviously incoherent or impossible to defend, entailing a denial that persons are identical with bodies. It must be the case, therefore, that Williams could not show the justification for conflating his strong claim about necessary conditions with the weaker concession about the relevance of bodily considerations, without some theory of the nature of persons. But he nowhere supplies the theory. Secondly, to turn to potential counterinstances, there is no reason Williams supplies for thinking that there could not be more than one person sharing a particular body. That is, there is no clear reason for supposing that it is incoherent to claim that, possibly in normal cases, certainly in at least some abnormal cases — as in the famous experimental cases discussed by R. W. Sperry [1966, 1968] regarding cerebral commissurotomy — we may be able to associate one person with each of the hemispheres of the brain. The anomalies of Sperry's cases show the conceivability (though not necessarily the advisability) of individuating persons with respect to (but not identifying them with) the hemispheres of the brain (Puccetti [1973]; T. Nagel [1971]; Margolis [1975c]). But if persons were, either under normal or abnormal circumstances, individuated with respect to the hemispheres of the brain, then, clearly, bodily identity could not be taken as a necessary condition of personal identity. Furthermore, if such cases were conceded, then the puzzle cases introduced by Shoemaker and Wiggins and others might be considerably strengthened. Hence, we may safely conclude that Williams' arguments are quite inconclusive.

The force of the counterconsideration needs to be made clear. Williams maintains that bodily identity is a necessary condition of personal identity. But in order to give even initial plausibility to his view, he would have to show that the thesis that there may be plural persons "associated with" or "in" the same body is conceptually incoherent. What Williams asks, however, is, assuming person A associated with body A and person B associated with body B, is it conceivable that A and B could be identical if body A and body B are not identical? and could person A somehow become associated with body B in the way in which he was associated with body A? Those questions presuppose an answer to the question, what *is* it to be a person and how is a person related to a body? But if it is not inconceivable that there may be plural persons inhabiting the same body, then it cannot be the case that bodily identity is a necessary condition of personal identity. Williams never shows that the possibility is incoherent. In fact, no one has ever shown that, and there is good reason to think that it is not incoherent. If it were conceded, then we should, at best, be obliged to retreat to the weaker thesis – which Strawson was already willing to adopt – namely, that personal identity "involves" considerations of bodily identity. But that thesis, as we have seen, is a remarkably weak one.

To say that much, however, is neither to advocate nor to reject out of hand the theory of plural persons in the same body. It is clear that the thesis may become an extravagance and may even, characteristically, be unnecessary. But the question is, in a large sense, an empirical one. That alone decisively defeats Williams' contention. Having said that, however, we should properly guard against anomalous views.

Roland Puccetti [1973] is perhaps the most strenuous proponent of the view that, even in normal cases, there are two persons inhabiting the human body. Puccetti bases his account on the brain-bisection literature (Bogen [1969a], [1969b]; Bogen and Bogen [1969]; Bogen, DeZure, Tenhouten, and Marsh [1972]; Gazzaniga [1970]; Geschwind [1965]). His principal concern lies with whether there could be two minds in one person or whether the admission of two minds entails the admission of two persons. One is tempted to think that the empirical data regarding brain-bisected subjects are not in dispute, that only the interpretation of those data is in dispute. But the least scanning of the literature shows a characteristic uncertainty in identifying the proper subject or subjects of perceptual, behavioral, and cognitive ascriptions. Summarizing a specimen study, Puccetti says: "In the commissurotomy patient under test conditions, the minor hemisphere is still dominant for recognizing faces, so where a manual response is indicated *it points* with either hand to the face *it saw* and the speech hemisphere *goes along*, being much less sure what *it saw*" (italics added). The trouble is that the ascription of personal and mental attributes to the two hemispheres lies at the very heart of the conceptual puzzle, and yet there is really no argument in Puccetti's account to justify these ascriptions. Perhaps this is intended to be an elliptical way of speaking of the data under the control of the explanatory theory favored in the experimental literature. But there is no sustained argument there supporting the thesis of two distinct minds (Levy, Trevarthen, Sperry [1972]); and it may be doubted whether the principal contributors have distinguished satisfactorily between *two brains, two minds, two persons*, and *two modes of thinking*. Also, the literature does not even provisionally settle the question of whether the idiom of two minds is to be construed metaphorically or literally. Sperry [1968], for instance, says, cautiously and justifiably, that the commissurotomy patients "behave in many ways as *if* they have two independent streams of conscious awareness" (italics added). The existence of two brains is, in an obvious sense, relatively uncontroversial; the existence of two persons in one body is hardly considered at all, except for Puccetti's account; the existence of two modes of thinking proves to be irrelevant; and the evidence regarding two minds is, in all fairness, not at all informed by philosophical considerations regarding the identification and numerical identity of minds and persons. (We may assume, here, that to speak of two minds is (i) to speak predicatively of persons, and (ii) to draw attention to anomalies of behavior and thought.)

Puccetti takes it as flatly self-contradictory to admit two minds without admitting two persons. He says, for instance, "I am arguing that two minds is logically equivalent to two persons." But the argument is inconclusive. First of all, Puccetti himself acknowledges the possibility of "a schizoid personality with divergent impulses; or of dissociative reactions in the same person". We may admit, with Puccetti, that the commissurotomy patient doe not exhibit these syndromes. Still, either they show how it is possible for there to be two minds in one person or else they suggest that Puccetti has not helped us to see how to determine whether there is one mind or two minds, or more than two minds, in one person or experimental subject. The scientists in the split-brain field are inclined to hold that, among commissurotomy patients, "two minds" coexist in one person. Puccetti's sole argument appears to be that if this is so, "we should [speaking of a certain experimental case] be able to say intelligibly of P at time T_1 that he both knew and did not know he held a key in his left hand"; and that, he says, "certainly sounds contradictory". But his move is complicated because it conflates two independent issues: (a) that the admission of two minds *entails* two persons (speaking of *human beings*); and (b) that commissurotomy *results* in two minds (and therefore, or possibly, two persons). At this point, only thesis (a) is decisive, and Puccetti's argument here is simply not adequate. For, apart from the clear lead suggested by schizophrenia and dissociative personality, *if*, in context, two minds be admitted, then we have only to subscript the use of 'know' for each mind — in a way not altogether unlike what is said in multiple personality cases — and we can say (if we wish) that P (the subject) knows$_1$ (by means of mind$_1$) that he has a key in his left hand but does not know$_2$ (by means of mind$_2$) that he has a key in his left hand. We should thereby merely have complicated the problems connected with the intentionality of cognitive states. This is not to recommend this way of speaking, only to show that it is relatively easy — particularly in the absence of an articulated theory of minds and persons — to speak of two minds in one person. The argument against subscripting 'know' appears to provide a fair objection as well to subscripting 'mind'. Either we have no very clear way to count minds in one body (hence to ascribe attributes to putatively plural minds) or else the ways in which, at times, we do, demonstrates that it is not in the least logically impossible to attribute two minds to one person. The truth of the matter is that we have no very clear way in which to count either persons or minds associated with one body, as soon as we are tempted to think that there may be more than one (T. Nagel [1971]). Normally, the numerical question returns us to the relationship between persons and bodies. Once it is freed from that constraint, we require a supplementary criterion, which neither Puccetti nor the experimental literature supply.

Puccetti argues further that it is implausible to hold that "commissurotomy *create*[*s*] two minds or persons [where] there was just one before". He concludes that "*even* in the normal cerebrally intact human being there *must* be two persons [*a fortiori*, two minds], though before the era of commissurotomy experiments we had no way of knowing this". The argument seems to echo that of the alleged contradiction of two minds in one person and is equally unconvincing. Every analogy regarding the puzzles of numerical identity — for instance, fission — makes it quite clear that one entity of a given kind may, under specifiable circumstances, yield two entities of that kind. There simply are no fixed rules regarding the individuation of things that would preclude such a possibility, either where amoebae or commissurotomized patients are concerned: the criteria needed are, precisely, proposed *ad hoc*, in order to preserve consistency of usage in enlarged, hitherto unexamined, and anomalous situations. Puccetti seems to be asking for decisive observational evidence as to whether there are two minds or not, but the question calls for a ruling or revision of some sort — though it is not, for that reason, any the less empirical.

Again, Puccetti must be equivocating in his use of the critical predicates — a charge that may be made with equal force of the experimental literature on which he depends. For instance, summarizing an important experiment, Puccetti says: "A figure presented to the left hemisphere of a normal is named verbally 14 *msec* more slowly that if first presented to the right hemisphere, suggesting that *visual information* of this sort is *sent over* to the minor hemisphere for processing" (italics added). Puccetti rightly concludes that "there will always be some difference in the *information* content of each brain" (italics added); but he says that he can explain this only by denying that normals are unitary persons, holding instead that "he or she was a compound of two persons who *functioned in concert by transcommissural exchange*" (italics added). Sometimes, the critical terms — for instance, 'information', 'processing', 'function in concert', 'exchange' — concern *cognitive ascriptions* made of *persons*; sometimes, they concern *noncognitive* ascriptions made of *brains* or processes within brains that facilitate but are not identical with cognitive processes.

"Transcommissural exchange" of information from one hemisphere to another neither entails, nor renders probable in the least degree, the thesis that there are two persons associated with one hemisphere each, exchanging information, cooperating, synchronizing their respective "memory traces", emotional states, perceptual experiences, and so on. The plain fact is that there appear to be *no circumstances at all* where, among normals, "dual persons" are aware of one another cofunctioning, cooperating, exchanging information and the like; and, of course, on the hypothesis, the dual persons of commissurotomized patients are now total strangers to one another. Every analogy between clearly independent persons breaks down. Puccetti would have us believe that "our" own dual persons are never aware of being in contact with one another in spite of their quite remarkable cooperation; as he says, "I cannot believe my right-side cerebral companion contributed much to the writing of this paper, for example, or understood it as he saw me writing it out. He leaves the philosophizing to me."

Our conclusions thus far, then, are these: (1) it is logically possible to ascribe two minds to one person, though Puccetti denies it; (2) it is logically possible that commissurotomy creates two minds or two persons where there was one mind or one person before, though Puccetti denies it; (3) what are described as cognitive states depend upon what are described as noncognitive neural processes and the like: they ought not, lacking a suitably reductive argument, to be identified with one another and ought not to be taken as supporting the ascription of univocal cognitive predicates – both of which issues Puccetti fails to consider.

A few other observations are in order. First of all, much speculation about the two-minds issue really concerns two putatively different *modes of thinking*. Following Bogen [1969b], these – which Bogen terms the propositional and appositional modes – are normally (but only normally and never exclusively) associated with the left and right brains respectively. Still, it is reported (Bogen [1969a]) that, with regard both to hemispherectomy cases (where one hemisphere is removed) and cases of hemispheric atrophy (where one hemisphere simply shrivels to a small, inoperative brain), both the so-called propositional and appositional modes may function through one hemisphere, relatively well or weakly depending on the age and intelligence of the subject in the critical interval. The distinction between the two modes is, at present, hardly more than impressionistically construed (though it is an important distinction); but it has nothing whatsoever to do with the thesis about two minds or two persons in the same body. Since normals coordinate these two modes of thinking without any sense of the intrusion of one mind in the activities of the other, we see that Puccetti's thesis, in certain contexts at least, may well require the admission of a third person who coordinates (always without knowing it) the informational input of the two hemispheres. For example, in binocular stereoscopic vision, there is always a perspectival disparity between the optic array admitted to one eye and admitted to the other; but what the subject can report he sees are, normally, not such disparities (the stereoscope apart) but objects in an environment, where we may theorize that the perception of their relatively invariant visual attributes is informed by some *sub*cognitive pickup of the disparity information. Gibson [1966], for example, says flatly that the "compulsory convergence" of the eyes of primates "seems to entail a complete loss of the ability to perceive two different objects at the same time with two eyes, or two scenes at the same time". But then, the putatively third "person" cannot be affiliated with either hemisphere in the way in which the other "two" are; and, *if* the third may be admitted to play such a role, it seems quite easy to deny the existence of the other two.

There is, also, a large, scientifically unanswered question, in cases of agenesis (where the corpus callosum is absent at birth), whether the achievement of the subject can be accounted for without *some* compensating inter-hemispheric exchange. Puccetti himself reports (following Saul and Sperry [1968]) a subject above average in verbal I.Q. and subnormal in perceptuo-motor tasks. But it is not entirely clear that high verbal I.Q. is possible without being linked to perceptuomotor abilities of some minimal sort or that even subnormal perceptuomotor abilities can be satisfactorily accounted for on the thesis of no interhemispheric dependence whatsoever; nor is it clear, for that matter, how such a creature could develop as a relatively well-coordinated subject. Along these lines, Saul and Sperry actually note that there is evidence that the brain stem (which, after all, is common to the neural system of which the two hemispheres are an integral part) may itself develop compensating processes for interhemispheric exchange, precisely under the conditions of agenesis. If this be admitted, then, even if we should allow the creation of two persons under the conditions of commissurotomy, this need not be permanent in principle and we need not suppose that agenesis patients were ever dual persons (having been single organisms and having evolved as persons only over a long period of time). Apparently, there is no very clear picture about the functional capacity of the brain stem in split brain phenomena and there is no prospect of splitting the brain stem itself in a viable way. But, bearing in mind the familiar puzzles of numerical identity, just such considerations may be decisive.

Finally, there remains the complex question about the nature of what we call the unity of mind and person. Puccetti pretty well discards Sherrington's [1906] pronouncements about the unity of the self; but he nowhere considers carefully what we mean by individuating persons and minds. For example, should we say (dealing with people who are markedly absentminded), that the mind (and possibly the person associated with that mind) that was conscious of certain events and, for a while, of certain memories of those events is and must be different from the mind (and possibly the person associated with that mind) that is now unaware of those events and lacks those memories and cannot in any way recover them? This suggests what may be called longitudinal analogues of the split brain cases. If, that is, Puccetti claims that there are minds (and persons) side by side at any given moment *T*, within the same body, why should we not hold also that there are plural minds (or persons), time slice by time slice, within the same body? (Parfit [1971]). The truth is that the so-called unity of minds and persons is designed to accommodate all sorts of anomalies — for instance, self-deception, contradictory beliefs, aphasias, loss of memory, compulsions, ignorance about one's own motives and intentions, dreaming and sleepwalking, the subconscious, amnesia, schizophrenia and dissociative personality. Admittedly, the question remains what the best proposal is for the bisected brain phenomena, but it is certainly not obvious that the evidence simply *shows* that there are two minds at work both in normal and in commissurotomized subjects. It also fails to show that there are no empirical circumstances under which the hypothesis of plural persons in one body is not more reasonable than that of "one person, one body" (Strawson [1959]).

This returns us to the original point of departure. The most interesting theories concede that there is *some* important relationship between persons and bodies, either identity or one or another form of emergence — which is to say that the most interesting theories are likely to be reductive or non-reductive forms of materialism. But there is no decisive argument at the present moment that shows that identity should be preferred to emergence (unless it is the obviously questionbegging one) and there is no way to decide the question, from which Strawson and Williams select their characteristic concerns, without a full theory of the nature of a person. Strawson's insistence that the concept of a person is primitive is simply a version of emergence theories; and Williams' insistence that bodily identity is a necessary condition of personal identity is most clearly arguable on the assumption of some version of reductive theories. But whether either one is right — and if right, for what reasons — depends on considerations that neither introduces and that have not been adequately explored as yet.

CHAPTER 7

LANGUAGE ACQUISITION. I:
RATIONALISTS VS. EMPIRICISTS

If we reflect on the argument thus far, we shall see that reductive accounts of both mental states and of persons have been resisted and provisionally stalemated. Against mind/body identity theories and eliminative materialism, we have argued that mental and psychological attributes are ascribed that, though they must be suitably associated with physical processes, do not plausibly lead to the theories favored; and against reductive accounts of persons, we have argued that the distinctive abilities of persons and the potential complexity of individuating persons once again lead us away from the theories favored. These maneuvers are not unreasonable, but it must be admitted that they are insufficiently developed. What we need to know, rather more precisely, is just what sort of abilities we ascribe to persons that would, at one and the same time, tend to undercut both forms of reductionism. The answer is, language; but its full implications cannot be sketched at a stroke. Curiously, also, an adequate theory of language illuminates the distinction of sentient and languageless creatures as well.

But the important thing to bear in mind is the strategy of the argument. The question of language and of language acquisition is so complex that, in our effort to understand it, we risk failing to perceive its relationship to the entire mind/body problem. We shall have to content ourselves, in the present context, with the barest sketch of the import of that question on our larger issue; for, the clarification of the central features of language will be found to facilitate as well — however roundabout and seemingly digressive the approach — a grasp of the essential features of human culture and of the limitations of the sentient but languageless world. For the sake of the ultimate unity of those issues, we shall have to make a fresh start — without much attention initally to the arguments that have been scanned before.

The most distinctive attribute of persons, then, is their linguistic capacity. It may not unfairly be claimed to be the necessary and sufficient condition of personhood. Let us provisionally regard it as such. We are thereby enabled at once to set persons apart from sentient creatures (or, "sentient bodies"), by contrast with Strawson's [1959] indecisive account; we also gain thereby a purchase on the theory that persons are cultural entities, for languages are peculiarly cultural phenomena. Also, they do not in any obvious way, on the view of even the most strenuous reductionists (Sellars [1963a]), reduce to physical phenomena or lend themselves to "purely physical explanations".

The most strategic question that language poses is that of its acquisition. For, its acquisition bears on its nature and its nature, on the means of its acquisition. The question, what kind of creature can acquire language thereupon becomes a pertinent query; and the question, what kind of creature results from its acquisition comes to bear on the problem of reductionism. The solution of these puzzles suggests at once a way of construing the continuum that includes inanimate physical nature, the animate world of plants, the sentient world of linguistically competent persons and their cultural products, including (conceivably) the production of artificially intelligent entities. Much, therefore, hangs on it; the intended associations are clear.

The acquisition of a natural language, that is, the acquisition of a first language by human children learning in whatever way membership in a human society habitually facilitates, has, in our own time (Chomsky [1965], [1966]), been thought to affect decisively the tenability of an empiricist or a so-called rationalist theory of mind. By a rationalist theory, is meant a theory, not about an *a priori* source of indubitable truths, but about a certain structuring of the mind before birth, before induction into a culture, before the initial acquisition of a first language — in accord with which the mind "is 'preset' with a severe restriction on the form of grammar" favoring the universal rules of natural languages (Chomsky [1972]). The issue deserves our attention both because of its intrinsic interest and because of the considerable economy in argument that it affords. Roughly, what we need to demonstrate is that a rationalist theory of mind and language is impossible or at least inexplicable on any known explanatory strategy or would require assumptions that are themselves entirely implausible, that specifically linguistic competence cannot be ascribed to children before their induction into a culture, and that, therefore, the theory that persons are distinctively cultural entities is both viable and pointedly reasonable. For, any theory that can account for the mastery of language in pre-cultural terms will, to that extent, undermine the thesis that persons are essentially cultural entities. This would not in itself reinstate the mind/body identity thesis, though it would facilitate it enormously and though arguments very similar to Chomsky's have encouraged reductionism. In fact, rationalism holds that the creature prior to first beginning to learn a native language and the creature that learns it are not merely phases of the same biological organism (Chomsky neither restricts language acquisition to organisms nor specifies linguistic ability in any way that presupposes "realization" in an organism or machine or the like) but have in all respects the same essential competences. Abilities native to a given system simply develop or mature. If, however, linguistic ability is *sui generis* (in the sense that it cannot be physicalistically reduced) and if the human person is essentially distinguished by his linguistic ability, then, in effect, empiricism is committed to the thesis that the "creature" that achieves language is not one and the same as the creature that first begins to acquire language. The reason is that they are not entities of the same kind: the first is distinguished by its linguistic ability; the second, at least negatively, by the absence of such ability. Hence, on the argument, human persons may be biologically continuous with members of *Homo sapiens* but not identical with them. There is no consistent way to maintain such a thesis except by conceding a relationship like that of embodiment, for there is no way otherwise to accommodate the peculiar emergence involved. Nevertheless, it is notorious that empiricists about language acquisition (Putnam [1967b]; Quine [1960], [1974]) are characteristically committed to reductionism of one sort or another. One obvious counterstrategy involves denying that language acquisition *is sui generis*. We shall return to that pivotal issue shortly. Contemporary rationalism, for its own part, is a noticeably incomplete doctrine, in that it fails to specify the nature of the creature, man (that is, the species that, on the evidence, successfully acquires language), in virtue of which innate universal rules of grammar may be ascribed to individuals of that kind (G. Miller [1970]); nevertheless, though it provides no explanation, it precludes, if confirmed or adopted, radical differences in kind among bodies, sentient creatures, and persons.

Chomsky [1972] regards the confirmation and disconfirmation of rationalist and empiricist theories of language acquisition as *empirically* accessible. The decisive evidence against *all* empiricist theories, he supposes, is the remarkable rapidity with which children master their own language, from "a highly degenerate sample ... much of [which] must be excluded as irrelevant and incorrect", issuing in a command of language that "obviously extends far beyond the data presented ... [with] a predictive scope of which the data on which it is based constitute a negligible part". Chomsky's immediate opponents are empiricists who advocate behavioristic theories of language – Quine [1960] and Skinner [1957], for instance. The inadequacy of such theories (Chomsky [1959]; Margolis [1973b]) is important to draw out both for intrinsic reasons and for its service in clarifying the untenability of radical behaviorism. But though, frankly, we lack a competent empiricist theory of language acquisition, conceptual as well as empirical considerations count heavily against the rationalist theory. In any event, the possibility of constructing an empiricist account of language acquisition is hardly exhausted by behavioristic theories.

Irresistible as Chomsky's facts are, it is rather more difficult than at first appears to disconfirm empiricist theories of language learning. For one thing, there is, on historical grounds, no simple line of demarcation between rationalism and empiricism with respect to the doctrine of "innate ideas", the issue that has traditionally separated rationalists and empiricists and that, curiously, has dominated current quarrels about language acquisition. As Chomsky himself makes clear, following Leibniz, it is not the case, even for Locke, that empiricists deny innate capacities of mind (Chomsky [1965]; Chomsky [1966]). The doctrine of the *tabula rasa* has never actually been relevant in sorting out the partisans of these opposed points of view, though prominent empiricists (Goodman [1967]) may have taken Locke to have disposed of innate ideas once and for all. Secondly, contemporary empiricists are entirely willing to postulate innate capacities of mind on which language learning depends. Putnam [1967b], for instance, attempts to account for language acquisition in terms of such intellectual capacities as those affecting memory. The thesis is broadly Humean – even, perhaps, Lockeian. Putnam's view, however, is characterizable both as construing language acquisition as a relatively simple achievement – hence, as not requiring a very exceptional version of the doctrine of innate ideas – and as postulating that what are innate are merely general intellectual (empiricist) competences, not specific, complex, and inborn linguistic structures. The rationalist argues, by contrast, that the innate component required is remarkably detailed, remarkably complex, specifically linguistic, utterly alien to empiricist admissions about learning, and "species specific".

Chomsky's governing thesis is, quite simply, that a proper study of the grammatical structure of natural languages viewed in terms of the strikingly efficient, rapid, convergent command of given languages by human infants initially totally ignorant of those languages argues that linguistics is essentially a specialization within cognitive psychology: in particular, it commits us, on empirical grounds, to a rationalist conception of the mind.

The empiricist, say in the spirit of Hume, would argue that human beings are innately capable of certain general intellectual strategies, prompted by sensory experience: principally, they are capable of associating ideas affecting the ability to name, remember, abstract, and the like; consequently, learning a language is regarded by empiricists as a specialized task within the general innate competence of men, a task that does not presuppose initial capacities specifically and antecedently structured for mastering grammars. The rationalist denies this, insisting that what the infant learns in learning a language is a deep structure that is highly abstract, normally not accessible introspectively, not clearly linked to any usual run of empirical cues, and enabling the speaker regularly to improvise grammatically sound sentences not empirically or straightforwardly dependent on the range of sentences to which he was first introduced; hence, that linguistic acquisition presupposes that the mind is antecedently and in a detailed way structured to learn languages (Chomsky [1972]).

There are at least two very general considerations that count against the rationalist claim, that do not require any close analysis of putatively local or universal features of language. Suppose we grant the thesis provisionally. We must still concede that the infant not only recovers the allegedly universal grammar that sets constraints on the local grammar of the particular natural language he masters but also that he masters (but does not *recover*) the local grammar of his actual language. We may reasonably suppose, on the rationalist thesis, that the acquisition of a particular language is a more difficult feat than the recovery of some inborn universal grammar. For, after all, a given natural language will have features not only assignable to the universal grammar but its own distinctive features as well; and its own will be somewhat idiosyncratic, linked to historical accidents, complicated by a large number of causal factors not bearing directly on the evolution and genetic inheritance of the human brain. A human child, for instance, will have to judge that the phonological variants that strike his ear fall within an acceptable range in order to count as a familiar word having a familiar sense: he may hear the word 'car' pronounced by a Georgian, a downeaster from Maine, and a Hungarian refugee. Even if he has never heard these pronunciations before, there is no clear sense, given a fragment of language, in which he could draw — in any way whatsoever — on innate grammatical or phonological rules to decide determinately that the word is 'car' and not another word. The problem clearly affects every aspect of language, even the syntactical, if ambiguity and contextual reference and the difficulty of specifying grammatically deviant sentences be admitted (Ziff [1965]; Putnam [1961]). Two powerful qualifications suggest themselves: first, the essential importance of contextual clues in deciding the semantic import of words presumably conveyed by sounds (embodied in sounds); second, the prospect that the syntax of linguistic utterances cannot be determined apart from contextual clues bearing on sense. But if that is so, then it is a foregone conclusion that the mastery of a natural language cannot be accounted for in the way in which the rationalist supposes, that is, the *ability* to speak a particular natural language as opposed to what

Chomsky calls linguistic *competence* (linked to the recovery of the universal grammar) *and* opposed to actual linguistic performance (that depends on external factors as well [Chomsky (1965)]). The reason is elementary. The specific grammar of a given natural language is not innate to the human infant; in fact, infants will learn any natural language with the same facility if properly associated with competent speakers: a child of French-speaking parents will speak Eskimo and not French if only he is reared among the Eskimo and not among the French. But that means that the infant must learn the intricate grammar of a natural language that is not innate even if *that* grammar is constrained by a deep grammar that is innate. He must, that is, have a general intellectual capacity to discover the local grammar (and other local features) of his language *under conditions essentially like those under which the rationalist supposes empiricism cannot but be inadequate.* In a word, *only* an empiricist theory of language acquisition, governed, on the hypothesis, by a rationalist theory of universal grammar, can account for the mastery of the idiosyncratic features of given natural languages under conditions of fragmentary, degenerate, ill-formed, divergent empirical cues. (This is the distinction we may register by speaking of linguistic *competence* and linguistic *ability*, the *recovery* of an innate universal grammar and the *mastery* of a particular natural language.) But if this is so, then it becomes argumentative whether the recovery of the allegedly deep grammar could not also be accounted for on empiricist grounds: whether, that is, the "recovery" is not actually a "mastery" or whether indeed there is even a need to postulate a fixed, innate, deep, and universal grammar. In any event, if an infant cannot but discover the structure of his local language by means of general intellectual capacities, then it becomes an open question whether such empiricst capacities are merely supplementary to a deeper rationalist, specifically grammatical, competence. To put the matter this way is not, then, to press for a stalemate; on the contrary, the burden rests once again with the rationalist to show what more is needed. In fact, the very uncertainty of contemporary grammarians (Chomsky and Halle [1968]) as to whether any of their hard-won generalizations about grammatical or phonological rules — which, on the hypothesis, children must have internalized — actually are linguistic universals argues that rather extraordinary empiricist capacities must be assigned them whether or not rationalist capacities are assigned as well.

The second consideration is this. Suppose that, as experimental evidence seems to bear out, the primates are capable of learning some range of the grammar of human languages (Gardner and Gardner [1969]). This is a much more significant achievement, relative to our question than that some creature other than man (the dolphin, say) actually has a language (Lilly [1967]), though the communications of other animals generate other puzzles. Chomsky holds that language is "species specific". Sometimes, he seems to say that only man can master language, but, sometimes, he admits the possibility that other creatures may, though they appear not to, have a language. Should dolphins or Martians be shown to have a language, the rationalist thesis would not be seriously affected. But it *would* be seriously affected if the chimpanzee could master some part of *human* language. For, on Chomsky's view [1972], a grammar "can be acquired only by an organism that is 'preset' with a severe restriction on the form of grammar"; "this innate restriction", he says, "is a precondition, in the Kantian sense, for linguistic experience". (We may note, here, in passing, that, whatever the "preset" grammatical constraints on language acquisition may be, they *cannot*, on Chomsky's own view, be Kantian in nature: the reason is simply that, on Chomsky's view, one can learn languages that are not thus constrained.)

On empirical grounds, it appears that chimpanzees neither speak a natural language of their own nor are "preset" to master human languages. Conse-quently, if the chimpanzee (Premack [1971]) with his alien experience and evolution can master a portion of human language (both putatively universal and local grammatical features or at least what must be an effective portion of the local grammar), there would seem to be no plausible hypothesis except the empiricist's for accounting for his achievement. But, in that case, it would be an open question whether human infants *could* master human languages on the basis of innate capacities characterized solely in empiricist terms. At the very least, the rationalist thesis would not be able to be confirmed – at least on the basis of such linguistic behavior. More than this, it is not entirely clear *what* evidence would be decisive for confirmation. Consider, in this regard, a human society that speaks an *artificial* language, having abandoned, say, the natural language by means of which its members formulated their present language, and that attempts to rear offspring in the artificial language only, by the same general instructional methods that obtain for natural languages. If their offspring could learn that language, then, on the hypothesis – countenanced and, in a sense, pressed by Chomsky – that an artificial language may well be coherent and yet fail to be based on given linguistic universals, there would, for empirical reasons, be no basis at all for holding to the rationalist thesis. On the other hand, the failure of children to learn such a language may, conceivably, be due to non-linguistic limitations; for instance, it may be due to the limited competence of human memory. (Imagine, in this connection, that such a society had the use of devices for fixing the serial order of rather long "structure-independent" strings of words.) Until a significant run of genuine linguistic universals were actually in hand, it would be impossible to confirm rationalism and to disconfirm empiricism: the only evidence for the rationalist thesis, at the present time, seems to be that certain grammatical generalizations *may* be approximations of innate linguistic universals; but that is hardly enough.

The grammatical convergence of human languages is not only idealized but difficult to fix in terms of determinate rules, partly because the putative rules of deep grammar and of grammaticality itself may not be formulable except as relativized to the learned presuppositions of speakers regarding practices in their world. George Lakoff [1971a], for instance, is of the opinion that "The study of the relationship between a sentence and those things that it presupposes about the nature of the world by way of systematic rules is part of the study of linguistic competence. Performance is another matter. Suppose that S is well-formed only relative to PR [a set of presuppositions]. Then a speaker will make certain *judgments* about the well-formedness or ill-formedness of S which will vary with his extralinguistic knowledge. If the presuppositions of PR do not accord with his factual knowledge, cultural background, or beliefs about the world, then he may *judge* S to be 'odd', 'strange', 'deviant', ungrammatical', or simply ill-formed relative to his own presuppositions about the nature of the world. Thus, extralinguistic factors very often enter judgments of well-formedness. This is a matter of performance. The linguistic competence underlying this is the ability of a speaker to pair sentences with the presuppositions relative to which they are well-formed." If Lakoff is right, then the transformational rules of language are themselves a function of the presuppositions that obtain; but if so, then the concept of "autonomous syntax" essential to the nativist position (Lakoff [1971b]; Stalker [1976]) must be abandoned and with it the thesis that the mind is linguistically preset. (Lakoff apparently had at one time restricted the "deep" syntactic categories to "Sentence, Noun-Phrase, Verb-Phrase, Conjunction, Noun, and Verb" but others have whittled away at the list — and it is, in any case, noticeably less determinate that the original Chomskyan claim would require (McCawley [1971a]).) In fact, even where Lakoff's views (and other variants) are rejected, so that presupposition is not taken to affect the semantic component of the model of linguistic competence (for instance, Kempson [1975]), it seems to be necessary to introduce at least a "performance model" which does concede the "pragmatic" force of presupposition (cf. Grice [1957]; Searle [1969]; Bennett [1976]). In particular, Ruth Kempson concedes (rather, insists) that there are pragmatic aspects of the use of "definite noun phrases" (Russell [1905]; Strawson [1950]) that cannot be explicated in terms of the semantic component of the model of competence. The internecine quarrels of contemporary linguistics are of slight concern here, but it is difficult to see how, if the point be conceded, a clear demarcation can be maintained between the conditions of linguistic competence and of linguistic performance. Kempson's presumption regarding the adequacy of a formal semantics rests on her adoption of a truth-conditional definition of meaning. But that thesis itself presupposes that an adequate model of linguistic competence can be unequivocally applied to all relevant sentences (or utterances). Apart from the problem of separating the syntactic and semantic components of the required model and apart from the problem of providing the required transformational rules, there seems to be no satisfactory way of sorting semantically deviant and semantically nondeviant sentences. Without such a rule, there cannot be a way of defining meaning in terms of formal semantic conditions (*contra* Davidson [1967b]; cf. Hacking [1975]). (We shall return to the issue.)

Generally speaking, then, we must note (i) that actual languages appear to have variably "exceptional" features that violate putative linguistic universals; (ii) that reasonably detailed linguistic generalizations have never been universally confirmed; (iii) that such universals as "sentences" appear to be incapable of formal specification, are idealized to some extent or contextually inferred; (iv) that the regularities of language cannot be demarcated without reference to contexts of performance, which introduce extralinguistic presupposition; (v) that problems of reference, ambiguity, and the difficulty of sorting deviant and non-deviant utterances favor the inseparability of syntactic and semantic structures and the ineliminability of contextual cues affecting the analysis of the meaning of actual utterances; (vi) that the acquisition of actual languages requires, even on the rationalist thesis, a strong empiricist model of learning; (vii) that the evidence of animal learning either tends to disconfirm the rationalist thesis or renders it somewhat less open to empirical confirmation and disconfirmation; (viii) that the evidence regarding infants' acquisition of language is so idealized as to fail to serve as empirical confirmation of the rationalist thesis; and (ix) that the very model of rationalism is anomalous with respect to the explanatory patterns of science.

There are deeper considerations. Natural languages appear to be cultural achievements. Feral children, for example, cannot master language or cannot perform significantly better in this regard than the primates. It is quite possible that their inability to perform linguistically depends on more fundamental physical changes — for instance, on the decline of babbling, though there are difficulties with this view (Gardner and Gardner [1971]). But it is hard to see in what sense an innate grammar may confidently be assigned to them, on empirical grounds, and it is difficult to see how whatever marginal linguistic ability they may exhibit would incline us to a rationalist rather than an empiricist thesis. Nevertheless, Chomsky's theory would oblige us to treat natural languages as mastered partly under conditions of induction into a culture and partly under conditions of activating the recovery of pre-cultural, genetically determined grammatical rules — what, in effect, is a sort of Platonism (Chomsky [1966]). (This is not to say that language as such need be characterized in any but a functional way; but the question at stake concerns language *acquisition*, by determinately endowed creatures.) Chomsky [1972] himself claims that the universal, "deep structures of the sort postulated in transformational-generative grammar are real mental structures". He does not explain how this is possible. But his followers (Katz [1964]) explicitly state that "the structure of the mechanism underlying the speaker's ability to communicate with other speakers . . . is a brain mechanism, a component of neural system"; there appears to be no other account consistent with materialism that could be offered — requiring, that is, an internal representational system. (We shall return to the issue.)

Actually, the universal and local grammatical features of given languages are empirically discriminated in essentially the same way, by considering the scope of given hypotheses for given runs of linguistic data. The universal grammar is simply what, on the evidence, proves to be invariant and universally binding on the entire range of natural languages. It must be emphasized that, on the rationalist thesis, it is quite possible to construct artificial languages that do not behave in accord with alleged linguistic universals; hence, the importance of theorizing about the infant's language acquisition. On the thesis proposed, the local grammatical features of a language will be assigned to certain culturally acquired rules and the universal features, to a *pre-cultural* mental structure (whether materialistically defined or not being, at this point, not regarded as particularly significant [Chomsky (1972)]). The universal grammar will be a set of determinate rules "that relate sound and meaning in a particular way" (Chomsky [1972]).

The rationalist is committed, then, to the strenuous theory that the human mind, apart from cultural influence, is so structured as to be innately disposed to follow determinate rules that have somehow become "internalized" for the race. It is not merely that the mind is so structured that mental phenomena accord with certain *lawlike* regularities, but that it is so structured that even the infant mind hypothesizes, or behaves in a way suitably analogous to forming hypotheses, about how culturally relevant data may be assigned properties conformable with pre-culturally held universal *rules*. Of course, the thesis that infants form hypotheses commits us to an even more strenuous theory about the innately "preset" rules under which first languages are acquired — the "rules" for successfully appraising hypotheses about language cannot be the same as the "rules" of language itself.

The difficulties with this thesis are quite complex and not entirely easy to specify. But consider that a human *person* is a creature of a certain physically endowed sort that, under conditions of cultural training, acquires the ability to use a language (where 'ability', as noted above, signifies more than [and also something quite different from] what Chomsky calls 'competence'). An empiricist account would admit innate intellectual capacities to determine operative rules for a given domain, in particular, the rules of language; it would normally do so by supposing that a potential speaker of a language develops *as* a person *as* that creature, by strategies that are at present largely a mystery, actually learns the rules of a particular natural language. The rationalist is bound to hold that the local rules of a given language are discernible as such by an infant who has not yet developed as a speaker of the language but who develops by *testing hypotheses about its rules by reference to universal rules that it is, somehow, already in possession of*. For instance, the rationalist must explain an infant's ability to learn that a local language has "exceptions" with respect to a putatively universal grammar. Hence, the rationalist has to explain the sense in which a merely sentient organism, prior to cultural or societal training, at the very beginning of its life, can be said to possess rules, in spite of the fact that the very notion of a rule seems to entail norms governing admissible and inadmissible instances of some determinate sort, that is, in spite of the fact that the very notion of a rule seems to make no sense apart from institutionalized forms of life. The institutions appear to be fully cultural and complex where language is concerned and at least proto-cultural where relatively complex, socially learned, and distinctly alterable social patterns are concerned.

On the rationalist assumption, the human infant is already, in some sense, oriented to the discrimination of rules because it is pre-culturally endowed with a set of *invariant* rules to which whatever rules it may provisionally posit for any culturally confronted language must finally conform — in order, precisely, for that language to be discernible *as* a language. Machine analogues are both relevant and irrelevant (Putnam [1960]; T. Nagel [1969]), since machines, paradigmatically, are known, by their inventors at least, to be programmed to follow certain rules. The rationalist hypothesis was more plausible in the seventeenth century, since God was thought, then, to be the artificer of man. And, indeed, for Descartes, the mind is *thinking substance*, substance inherently so structured that it innately adheres to the *rules* of thought and reason (whatever those may be taken to be — for instance, the principle of sufficient reason [Leibniz]); whereas the empiricists admit, speaking of the association of ideas and of the conditions of memory, only certain innate *lawlike* regularities governing the processes of thought. Hence, the rationalist and the empiricist are more fundamentally opposed to one another than might otherwise have appeared. That Locke is in some respects a rationalist in spite of himself is, in a sense, irrelevant. The main thrust of the rationalist-empiricist quarrel concerns whether the human infant is so endowed that it can *discover* (invent or master) the rules of reason and the rules of language or whether it is, in some sense, already endowed with such rules that it may, under conditions of sensory experience, *recover* the essential structure of its own mind. Both rationalists and empiricists admit innate ideas; but empiricists admit only lawlike regularities and rationalists include as well rulelike universals. The reason for stressing the difference is that one sees thereby that the issue cannot be straightforwardly empirical, since there appear to be no empirical ways of assigning determinate rules to the innate structure of the mind, unless the mind is actually programmed in the manner of a Turing machine. This critical issue is, as we shall see, the fulcrum on which the adequacy of any theory of persons depends: it is, for instance, a decisive problem for all forms of reductive materialism. But, in any case, in the context of language acquisition, it is reasonably clear that the child learning one natural language for the first time and the field linguist surveying the entire range of natural languages and the historical features of their development and the like, simply do not have comparable data on which to theorize (or, perhaps, comparable abilities to theorize) regarding their probable structure. Hence, there is reason to think that the regularities the linguist generates are artifacts of his directed inquiry, at least in the sense in which he takes his findings to approximate the structure of the infant mind. An "inductive requirement" or constraint (Derwing [1973]) seems reasonable, therefore: "some reasonable provision must be made for the 'learnability' of a (linguist's) grammar by a child *solely on the basis of the data which is available to him* before we elevate such a grammar from the domain of 'scholastic fiction' (Jakobson [1961]) to that of a plausible model of the 'real', 'internalized', or 'psychologically valid' grammar of some language." Resistance to Chomsky's thesis, that continues to respect the deep uniformities of natural language, will tend to hold (i) that "deep structures are much more abstract than had been thought" (Bach [1968]); (ii) that linguistic universals are idealizations of the actually variable regularities of particular natural languages (Steiner [1975]); and/or (iii) that the convergences of natural language depend on non-linguistic uniformities of some sort (physiological, neurological, perceptual or the like) in the accord with which economies of memory, uniformities among human concerns, historical contact and comparison among distinct cultures, even the perceivable structures of the external world as well as logical constraints may cooperative to yield the linguistic consequences observed. (i) constitutes a retreat to the non-falsifiable; (ii) is nothing more than the utter defusing of a distinctive thesis (innatism); and (iii) is merely the determinable form of all empiricist theories. In short, attention will be focussed on the historically shaped and somewhat idiosyncratic regularities of particular languages, concessive to the thesis of a grammar incorporating underlying uniformities but favoring a grammar not so "deep" as to be not primarily concerned with the surface structures of such languages.

We may press our charge in a number of ways. For one thing, *if* Chomsky were a materialist, which is not required, then if he held that the rules of universal grammar innately structured the brain, he would be obliged to treat man as a machine, that is, as not merely analyzable by way of analogy with a machine — or he would be obliged to take God as man's artificer or something of the sort. Otherwise, he would not be able to account for preferring a rationalist thesis over an empiricist: the notion of a physical brain innately structured to "follow rules" is, to say the least, anomalous. The sense in which a machine is actually programmed to follow rules is, on the face of it, always reducible, in the sense that the relevant changes of state of an actually "realized" machine are always explicable in causal terms restricted to purely physical factors. In that sense, to speak of such a machine as following rules is invariably to employ a mere *façon de parler*. It cannot relevantly illuminate the nature of a human language user, who is not known to have been programmed in the same sense and whose linguistic performance cannot, on any known basis, be reduced to purely physical phenomena. Put another way: the justification of speaking of a machine's following rules is that it has been programmed by a human agent (which is obviously not true of human beings themselves); but, given such justification, it is always possible to replace the functional description of the machine (linguistic or otherwise) by some extensionally equivalent, purely physical description (which is not feasible for the linguistic behavior of humans). Hence, Chomsky could not be justified in treating the human mind as linguistically "preset" unless (a) he had evidence that the mind was actually programmed and/or (b) he was able to provide an account of the regularities of language in purely physical terms – which seems impossible (Sellars [1963a]). In this sense, holding to the uniquely species-specific nature of linguistic universals, Chomsky opposes the thesis that men are machines: they have, on the contrary, some innate and nonreducible *cognitive* competence to which their molar abilities regarding performance may, relevantly, be reduced. Here, the difference between the (rationalist) view Chomsky favors and the (empiricist) view Putnam favors becomes entirely clear.

Secondly, consider the interesting thesis that, in the so-called holophrastic period of development, not only do "young children express something like the content of full sentences in single-word utterances" but also "the concept of a sentence undergoes a continuing evolution through the holophrastic period" (McNeill [1970]). For example, a child is observed to say *hi* "when something hot [is] presented to her" (at 12 months, 20 days) and *ha* "to an empty coffee cup" (at 13 months, 20 days) and *nana*, pointing to the top of a refrigerator, "the accustomed place for finding bananas", even though there are none (at 14 months, 28 days). There is, perhaps, some inescapable ideal- ization regarding the verbal behavior of very young children; but, more than that, it is quite impossible to provide evidence bearing on the use of holo- phrastic expressions that confirm rationalist hypotheses about language acquisition. The evidence of the holophrastic level appears both idealized and insensitive to the competing theories. In fact, the idealization involved in holophrastic speech has to do with the (reasonable) importation of a prelinguistic model of rationality – of coordinated desires, needs, intentions, sensations, perceptions, and activities – in virtue of which and of which alone, *in the context of given stimuli and responses*, holophrastic utterances are construed as the uttering of sentences having the implicit structure they are assigned. Here, we have a clear instance of the kind of case in which ascriptions of intentional states are made on the basis of evidence involving the physical states of a creature, but in a way that cannot reasonably lead to the identity thesis or to reductionism. It may serve as a paradigm of a more pervasive phenomenon. What is absolutely crucial to the characterization of early linguistic responses is that the conception of infant rationality – involving desire, intention, belief, and the like – is for that very reason *already characterized in propositional terms*, that is, in a form that can only be rendered in terms of a linguistic model. Hence, there is every reason to believe that the putative structure of infant speech is an artifact of the theory on which particular utterances are ascribed. (We shall return to the problem of rationality in prelinguistic and nonlinguistic creatures.)

David McNeill [1970] insists that there are "reasons for supposing that the concept of a sentence is not a product of learning", that "Children everywhere begin with exactly the same initial hypothesis [*sic*]: sentences consist of single words." He also argues that the linguistic universals of language acquisition, considered diachronically through the stages of learning, are everywhere the same. And he concludes that it is not difficult to account for children learning the universal abstract structure of natural languages because they actually "begin speaking underlying structure directly" [*sic*] and, only later, learn the transformational idiosyncrasies of particular languages. But, though he shows the differences between an empiricist and rationalist conception of language learning, he does not demonstrate either than an empiricist account is inherently inadequate or that the rationalist account is intrinsically coherent or empirically confirmed. In particular, not only are the early phases of language acquisition so highly idealized that they outstrip the empirical evidence, perhaps in principle, but the so-called universals are so extremely abstract that it is difficult to see in what sense they are specifically *linguistic* rather than cognitive universals (which are quite different) and, in fact, cognitive universals learned rather than innate. For instance, as McNeill says, "permutation ... is a universal transformational relation ... used in a unique way in English and French. Other universal relations are deletion and addition; there are perhaps only a half dozen varieties of universal transformations." But it is difficult to construe the rules of permutation as essentially linguistic or essentially innate, though it obviously concerns the limits of possible combination. Furthermore, there is absolutely no reason to suppose that children learning the "unique" forms of permutation of English and French must either have learned or have been "preset" for the "universal transformational" forms or rules of permutation. To say that they must would not be altogether unlike saying, assuming Goldbach's conjecture to be true for natural numbers, that children who learn the rules for number games having idiosyncratic, but not incoherent or inconsistent, rules are obviously "preset" in accord with Goldbach's conjecture, which they somehow use "directly" at the earliest stage of grasping numbers. That the (Goldbach's) conjecture may not be a universal corresponds to the possibility that putative linguistic universals may not be universals at all; that it may be a universal corresponds to the possibility (the Kantian-like thesis) that putative linguistic universals are universal only in the sense of being logical or conceptual constraints that cannot be violated, saving coherence; *and* that it may be an unfalsified generalization corresponds to the possibility that children may be capable, on empiricist grounds, of extraordinarily powerful linguistic generalizations. Also, the notion that there exists an innate rule governing holophrastic sentences, where the stipulation that a sentence obtains in infant speech depends and must depend on the "field observer's" idealization of the infant's *intentions*, utterly trivializes the concept of a linguistic rule. In fact, McNeill merely assumes the rationalist thesis. Beyond this, it is an extraordinary irony that the search for determinate linguistic universals should end with the provision of the rule of sentence-formation as the initial paradigm: there seems to be no prospect of formulating a determinate rule of that sort that would be remotely adequate.

Consider, then, Chomsky's linguistic universals. As Chomsky (with Halle [1968]) says: "a general principle counts as a linguistic universal if it is compatible with the facts for all human languages. As linguists, of course, we are concerned not with principles that happen by accident to be universal in this sense, but rather with those that are universal in the domain of all possible human languages, that is, those that are in effect preconditions for the acquisition of language." *If* Chomsky were concerned with the *lawlike* preconditions of language, empiricists would give no quarrel: there is every reason to think that acquiring a language is a natural phenomenon for man, hence subject to regularities comparable to what may be found elsewhere in nature, for instance, regarding the non-linguistic behavior of men; though it is hard to see that there could be any nomic universals that would explain the acquisition of language. In fact, in ethological studies, quite interestingly (Lorenz [1971]), emphasis is placed, precisely, on "the presence of individually invariable species-specific structures in human behavior as [causal] determinants of certain species-typical characteristics common to *all* human societies"; the theme is elaborated for animals as well. The parallel with Chomsky's characterization of his own work – but also, the difference – is striking. If, however, *that* were Chomsky's objective (that is, nomic invariances), his universals would not be *linguistic*, since linguistic universals are violable and alterable rules. So Chomsky seeks rather to isolate *rulelike* universals, linguistic analogues of the universal laws of nature. (In that sense, Chomsky could not retreat – he does not wish to – to a machine model.) Nevertheless, however comprehensive they may be, putative linguistic universals cannot be marked as such without some theoretical basis for distinguishing them from accidental generalizations, as Chomsky acknowledges; and, there seems to be no foundation for that distinction except the evidence that "every normal child acquires an extremely intricate and abstract grammar, the properties of which are much underdetermined by the available data" [1968]. But *that* fact, as we have already seen, does not decisively favor the rationalist account over the empiricist and may not even (*contra* Chomsky) directly bear on the child's psychological capacities.

In a word, the argument involves a circle: we suppose that the most comprehensive linguistic generalizations are linguistic universals because we are already committed to the rationalist thesis that the mind is "preset" to learn all possible languages; and we adopt the rationalist thesis because we suppose that the acquisition of language, taking place "with great speed, under conditions that are far from ideal, and [with] little significant variation among children who may differ greatly in intelligence and experience" [1968], cannot be accomplished unless the mind is appropriately supplied with linguistic universals — of which our generalizations *are* approximations. There seem to be no independent considerations.

On the other hand, there may well be conceptual constraints on all possible languages, in effect, universal "rulelike" regularities that *cannot* be violated without losing some measure of coherence, intelligibility, or the like. For example, it may be impossible to admit thought — *a fortiori*, language — as coherent insofar as it violates the rule that nothing can be both A and not A in the same respect, though actual violations may be accommodated by compensatory processes. There is no need to attempt to formulate any such "rules" carefully; for if there are any, they cannot be of the sort Chomsky has in mind in speaking of *linguistic universals*. The reason is simply that it is, for Chomsky, theoretically possible to formulate an artificial language, a language which human infants do not and could not actually learn in the manner of natural languages but which competent language users would be capable of learning as a second language. Chomsky [1972] himself stresses that "there is no *a priori* reason why human language should make use of [the putatively universal rulelike operations it does, rather than of alternative operations that do not actually obtain in natural languages]. One can hardly argue", he says, "that the latter [of which he provides conceivable instances] are more 'complex' in some absolute sense; nor ... more productive of ambiguity or more harmful to communicative efficacy. Yet, no human language contains structure-independent operations among (or replacing) the structure-dependent grammatical transformations." All this may be granted, but it falls noticeably short of the requirements of the rationalist. Rulelike generalizations will hold on empirical grounds and may be converted into linguistic universals only on the assumption of the rationalist thesis, which is itself presumably supported by the empirical discovery of linguistic universals; and conceptual or "rulelike" constraints governing thought and language (transcendental constraints, in the Kantian sense) are *too* comprehensive to count as linguistic universals: linguistic universals are not the minimal price, but conceptual constraints are, of coherence and intelligibility. In general, we may distinguish among nomic universals, rulelike regularities, and (universal) conceptual limits. All are associated, in some way, with putative "invariances". The last is best associated with the Kantian enterprise, even if relativized to an historically developed understanding (Strawson [1966]). Where valid, its would-be violation defines the logically impossible; hence, it affords no basis for the demarcation of the empiricist and rationalist alternatives. The first, paradigmatically associated with the uniformities of physical nature, defines the physically impossible (Smart [1963]); hence, it affords no more than a minimal constraint on the formulability of rules. Rulelike regularities, however, are either reducible or not reducible to universals of the other two sorts. Where they are, as by some extensionally equivalent formulation, reference to rules is no more than a *façon de parler* (for instance, as in speaking either of the rule-following behavior of a realized Turing machine or of the "rules" of permutation); and where they are not, as apparently in the linguistic behavior of human persons, given "invariances" are in the nature of the case open to revision by the very creatures that conform to them. (This, as we shall see in another context, is decisive in appraising teleological descriptions of physical nature, ascribing rules to animal societies, gauging the import of speaking of intelligent machines.) Hence, there seems to be no relevantly viable empirical sense in which to construe a generative-transformational grammar as favoring the rationalist over the empiricist. In fact, on the machine-like reduction of human language, there remains no relevant basis for contrasting the rationalist and the empiricist. But to say that is not to deny the empirical defensibility of such a grammar itself.

We may put our findings in the form of a dilemma. Either the rationalist is a dualist, a true Cartesian, or else, advocating a psychology that is, in some sense, compatible with an adequate theory of the human body, he can offer no empirical grounds for preferring his own thesis to the empiricist's. The irony is that Chomsky had supposed his theory to restore linguistics to the discipline of psychology, contrary to the taxonomic theories of Bloomfield [1933] and others, and to have exposed the inadequacy of a behavioristic linguistics. Nevertheless, Chomsky fails to explain the sense in which it is coherent or confirmable to hold that the mind or the brain, innately and prior to any cultural influence, can be said to be so structured that it is disposed, not in the sense of habits or the like but in the sense of being in a certain formal or "logical" or "functional" state (Putnam [1960]) to "follow" determinate and detailed rules determinately ordered by a hierarchy of rules.

The point is that it hardly pays to construe linguistics as a branch of cognitive psychology if the theory of mind that it entails posits an empirically inaccessible and theoretically inexplicable feature of the mind or brain. (We shall have to return to the issue in a more frontal way.)

There is a deeper significance to the quarrel. Rules must be instituted or at least develop in some recognizably social way; must be capable of being viably replaced by alternative systems of rules; must be capable of being followed and violated by beings themselves capable of recognizing that rules obtain and that rules are followed or violated; and must be capable of being conformed to and reformed or revised for reasons to which the beings affected subscribe (Schwayder [1965]; Lewis [1969]). Conceivably, some relatively weak qualification under these conditions would count as rule-following behavior. But a theory of rules is inseparable from a theory of societal life in which common norms and purposes, criteria for discriminating conforming and non-conforming behavior, and evidence for a sufficiently advanced level of intelligence among the beings affected may be specified. The simple truth is that we utterly lack a conceptual model in which the *brain* may be supposed to be programmed for such *behavior*, or the pre-cultural *mind* of infants. The first alternative will not do, because, regarding the physical brain, we must suppose that "physical phenomena have none but purely physical explanations" (Lewis [1966]) – which leads (against Chomsky's apparent intention) to reductionism; and the second fails, because, regarding the infant mind, we must suppose that, except on some extreme and literal-minded Platonistic theory, infants could hardly be said to be capable of even the minimal discriminations that the recognition and use of rules entail.

These considerations, stressing the cultural or at least proto-cultural nature of rules, confirm that if persons are essentially distinguished in terms of their mastery of a language, their mastery of a peculiarly complex rule-governed system, then persons must be distinctively cultural entities. But there are other consequences. The very idea of rules, of grounds for distinguishing between legitimate and illegitimate or admissible and inadmissible behavior, implies that conformity and judgments of conformity obtain only *in intensional contexts*: behavior under some descriptions but not under every coextensive description will be able to satisfy given norms. So construed, Chomsky's theory appears to entail that infants are programmed to maintain intensional regularities. Seen thus, the thesis risks incoherence. The upshot is that in holding that persons are essentially cultural entities we are holding that persons cannot be identified as such without reference to phenomena that cannot themselves be specified in non-intensional terms – which, of course, is not to deny that extensional uses of language may be readily detailed. Here again is the key to nonreductive materialism, to the advantage of linking the identity of persons with that of bodies as well as to the lacunae of the usual reductive arguments − for instance, as in the confused view that the (lawlike) coding of biological systems provides the structural clue to the deep "coding" (of the intensional distinctions) of human societies (Jacob [1974]; Monod [1971]).

Thus, François Jacob pronounces, on the basis of detailed studies of the coding of macromolecules ("integrons"): "A new hierarchy of integrons [obtains], from family organization to modern state, from ethnic group to coalition of nations, a whole series of integrations is based on a variety of cultural, moral, social, political, economic, military and religious codes." What he fails to notice is that the "rulelike" ascriptions to molecules cannot but be a *façon de parler*. The essential difficulty, linking Chomskyan linguistics, structuralism (Lévi-Strauss [1963]), and information-processing models, lies in conflating molar and molecular levels of discourse − the terms are Tolman's (1932) − and in assuming that because nomic invariances occur on the molecular level and because, regarding machines, such invariances as well as invariances of rulelike programming occur on both the molecular and molar levels, it must be the case that rulelike (intensional) invariances occur, among the higher sentient creatures and persons, on the molecular and molar levels as well, or that rulelike phenomena must be reducible to lawlike phenomena. Thus Jacques Monod holds that "one of the fundamental characteristics common to all living beings without exception [is] that of being *objects* endowed *with a purpose* or project [a molar consideration], which at the same time they exhibit in their structure [a molecular consideration] and carry out through their performances [equivocally, having molar or molecular import]". This property, Monod terms "teleonomy", which is itself instructive in collapsing the distinction between rules and laws, intensional and extensional order − and, most important, distinct varieties of teleology. Furthermore, in characterizing "the *principle* of a definition of a species 'teleonomic level'," Monod explains that "All teleonomic structures and performances can be regarded as corresponding to a certain quantity of information which must be transmitted for these structures to be realized and these performances accomplished".

The corresponding Chomskyan error consists in supposing that, since language is functionally described in being grammatically described (though language is a molar phenomenon), putative invariances may be specified for some molecular level (the representation of linguistic universals) regardless of the purposive (molar) informalities of speech itself. The development of so-called "generative semantics" (Lakoff [1971b]; McCawley [1971a]) attests, in part, to the inadequacy of the view, maintaining (McCawley) that "there is no natural breaking point between a 'syntactic component' and a 'semantic component' of a grammar such as the level of 'deep structure' was envisioned to be in Chomsky" and even moving to resist, as in referential contexts (McCawley [1971b]), the provision of a breaking point between "surface" and "deep structures". Broadly speaking, invariances on the molecular level are nomic and not teleologically significant; or else, when they are teleologically interpreted, *though nomic*, they are specified, as in an information-processing model, relative to the molar behavior of a programmed machine or, metaphorically, relative to the molar behavior of a purposive system for which no known program exists. The use of an informational model does not insure that every system to which it is applied may be construed as a machine with a finite program of some sort.

But, so speaking, we introduce a new source of puzzlement regarding the nature of cultural entities and, ulteriorly, of mental states and molar behavior.

CHAPTER 8

LANGUAGE ACQUISITION. II:
FIRST AND SECOND LANGUAGES
AND THE THEORY OF THOUGHT AND PERCEPTION

In a sense, we must review the foregoing argument from another perspective. For we have not yet succeeded in isolating what is distinctive of language acquisition and what separates languageless creatures from those that have language. As we shall see, the account required will lead us to further difficulties. Nevertheless, the most strategic question about linguistic mastery, here, asks whether acquiring a first (natural) language is like acquiring a second. Since we are reasonably clear about some of the salient features of acquiring a second language, the move to construe acquiring a first in terms appropriate to acquiring a second suggests a clear economy and the resolution of a deep puzzle. In an interesting sense, the affirmative view need not be favored by so-called linguistic empiricists as opposed to linguistic rationalists — that is, by those who concede only innate lawlike dispositions of the mind as opposed to those who concede also innate rulelike dispositions: it is quite possible that empiricists about language acquisition should forego that view and search for an alternative theory of language learning.

Colin Turbayne [1972], who is strongly attracted to empiricism and opposed to linguistic rationalism, speaks quite straightforwardly of "the 'code' of visual language", which he admits is "chaotic"; but, Turbayne thinks, one eventually "learns to 'read' this language [that is, the 'code' of visual discrimination] like a native 'decoder', and finally manages to fuse or complicate the items of the two languages [that is, the visual and haptic 'codes']" (which yields a theory of vision rather like Berkeley's [Turbayne (1969)].) Turbayne says that "perceiving is modelled on reading", by which he obviously means *not* that it may be *heuristically* useful to construe perceiving (cognitively) in propositional and, therefore, linguistic terms, but rather that perceiving actually entails mastering a skill that is *essentially* one of reading a kind of visual code or language. He summarizes his view in the following way: "According to the [traditional rationalist doctrine resurrected in recent years], the mind comes equipped with certain innate ideas or principles in the form of knowledge of language structure. This knowledge it applies to the mastery of its first language. It seems to me, however, that we are able to acquire this 'first' language, not through knowledge of any innate ideas, but because all of us have been mastering code-breaking and encoding skills from earliest infancy. Some of us more readily broke the code of written English because we had already broken the simpler code of I.T.A. [Sir James Pitman's Initial Teaching Alphabet]. Most of us were helped to acquire our 'first' language because we had already broken the code of visual language in the first months of life". Turbayne is particularly agile in sorting the usual metaphoric ways in which the mind is described — which he strenuously resists. It is fair to say, therefore, that he intends his account quite literally. He draws attention as well to a similar view held by Nelson Goodman.

It is quite true that Goodman [1967] holds that "acquisition of an initial language is acquisition of a secondary symbolic system" and, consequently, rather like the acquisition of a second language. But it is precisely Goodman's position that Chomsky [1972] has himself so strenuously opposed. Chomsky stresses Goodman's confidence that "once one language is available and can be used for giving explanation and instruction", the acquisition of a second language poses no difficulties and obviates the need for an appeal to innate ideas. But, Chomsky holds — quite reasonably — Goodman must be speaking metaphorically since (1) there is not the slightest reason to suppose that "the specific properties of grammar — say the distinction of deep and surface structure, the specific properties of grammatical transformations and phonological rules, the principles of rule ordering, and so on — are present in these already acquired prelinguistic 'symbolic systems' "; and (2) these putative systems, "whatever they may be, cannot 'be used for giving explanation and instruction' *in the way in which a first language can be used in second-language acquisition*". Hence, the problem of first-language acquisition remains unresolved, viewed from the empiricist's vantage — when, at least, it is based on construing first-language acquisition as a sort of second-language acquisition. In fact, Goodman [1968] holds elsewhere that languages are symbol systems "of a particular kind", that satisfy minimally the "syntactic requirements of disjointness and differentiation" — that is, roughly, the requirement that replicas of given marks or inscriptions are syntactically equivalent to one another and that, as a consequence of being "character-indifferent", "no mark may belong to more than one character"; and the requirement that it is theoretically possible that, for any given mark or inscription that does not belong to two given characters, it may be determined that the mark does not belong to the one character or does not belong to the other. Apart from the strenuousness of applying these criteria to actual languages, it is extremely difficult to see how Goodman could conclude, on his own grounds, that we possess initial "symbol systems" sufficiently like linguistic systems that we may thereby undercut the plausibility of "the claim that there are rigid limitations upon initial-language acquisition".

But the rationalist tends to speak in much the same way — though, obviously, for very different reasons. David McNeill [1970], for example, pursuing a position explicitly indebted to Chomsky's, begins his account of first-language acquisition by holding that "virtually everything that occurs in language acquisition depends on *prior* knowledge of the basic aspects of sentence structure. The concept of a sentence may be part of man's innate mental capacity. The argument of the book is designed to justify this assertion." "Children", he says, "everywhere begin with exactly the same initial hypothesis; sentences consist of single words." The upshot, he thinks, is that "one can say that children begin speaking underlying structure directly" (that is, because they do not initially grasp the idiosyncratic aspects of the different natural languages). This is tantalizingly close to providing a rationalist counterpart to Goodman's and Turbayne's empiricist accounts. Here, more comppellingly than for the empiricist, there is no problem in explaining and instructing, because what is essentially required in acquiring a second language *or* a first is already innate in the infant. In particular, this hypothesis takes care of Chomsky's [1972] objection to empiricism, since it is no longer necessary, in instruction, that "one have enough explicit knowledge about [the universal deep] structure [of a first or second language]". No one has that knowledge but no one needs it for the task at hand. Zeno Vendler [1972], arguing along somewhat different lines but as a rationalist, holds that all thought is propositional in nature; but since he means this in the literal sense that, although we do not need to think in terms of language (some particular natural language), we do nevertheless think in terms of the very same deep structure that underlies language, animals cannot think. He concludes from this that "a child must learn his native tongue in a way similar to the way one learns a second language", that is, *via* something like Chomsky's deep structure. What we see, then, is the strategic connection between the first-/second-language problem and the theory of thought and perception.

The trouble is that not only are linguistic universals difficult to specify *if*, as Chomsky apparently wishes (Chomsky and Halle [1968]), they are to be made suitably explicit: McNeill's *sentence* is obviously inadequate and questionbegging (particularly, as we have seen, allegedly holophrastic sentences); it is, also, extremely problematic what to make of the notion of *rulelike* dispositions in infants. Certainly (as has been argued), there is no straightforward account of genetics that could countenance the inheritance of rulelike as opposed to lawlike regularities: there is no remotely plausible conceptual model by which to account for the transmission of such an organization. But the problematic nature of both the rationalist and empiricist discussions of first- and second-language acquisition suggests the need for more fundamental distinctions.

A promising beginning may be made by considering, briefly, the relationship between speech and thought. Empiricists like Turbayne and Goodman evidently take it for granted that there is a very strong structural similarity between cognitive perception and reading a language. But a rationalist like Zeno Vendler also holds that "you can say whatever you think, and you can think *almost* whatever you can say" (where the restriction is irrelevant to our concern) because, as Vendler argues, the structure of thought and speech is the same — literally, the same. He means by this that speech and thought both rest on innate ideas, in Descartes's sense; though he seems also to hold that we think directly in terms of Chomskyan linguistic universals. Now, the trouble with all such views — whether empiricist or rationalist — is that, on the face of it, (a) animals may be said to perceive (cognitively), though there is no reason to suppose that in learning to discriminate perceptually they are learning to master some prelinguistic "symbolic system"; and (b) *if* animals are conceded to perceive in a cognitively pertinent sense, then they cannot altogether be denied the ability to have beliefs and, in that sense, to think, despite the fact that they lack language and the capacity to master language (cf. Malcolm [1973]).

There is, furthermore, the intriguing recent evidence, already mentioned, of the ability of chimpanzees to master a portion of natural language. Roger Brown (1970) cites the early views of Chomsky and Eric Lenneberg against animal language: "acquisition of even [the] barest rudiments [of language] is quite beyond the capacities of an otherwise intelligent ape" (Chomsky); "There is no evidence that any nonhuman form has the capacity to acquire even the most primitive stages of language development" (Lenneberg). But Brown himself had held essentially the same view and has revised it cautiously under the pressure of the work of the Gardners (Gardner and Gardner [1971]) and Premack [1971]. In any case, if chimpanzees can learn to perform linguistically, then the doubts that have been professionally aired about that accomplishment imply that the learning of a first language cannot be relevantly like the learning of a second and, in particular, that the perceptual competence of the chimpanzee cannot be construed as the mastery of a "symbolic system" sufficiently like a language that it would make the mastery of a first language likely. Alternatively, if it is held (against the evidence) that chimpanzees do not actually exhibit a minimal command of language, then it could hardly be supposed that the prelinguistic perceptual abilities of the human infant render *its* eventual mastery of language the least bit likely.

There is, then, very little reason to suppose either (i) that perceptual discrimination is or entails the mastery of a "symbolic system" or "symbol system" structurally similar to a language; or (ii) that prelinguistic thinking or even nonverbal thinking on the part of linguistically qualified subjects exhibits the structure of speech. (i) seems to be the thesis favored by empiricists in order to overtake the difficulty of first-language acquisition; and (ii) seems to be the thesis favored by rationalists in order to overtake that same difficulty. Furthermore, although (i) suggests a parallel between visual and haptic perception corresponding to that between spoken and written language, it does not provide us with a linguistic-like analysis of perception as such; and, although (ii) suggests that speech and thought have the same structure because they jointly rest on the same innate conditions on which language acquisition itself depends, it does not provide us with a way of determining independently what the structure of thinking is. These omissions are so remarkably similar that, in the absence of a plausible account of the genetic conditions of innate ideas and of a detailed linguistic model for the characterization of vision, it seems reasonable to turn to other alternatives. Here, the similarities between perceptual cognition and thought are instructive.

Of course, even if we debate the true nature of chimpanzee linguistic competence, we cannot doubt that these creatures are intelligent and capable of perceptual cognition. Even if we are not sure what to make of Washoe's proto-linguistic responses to linguistic cues, we cannot deny that Washoe *sees what* the Gardners are doing on the occasion of her linguistic attempts; that is, we cannot deny that Washoe sees *that* this or that occurs. Obviously, then, in ascribing perceptual cognition to Washoe, we find ourselves obliged to formulate her perceptual discriminations *propositionally*, whether or not we are prepared to ascribe linguistic abilities to her. *A fortiori*, we do the same for human infants and for adults who have mastered language, without supposing that when human beings may correctly be said to perceive *that* such-and-such is the case they must have formulated — or must have been capable of formulating, linguistically — whatever propositional content is assigned to their perception. Similarly, if Washoe may be said to *believe that* such-and-such is the case, for instance on the basis of perception, then since to believe that such-and-such is the case is to think or to be able to think or to have thoughts, Washoe's thoughts may be linguistically formulated whether or not we ascribe linguistic abilities to her. *A fortiori*, we do the same for human infants and for adults who have mastered language, without supposing that when human beings may correctly be said to think *that* such-and-such is the case they must have formulated — or must have been capable of formulating, linguistically — whatever propositional content is assigned to their thought. In a word, it is quite impossible to ascribe cognitive states to any subject without specifying the content of such states propositionally; and it is quite impossible to specify *propositions — on any theory* — independently of *sentences* by which they are putatively conveyed. Not that we require sentences (as we do) merely to formulate propositions; rather, that propositions are linguistically modelled. But, since we can ascribe cognitive states (perception and thought) not only to animals lacking language but also to human beings when they lack language or when they have not actually used their linguistic abilities, it is very reasonable to suppose that linguistic formulations of the propositional content of their cognitive states, in the absence of explicit speech acts, must be construed *heuristically*. By this is meant: (a) that there is no propositional structure that can be independently discerned in perception or thought as such and that no independent access to such structures is needed (*contra* Geach [1957] and Armstrong [1973]); (b) that perception and thought must be assigned propositional content (cf. Chisholm [1966]; Vendler [1972]); and (c) that in using the sentences of some natural language in order to convey the propositional content of perception and thought, no assumptions need be made about the correspondences between the actual grammar of that language and the propositional structure of either perception or thought. Perception and thought actually obtain but, whatever their structure, their propositional structure is only heuristically assigned.

If this be so, then attempts by both rationalists and empiricists to conflate first- and second-language acquisition is at least not required in order to make sense out of perception and thought. For, contrary to Turbayne and Goodman, language does not depend on a visual code of any sort but, propositionally construed, vision is itself parasitically characterized in linguistic terms. And, contrary to Vendler and Geach, though thoughts may be linguistically expressed, the linguistic reporting of thought by means of *oratio obliqua* constructions does not entail that there is an independently accessible structure of thought that is either the same as or analogous with the structure of language. The thesis that the propositional content of cognitive perception and thought may be heuristically ascribed accommodates the relevant reporting of the content of a languageless creature's states, since it is our very theory of cognitive states that justifies the ascription of propositional objects to perception and thought; that is, our theory assigns objects of such a sort that only a model for reporting propositional objects will suffice, and the only model we have for formulating or fixing propositions expressed or conveyed requires the use of sentences. (This, of course, does not mean that propositions can be conveyed or expressed only verbally.)

Should it turn out, on independent empirical investigation, that there is indeed a discernible propositional structure to perception and thought (the meaning of which possibility is by no means entirely clear), the heuristic thesis may be replaced by the literal one. For example, perhaps there is evidence of some internal (molecular) "representation" of the content of thought and perception (Fodor [1975]). What is here being argued (thus far) is only that the heuristic thesis is both economical and reasonable and that there is no independent evidence or evidence free of questionbegging interpretations that points to grammatical structures somehow embedded in the processes of perception and thought.

Roger Brown [1973], in fact, having qualified resistence to chimpanzee language, concludes that Chomsky's view of the "barest rudiments" of language is far too restrictive, that on that view even children are not producing language (at the levels Brown distinguishes as Stages I–III), and that, in general, "what goes before 'language' in development is only linguistic by courtesy of its continuity with a system which in fully elaborated form is indeed a language". Washoe, it now turns out, compares rather favorably with so-called Stage I "linguistic" performance, essentially because "appropriate word order is not strictly *necessary* for purposes of communication for either the Stage I child or the Stage I chimpanzee". The reason, apparently, is "because most of these sequences are produced concurrently with a referent situation which would ordinarily admit of only one sensible interpretation whether the order was right or wrong". Brown concludes that Washoe's accomplishment seems to entail "enough of a linguistic capacity to have supported a considerable degree of cultural evolution"; "I would not rule out", he says, "the possibility that chimpanzees in fact make more use of a linguistic capacity than has generally been supposed." Furthermore, the thesis relies heavily on contextual interpretation and idealization — in effect, on presuppositions regarding the chimpanzee's rationality (propositionally rendered). But what this really means is that, even in the context of language acquisition, a heuristic model of first-language learning is inescapable. Brown [1956] himself, however, draws attention (without elucidation) to the important fact that "first-language learning ... is a process of cognitive socialization", by which he means "the taking on of culture". Here, the difference between first-language and second-language learning is impossible to ignore. Still, when he introduces what he calls "the Original Word Game", by which some tutor trains a player in at least a first language, Brown straightforwardly says that "the player forms hypotheses about the nonlinguistic categories eliciting particular utterances". Clearly, to admit that the acquisition of a first language is part of the first "taking on of culture" entails a reliance on a heuristic model of propositional ascriptions. It is just the failure to recognize the adequacy of a heuristic model for assigning propositional content to the perception and belief of creatures lacking language that has obliged *both* rationalists and empiricists to construe the learning of a first language on the model of learning a second. How else, one can imagine them asking, can language-less creatures *understand* the nature of the first language they acquire? But how, we may ask in turn, are we to understand the notion of prelinguistic hypotheses? Essentially the same point is succinctly pressed against the theories of William Stern [1914] by the Russian theorist, L. S. Vygotsky [1962]. Attacking Stern's intellectualistic conception of language learning, Vygotsky remarks: "One might expect . . . that much light would be thrown on the relation between speech and thought when the meaningfulness of language is regarded as a result of an intellectual operation. Actually, such an approach, stipulating as it does an *already formed* intellect, blocks an investigation of the involved dialectical interactions of thought and speech." Clearly, both the empiricists and rationalists here considered are struggling to preserve just the futile form of intellectualism that Vygotsky has exposed.

There are a good many questions that the heuristic model itself generates, that deserve a separate airing. But there are two considerations that may be mentioned that will at least suggest the resilience and power of the model. For one thing, heuristic ascriptions of propositional content to thought and perception entail a richer conception of the use of *oratio obliqua* constructions than is usually conceded. *Oratio obliqua* may be used (1) to report the propositional content of what someone *said*; and (2) to report the propositional content of what someone *perceived* or *thought*, even when the subject is incapable of speech or cannot be said relevantly to have exercised or to have been disposed to exercise his linguistic ability. Vendler concedes as much, though for a different purpose, when he acknowledges that indirect discourse may be used "for the reproduction of someone else's, or my own, thought as well" as for reporting the message or propositional content of someone's speech-act. *If* thinking does not presuppose the capacity to speak, then it is impossible to deny that *oratio obliqua* has this larger (and heuristic) function. Only a rationalist could avoid the conclusion. But *which* propositions to assign to a creature on the occasion of a particular ascription of perception or thinking will depend on our theory of the biologically developed capabilities of the creature in question: in fact, the very notion that a given creature is capable of cognitive perception and thought entails some constraint on the conceptual capacities of the creature itself. Hence, in determining what the range of perception and thought is that may be ascribed to a given creature, we determine as well the repertory or propositions that may be assigned as the pertinent content of particular perceptions and thoughts *and*, at the same time, the range of concepts that the creature is capable of using (*contra* Geach and Armstrong). The elucidation of these issues is obviously strenuous; but the point at stake here is merely one of sketching the orienting features of the theory within which heuristic ascriptions are actually made.

The second consideration concerns the intensionality of mental states like belief, thought, mood, attitude as well as of cognition in genera. Schematically, to believe *that a&b* does not entail and is not the same thing as believing *that b&a*. The puzzles of intensionality are well known and are regarded as particularly troublesome for a thoroughgoing materialistic interpretation of the mind (cf. Dennett [1969]; Armstrong [1973]). Be that as it may, the heuristic model entirely obviates the paradoxes of intensionality: mental states remain inten*t*ional, in the sense that they may be "about" or "directed to" propositions; but the ascription of propositional content need not generate any intensional puzzles. The reason is elementary. Since the heuristic model does not presuppose a mastery of language or, for those who have linguistic competence, an actual use of that competence, no intensional considerations bearing on relations between sentences is the least bit relevant. If, for a given creature, we wish to ascribe the belief that *a&b* and the belief that *b&a*, we cannot do so on the basis of what is entailed or logically equivalent among sets of sentences; we can do so only on the evidence — for instance, behavioral evidence relative to our theory of the interests, desires, skills, capacities, and the like of the creature in question — that (i) both may be independently confirmed; or (ii) that the ascription is indifferent to either sentential formulation. In short, the heuristic model illuminates the important finding that the puzzles of intensionality arise not where ascriptions of mental states are involved but only where such ascriptions are made of creatures actively employing or disposed to employ speech in the expression or reporting of their thoughts and perceptions. Here, again, enormous conceptual complications arise. Nevertheless, the considerations provided suggest that we may pursue these without any danger of an immediate stalemate. And we may pursue them, without resolving the rationalist/empiricist controversy and without confusing first- and second-language acquisition with the capacity for cognitive perception and thought. What the conditions are for successful first-language acquisition remain, however, a profound empirical mystery.

Vygotsky's views, here again, are instructive. "If we compare", he says, "the early development of speech and intellect — which, as we have seen, develop along separate lines both in animals and in very young children — with the development of inner speech and of verbal thought, we must conclude that the later stage is not a simple continuation of the earlier. *The nature of the development itself changes*, from biological to sociohistorical. Verbal thought is not an innate, natural form of behavior but is determined by a historical-cultural process and has specific properties and laws that cannot be found in the natural forms of thought and speech." In effect, what Vygotsky points to, in his own idiom, is that there is and can be no purely biological accounting for the culturally distinctive (rulelike) regularities of language and that ascriptions of prelinguistic communication by sound and gesture (what he sometimes calls animal language) and prelinguistic thought (which two processes develop separately, as evidenced by the solution of problems and the expression of emotion by voice and gesture) provide the genetic basis for the *gradual* emergence of "verbal thought" and "intellectual speech". What Vygotsky means by these two phrases is (i) that verbal thought is, in effect, "inner, soundless speech" — *functionally* considered, the result of a gradual series of "molecular" changes culminating in the "fusion" of the separate and increasingly altered (that is, linguistically altered) processes of (prelinguistic) thought and (prelinguistic) "speech"; and (ii) that intellectual speech is "external speech" (the mastery of "the correct use of grammatical forms and structures", which may precede a grasp of "the logical operations for which they stand") *plus* the requisite grasp of their logical function. What this suggests, in effect, is that the beginning of human speech must be, initially, functionally redundant with the prelinguistic communicative (and perceptual) abilities of infants at the same time that the redundancies may gradually be learned to manifest structures of a distinctly linguistic sort.

One of Vygotsky's principal concerns is to demonstrate that the transitional phase in this development is precisely what has been characterized by Jean Piaget as "the child's egocentric speech" (though without adopting — in fact, reversing — Piaget's own explanatory account) (Piaget [1923], [1926]). Here, the emphasis is placed (correctly) on the fully social character of learning (even) the forms and structures of a language though the language learned is, on the thesis advanced, used in a way that is not socialized but "incommunicable" (egocentric). What Vygotsky says is extremely suggestive leading on to an account of "inner speech" (that is, verbally informed thought); but the truth is that it, too, presupposes an essential feature of the learning of a first language, that is not supplied. For, for one thing, what it is to say that a child comes to *grasp* the functional properties of language is never explained: here, Vygotsky is in just the same position as Stern, though he has cautioned us to attend to a gradual process. And for another, Vygotsky has nothing to say about the inescapability of analyzing prelinguistic thought and perception in terms of a linguistic model; hence, he provides no ground on which to facilitate our understanding of the transition from the prelinguistic to the linguistic. In fact, even in his investigation of concept formation, Vygotsky confines himself to what he calls "the new significative use of the world, its use *as a means of concept formation*", which he claims (in opposition both to associative theorists and to those who favor teleological causation by way of cultural tasks) "is the immediate psychological cause of the radical change in the intellectual process that occurs on the threshold of adolescence".

The point is that, along Vygotskyan lines precisely, the connection between the two must lie with their functional convergence; that since an *awareness* of the propositional function of language and all that that entails cannot pop up *ex nihilo*, the only reasonable assumption is that such an awareness is itself the result of a dawning and reflexive grasp of what is already functionally present in the prelinguistic material from which it emerges. Only a theory like that of the heuristic analysis of prelinguistic thought and perception could, therefore, sustain an empirical account that, like Vygotsky's, eschews the charge that learning a first language is like learning a second. Here, then, Vygotsky fails to examine the implications of concept formation on the part of prelinguistic creatures (animals or human infants) and concerns himself only with the (admittedly important) question of the threshold phenomenon of learning to conceive by means of the use of words. Hence, he neither specifies the nature of linguistic mastery nor the functional nature of pre-linguistic conception on which verbal conception must depend. He is primarily concerned with the continuity between the two phases of development, but he has no way of specifying the functional resemblance among the developing stages. The force of this conclusion may be appreciated merely by considering that, in what Vygotsky calls "the second major phase on the way to concept formation" − "thinking in complexes", a child "unites" objects by way of "bonds actually existing between these objects" whenever the child notices that one object is similar to a nuclear or sample object − say, "in shape or in size, *or in any other attribute that happens to strike him*". (Italics added.) But to say this is just to fix the puzzle that needs to be explicated. One may, therefore, agree, with Vygotsky, that "there is no rigid correspondence between the units of thought and speech", but the question remains, what is the structure of thought? One may agree that "a word devoid of thought is a dead thing", but it is either false or trivially true (because verbal thought, thinking linguistically, is intended) to hold that "a thought unembodied in words remains a shadow". Vygotsky's own genetic method precludes the claim, calls for an explanation that he apparently fails to supply. The heuristic model, it may be said, accommodates the "different structures" of thought and speech, obviates the need to reduce first-language learning to second-language learning, and provides for the functional continuity of prelinguistic and linguistic competences.

Having said this much, we must consider, further, whether the heuristic model is a reasonable one or whether it may be effectively challenged by further considerations that bear on the ascription of thought and perception. We have, in effect, merely sketched an empiricist theory of language acquisition; but the conditions on which it is to obtain presuppose that it properly applies to non-linguistic cognitive achievements as well. To demonstrate the force of the thesis in that regard invites us to look at the issues we have been canvassing in any entirely different light. So let us make a fresh start once again. Whatever else they may be, let us say, persons must be sentient entities. That is, they must possess states of a cognitively relevant sort attributed in virtue of having exercised and of being able to exercise abilities suited to scanning the discernible features of the world, including, reflexively, their own mental states. That they are capable of cognition does not, on the usual admissions, distinguish persons from the higher animals (cf. Strawson [1959]). Also, it can hardly be supposed that the denial of cognitive achievements to the lower animals, that are at least "irritable" and "sensitive" and by which sentient "information" may in some sense be said to be processed, entails the denial of cognition to the higher animals; or, that the denial of cognition to the higher animals, should that prove viable, entails the denial of cognitive achievements to (human) persons. In this regard, the issue of cognitive ascriptions is empirical, although it seems conceptually impossible to deny that human persons are cognitive agents. We should be denying what the denial itself would entail. Essentially, this is the Cartesian insight stripped of indubitably, egocentricity, and metaphysical extravagance. Denial and speculation are simply particular manifestations of just the sort of (cognitive) activity in virtue of which something could be counted a person at all. In our own case, of course, the ascriptions are reflexive. But the argument is incomplete.

To say that persons are capable of perception and introspection is to say nothing about the analysis of such capacities in terms of sub-cognitive processes that they presumably include. There are bound to be disputes about such processes that are relatively neutral to the mere ascription of cognitive capacity. Nevertheless, to perceive — in the cognitively relevant sense — is at the very least to have perceptual beliefs, either because perceiving is having perceptual beliefs or in the sense that perceiving produces perceptual beliefs (cf. Pitcher [1971]). We cannot, therefore, deny that belief states are real without in effect denying that persons are real. One cannot be said to perceive cognitively unless one may be said to believe — because of what one perceives — *that* . . . , where what is introduced by 'that' is the propositional content of the belief in question. Furthermore, if we admit cognitive agents that are not persons — in at least the strongly plausible sense in which persons are just those entities that have a mastery of language and, because of that, a capacity to refer to themselves and to the things of the world — then we cannot deny that belief states are real for such creatures as well. Also, if it is true, as seems eminently reasonable, that the ascription of beliefs makes sense only in a context in which some set of related mental states may be attributed as well — for instance, desires, intentions, volitions, memories, experiences, inferences and the like, and some set of actions informed by such states — then the admission of persons and animals capable of cognition entails the admission of a variety of real mental states. Since, however, animals lack a language, since belief states and the like are individuated propositionally, and since propositions can be specified only by means of sentences, the admission that animals think or perceive or have beliefs entails that the propositional content of such states may be specified only by a *heuristic* use of language and, as a consequence, that animal psychology must be inherently anthropomorphized (cf. Bennett [1964]).

A *fictive* theory of beliefs holds that beliefs are not real, are ascribed only as a *façon de parler*, as for instance instrumentally useful in moving predictively among the real states of some system (Gibson [1966]; Dennett [1969]). In this sense, a fictive theory of beliefs is inherently reductionistic, in eliminating agents actually capable of cognition, though it need not be reductionistic at the level at which the fiction is thought to be operative. Persons must go, one may argue, but biology need not be reducible to subatomic physics, or functional characterizations to structural ones. If beliefs are essential to persons or other cognitive agents, then the denial of the reality of beliefs is tantamount to the denial of the reality of such agents. A *heuristic* theory of beliefs, on the other hand, holds that beliefs are real states of organisms or entities; furthermore, since, on the theory, belief states are propositionally structured, particular beliefs have the actual structures they do. Still, because propositions can be specified only linguistically and since animals lack language, we face a fundamental difficulty in specifying the actual structure of animal beliefs — or of human beliefs manifested nonverbally. We theorize about the conceptual capacity, interests, needs, desires, intentions, and characteristic behavior of a particular animal and, on the evidence, we ascribe particular beliefs to it. We characterize an animal's beliefs heuristically, then, because we lack a direct means for scanning the structure of such beliefs — not because we deny that animals have beliefs or that their beliefs have the structure ascribed to them. On the heuristic view, they have the structure they have; but since that structure must be specified propositionally and since propositional structure can be specified only by means of sentences, we theorize that the *real* structure of animal beliefs can only be analogically approximated (cf. T. Nagel [1974]). We judge our approximations to be defensible in virtue of the explanatory and predictive power of such specifications within the scope of the governing assumption that animals are cognitive agents. The thesis that they are incapable of thinking, for instance because thinking presupposes language (Davidson [1975]; Vendler [1972]), is undermined by the admission that animals are capable of perceptual belief. Donald Davidson for example concedes that animals do perceive in a cognitively relevant sense, but he also claims that they are incapable of thought; the two theses are, however, incompatible, since cognitive perception has the same propositional structure as thought. So a fictive theory of beliefs holds that beliefs are not real, and a heuristic theory of beliefs holds only that the *characterization of real beliefs* depends on the use of a linguistic model that cannot be independently tested for fit, because either the creatures to which beliefs are ascribed lack a language or the linguistically competent creatures that have beliefs do not, on some occasion, form them linguistically.

Conceivably, the argument may be outflanked in various ways. The available strategies seem to be the following: (i) beliefs may be straightforwardly denied reality — and with them, persons and animals as cognitive agents; (ii) animals may be said to have a language in some sense, precisely because they are capable of perceptual cognition; (iii) beliefs may be said to be characterized and individuated adequately on the basis of a nonlinguistic model; (iv) beliefs may be denied reality, without denying the reality of cognitive agents, by replacing belief-ascriptions with ascriptions of certain real states to the sub-cognitive parts of the system that is the cognitive agent. We need not consider these alternatives separately, for there are certain key maneuvers that would decide the fate of all relevant theories, though they are not readily sorted in just the terms given.

A key consideration is this. Propositional content (and, by parity of reasoning, intentional objects) can be assigned only to mental states (as opposed to physical states), mental episodes, actions and the like, themselves directly ascribed only to persons or other cognitive agents; where they appear to be assigned to states, processes, episodes, and the like that obtain on some *sub*-cognitive level, or are ascribed to *parts* of a system that is otherwise counted as a cognitive agent, they are dependently so assigned precisely in virtue of counterpart ascriptions made of the cognitive agents themselves. *Information*, said to be processed in any of a large variety of ways — consciously, neurologically within the brain or through the nervous system as a whole or by some biological organism — is specified propositionally (Arbib [1972]). Hence, if the thesis about propositional content were sustained, it would be conceptually impossible to speak of the informational input and output of the sub-cognitive parts of a system without providing for cognitive access to some portion *of* that information *by* the system (the cognitive agent) itself. The critical reason for so speaking is a simple one: propositions are specifiable only by means of sentences used to perform speech acts, cognitively significant behavior, even though propositions are not linguistic "entities" (cannot be linguistic " entities" if, at the very least, animals have beliefs though they lack language); but the use of sentences in the performance of speech acts (and the behavior of animals justifying the heuristic analogue) is, precisely, just the activity that marks persons (and animals) as the distinctive cognitive agents that they are. The ascription of states having propositional content to *non*-cognitive systems must, therefore, be either incoherent, metaphorical, or parasitic on ascriptions to genuine cognitive agents. Alternatively, when information or propositionally qualified states are ascribed to purely physical systems, they are ascribed either fictively or as a *façon de parler*.

When we use the linguistic model heuristically, therefore, whether with respect to information processed at a sub-cognitive level or with respect to a languageless creature, we presuppose the presence of a cognitive agent regarding the beliefs and related states and episodes of which the relevant ascriptions may be defended — either by direct analogy with persons or derivatively, by considering the function of such putative information for whatever information the system as a whole, functioning cognitively, has access to. This is simply another way of stating the thesis that real cognitive agents must have real beliefs and that real beliefs presupposed real cognitive agents. This is in general accord with Daniel Dennett's view [1976] that the "information or content an event [has] within the system [it has] for the system as a (biological) whole"; also with his view that the content of some event transferring information from one sub-cognitive area to another "is to be understood as a function of the function within the whole system of that event". These formulations constitute his gloss on Michael Arbib's witty emendation of the expression "what the frog's eye tells the frog's brain" as "what the frog's eye tells the frog". At this point, it does not matter whether the cognitive agent is a living creature or a machine of some sort: any ascription of information said to be processed from one physical sub-system to another will be so characterized only if the system of which the other is a part may, rightly, be characterized as capable of cognitive states (Crosson and Sayre [1967]; Mackay [1969]).

On the most generous theory, "every physical channel has a definite numerical capacity for conveying information", and "an event y provides an amount of information about the occurrence of an event x" if observing that y (in whatever cognitively relevant sense of 'observing' we may choose) alters the valid assignment of a probability to the occurrence of x (Massey [1967]; cf. Shannon and Weaver [1949]). The information assigned to an event, therefore, is specified propositionally in just the same way as beliefs are specified. It is sometimes even argued that "such simple Informational processing mechanisms as thermometers, radios, voltmeters, and telephonic systems will *also* qualify [for knowledge (and other mentalistic predicates)]" (Dretske [1976]). On the thesis, the critical difference between such systems and living animals and human persons lies in the fact that systems of the first sort, unlike the latter, appear to be "incapable of distinguishing between Informationally equivalent [states of affairs]"; that is, "their internal states have a [propositional] content ... but a content that is transparent to the substitution of informational equivalents" (Dretske). But since propositional attitudes and intentional objects behave intensionally, this is an elliptical way of saying that cognitive agents will find that, if *they* construe such systems as conveying information or as believing or knowing that something is the case, they will be bound to construe them as incapable of sorting or preferring alternative extensionally equivalent messages. Which is precisely what cognitive agents are supposed to be capable of doing. There is, therefore, a double distinction favoring proper cognitive agents: (i) a capacity to *have* intentional states, states assigned propositional content; and (ii) a capacity to distinguish between at least *some* informationally equivalent messages or to favor disjunctively some alternatives among informationally equivalent messages. In this regard, to speak of a thermometer as "knowing" or "believing" that p is merely a *façon de parler* – one in fact that construes causal sequences informationally (Ashby [1956]); alternatively put, the thermometer conveys information in conveying information *for* a proper cognitive agent: here, there is an ellipsis rather than a *façon de parler*.

What we may say, then, is this. A cognitive agent must have beliefs. But having beliefs presupposes conceptual capacities of some sort, in virtue of which such agents cannot but behave asymmetrically with regard to *some* otherwise extensionally equivalent messages. For instance, Fido may be said to believe that his master is at the door, but it is entirely possible that, though his master be the president of the First National Bank, Fido, lacking the concept of *the president of the First National Bank*, cannot be said to believe that the president of the First National Bank is at the door. Ascriptions of belief to Fido are ascriptions of real states that, because Fido lacks language, can be made only heuristically. But since Fido is a cognitive agent, some intensional asymmetries must be preserved (ascribed to *conceptual* limitations. No such asymmetries regarding information arise with respect to such systems as thermometers and thermostats. It is only by a fictive ascription that they can be said to be capable of knowledge and belief; and it is only by an ellipsis that they are said to convey information. They convey information in that a cognitively competent agent can, on an interpretation, construe the physical states of such systems as having a certain informational function. Linguistically competent agents formulate and follow *rules* or rulelike regularities, which they grasp and can violate and which permit intensional distinctions. Animals lacking language cannot formulate such rules but, being cognitive agents and capable of understanding concepts, they behave in intensionally asymmetrical ways; these are detailed heuristically, as has been said. Systems incapable of cognition may nevertheless be construed informationally, which is to say that the nomological regularities among the physical states of such systems are, on an interpretation, assigned propositional content. For instance, a thermostat set at a certain temperature cuts off the heat; in effect, the physical sequence conveys, on an interpretation or *rubric* (which may be a program actually imposed by a cognitive agent or a natural *telos* assigned as the best explanation of the behavior of, say, a plant system or an interpretation justified solely in accord with the instrumental strategies of a cognitive agent), *that* something or other is the case or ought to be done or the like. The thermostat's cutting off the heat (or better, the "perception" that informs that "act") is an interpretation, functionally equivalent to the assertion of some appropriate proposition.

The issue is a strategic one and has been much disputed. But there is a way of strengthening our account that may seem at first a little distant. Consider that animals incapable of mastering a language can have no concept of predication — on any plausible theory of concepts. Nevertheless, *if* animals are conceded to be capable of perceptual cognition, and if the propositional content of the perceptual beliefs of animals must be formulated by a heuristic use of language, then it is quite impossible that the individuation of animal beliefs will not involve a heuristic use of the predicative relation. Fido may be said to see that his master is at the door in spite of the fact that, lacking language, Fido has no concept of predication. The complexities of heuristic ascriptions need not detain us here. (We shall return to them, however.)

On a theory of Fido's interests, capacities, desires, range of behavior and the like, and on the evidence that Fido did perceive something, the point at stake is simply that the *functional* import of Fido's perception is best approximated by some such verbal report as "I see my master at the door". The theory of Fido's capacities is an induction to the best explanation regarding Fido's life, and the putative functional equivalence of the perceptual episode and the heuristic report does not require any linguistic capacity on the part of Fido — *a fortiori*, does not require a capacity to use the linguistic concept of predication. We may then say that the propositional content of Fido's perceptual belief is the functional import of that belief. Furthermore, *if* its propositional content is formulated heuristically, *there is no reason to hold that the belief's message must be represented in some independently recoverable way in the sub-cognitive processes or cognitive sub-processes of the dog's internal system* — certainly none that the heuristically ascribed structure will be so represented. The heuristic characterization of the structure is an artifact of the theory; the real structure is functionally assigned on the theory and the evidence. It is quite sufficient that Fido's sub-cognitive information-processing channels be in some appropriate structural state compatible with an ascription of perception and that, on the theory favored, Fido's behavior justify the ascription of the particular perceptual belief in question. In other words, once we admit heuristic ascriptions of belief, we may treat particular beliefs as functionally real in spite of the fact that they are not represented structurally (that is, in a way that is independently accessible *qua* representational medium) in the sub-cognitive processes (or cognitive sub-processes) of an animal; or we may treat particular beliefs as structurally represented by the relevant portions of the animal's entire state and behavior. Which is in effect to say: either (i) impute the relevant belief on the evidence and then construe some portion of the evidence as the representation of the belief; or (ii) construe some state or behavior of the animal as the expression of the imputed belief and then assign the structure of the belief expressed as the representational structure of that expression. In either case, there is no independent access to the representation of the belief structure.

That Fido sees his master at the door is represented, then, either by whatever relevantly selected images, organic processes, neurological events or the like happen to obtain in the interval bearing on the perception or by Fido's behavior and general condition.

In any event, the detailed message of Fido's perceptual belief is ascribed on the basis of interpreting the relevant physical evidence in accord with a theory that already ascribes characteristic propositional attitudes to Fido, not on the basis of independently decoding the propositional import of some physical sequence in Fido's sub-cognitive systems. Unless something like Chomsky's theory of innate linguistic competence were valid *and* independently accessible, the account regarding heuristically ascribed beliefs to animals would apply as well to human infants that lacked language. For example, an infant's cry may at first simply be causally produced by hunger, though it may also be *interpreted* as a natural expression of hunger by some linguistically competent adult; and then, on the evidence of the infant's developing behavior, the cry may be functionally construed as the infant's intended communication *that it is hungry*. If so, intensional constraints will have to be imposed. The higher animals and infants behave in rather similar ways in this respect, though their capacities for rational behavior are clearly different. But on that evidence alone, it is not necessary to maintain that perceptual beliefs, intentional behavior, and the like cannot be attributed to cognitive agents without attributing as well some independently identifiable and determinate internal representation of the relevant propositional content or intentional object of such beliefs and behavior.

It is theoretically possible — therefore, also, a potentially desirable economy, should there be no clear evidence of internalized or innate linguistic schemata — that the internal states of an organism, causally effective in producing behavior (hence, undermining logical behaviorism) (Fodor [1968, 1975]) need be structured only in the sense that the representational schemata fitting the propositional or intentional content of the beliefs and behavior of animals are construed as the functionally real import of whatever physical structures obtain, in the light of the heuristically approximated structure of functionally real beliefs. On the theory, the beliefs are real; also, they are really propositionally structured. But the linguistic representation of their structure may be only heuristically assigned; hence, whatever physical structure is exhibited by the central states of an animal may, on the same theory, be assigned, parasitically, a representation of those (functionally specified) beliefs.

These considerations expose in effect the extraordinary doctrines recently advanced by Jerry Fodor [1975], diametrically opposed to the views here defended. Three of Fodor's claims may be mentioned: "(a) ... the sorts of data processes I have been discussing, though they may well go on in the nervous systems of organisms, are presumably not, in the most direct sense, attributable to the organisms themselves .... But whatever relevance the distinction between states of the organism and states of its nervous system may have for *some* purposes, there is no particular reason to suppose that it is relevant to the purposes of cognitive psychology. (b) ... if you want to know why the organism behaved the way it did, you must first find out what description it intended its behavior [or, response] to satisfy; what it took itself to be doing. [Alternatively put,] the 'promimal stimulus' is a proximal *representation* of the *distal* stimulus, and the 'proximal response' *stands for* an overt act. But representation presupposes a medium of representation, and there is no symbolization without symbols. In particular, there is no internal representation without an internal language. (c) If learning a language is literally a matter of making and confirming hypotheses about the truth conditions associated with its predicates, then learning a language presupposes the ability to use expressions coextensive with each of the elementary predicates of the language being learned. But, as we have seen the truth conditions associated with *any* predicate of L can be expressed in terms of the truth conditions associated with the elementary predicates of L. The upshot would appear to be that one can learn L only if one already knows some language rich enough to express the extension of any predicate of L. To put it tendentiously, one can learn what the semantic properties of a term are only if one already knows a language which contains a term having the same semantic properties." Briefly, the account already sketched conflicts with Fodor's in the following respects: against (a), it has been maintained that no ascription of propositional or intentional content can be made of sub-cognitive processes or of the parts of a system except derivatively, in the sense in which such content is functionally linked with the belief states or informed behavior of such a system construed as a cognitive agent; against (b), it has been maintained that the ascription of cognitive states to an animal (or pre-verbal infant) does not entail an independently confirmable internal language or symbol system; and against (c) it has been maintained that cognitive achievements − *a fortiori*, learning a language − does not presuppose an innate language.

It is true that Fodor explicitly says that his goal "is not to *demonstrate* that psychological processes are computational, but to work out the consequences of assuming that they are". But this is to say, precisely, that, assuming a computational model, (a)–(c) are unavoidable, on Fodor's view. Our own account, therefore, may be fairly construed as demonstrating how to avoid (a)–(c) *on* a computational model. On Fodor's view, for instance, "deciding is a computational process; the act the agent performs is the consequence of computations defined over representations of possible action. No representations, no computations. No computations, no model." But on our view, since the computations, though functionally real, may only be heuristically characterized, the representational scheme (or internal language) need only be functionally assigned to match the other; in fact, the computations (which will be intensionally qualified) cannot be identified in any other way in animals and pre-verbal infants, that is, in creatures that genuinely lack language.

(c) is the most curious and vulnerable of Fodor's claims. On (c), it appears that one can never actually learn a new concept (on any plausible view of what a concept is). Thus, Fodor says flatly that "the concept-learning task cannot coherently be interpreted as a task in which concepts are learned"; hence, on his view, "the only coherent sense to be made of such learning models as are currently available is one which presupposes a very extreme nativism". (Fodor also emphasizes that "barring rote memorization, 'concept learning' is the only sort of learning for which psychology offers us a model".) The reason is, roughly, that if the learning of concepts "is the projection and confirmation of hypotheses", then the acceptance of the relevant hypothesis that a certain concept obtains already presupposes an understanding of the concept in question. In effect, then, "learning concepts" is really nothing but learning "exemplars" of the concepts one already has or learning which concepts serve as "criterial" for the concept in question. But it seems preposterous to hold that one never learns a new concept (on any plausible view of what a concept is). For one thing, it seems more than reasonable to hold that at least some new concepts are sometimes learned: Fodor's theory is, in effect, a fashionable version of Plato's myth of recollection. For another, it seems peculiarly implausible to deny that such particular concepts as *one's unborn brother, indenumerably infinite, Dada, atomic fission* are not fairly treated as fully learned concepts. And for a third, it seems utterly implausible to suppose that the whole of human culture is, in effect, merely the exemplification of a repertory of preculturally fixed concepts — even of those that are essentially developed with the historical transformations of human culture. Certainly, there is no evidence (a) that the entire range of concepts available to linguistically competent humans are complex combinations of some finitely denumerable set of simple concepts of any sort whatsoever, or (b) that any promising portion of such a set of simple concepts could be accounted for in terms independent of cultural experience.

In fact, there seems to be no way of demonstrating the learning of a concept that is independent of learning beliefs. The only question that arises is whether, on the evidence, the new belief involves a new concept or does not; and that, again, is a question of the best explanation — without assuming extreme nativism. Chomsky's theory of course maintains that only an extreme nativism can explain the rapidity and convergence of language learning from degenerate samples. Fodor's maintains that learning in general can be explained only on the assumption of an extreme nativism. But the heuristic model already sketched shows at a stroke both that nativism is not entailed either by the learning of language or by the learning of concepts and that the learning of a concept does not entail the prior understanding of that concept.

Consider merely that a languageless animal may be ascribed the learning of a concept, for instance, *obedience*, on the basis of heuristically specified beliefs. Fido may be trained to be obedient and, on the evidence that Fido has acquired new propositional attitudes regarding relevant matters of obedience, it is entirely reasonable to suppose that Fido learned a concept that he did not formerly have, that is, for which there is no remotely favorable inductive evidence apart from the thesis in question. Since Fido is languageless and since the original ascription is heuristically specified, the only evidence that we require is that Fido *now has an understanding of obedience when, before, he did not*.

Fodor's model is initially plausible *only* where it is confined to explicitly linguistic formulations: concede that there is pre-linguistic learning — even the pre-linguistic learning of language — and non-linguistic learning of concepts even for the linguistically competent, and you will have fixed the literal-minded sense in which Fodor thinks that learning a new concept involves "hypothesis and confirmation". "Hypothesis and confirmation" is no more than a heuristically specified approximation of a learning process that is functionally best represented in linguistic terms. On empirical grounds, assuming nativism itself to be in doubt, there is not the slightest evidence that cognitive agents, whether animals or human infants or linguistically competent adults, never acquire substantively new concepts. What Fodor may have conflated is the native capacity of any creature to learn whatever it eventually learns and the combination of native and acquired capacities (including conceptual capacities) on which the learning of new concepts depends. In an obvious sense, the capacity to understand concepts is native but not necessarily all the concepts that one understands. So there is an equivocation on conceptual capacity: a creature, lacking concept C may be said to have the conceptual capacity to understand C; and a creature that understands C has the conceptual capacity to understand things in terms of C. When Fido learns the concept of *obedience* (or, for that matter, when Washoe learns the concept of the preposition *on*), we may fairly (and vacuously) say that Fido must have had the native (conceptual) capacity to learn that concept; but the evidence is that Fido lacked that concept natively and came to learn it. How could the *possibility* be denied, once the linguistic model is construed heuristically? But, *if* this be admitted for languageless animals, how could it be denied for human beings — either infants or adults?

One need not subscribe to Piaget's entire system in order to appreciate the fact that there is empirical evidence that children acquire new concepts in the course of their maturation (Piaget [1970]). It is only when something like an explicitly formal model is proposed that the original Platonic paradox arises: S learns concept C; that is, S learns that concepts $A_1 \ldots A_n$ serve as criterial conditions for concept C; hence S must have known concept C in order to learn that $A_1 \ldots A_n$ are thus criterially linked. But on the heuristic reading, the explicit model need not be literally adopted. Furthermore, the empirical situation appears to be as follows: at t, S does not understand the concept C; at t', S learns the concept. All that is needed to avoid Fodor's paradox is simply to concede that beliefs and concepts are functionally real and that the specification of the propositional content of beliefs and the learning of concepts is, where language is lacking, purely heuristic. The behavior at t and t' confirms S's not understanding, then understanding, C and S's having learned C in the interval. What is needed is a model for making sense of the facts, not a denial of the facts because of paradoxes that are artifacts of the model itself.

In summary, what we may say is this. Cognitive agents that have and use a language are able to represent their calculations (linguistically); *they* need no other (internal) representation of those calculations and there is none (*contra* Fodor) that "the agent *has access to*" (italics added). For languageless animals, the ascription of such psychological states as believing, valuing, intending, perceiving and the like (which Fodor concedes) is itself based on the heuristic use of a linguistic model, hence, on the heuristic use of a representational system; *a fortiori*, there is no "availability, to the behaving organism, of some sort of [internal] representational system". In any case, attribution of an internal representational system signifies only (i) that the propositional or intentional import of given behavior is *assigned* to whatever neurophysiological processes may, on a theory, be supposed to "realize" the mental states in question; and (ii) the internal representation cannot be anything but the counterpart of the explicit (linguistic) or heuristically imputed import of such behavior. There is, in short, no way in which the putative internal representation could be matched with the linguistic representation or the heuristically imputed import of actual behavior. The nativist theory of thought attempts somehow to ascribe as a prior, independent, and determinately articulated competence what can only be abstracted as the sub-processes of the actual ability of an agent to perform at the molar level.

The essential weakness of Fodor's account may be put in a word: Fodor cannot provide a schema that (on the evidence) is a possible candidate for the molecular (or internal) representation of what is thought or said at the molar level. "Messages", Fodor holds, "are most plausibly construed as formulae in the language of thought"; and messages are mediated by "intervening representations", "linguistic structural descriptions", that are "psychologically real". But what is the nature of these real internal representations with which agents are said to compute? In effect, Fodor subscribes to Donald Davidson's application [1967b] of Tarski's semantic conception of truth [1956]: "a theory of meaning", he says, "serves . . . to pair natural language sentences with some sort of canonical representation of their truth conditions". We have already seen, however (*contra* Quine [1960]), that there is no perspicuous extensional replacement for sentences involving propositional attitudes. Tarski himself despaired of fitting his conception of truth to natural languages. But Fodor actually says that "the heart of the computational approach to psychology is the attempt to explain the propositional attitudes of the organism by reference to relations that the organism bears to internal representations". Hence, he supposes (i) that there is some extensional paraphrase of the propositional object of a verb of propositional attitude ('believes', 'fears', 'forgets', and the like), and (ii) that there is some independent way of relating an instantiated propositional attitude to a particular proposition. He apparently believes that the propositional attitude may be construed relationally, *once* the (extensionally characterized) propositional or intentional object (in effect, some proposition) is specified. But that begs the very question at stake. We cannot detach *the proposition*, representing that about which one has a certain attitude until we fix which proposition represents what one has an attitude *about*, that is, until we analyze the mental state itself. In the same spirit, Fodor acknowledges: "Among the niceties that I am prepared to ignore at this point is the treatment of indexicals. If one were being serious, one would have to ensure that F [a formula of the internal code which corresponds to the English sentence 'There's an ink-blot on this page', ('S')] determines a definite referent for 'this page'. A standard proposal is to take F as containing a schema for a many-place relation between a speaker, a location, a time, etc; the arguments of this relation would thus differ for different tokens of S." But this ignores both the intentional features of reference that cannot be represented internally as the analysis of standard sentences (for instance, the referential use of definite descriptions (cf. Donnellan [1966]) and the fact that, even if the identity of indiscernibles be admitted, there is no manageably finite set of general descriptions that could individuate all objects uniquely and there is no sense in holding that, innately, we already have a schema for marking out just the particular objects that we encounter in experience at the molar level. The result is that if Fodor is right (as he seems to be), that the "heart" of the computational approach requires the success of defining meaning in terms of Tarskian-like truth conditions, then the enterprise is fairly doomed. Fodor's view about propositional attitudes is similarly unpromising. For he holds quite explicitly that "to have a certain propositional attitude is to be in a certain relation to an internal representation" and that "being in that relation to that representation is nomologically necessary and sufficient for (or nomologically identical to) having the propositional attitude". Since, however, the relation is a computational one, the theory must fail if the computational model is, as it appears to be, inadequate; also, there is every reason to believe that propositional attitudes can be specified only in contextually relevant terms and only at the molar level (cf. Wittgenstein [1963]) – hence, never nomologically.

It should be noted that Fodor admits the possibility of mental states or propositional attitudes that are not produced computationally (for instance, ideas that pop into one's head), "the consequence of brute incursions from the physiological level". But he is concerned primarily with the prospects of a cognitive psychology, that is, of a psychology that explains *rational* relations holding among the mental events within a given life. "Cognitive explanation", therefore, "requires not only causally interrelated mental states, but also mental states whose causal relations respect the semantic relations that hold between formulae in the internal representational system". It is quite possible that mental states be causally connected without being connected "by virtue of their content" (for instance, when some perceived episode functions as an arbitrary mnemonic device for remembering to do something utterly unrelated). Hence, for Fodor, cognitive psychology depends on the defense of a *cognitively* accessible computational model at the molecular level. But if the force of the counterarguments offered be conceded, then: (a) computations at the molecular level can only be dependently assigned as the sub-processes relative to cognitive performance at the molar level – hence, are never empirically accessible in an independent way; (b) there is no evidence that we possess innately, that is, independent of cultural experience, some finitely denumerable set of simple concepts sufficient to provide an analysis of all the concepts that we actually learn to use; (c) there is no prospect, short of giving an extensional analysis of intentional sentences and of reference (which appears impossible), of construing the meaning of utterances in natural languages in terms of internally accessible truth conditions of any sort. The importance of these conclusions attests to the importance of countering Fodor's claims. For, if Fodor is mistaken, then no other *cognitive* version of an internal computational model could be defended and no *non-cognitive* version (failing to reduce intentional contexts) would be remotely relevant: the first, because the task would remain the same; the second, because the intentional is irreducible.

Having said this much, we need only add some conveniently selected measures of the difference between the account offered and otherwise attractive alternatives that might conceivably outflank or undermine that account. Thus, for instance, our view converges with Daniel Dennett's to the extent that Dennett [1969] holds that "something is a message or a signal only when it goes on to effect functions in some self-contained Intentional system [that is, a person or other cognitive agent]". But then, Dennett concludes his account in the following way: "Thoughts, for example, are not only not to be identified with physical processes in the brain, but also not to be identified with logical or functional states or events in an Intentional system (physically realized in the nervous system of a body). The story we tell when we tell the ordinary story of a person's mental activities cannot be mapped with precision on to the extensional story of events in the person's body, nor has the ordinary story any real precision of its own. It has no precision, for when we say a person knows or believes this or that, for example, we ascribe to him no determinable, circumscribed, invariant, generalizable states, capacities or dispositions. The personal story, moreover, has a relatively vulnerable and impermanent place in our conceptual scheme, and could in principle be rendered 'obsolete' if some day we ceased to treat anything (any mobile body or system or device) as an Intentional system — by reasoning with it, communicating with it, etc." If what has gone before is tenable, then it is quite impossible, on any relevant model, to ascribe "content or meaning or particular central states of the brain" (Dennett) without admitting real cognitive agents and real belief states. Dennett is quite wrong in supposing that if we only "ceased to treat anything" as a person or cognitive agent, we could in principle quite easily eliminate persons from our ontology. If *we treat* anything in any way at all, *we* cannot eliminate the "intentional systems" that are persons. The very admission of science entails the admission of real cognitive agents, though it is conceivable that systems hitherto treated as cognitively qualified may, by way of a theoretical economy, cease to be so construed. Knowledge is an intensional array of some sort; it cannot be preserved on some "sub-personal" or sub-cognitive level, however it may be linked to processes on that level (Sellars [1963a]).

Another important point of divergence is afforded by a comparison with D. M. Armstrong's account of beliefs and concepts [1973]. Armstrong attempts, ingeniously, to adapt Geach's theory [1957] of concepts and Ideas (that is, "exercises of concepts") to a physicalist account: "Suppose I have the concept of X. This entails that I have a certain capacity. This capacity is a necessary (although insufficient) condition for having belief-states, or thoughts, involving propositions in which X figures." Armstrong develops a distinctively non-Lockean interpretation of the difference between what he calls simple and complex Ideas, which in a way need not concern us except to note that he means to explain "the self-directedness of beliefs (and thoughts) [that is, the intentionality of beliefs, as characterized by Brentano; presumably, therefore, their intensionality as well]" by explaining "the self-directedness of our *simple* concepts and Ideas" − since "complex Ideas are simply complexes of simple Ideas". Roughly, then, Armstrong holds that "if our beliefs are to be conceived of as like maps of the world, they must also involve [certain] fundamental 'representing' elements and relations. Such fundamental features will be called '*simple* Ideas'. Corresponding to simple Ideas there will automatically be simple concepts: concepts for having such Ideas". So Ideas, in effect, *represent* the elements and relations of belief-states. But, at this point, Armstrong states that he believes "simple Ideas can be contingently identified with physiological features of states of the brain . . . (Although such a thesis is not argued for in this work)."

Here, Armstrong diverges from Dennett's and our own account, for he fails to accommodate the double constraint that the attribution of intentionality to sub-cognitive states can only be defended on the basis of relevant attributions to cognitive agents themselves and that the intensionality of belief-states cannot be captured by the intended idiom − either because the description of physiological states excludes intentional considerations or because, interpreting those states informationally, their content is, as Dretske observes, "transparent to the substitution of informational equivalents". This is precisely why Armstrong's reduction of intentionality or self-directedness is inadequate. Thus he says: "My contention is that [simple] concepts are certain sorts of selective capacity towards things that fall under the concept in question. And this, I suggest further, *constitutes their self-directedness* ... simple concepts *must* be selective capacities. And, *qua* simple concepts, they are nothing but such selective capacities [that is, *states* of the thing that has the capacity]." But if the selective capacities involved are, as apparently intended, capacities of the cognitive agent as such, then, on the foregoing argument, intensional considerations will obtain and the states in question could *not* be physiological states; and if the capacities are physiological capacities of a "selective" sort, then they cannot be made to *represent*, qua physiological, the intensional features of belief-states or the intensional asymmetries of cognitive behavior.

The alternatives suggested by Dennett and Armstrong permit us, therefore, to scan rather economically the strategies noted earlier on by which our central thesis might possibly have been undermined. But we see now that there is no plausible basis for denying the reality of beliefs and persons or other cognitive agents, or for supposing that beliefs may be suitably charac-terized on the basis of a non-linguistic model, or for supposing that belief-states might be replaced by states lacking intensional features consistently with the admission of cognitive agents themselves. Also, whether animals have language or not is an empirical question. But whether they do or do not, they remain cognitive agents; hence, whether by heuristic or literal ascription, the very same problems confronting the analysis of persons (in this respect) confronts the analysis of animals. The failure of the alternative strategies marked earlier as (i), (ii), and (iv) must, therefore, count as a substantial weakness of all forms of mind/body reductionism. (iii), of course, has already been discounted by physicalists themselves.

CHAPTER 9

PROPOSITIONAL CONTENT
AND THE BELIEFS OF ANIMALS

Having formulated a heuristic model for the ascription of intentional mental states, we must consider more closely its application to languageless animals and its import for distinguishing between sentient animals and human persons. Reflection here serves to advance a number of critical themes. For one thing, it focusses our attention on how substantially different (non-intentional) sensations and (intentional) thoughts are — which bears on the general prospects of reductionism. For another, it clarifies the inherently anthropomorphized nature of animal psychology and the recalcitrance of intensional distinctions on the linguistic level — which confirms the strategic difference between attempting a reduction of animal sentience and of human linguistic ability. For a third, it draws attention to the dawning importance of teleological and non-teleological accounts of natural phenomena, varieties of teleology, and the distinction of human culture — which suggests the possibility of an ordered but nonreductive account of the conceptual distinctions required in explanations covering graduated stages of the continuum of things that include inanimate physical phenomena, plants, sentient animals, and human persons. For the present, let us confine our attention to animal sentience and the nature of intentional states.

We are inclined to concede that animals have sensory perception in spite of the fact that they lack language. It is, by a sort of Cartesian extreme, as possible to deny that animals are capable of perception as that they are capable of sensation and affect. But it is not enough to claim that they are automata. Cartesian automata lack a thinking substance, but functionally defined automata may, conceivably, be ascribed perceptual, sentient, and conative capacities (Fodor [1968] ; Mackay [1969]). If however, a perceptual capacity can be ascribed to a creature or entity, then perceptual knowledge and perceptual belief can be ascribed as well; and those conditions cannot be ascribed except in propositional terms (Margolis [1973a] ; Armstrong [1973] ; Sibley [1971]). Of any creature S to which cognitive perception may be ascribed, it must be possible to affirm both that

S perceives P,

for some perceivable object P, and that

S perceives that p,

that is, knows or believes by perceiving P that a certain proposition p is true. The verbs of perception, construed in a full epistemic sense, are jointly read in a propositional and a non-propositional way (Chisholm [1966] ; Dretske [1969] ; Margolis [1972b] ; Sibley [1971]). The schema is sufficiently flexible to accommodate perceptual illusion, perceptual error, and even ignorance of what one perceives (within limits).

These distinctions are familiar and relatively uncontroversial. Still, it is often supposed that the capacity for belief entails a linguistic capacity. (Vendler [1972] ; Hartnack [1972]). Norman Malcolm [1973], for instance, distinguishes between thinking and having thoughts: the latter are denied animals; and, more recently, Donald Davidson [1975] has maintained that "a creature cannot have thoughts unless it is an interpreter of the speech of another" *and* that "central to interpretation is a theory of truth that satisfies Tarski's convention T" (cf. Tarski [1956]). Since animals lack language, it would, on Davidson's view, have to be concluded that animals lack thought and belief as well. But if animals are capable of perception and if perception cannot be specified except in propositional terms — or, alternatively, if the capacity to perceive is the capacity to have perceptual knowledge and perceptual beliefs (Pitcher [1971]) — then it must be false, on some appropriate interpretation, that belief and thinking require language. Certainly, *some* thoughts and some beliefs cannot be ascribed to creatures that lack a language. But if Fido sees his master at the door and, seeing his master at the door, he sees that his master is at the door, then, *in some sense*, Fido knows or believes or thinks that his master is at the door. So it cannot be the case both that

(i)   Animals are capable of cognitive perception

and

(ii)   Belief and thought presuppose linguistic ability.

This is a sketch of a very simple and powerful argument. But it is a small gain if we cannot provide a theory of the way in which beliefs are ascribed to creatures lacking language or to creatures that, possessing linguistic ability, have not, on some occasion on which belief may be fairly ascribed, actually exercised that ability. Lacking language, Fido may not be capable of believing that his own beliefs are silly or that some of his beliefs are false, even if he is capable of believing that a certain dog is hostile or (even) that that dog believes that Fido is hostile. But in what way may we ascribe determinate beliefs to Fido if

(iii)   Beliefs are propositionally determinate,

and

(iv)   Propositions may be individuated only by the use of sentences by which, on some theory, they are properly conveyed?

If, therefore, propositions are identified with sentences or *any* functional elements of speech, or if belief states presuppose *any* constitutive condition of speech, then it will be impossible to hold that animals are capable of perception. But since propositions cannot but be linguistically specified – not in the sense that any description is a piece of language but in the sense that the specification of a proposition must be made on a linguistic model – there must be a very limited number of strategies by which belief, thought, and perception can be plausibly characterized.

Furthermore, returning to Davidson's claims, it is not in the least clear that natural languages *can* be shown to satisfy Tarski's convention T, simply because natural languages have not been shown to be fully formalizable. Tarski himself concedes that "the attempt to set up a structural definition of the term 'true sentence' [in effect, a definition in accord with convention T] – applicable to colloquial language is confronted with insuperable difficulties"; and he himself explicitly abandons the effort, restricting himself "henceforth entirely to *formalized languages*". In the sense in which the "semantic conception of truth" imposes an "adequacy condition" on all epistemologically relevant theories of truth (Tarski [1944]), Tarski's conception is entirely neutral, as he himself says, to any otherwise viable epistemological or ontological options (cf. Rescher [1973]). More than this, the critical question remains, whether an animal lacking language can be said to think or have thoughts; *if* having language is essential, then satisfying Tarski's convention T is necessary *if* it can be shown that a natural language satisfies and must satisfy convention T. On the argument, however, either (as Tarski holds) that cannot be shown or else, in the sense in which it may be taken to hold, it holds trivially for every natural language (though the theory is not unimportant for that reason). Hence, even for a language user, it is not necessary in order to have thoughts that one actually *subscribe* to convention T (or, if the thesis is trivial in the sense sketched, then, effectively, every speaker does subscribe whether he is aware of it or not). By parity of reasoning, *if* an animal may have thoughts though it lacks a language and if thoughts, perceptions, and the like have propositional content, *and if* such content is formulable only on a linguistic model, then, in perceiving, intending, thinking, and the like, an animal is functionally committed to convention T though it is not aware of being so committed. *Our* heuristic ascriptions of the propositional content of an animal's thoughts will satisfy convention T *if* convention T must be satisfied by every natural language. So Davidson's thesis cannot be made to depend on that consideration; but without it, it must count as no more than an unfavorable intuition.

Apart from the puzzles of a child's acquisition of a first language and of a chimpanzee's learning a portion of English, and apart from what might be regarded as the merely questionbegging phenomena of the hunting behavior of lions or the guarding behavior of dogs, one may consider the following striking instance involving the training of dolphins (taken from the Nova film series). The human trainer trains dolphin A to perform a task that is not part of its natural repertory, for instance, carrying a man-made object and depositing it on a signal in a precisely designated location. Dolphin B is permitted to "watch" the training, and dolphin A is trained to train dolphin B to perform the task — which it does. Now then, dolphin A, trained to train another dolphin to perform the task that it has been trained to perform, is "directed" or signalled to train dolphin C, which has not "watched" the earlier performance or the training of dolphin B. Dolphin A seems to train dolphin B by a combination of auditory signals (from its repertory of distinctive whistles, clicks, barks, "humanoid" sounds [Lilly (1967)]) and (perhaps) the directional positioning of its own body; and dolphin A seems to train dolphin C similarly. Now, the success in training dolphin C must depend on some powerful communicational system (not necessarily, *contra* Lilly, a language in our sense) involving high-level learning and what can only be called thinking (intending, deliberately directing, correcting, transmitting instructions, and the like). What one sees, therefore, is that, in any reasonably empirical sense in which the question of animal thinking arises, behavioral considerations are bound to take precedence over assumptions about the necessity of "interpreting speech", where the mastery of speech may be independently confirmed. (Our example suggests at least two critical themes that we shall have to return to: first, the implications of learning *vis-à-vis* intelligence and thinking; second, what may be termed "biological universals", that is, the discernment of [functionally informed] similarities relative to some purposive or teleological goal.) Certainly, at the very least, the success of the peculiarly complex achievements of dolphins and the success of chimpanzees in learning portions of human language argue at the very least a measure of intention, perceptual awareness, coordination of instruction and learned behavior that could hardly be denied the status of thinking (cf.

Wittgenstein [1963]; Griffin [1976]). Even without claiming language for animals (Black [1968]; Langer [1972]; Chomsky [1972]; Kenny [1973]), communication is apparent, often of such a seemingly ingenious sort that intentional behavior, strategy, even deliberately withholding information is difficult to deny (Schrier and Stolnitz [1971]; Jarrard [1971]). Still, the ascription of awareness to animals and of particular forms of awareness (to some extent, *contra* Griffin) requires essential distinctions that are not as yet satisfactorily supplied. This is particularly noticeable, for instance, in the analysis of the *Tanzsprache* of honeybees, whatever its versatility and possible lack of complete invariance (cf. Frisch [1967]; Gould [1974], [1975]).

There are a good many consequences that may be drawn from these preliminary observations. First of all, animal psychology must be inherently anthropomorphized *if* perceptual cognition be admitted. It is conceivable – with what success may be queried – that perceptual knowledge and belief may be reduced to physical processes that require no attention to linguistic or other intentional (and intensional) considerations (cf. Dennett [1969]; Armstrong [1973]). But in that case, our initially anthropomorphized account of animal perception and behavior may be reduced as well. It cannot be the case, as B. F. Skinner sometimes suggests (cf. W. K. Estes *et al.* [1954]), that the intentional idiom is merely a *façon de parler* unless one can demonstrate how the required reduction proceeds. Secondly, although not all teleological or purposive systems presuppose a linguistic model – simply because not all such systems presuppose perceptual cognition – it is clear that the comprehensive program known as the unity of science (Neurath *et al.* [1955]) depends fundamentally on the prospects of reducing linguistic phenomena to the paradigms of physical science. It is hard to see how this reduction is to be achieved.

On the other hand, it is often thought that there are anomalies that result from ascribing propositional content to the belief states of creatures that lack language. For, on the challenging argument, since animals lack language they cannot have a grasp of the logical and grammatical structure of the sentences that convey the putative propositional content of what they believe; there is no reason to suppose that their mental states have a structure analogous to that of what they lack; such structure as may be imputed to their mental states is inaccessible to independent inspection and cannot be reported; their brain states and behavior must, on the very linguistic model in question, be favorably (and, perhaps, circularly) interpreted as signifying certain perceptual beliefs and the like in order to permit us to infer from their behavior and brain states what it is that they actually believe; we cannot suppose that animal concepts — granting that animals have concepts or conceptual abilities — are so similar to human concepts that anthropomorphized ascriptions of belief and the like are literally valid; and, finally, we have no way of determining whether, if one belief is acribed to an animal, other beliefs or other formulations of the assigned belief, equivalent to or entailed by the propositions conveying the former, may also be validly ascribed. These are formidable difficulties, but they are surprisingly easy to offset.

What is needed is a defense on two fronts. We must be able to show (a) that the puzzles of logical and grammatical transformations and semantic substitutions need not generate anomalies for any otherwise viable theory that ascribes beliefs to creatures lacking language. And we must be able to provide (b) a way of accounting for the ascription of the relevant mental states to animals, that is both compatible with the initial assumption, viz. that animals lack language and lack linguistic concepts, and that is also reasonably congruent with the general constraints of observationality. These are not independent issues: the solutions to the special puzzles of the first sort only come into play, as do the puzzles themselves, if a tenable theory of the second sort can be provided. Nevertheless, it is convenient to assume a successful way of meeting (b) in order to isolate certain particularly persistent questions involved in (a) and to do so without making any strenuous commitments to particular theories of the animal mind.

The issues of the first sort fall into a fairly neat array that promises to be exhaustive of the complications that must be met. Here, it will be useful to select as specimens, sentences that permit us to move easily between ascriptions of perception and belief, that are as likely as any to be used in making relevant ascriptions, and that isolate the central puzzles with the least amount of extraneous complication. Consider, for example, the sentence

(1) Fido sees (believes) that his master is throwing the stick.

We are to understand, of course, that Fido believes, because he sees what he sees, that his master is throwing the stick. Using 'see' in the propositional sense, we must attribute to Fido a perceptual belief, though this does not involve us in supporting any detailed theory of perceptual cognition and belief. If we attend to the *proposition* 'that his master is throwing the stick', it is clear that, solely by logical processes and treating (1) extensionally, we might conclude that

(2) Fido sees (believes) that his master is throwing the stick or that Wellington defeated Napoleon at Waterloo,

or that

> (3) Fido sees (believes) that someone is throwing the stick.

Of course, on perceptual considerations, one might refuse the second disjunct of (2) as visually inaccessible; but that would not be a responsive move. Provided that the first disjunct is visually accessible, then Fido could have a belief based on what was visually perceived, in which the second disjunct was not itself visually accessible; the distinction between, say, narrowly visual beliefs and beliefs that essentially involve what is visually perceived does not, however interesting it may be in its own right, affect our present issue (cf. Dretske [1969]). Similarly, one might balk at (3), thinking that there must be an equivocation on 'someone', since, in the perceptual situation, 'someone' must be taken indexically as identifying a unique individual whereas, in the purely formal context, 'someone' is no more than an existential variable (cf. Margolis [1972c]). But, again, this is not responsive; for both (2) and (3) are to be considered as reports of what Fido sees or believes on the strength of the truth of (1). Hence, even if 'someone' in (3) functioned as a variable, (3) would be based on what was visually accessible.

One critical consideration is that, even for those who are linguistically competent and therefore to some extent competent regarding logical transformations involving language, no inferences on our part comparable to (2) and (3) are *empirically* valid without independent evidence. For instance, if

> (4) Tom believes that roses are red,

we would hardly be prepared to attribute to Tom, on purely logical grounds, a belief corresponding to the inference

> (5) Tom believes that roses are red or that Wellington defeated Napoleon at Waterloo.

Generally speaking, it is preposterous to assume that if a creature believes something, has a particular belief, then that creature believes whatever is logically equivalent to, or logically entailed by, what he believes. There is at least the reason that any creature's beliefs are fairly regarded as finite in number at any given time t, but that, at t, what is related by equivalence and entailment to the proposition conveying his belief are an infinite number of propositions. Also, statements reporting the empirically contingent beliefs of any creature may well expose the important truth that such a creature does not actually believe, for some conceivable beliefs at least, what *is* logically entailed by what he does believe (cf. Hintikka [1962]). The general reason for the constraint is simply that beliefs are determinate psychological states (cf. Margolis [1973a]).

The problem regarding Fido is, in a way, a bit more strenuous. Because, on the hypothesis, Fido is incapable of language and therefore incapable of inferences using language. Notice, by the way, that we need not at this point deny that animals are capable of inference. The same considerations, whatever they may be, that permit us to ascribe perception, knowledge, and belief to animals may support the ascription of (functionally specified) inference as well. If a lion sees an eland beside the pool, it may well be that we can ascribe to the lion the inference that he would startle the eland if he growled or made a commotion. In fact, it may reasonably be doubted that perceptual cognition *can* be conceded to animals without conceding some inferential abilities as well (cf. Harman [1973]). One sees, here, that other complications loom; but, clearly, if belief may be ascribed to animals lacking language, then there is as yet no decisive reason, assuming inference to be a psychological process of some sort relating ordered beliefs, why inference could not be ascribed to languageless animals. No, the problem regarding animals is, in a way, the reverse of the problem regarding creatures that have mastered language. With human beings, we may be philosophically worried by the possibility that belief contexts do not yield to a completely extensional analysis. Though the embedded propositions of (4) and (5) are truth-functionally connected, (4) and (5) are not in any obvious way also truth-functionally connected (cf. Quine [1960]; Margolis [1977e]). But the problem regarding animals is that, since the intensional complexities arising for language users *cannot arise for languageless animals*, we are tempted to concede that *if* an animal may rightly be said to believe that *p*, then there is no alternative but to admit that that animal must also be said to believe whatever is logically equivalent to, or entailed by, what it does believe. But that obviously leads to difficulties. For, one thing, an animal would have to be said to have a vastly larger number of beliefs if it believed that *p*, for any *p*, then could reasonably be ascribed to any linguistically competent human in a similar situation. For another, an animal would have to be said to have beliefs (detailed by complex but purely formal maneuvers) that must exceed even the wildest view of its conceptual capacity.

So it cannot be true that, since intensional complications (regarding equivalence and entailment) do not arise for a languageless creature, the beliefs of an animal must be treated extensionally — in the sense that, believing that *p*, the animal must be said to believe whatever is logically entailed by what it is conceded to believe. There is only one other alternative possible, viz. that the beliefs ascribed to animals must be ascribed *singly*, that is, taking every belief as provisionally distinct that is propositionally distinct. It is quite possible that the empirical evidence supporting the ascription of belief A may, independently, support the ascription of belief B, where the propositions conveying A and B are related by entailment. The facts regarding such an entailment *never* bear on the ascription of a belief to an animal (or other propositionally qualified mental state). The usual intensional/extensional puzzles regarding human belief contexts simply do not arise for creatures lacking language (cf. Close [1976]). So it is never appropriate either to attribute beliefs that presuppose some linguistic mastery to animals or to attribute to them beliefs that, given certain initial beliefs, are related to the first solely in virtue of the entailment relation holding between (linguistically formulated) propositions conveying the beliefs in question. This seems to capture our most reasonable intuitions about the beliefs of animals.

Now, then, a comparable constraint obtains for grammatical and semantic equivalences. For, if, as before, it is true that

(1) Fido sees (believes) that his master is throwing the stick,

it does not follow that

(6) Fido sees (believes) that the stick is being thrown by his master.

Correspondingly, if (1) be true, and if Fido's master = the president of the First National Bank, it does not follow that

(7) Fido sees (believes) that the president of the First National Bank is throwing the stick.

Some further distinctions are called for, however. (6) and (7) do not behave in the same way. The defense of (6), *given* (1), may be attempted in either of two quite different ways — one illicit, the other not. (6) may be defended: (a) by appeal to the active/passive transformation; or (b) by noting that the belief in question may be *indifferently* specified by using either the active or the passive formulation. On the assumption that Fido lacks language, strategy (a) is illicit, since there is no empirical basis for ascribing to Fido any grasp of the grammatical transformation itself. It is quite reasonable, in *normal* human contexts (but not in all), that if

(8) Tom sees (believes) that Jack is throwing the stick,

then

(9) Tom sees (believes) that the stick is being thrown by Jack

is also true. The reason, in the human case, is that, for a language user, the active/passive transformation is so fundamental that one's capacity to draw the inference even if the inference has not been drawn, either consciously or unconsciously, is thought to be sufficient to justify ascribing the second belief if the first be granted. This shows, incidentally, at least one respect in which the ascription of belief and knowledge cannot but be contextually and informally supported. Strategy (b), however, depends on the fact, precisely, that Fido is not a language user and that the difference between Fido's beliefs and analogous human beliefs is such that, where intensional puzzles would arise in the human setting, we are *sometimes* prepared to treat alternative propositional formulations as simply indifferent to what it is that Fido believes. This is easily misunderstood. First of all, such indifference cannot hold for *all* of an animal's beliefs: if it did, then the anomalies already noted in the extensionalist reading of belief would obtain. Secondly, whether such indifference is or is not misleading always arises wherever equivalent replacements of a logical, syntactic, or semantic sort are at stake. Since such replacements *always* arise in animal contexts, because animals lack language and because their beliefs are conveyed by the use of a linguistic model, *some* measure of indifference is bound to be admitted. Were this not so, we could never hope to specify an animal's belief; it would be as if animals had a secret language that we had never mastered and that, on comparatively gross-grained behavioral evidence, we tried to guess at the exact formulation required.

F. N. Sibley's [1971] views on animal perception are instructive here. Sibley wishes to refine D. M. Armstrong's [1968] thesis that animals perceive and have beliefs *and* that they cannot be said to perceive (cognitively) unless they can acquire beliefs *and* that they cannot acquire beliefs unless they have the requisite concepts. Sibley's summary suggests the heuristic model of belief-ascription already introduced: "no creature can have a belief without having the concepts requisite for that belief. As Armstrong himself says, 'If perception is the acquiring of beliefs or information then clearly it must involve the possession of concepts. For to believe that *A* is *B* entails possessing the concepts of *A* and *B*.' To this I would add what Armstrong omits to mention, that it also entails possessing the concept 'is' of predication or property possession. The other principle I shall follow is that, in being 'committed to the view that there can be concepts that involve no linguistic ability', we are normally justified in attributing a certain belief to *S* only if *S* is capable of responses appropriate to having the concepts and belief in question. We can attribute to a dog the belief that its master is about to take it out, but not that he is about to take it to the park rather than to the common if the dog's behavior, as the master picks up the lead, never exhibits any appropriate differences that would permit the alternative concepts to apply." Nevertheless, despite his caution, Sibley fails to draw the conclusion that *all* ascriptions to languageless creatures are heuristically ascribed on the basis of our theory of their conceptual abilities in the light of their behavior. For, he argues "that the *minimal belief* [italics added] we could attribute to [such a creature] would be the belief [given a perceptual context] (however brief or momentary) that *something* existed or happened (and that we might attribute this belief even though we cannot attribute to it the belief that something *is* somehow or *looks* somehow". Sibley's reason for qualifying the ascription is just that, say, a dog may not have the same concepts of the external physical world that we do. Hence, he wishes to treat 'something' as a "non-status-indicating concept" − that is, one that does not entail "a particularized physical-status concept". But he fails to note that the use of 'something', even on his own view, *does* entail concepts of individuation; and he offers no account justifying the claim that a languageless creature may have *that* concept. The point is, there simply is no "minimal belief" or minimal concept that we can ascribe to languageless creatures. *If* we are justified in ascribing the "minimal belief" Sibley favors, then we are justified in ascribing full-blooded beliefs specified in terms of some version of the conceptual distinctions accessible to ourselves. Two considerations are decisive: (a) the ascription of beliefs to languageless creatures presupposes a model of the rational coordination of a creature's interests, desires, needs, perceptions, sensations, beliefs, intentions, and informed actions, that already depend, parasitically, on a linguistic model for assigning propositional content to mental states; and (b) the relevant ascriptions are heuristic, in the sense supplied, and therefore implicitly concede the unavailability of such a creature's correcting such ascriptions by means of a linguistic exchange. But this does not lead to any form of skepticism (*contra* T. Nagel [1974]), since there is in principle no way in which the relevant ascriptions make sense except from the vantage of linguistically competent creatures. Hence it is that animal psychology is inherently anthropomorphized.

Notice, also, that a similar question of logical, syntactic, and semantic indifference arises, in human contexts, wherever *oratio obliqua* constructions are used in reporting beliefs. *Obliqua* constructions are used both to report what one may have said and what one may have believed or thought without having spoken (Vendler [1972]). Hence, the concession regarding animals is obviously required in human situations as well. In any case, it is just because Fido knows no grammar that it is not unreasonable to hold that both (1) and

(6) capture Fido's belief perspicuously, if either does. The reason is *not* equivalence of any sort, though equivalence raises the question of indifference. It is rather that we choose, at times, to hold that Fido's understanding of the relationship between his master and the stick is such that either of our formulations, the active or the passive, will do as well as the other. So indifference actually accommodates the important point that a dog's concepts will be different from human concepts in ways that cannot be more than approximately fixed.

The human analogue of inferring the truth of (7) from the truth of (1) generally raises intensional puzzles on the grounds of the so-called referential opacity of belief contexts. Obviously, a related problem arises in the human analogue of inferring from the truth of (1) to the truth of (6), that is, in the inference from (8) to (9). But in the latter sort of case, the intensional consideration cannot be assimilated merely to referential opacity. What this shows, neatly, is that belief contexts are intensionally qualified in a variety of ways and that the putative removal of one relevant intensional feature need not eliminate another. Quine [1969], for example, pretty well confines his attention to the alleged opacity of contexts in which co-designative terms cannot be substituted, *salve veritate*. But beliefs formulated merely in terms of active/passive transformations obviously cannot be thus construed: what they pose, rather, is the intensional puzzle of selecting among alternative but equivalent predications. In the human analogue, the intensional issue is always managed in terms at least of whether the believer could be said to have known or believed, under the circumstances, that what was grammatically or semantically equivalent was thus equivalent. In the instance of animals, that question never arises; in its place, where co-designative terms or extensionally equivalent predicates obtain, the important question is whether the animal has the relevant concept. If the animal lacks the concept, on the evidence on which other relevant concepts may be ascribed, then the equivalent ascription must be disallowed. But once again, this is not because of the usual intensional considerations: ascriptions to animals must be tested singly. Nevertheless, *if*, on the evidence, the animal has the relevant concept, the following alternatives may still obtain: (a) the evidence may confirm both ascriptions if it confirms either; (b) the evidence may confirm one ascription and fail to confirm the other; or (c) the evidence may confirm that the animal has a concept for which the alternative formulations, our formulations, are indifferent. Thus, in (1) and (7), it is reasonable to suppose that if Fido has the concept of one's being his master, he does not have the concept of one's being the president of the First National Bank. Hence, though (1) and (7) are, on the hypothesis, extensionally equivalent, Fido might well believe in accordance with (1) and have no belief corresponding to (7). Similarly, if (for the sake of the argument) having red hair was always and only correlated with having three kidneys, then, though it might well be true that

(10) Fido saw (believed) that the man with red hair threw the stick,

it could not be the case that

(11) Fido saw (believed) that the man with three kidneys threw the stick

was a merely indifferent and alternative formulation of what Fido actually believed; and indeed, so construed, it would doubtless be false. In short, where intensional puzzles arise in the human analogue, the question of indifferent formulations as well as the empirical evidence supporting *independent* alternative formulations arises with respect to animal beliefs; also, in the animal context, *no* intensional puzzles arise, that is, no intensional puzzles regarding the believer's state of mind *vis-à-vis* equivalences *qua* equivalences.

We may fairly claim, then, to have sketched an argument covering all the relevant anomalies that may (by the use of a linguistic model) be generated merely in attributing determinate beliefs to animals lacking language. There may be indeterminancies regarding the beliefs of animals, but then indeterminacies appear as well where language users are involved. I may, on some occasion, not know what you believe at all, and I may not know whether you believe A or B. There is no reason to think that such indeterminacies must be eliminated in making ascriptions to animals. But apart from that, all of the puzzles regarding intensionality and extensionality may be obviated merely by adhering to the following constraints:

(v)   Belief ascriptions to animals are confirmable only taken singly; that is, languageless animals are assumed incapable of beliefs about equivalences and entailments;

(vi) No beliefs that presuppose linguistic ability can be defensibly ascribed to animals lacking language;

(vii) Animals may be assumed to have concepts different from human concepts, if concepts may be ascribed to them at all; hence, differences in equivalent formulations marked in terms of our own concepts may, at times, because of the heuristic nature of animal ascriptions, be regarded as indifferent to the content of animal beliefs.

Having said this much, we are still faced with the puzzles bearing on part (b) of our originally sketched defense, that is, bearing on the need to provide empirically manageable grounds for the ascription, to animals, of propositionally specified mental states. Here, again, the strategy is surprisingly straightforward. Consider, first of all, that physical objects, physical states and events can be specified in extensionally satisfactory ways indifferently to intensional distinctions. However, extensionally equivalent propositions may differ intensionally. Hence, one way in which a physically reductive account of belief might be favored would require that, although belief A and belief B differ intensionally (that is, in the intensional rendering of their intentional propositional content), all propositional formulations (of the putative content of a belief) must, if they are equivalences, be *indifferent formulations of one and the same belief*; and all propositional formulations (of the putative content of a belief) that are entailments of one another must be formulations of *parts of one and the same belief*. But this goes flatly contrary to the intensional nature of belief contexts. No one is thought to believe whatever is equivalent to or entailed by what he believes. (Of course, this does not mean that S and S′ could not have numerically different beliefs of the same kind or that S could not have numerically different beliefs of the same kind on two different occasions.) The only conceivable way in which the puzzle of intensionality could be resolved favorably for reductive materialism would require that, in addition, each creature capable of belief states could be fairly described in terms of a Turing machine model (Putnam [1960]; Fodor [1968]). This suggests the empirical barrier confronting Armstrong's [1968] and Daniel Dennett's [1969] programs of physicalism, for there is simply no evidence that any subset of what would be equivalent to, or entailed by, the propositions conveying one's beliefs, characterize a set of beliefs that any agent must believe if he believes the initial beliefs in question.

Apart from these considerations, we may note that there is no independent way of analyzing the putative structure of a belief state; that is, there is no way to *compare* the structure of a belief state and the structure of a proposition presumed to convey its "intentional" content — which of course constitutes an insuperable barrier to the identity thesis. Since we hold that beliefs can only be determinately specified by propositions, by the use of a linguistic model, our theory justifies our ascribing a particular propositional content to a particular belief. But there is no way to test the fit *by comparing independently the structure of the one and the structure of the other*; we justify the fit, empirically, by reference to a wider theory on which beliefs are systematically linked with behavior and intentions and desires and perceptions and the like — broadly speaking, a theory about the rationality and purposiveness characteristic of distinct species. This suggests what is basically wrong with Armstrong's use [1973] of Peter Geach's theory [1957] of "concepts" and "Ideas" (cf. Russell [1966], [1956]; Pears [1967b]). The very conditions therefore, under which we ascribe belief states favor the heuristic model. In any case, the physicalist utterly lacks a foundation on which to *detect* the intentional content of any belief state by an inspection of central nervous states — *a fortiori*, the intensional variability of belief states. The principal difficulties, then, include the following: (a) there is (*contra* Putnam [1960]), on both conceptual and empirical grounds, no basis for believing that the mental states of human beings, in particular, linguistically informed states, can be satisfactorily described in terms of a Turing machine model; (b) the ascription of intentional states or states of thinking does not require (*contra* Fodor [1975]) that there be an internal representation of validly ascribed states; (c) intentionally qualified mental states are functionally ascribed (*contra* Armstrong [1973]) on the basis of behavior and in accord with a governing model of rationality and purposiveness, for both languageless and linguistically competent creatures; (d) intensional differences in the propositional content of beliefs (essential to the characterization of human and animal behavior) — involving either linguistic capacities or conceptual limitations — can only be *assigned* to events in the central nervous system (*contra* Sellars [1963a] and Dennett [1969]).

We may recapitulate our findings thus:

(1) we ascribe beliefs to animals;
(2) animals lack language;
(3) belief does not presuppose linguistic ability;
(4) beliefs are propositionally determinate;
(5) beliefs are determinately specified only through the use of a linguistic model;
(6) propositions differ intensionally;
(7) the structure of belief states is not independently accessible;
(8) beliefs are ascribed to animals on the basis of evidence relating to perception, behavior, intention, and desire, that are themselves ascribed by reference to the same linguistic model.

The admission of (1)–(8) appears to be compatible only with the heuristic model of ascribing mental states.

The beauty of the model lies, precisely, in relieving us of utterly futile efforts to understand, say, animal analogues of predication and the like. To admit for instance that no beliefs presupposing linguistic ability can be defensibly ascribed to animals lacking language entails that animals lack the linguistic conception of the 'is' of predication. Hence, to treat belief ascriptions heuristically *is to treat the ascription of concepts heuristically as well*. Furthermore, the ascription of concepts is parasitic on the ascription of beliefs. That is, if a belief that *p* may be ascribed to a creature, then we must ascribe to that creature the concepts, which on an analysis of the propositional content of *p*, are taken to be the "constituents" (somehow) related in the belief or judgment that *p*. D. M. Armstrong [1973] has suggested a useful way of construing the relationship between concepts and beliefs − if we ignore his adherence to Geach's thesis about the analogy between the structure of thought and the structure of language and if we put aside the question of materialistic reduction. "A's concept of red", Armstrong says, "is a *second-order* capacity − a capacity to acquire the capacity to react towards the red object when the latter acts upon A's mind. . . . the *first-order* capacity is rather to be identified with a certain . . . type of belief". Just so. Concepts would be heuristic entities on any theory that did not suppose that they were empirically accessible. Even with language users, the assumption is that the concepts used in making a judgment or evincing a belief correspond, in some way that is not independently accessible, to the structured relationship that unites the parts of a sentence conveying the relevant proposition. So, for language users − or, more accurately, for language users on occasions on which they actually express their beliefs and judgments linguistically − beliefs need not be heuristically ascribed; but their concepts would be heuristically ascribed even then. *A fortiori*, concepts must be heuristically ascribed to animals lacking language.

It is, so to say, the ubiquity of predication in language that permits us, heuristically, to treat animals as holding beliefs involving predication. Here, questions of indifference normally do not arise. To reject predication is, effectively, to preclude the grounds on which beliefs may be ascribed to animals. It is only within the range of the heuristic device itself that we may ask whether alternative formulations are or are not indifferent to the content of an animal's belief or whether the evidence regarding *which* concepts may be ascribed to an animal would definitely disqualify one or another member of a set of equivalences otherwise (indifferently) employed in formulating that belief.

Within limits, comparable problems arise in ascribing beliefs to creatures that are linguistically competent but that do not, on a given occasion, actually express their beliefs linguistically. Here, however, even in the absence of an actual use of language, intensional problems may be conceded. For if S (a language user) believes that p, and q is either equivalent to or entailed by p, it is a fair question to ask whether S's linguistic competence *and* linguistic experience justify us in ascribing to S the further belief that q. In short, in the context of linguistic *ability*, considerations of skill and ability are invariably relevant in ascribing belief and knowledge (cf. Margolis [1977f]). But to mention such cases draws us on to the full-blooded intensional contexts of linguistically expressed beliefs. The twilight area marked here must be analyzed in some one of alternative ways in which the fully intensional account of beliefs and the heuristic account of belief ascriptions are plausibly joined.

In any event, it is important to emphasize that propositions, like concepts (and like facts, to which when true, they are alleged to correspond) are heuristic entities. For, if they are, then it is quite reasonable to suppose that only a heuristic model for ascribing mental states is plausible. Conceding the reality of mental states, then, is tantamount to undermining reductionism: there is, *in principle*, no access to the propositional content of mental states by way of an analysis of the physical properties of neurophysiological states, and the imputation of such content on the basis of a machine program presupposes a range of mental states for which, on conceptual and empirical grounds, there is no prospect of a comparable reduction.

Consider propositions, then. A proposition, Zeno Vendler [1972] supposes, "is the message expressed in a speech-act"; he says as well that a proposition "can also be entertained, in the form of a thought, in a variety of mental acts and states" (cf. Jones [1975]; Margolis [1977g]). These remarks are not unreasonable, but they rest on a crucial weakness. For Vendler says, quite rightly, that "indirect quotation [or discourse] is not a repetition of a sentence somebody uttered, but a report on a speech-act somebody performed"; he also speaks, however, of the use of indirect discourse "for the reproduction of someone else's, or my own, thoughts as well". The conjunction raises a difficulty because Vendler has insisted that though "speech needs a language; thought does not". The question looms, therefore, *why* indirect discourse can be used to report the propositional content of what one thinks or believes, where one's thought or belief is not linguistically expressed or formed. Peter Geach [1957] had strongly warned against construing thoughts or "acts of judgment" (mental acts) as expressed in a kind of "inner language" (what he calls "Mental", which, he says, William of Ockham thought to have a grammar remarkably like Latin). Nevertheless, Geach himself holds to an analogical theory between speech and psychological states (those states at least that depend on acts of judgment); and in this, Vendler appears to follow Geach rather closely. For Geach says: "The primary role of *oratio recta* is certainly not psychological; it serves to report what somebody actually said or wrote. But *oratio recta* can be used metaphorically to report what somebody thought, 'said in his heart' (without, of course, implying that the thinker had the quoted words in his mind); such constructions are frequent in the Authorized Version of the Bible: 'The fool hath said in his heart "There is no God" '; 'They said in their heart "Let us destroy them together".' Clearly we could *always* describe judgments by using *oratio recta* in this way; *oratio obliqua* is logically superfluous." Geach's metaphorical extension rests on his own theory of a psychological Idea ("the exercise of a concept in judgment") – which, unfortunately, is as inaccessible to independent specification as propositions are with respect to sentences.

But more than this, Geach's insistence that *oratio obliqua* is superfluous rests squarely on the force of the metaphor – that, in thinking and believing, one performs an act of judgment properly captured by the formula '. . . said in his heart.' Were that theory rejected, for instance because of the recalcitrance and lack of independent accessibility of those psychological phenomena Geach calls Ideas ("exercises of concepts"), there would be no proper basis for maintaining that *oratio recta* constructions could justifiably be said to capture the content of thoughts and beliefs. That is, there would be no basis for the claim *if* we were obliged, in order to sustain it, to *compare* the actual structure of speech and thought. Vendler is in precisely the same position, except that he simply claims that *oratio obliqua* constructions may be used to report the content of thought and belief. He holds that "you can say whatever you think, and you can think *almost* whatever you can say". He appears to rest the argument on Descartes' doctrine of innate ideas, so that we are bound to hold that the structure of thought and speech is the same. Otherwise, since thought need not be linguistically encoded, the appeal to *oratio obliqua* would be anomalous. Geach's theory, then, we may say, rests on an analogy between speech and thought; Vendler's rests more nearly on an alleged isomorphism. In fact, Vendler favors "the rationalistic idea of a 'perfect' language, a language isomorphic with the structure of thought; and, holding that "we think in concepts", he claims that "the linguistic expression of a concept is a sentence frame partly filled by dummy words". It turns out, then, that animals cannot think because they cannot understand sentence frames. This is the reason, as we have seen, that Vendler is led, in the Chomskyan spirit, to maintain that "a child must learn his native tongue in a way similar to the way in which one learns a second language. He must have, in other words, a native equipment that codes the fundamental illocutionary, syntactic, and semantic features of any possible human language." He concedes, therefore, that animals can have "internal experiences" like images and the like but they cannot think because they lack the conditions on which a language depends, on which understanding thinking itself depends (cf. Malcolm [1973]). Hence, he is led to concede that "animals may feel without thinking, as we humans often do", at the same time that he denies that animals are conscious "because they have no thoughts".

Anthony Kenny [1975] also follows Geach's lead, though he maintains the seemingly paradoxical thesis that animals can think though they have no minds. His point is that animals are incapable of both intellectual activities and volition, since both involve "the creation and utilization of symbols". Animals are, however, capable of sense perception (involving "the awareness of, and ability to respond to, changes in the environment" by means of the senses); capable of thinking (since "a dog may well think that his master is at the door"); capable of agency; capable of having concepts (since even desire, sensual or felt desire, involves "the exercise of simpler and more rudimentary concepts [than volition], which can be manifested in non-linguistic behavior"); capable of acting "for the sake of goals" and of being "conscious of their goals" ("in the quite literal sense they may see or smell what they are after"); capable of "recognitional capacities" (for "we cannot attribute desire to an agent which cannot recognize things as answering to its desires"); capable of intending to do things ("in the sense that it is often true of them that unless interfered with they will go on voluntarily to perform various actions"). What Kenny means, then, in denying that animals have minds is that they lack the "ability of *intention*", of acting *with* the intention of doing this or that, of acting "from a consideration of the act as answering to a certain linguistic description", of being able to "*give a reason*" for what they do, of having the reflexive thought "*that he is thinking that . . .*". All this is true. Yet nowhere does Kenny explain what the basis is for characterizing in *propositional terms* what an animal wants or sees. If, as he concedes, chimpanzees may actually learn language, then it is anomalous to deny that they have *some* intellectual and volitional capacities before they learn language; but if he insists on his definition of the mind, then, under the circumstances, he must fall back to a nativist conception of the mind, which he resists. For animals do seem to want things without sensual desire (for instance a dog's wanting its master to throw a stick that it has fetched), seem to be capable of acting for the sake of abstract or functional goals (for instance a seeing eye-dog's guiding its master around obstacles never previously encountered), seem to have intentions and seem to act for reasons (for instance a dog's going through the house room by room to search for its master who was not seen to leave), seem to be able to discriminate perceptually (for instance a dog's perceiving that food served on some occasions is not the kind it regularly favors and waiting expectantly for the other). Given capacities of these sorts, it seems excessive to insist that, where animals lack language, they also lack minds.

Also, if as has been argued, cognitive and volitional states are attributed to animals on the basis of interpreting their behavior in accord with a theory of the coherent ordering of their mental states and their behavior, then we see a very good reason for regarding the classical notion of practical reasoning as a heuristic schema — even among humans — linking cognition, volition, and power (the capacity to act congruently with cognition and volition; cf. Kenny [1975]).

Kenny's support of the theory of practical reasoning, in which beliefs and volitions regarding particular objectives are linked to particular actions in the manner of premises and conclusion, rests on his acceptance of Geach's [1957] theory of mental acts. But Geach specifically denies that "brute" animals have concepts, whereas Kenny restricts their concepts to those that do not require linguistic expression. Even more seriously, though Geach holds that concepts are "mental capacities", capacities to "perform . . . mental exercises of a specifiable sort", he does not provide any grounds for construing an Idea ("the exercise of a concept in judgment") as a real mental phenomenon; hence, the realistic theory of practical reasoning is correspondingly threatened. Geach maintains (on Kenny's convenient summary) that "a judgment to the effect that things stand in an n-termed relation R itself consisted of Ideas standing in an n-termed relation ZR. A judgment to the effect that gold is heavier than lead, for example, would consist of an Idea of gold standing in the relation Z (heavier than) to an Idea of lead." That is, the Ideas must stand in the relation of being Z-heavier than. 'Z' is an intensional operator, on Geach's view. But more than that, there is and can be no independent access to the putatively real ordering of Ideas signified by 'Z' applied to any relation. The introduction of 'Z' is parasitic on the use of a linguistic model (" 'Z' was to be defined by reference to the verbal expression of a judgment"). 'Z' is otherwise uninterpreted and undefined. And the alleged congruity between 'R' and 'ZR' — the one relating actual things, the other relating Ideas of things — is simply posited on the basis of the use of the very linguistic model on the strength of which Ideas were first introduced. Appeal to a linguistic model, however, cannot but be neutral as between a heuristic specification of the propositional content of mental states and the thesis that the propositional content thus specified constitutes the real expression of the relation of real Ideas in the mind. Hence, it neither provides for the denial of the intellectual or volitional capacities of animals nor for the affirmation of the psychological reality of the structure of the putative arguments of practical reasoning.

The paradox of weakness of will (*akrasia*) makes this abundantly clear. The Socratic resolution explains the incongruity of belief and volition, on the one hand, and action, on the other, in terms of a defect of cognition in the particular instance; the Thomist resolution explains it in terms of a defect of wanting. But it is entirely possible that the psychological effectiveness of believing that one ought to act in a certain way for a certain goal and of wanting the goal should be deficient in such a way that, without compromising the belief or the desire or want or the logical connection between the representation of these states and of the appropriate action, the actual capacity to perform in the way indicated remains contingently inadequate though not in general inadequate (*contra* Hare [1963]; Davidson [1969a]). Practical reasoning, on Kenny's view, is "a process of passing from one fiat to another [the propositional expression of a volition construed as an imperative, rather in Hare's (1952) manner] according to rules". And "rational appetite" (or will) "is the capacity to perform an action issuing from a certain kind of *thought*" (a certain mental state, a volitional state). It is, therefore, the thesis that rational appetite involves states the expression of which (linguistic or nonlinguistic) is really formulable as fiats (by Kenny's adaptation of Geach's theory of Ideas [cf. Kenny 1963]) that generates the problem of weakness of will. The classical argument in Aristotle (*Nicomachean Ethics*) justifies and encourages just such a development. If rational appetite were construed as really conforming to the rules of practical reasoning – though effectively, the premises and conclusion are mental states and actions – then weakness of will would be bound to be construed in terms of the *formal* failure of a would-be argument; whereas if the logic of rational appetite were construed heuristically, then the failure marked by weakness of will could be construed in *causal* terms, that is, without any loss of rationality as far as reasoning goes. This leads to the thesis that there is no difference between the logic of practical and theoretical reasoning, though there may well be a difference between the logic of imperatives and of constatives and there may well be a difference between consistency in behavior and consistency in argument. So there are substantive differences entailed by alternative characterizations of the propositional content of mental states.

But the tenuousness of these theories affects the question of what we may assign as the proper object of thought and belief. After all, *if* belief is a psychological state and *if* there is no independent access to the content of belief states unexpressed in language, then it is only by way of a theory that we may, at least heuristically, ascribe a propositional content to beliefs. That is, it is simply because we hold *that* whatever may be thought or believed can be expressed linguistically that, on the strength of behavior and other evidence, we *assign* a propositional content to belief (*contra* Armstrong [1973] and Dennett [1969]). We most certainly do not do so by an independent inspection of the (propositional) content of our (unexpressed) thoughts and beliefs. But this returns us once again to our query about propositions and facts.

Propositions, it seems, are themselves heuristic entities, if they are not identified with sentences or statements or the like; that is, they are "the message" or "what is expressed" in a certain set of sentences or speech-acts. When, therefore, we assign a *proposition* to a linguistically unexpressed thought or belief, we do so by formulating sentences by which it could be expressed — on the assumption that whatever can be thought can be said. Hence, there is something tendentious in Vendler's claim that "propositions are subjective entities", which, when formulated for a given person's statements, orders, promises and the like, require our "taking into consideration the speaker's mind". We cannot and do not take into consideration the speaker's mind, in the sense of examining *it* for the intended propositions (*contra* Fodor [1975]); rather, we posit or assign such propositions as we suppose, on the evidence, convey the speaker's mind — on the assumption that whatever can be thought can be said: by determining what one *would* say, we construct what one *has thought* or *thinks*. In this sense, propositions are not subjective — but heuristic. The point of the difference, of course, is just that the reduction of animal sentience (as far as intentional states are concerned) can only be effected by construing such sentience as the result of a mere *façon de parler* or as the functionally assigned counterpart of a biologically realized Turing machine (Putnam [1960]). Whether this can be justified in the case of the higher animals depends on certain decisive empirical considerations; but from the point of view of the argument's strategy, its success could not entail the success of a corresponding program applied to linguistically competent creatures (that is, creatures having a natural language). To say this, however, suggests very forcefully that there are bound to be pre-linguistic capacities (on which the acquisition of a first language depends) that, similarly, do not yield to the intended reductions; hence, that even animal sentience poses a critical difficulty for reductionism.

Perhaps a final caution is in order. Nothing said about the perceptual abilities of animals is intended to deny that non-epistemic perceptual abilities can be ascribed to lower-order animals where no epistemic ability obtains. D. M. Armstrong [1968] treats perception as the acquiring of beliefs, but shows some uneasiness about non-epistemic perception. And F. N. Sibley [1971], who chides Armstrong on the grounds that an animal's beliefs will normally not be beliefs about the physical world (since animals lack our conception of a physical world), nevertheless insists, with Armstrong, that "A creature perceiving will *always* be acquiring a belief of some sort, not an inhibited tendency to believe, and perception will still be, necessarily, a possible source of information about the physical environment". But the notion of perception without the *capacity* for belief is not conceptually incoherent and has some empirical plausibility; in fact, on evolutionary grounds, there is good reason to think that non-epistemic sensory discrimination or perception is more primitive than epistemic perception, even though epistemic perception is conceptually more fundamental in the sense that whatever *information* is assigned to the other exploits the cognitive phenomenon (cf. Dretske [1969]). (Sibley confuses, here, two senses of 'basic'.) Thus, if, say, the female preying mantis invariably acts to kill its mate upon the male's secreting a certain odor, information regarding the presence of which is processed through the female's olfactory sense, then there is fair reason to speak of the mantis's (non-epistemic) perception of the odor, without reference at all to any capacity for perceptual beliefs; furthermore, insofar as the behavior of the mantis is thought to be entirely or almost entirely instinctual, that is, biochemically programmed in some way, there may be no basis for admitting intervening beliefs — the ascription of beliefs makes sense only in the setting of an organism's life that displays a certain characteristic lack of invariance and of a developing behavioral flexibility that (to put the matter loosely) seems difficult to account for without postulating a wide range of different propositional attitudes (beliefs, intentions, desires, and the like). The invariant teleology of the mantis's life actually depends on its perceptual sensitivity; that is, sensory information relevant to its mode of behavioral functioning can and is actually picked up through the sensory organs with which it is endowed. But the invariance of its behavior precludes (so it may be argued) its having any perceptual beliefs at all. The argument against the capacity for beliefs does not in the least entail objections against perceptual capacity. J. J. Gibson [1966] reports for instance that "Female moths at the right stage of the reproductive cycle emit a scent so powerful that males of the appropriate species, but no other, find them by flying upwind to the source from a distance of several miles ... How does the appropriate male orient when his antennae pick up a trace, even the faintest trace, of this specific substance? What does he do? His compound eyes are inadequate to specify the female except at a very close range and, in any case, he may be miles away. The gradient of concentration of the odor is likewise insufficient to specify the direction of the female until he is almost upon her. He can equalize the bilateral pressure on the front of his body caused by airflow, and fly upwind. The streaming out of an odor field, in short, creates a sort of air track."

There is no need to postulate beliefs here (though this is clearly arguable), but there is no clear gain in denying perceptual discrimination of some sort. Obviously, non-epistemic perception is more primitive than epistemic perception in the sense, suited to biological evolution, that there exist creatures whose behavior, functionally invariant though it is, cannot be understood except in terms of some mode of perceptual triggering. It is difficult to see how this can be denied, once it be admitted that animals lacking language but possessing sensory organs are capable of perception. On the model of the insect or the earthworm, it is extravagant to maintain that perception either is or entails the acquiring of beliefs; more parsimonious is the view that perception is or entails the processing of sensory information: the information must be acquired through the activity of sense organs, and it may be regarded as processed in that its acquisition affects in functionally relevant ways the behavior of a given organism. That the most interesting perceptual systems are fully cognitive, involve consciousness, propositional attitudes and the like seems to be utterly irrelevant to the bare occurrence of the primitive perceptual processes of the lower animals. Nevertheless, the information assigned to such lower-order creatures exploits the same heuristic model as is used in ascribing beliefs to languageless animals, except that the rationality of the latter is replaced by an analogous functional teleology omitting consciousness.

On this view, the admission of non-epistemic perception entails ascribing a teleological model to a given species, in virtue of which *alone* propositionally specified) information is assigned as the functional import of internal processes. Here, we see, at one and the same time, the conceptual dependence of the teleological model of lower organisms on the sentient model suited to higher-order animals and the sense in which, where a finite-state machine program cannot be fitted to the non-epistemic sensitivity of an organism, biological reduction will be resisted. But whether it is or is not, the ascription of information presupposes a teleological model either instrumental for, or suitably analogous to, the functioning of sentient systems. In the same sense, therefore, where we assign a "natural function" to DNA, we assign as well its characteristic information, and we do so under the grip of a theory of the normal functioning of a given species (cf. Luria [1973] ; J. D. Watson [1970] ; Simon [1971] ; Vol'kenshtein [1970]).

CHAPTER 10

MENTAL STATES AND SENTIENCE

The force of the argument up to this point may be conveniently focussed in the following way. Consider W. I. Matson's [1976] Frankenstein Axiom: "An exact physical replica, however produced, of a sentient being would be itself a sentient being." Matson does not actually say what sentience is, but he somehow assumes that, whatever it is, its presence is entailed by some appropriate physical organization. He holds that the "axiom is weaker than the identity theory of mind and body . . . since [it] is compatible with epiphenomenalism". Since it is also entailed by the identity theory, he takes it that its falsity (which he denies) would falsify the identity theory itself. Nevertheless, in reviewing the arguments against the axiom, Matson claims that all "depend on the conceivability of a body's having the exact function and structure of one's own and yet being insentient" — which he believes yields no conclusive proof and is no more than a mere "autobiographical notice" of some theorist's imagined capacity to conceive what is required. Now, Matson holds "that sentience is just the functioning of the brain" — in what precise way is not clear; but on that view, it is trivially true that imagining "a body's having the exact *function* and structure of one's own and yet being insentient" is impossible. The important thing to notice is that the Frankenstein Axiom does not mention any functional properties at all: the thesis given is that a *physical* replica of a sentient being would be a sentient being. The *non sequitur* is apparent.

If there is a distinction between structural and functional properties (Putnam [1960]; Fodor [1968]), in effect, between physical and abstract properties, then it is an open question whether a physical replica would entail the (functional) property of sentience. A physical replica is simply a replica composed of the same substance (matter) as the original and exhibiting the same *physical* properties as the original. The relation of (at least certain) functional and structural properties is as yet entirely unexplained. The identity theory requires that sentient properties be physical properties; and the Frankenstein Axiom maintains, in effect, that at the very least a certain set of physical properties entails the property of sentience. It may trivially be conceded that any physically "realized" machine is composed of matter, hence that any actually instantiated functional properties are instantiated in

physically composed systems of some sort. Still, Matson concedes the following: "although the man who knows the design of a computer can in principle
read off from a flow chart the computation in which it is engaged, it is
doubtful whether any analogous translation procedure for, say, neuron firings
is possible. Nevertheless, we are forced to assume that there is some structural
correspondence between brain state and sentient conditions." In effect, this
is how Matson vindicates the Frankenstein Axiom (and, ultimately, the
identity theory). However, *if* it is conceded that functional and structural
properties are properties of different kinds, then it is reasonably clear that, if
sentience is a functional and not a structural property, the identity theory
could not possibly be defended unless for every system to which sentience
may be validly ascribed a suitable machine program could also be ascribed in
virtue of which the putative functional properties of the system correspond
invariantly with a certain finite set of the structural properties of the same
system. Matson both doubts that this is possible in the human instance and
insists that there must be "some structural correspondence between brain
state and sentient conditions". Of course, since if one coherent functional
account can be fitted to a given physical system, indefinitely many alternative
such accounts can be as well (rather in the spirit in which Wittgenstein asks
how one knows how to go on to the next member of an arithmetic series
[1963]), one cannot know what the function of any machine is from a
description of its structural properties; but the reason is a minor one as far as
reductionism is concerned — one must know the intention of the programmer
in order to assign *the* function, though any functional account may always be
discarded (in discarding the characterization of a physical system as a machine)
in favor of a purely physicalistic account. In this sense, to speak of a system
as a machine is to speak of a certain functional *role* assigned to a physical
system. The parallel with Sellars's [1963a] view of the difference between
bodies and persons is obvious. But if we wished to speak of machines, persons,
and other cultural items as entities of a distinctive sort, the maneuver would
be blocked. (We shall return to the issue.)

'Correspondence', moreover, is a peculiarly elastic term, particularly where
some strict isomorphism is denied. Hence, once we settle the *compositional*
question — in effect, adhere to ontic monism (materialism) — we may enter-
tain any number of alternative theories about the relations among the attributes of systems thus composed. This will be particularly true for systems
that lack a complete machine program. For instance, it is not too much to
hold that the functional properties of sentience may be *assigned*, on a suitable
theory, to neurophysiological events or processes the inspection of which

could not possibly (in the absence of an adequate machine model) serve to insure the occurrence of such properties. But now, if we review the arguments that have led up to this concession, we should remember: (i) that we have denied (*contra* Putnam [1960]) that the mind/body problem is a straight-forward analogue of the functional-/structural-attribute problem with respect to Turing machines; (ii) that we have rejected (*contra* Chomsky [1972]) the rationalist hypothesis that human beings are "preset" for language in terms of invariant linguistic universals; (iii) that we have denied (*contra* Fodor [1975]) that thinking and other intentionally qualified mental states presuppose an independently accessible internal representation of the propositional content of such states; (iv) that we have denied (*contra* Feigl [1967] and Cornman [1968a]) that there are one/one or one/(determinately) many or (determinately) many/one correlations between the mental and the physical; (v) that we have insisted (*contra* Sellars [1963a] and Armstrong [1973]) that intentional mental states, in particular, mental states involving linguistic ability, exhibit irreducibly intensional features; (vi) that we have argued (against a good many) that intentional mental states do not presuppose linguistic capacities; and (vii) that we have argued that the ascription of intentional mental states depends on interpreting the propositional import of the actual behavior of a creature in terms of a certain theory – a theory of the species-typical organization of the intentions, desires, needs, beliefs, perceptions, actions and the like of such a creature, a theory (of a creature's rationality) that is itself heuristically construed in terms of a model of language. The convergent force of all these considerations, particularly given the distinction between structural and functional properties, is simply that the only "correspondence" available to Matson (or anyone else), in the context of humans and at least the higher mammals, is the unhelpful one of actually assigning the propositional content of a mental state to a suitably selected neurophysiological state. Once we admit that sentience and intentional mental states are ascribed in terms of the molar behavior of a system construed as significant in terms of the sequence and order of such behavior *vis-à-vis* the heuristically assigned model of its characteristic form of life (or suitable analogue), we can readily see why it is that the Frankenstein Axiom is quite inadequate. Attention to the intentional import of behavior is simply not the same as attention to the central physical states of purely physical systems.

The trouble remains, however, that these considerations fail somehow to explain what the ascription of sentience and consciousness comes to in the first place.

The pivotal consideration rests with distinguishing the conditions under which functional properties are ascribed to systems and the conditions under which that subset of functional properties that we term sentience and consciousness are ascribed. It is reasonably clear that functional properties, even informational properties, may be ascribed to physical systems, machines, plants, lower animals, and the artifacts of human culture (including both language and works of art) in spite of the fact that such items are normally not regarded as sentient or conscious or capable of cognitive states or the like. In a sense, this last remark is potentially questionbegging, since it has not been settled why a "self-correcting" field gun equipped with "sensors" for "scanning" the horizon for relevant targets is denied sentience; or why the Venus flytrap or hydra is denied consciousness. But it is true nevertheless that in ascribing such properties, it is not entailed that the system involved be conscious or sentient or capable of cognitive states. (These formulations, incidentally, are taken, in the relevant sense, to be equivalent.) Still, on the argument that has gone before, *that* a nonsentient system has a determinate function depends on a certain intention or interpretation formed by a sentient system: the function of a machine is the function it is assigned by its programmer; the putative functions of the organs of the body, as in the medical setting, are assigned in accord with the prudential interests of sentient creatures (Margolis [1976]); the normal functioning of plants and lower animals is ascribed by way of analogy with the interests of sentient creatures. In the latter instance, questions arise about the sense in which a system may be said to *have* a function rather than to have a function imputed to it for explanatory purposes (Woodfield [1976]). To speak of the function of a system described in purely physicalistic terms is merely metaphoric or a *façon de parler*. To speak of the function or teleological organization of nonsentient biological systems is, normally, to signify either that a physicalistic account is as yet lacking or that there is reason to believe that no satisfactory account of such a sort can be provided for the biological phenomena in question. Some maintain that teleological explanations are nothing more than straightforward "covering-law explanations" (Ruse [1973]; E. Nagel [1961]); others insist that the empirical evidence does not show this and may in fact require its rejection (Taylor [1964]). (We shall return to the issue.) So, functional properties are ascribed in both reductive and non-reductive settings. The same is true of informational properties, except that, as has already been argued, a system can be said to store or convey information (non-metaphorically) only if it is part of a larger system that is sentient (and can *use* information) or if it is an instrument of an independent sentient system: the first possibility appears in the relation between the brain and a sentient organism; the second, in the relation between a computer and a human agent. Hence, informational ascriptions entail a concession to non-reductive accounts *if* sentience and consciousness cannot be physicalistically reduced; but the ascription of informational capacities to a given system does not entail that *that* system be sentient. A nonsentient system, then, may be ascribed functional properties, on a theory; but a system has informational properties only if it functions within or for a sentient system.

Consciousness is obviously a controversial topic. It is for instance often rejected as useless for productive work in the behavioral sciences (Lashley [1923]; Boring [1963]; Hebb [1974]). It is also peculiarly difficult to view as a theoretical concept because we ourselves are largely distinguished by our ability to report our inner experience and (however argumentative the proper description of the phenomenon may be) by our ability to attend to that inner experience (cf. Wittgenstein [1963]; Malcolm [1954]; Anscombe [1957]; Chisholm [1966]). Matson mentions what he takes to be "the mistake of thinking of consciousness as something that explains behavior causally ... consciousness as such [he says] never *does* anything". Part of the trouble, of course, is that the admission that consciousness (or better, conscious states or mental events of a conscious sort) play a causal role is thought to reinstate Cartesian dualism at a stroke; although obviously, a straightforward identity theory (Smart [1962]) entails that consciousness *does* have a causal role. In fact, the only plausible form of epiphenomenalism, in a materialist setting, holds (*contra* K. Campbell [1970]) that only the intentional or propositional content of a mental state lacks causal force — not that mental states and mental events themselves (being either identical with or suitably "realized" in physical states and events) lack such force. Others, notably Gilbert Ryle [1949], construe the admission of psychophysical interaction as a category mistake; and still others (for instance, Körner [1966]; Brodbeck [1966]) insist on precluding reference to the mental within the causal order that the sciences investigate. (These considerations bear on the prospects of psychophysical laws, a matter to which we shall return.) Also, it must be admitted, where psychophysical interaction is strongly championed (Broad [1925]), an incipiently dualistic account is often to be found.

The complexity of our issue may be grasped by noting that the reduction or elimination of mental states requires the reduction or elimination of persons or sentient animals or the like. The cavalier rejection of consciousness, therefore, whatever its proper analysis, leaves the behavioral sciences with the unresolved question of the nature of putative persons and sentient organisms

— to which *behavior* is ascribed. This may be seen by considering the conces-sions of D. M. Armstrong [1968] and Herbert Feigl [1967]. Armstrong holds that "The concept of a mental state is primarily the concept of *a state of the person apt for bringing about a certain sort of behavior.* Sacrificing all accuracy for brevity, we can say that, although mind is not behavior, it is the *cause* of behavior". Several things deserve our attention here. First of all, mental states are defined in terms of their characteristic causal role, not their experienced or phenomenal qualities (in a manner similar to that of Lewis's account [1966]). Secondly, so defined, though mental states are conceded to have a causal role, they appear (at least) not to be specified in terms of consciousness at all. Thirdly, they cannot be defined, apparently, without reference to the behavior of a certain kind of entity, in particular, a person (or, of course, a sentient creature if, as Armstrong elsewhere concedes, animals have mental states); but persons and sentient creatures, trivially, are just the kinds of entities to which sentience is ascribed as an essential attribute. Fourthly, 'behavior' becomes equivocal precisely in virtue of the consideration of whether any putative instance of behavior is or is not informed by conscious or sentient states, although the account is clearly incompatible with behaviorism. Now, Armstrong himself concedes the *prima facie* reasonableness of the charge that "consciousness is something more than the occurrence of an inner state apt for the production of certain sorts of behavior", particularly since, "unlike the gene, the mind is not a mere theoretical concept. In our own case, at least, we have a direct awareness of mental states." But his own solution is, however clever, essentially unresponsive. He holds that "conscious-ness is no more than *awareness* (perception) of inner mental states by the person whose states they are", that is, it "is simply a further mental state, a state 'directed' towards the original inner states . . . an inner state apt for the production of certain behavior". Nevertheless, in clarifying 'awareness', Armstrong says that "if this further mental state, which *qua* mental state is simply a state of the person apt for the production of certain behavior, can be contingently identified with a state of the brain, it will be a process in which one part of the brain scans another part of the brain. In perception the brain scans the environment. In awareness of the perception another process in the brain scans that scanning." The fundamental lacuna in the argument is simply that, as has already been shown, the use of an information-processing model makes no sense (because of its reliance on propositional import) with-out the admission of a sentient system: the part of the *brain* that, on Armstrong's view, is in effect aware of the environment or of another part of the brain, could not be so characterized (however metaphorically or elliptically) unless the person or organism relative to which the brain scans information were itself a sentient system. *But then, it is impossible to explain the sentience of that system in terms of the information-processing capacity (awareness) of any of its parts* (cf. Dennett [1969]). Armstrong has simply reversed the explanatory order of things. Hence, although he concedes the causal role of consciousness, he has no satisfactory account of it.

On the other hand, Feigl summarizes the materialist literature regarding the mind/body problem and his own position relative to it, in the following way: "Some philosophers feel that the central issue of the mind-body problems is that of intentionality (sapience); others see it in the problem of sentience; and still others in the puzzles of selfhood. Although I have focused my attention primarily on the sentience problem, I regard the others as equally important. But I must confess that ... the sapience and selfhood issues have always vexed me less severely than those of sentience." What is striking here is, precisely, that, unlike Armstrong, Feigl fails to see the conceptual connection between sentience, sapience, and selfhood (or, sentient creaturehood). He fails to see, that is, that (i) ascriptions of sentience and sapience are correlative — a creature cannot be said to perceive, for instance, if putative perceptions are not significantly related to putative wants and needs and coordinated behavior; (ii) cognitive or cognitively qualified states of no sort can be determinately ascribed except by reference to their propositional content — to see something, for instance, in the way that yields belief or knowledge is to see, or to believe one sees, *that* something is the case, where the relevant intentional content can be ascribed only on the basis of verbal and nonverbal behavior, in accord with a theory of the "sapient" interests of the creature involved. For example, a creature cannot be said to see *that p*, where no behavior suitably linked by way of a theory of the species-typical interests of such a creature ever issues on the occasion of the putative perception: Fido, said to see that his master is at the door, runs *expectantly* to the door because he *wants* attention or the like. It is in this sense that ascriptions of intentional mental states presuppose an entity of at least a *minimally* rational sort. A creature cannot be said to intend to do what it does not believe is not yet the case or what it believes it cannot accomplish; and a creature cannot be said to want or desire anything if there is no general congruence between its putative wants and its intentions and the actions it performs; nor can it even be said to know or believe anything if it does not generally act in ways that exhibit a suitable coherence between its putative information and its wants and desires (Rundle [1972]). The principal conclusion to stress is that "an event, state or structure [of the brain or nervous system or the like] can be considered to have [intentional] content only within a system as a whole" — hence, that the "fundamental problem [remains] of how the brain *uses* information intelligently" (Dennett [1969]). To put the point as a maxim: the brain *uses* information only if the creature *uses* information. On the face of it, inanimate physical systems cannot plausibly be ascribed the minimal rationality of sentient creatures. Living creatures, on the other hand, are said to be sentient insofar as they are also said to be intelligent: they are said to have certain sentient capacities only insofar as whatever putative belief and knowledge may be ascribed them conform, on some theory of their cognitive capabilities and characteristic wants, to what would minimally cohere with putative intentions, desires, and behavior also ascribed to them.

To speak of the *concepts* possessed by an animal, therefore, is simply to speak of the selective capabilities of sentience and intelligence ascribed to it, in virtue of which its putative mental states may be analyzed in the manner given. There can be no independent access to the concepts of a creature: assuming that it is minimally rational, in the sense sketched, the concepts assigned to it are simply the result of reading back, as potentialities relevant to its own teleological or goal-directed (goal-pursuing) pattern, whatever, on the empirical evidence, may be heuristically reported as the intentional import of its particular mental states. Consequently, we cannot sort the causal role of concepts distinguished either intensionally or extensionally.

Armstrong's view [1973] is instructive here because (inadvertently) it provides knockdown evidence that *if* one ascribes concepts and mental states to creatures, *it is impossible* to free such ascriptions from behavioral considerations that are themselves informed by a (heuristic, intentionally described) theory of the interests and rational organization of the life of such creatures. "The concept of red [Armstrong maintains] is said to be a certain selective capacity toward members of the class of red things. But are there not *other* possible concepts under which all and only members of the class of red things fall? And how would we distinguish possession of the concept of red from possession of one of these other concepts? If the class of red things is coextensive with the class of X's, then a selective capacity toward red things is a selective capacity towards things of the sort . . . [Here is] the solution of our problem. The concept of red is the concept of *red* because the red object that activates this concept . . . has this effect *in virtue of the object's redness* [sic] . . . And that is the criterion for calling it the concept of red." Armstrong, therefore, fails to link concepts to behavior. Nevertheless, he has difficulty differentiating concepts corresponding to coextensive classes: in speaking of the causal efficacy of properties [*sic*], he says that although "two properties are coextensive, . . . they are not both causally operative in the same way in the two [distinct causal] situations", but, in the same context, he admits that "it seems likely that . . . coextensive properties could not involve different causal powers in relation to *anything at all*". He wavers again, holding that perhaps the "distinction could be made in situations where the causal chain between object and mind was less direct" (presumably, less direct than otherwise straightforward causal linkages would be), but the claim is ultimately untenable. It is, in fact, unnecessary to speak of the causal efficacy of concepts: concepts are heuristically introduced in just the way in which the propositional content of non-verbalized mental states is introduced; mental states and events may be assigned a causal role; but distinctions between concepts impose no intensional paradoxes, for precisely the same reason no paradox arises in reporting, heuristically, the propositional content of mental states.

A causal account of concepts is inadequate, then, because it cannot provide for different concepts applying to coextensive properties; and it appears to be self-defeating, because, in order to test whether the alleged causal regularities hold between concepts and instances of certain classes of things that we encounter in certain ways, we must be able to discriminate different concepts whether or not they exhibit the causal regularities in question. So, a causal theory of concepts, even the theory (Armstrong's) that the concept of red "is a *second-order capacity* — a capacity to acquire the capacity to react towards the red object when the latter acts upon [one's] mind", is ultimately indefensible. The reason is already in our hands: where concepts are ascribed on the basis of linguistic behavior, we are faced with the nonreducibility of language itself; and where concepts are ascribed on the basis of mental states that are not linguistically informed, we are faced with the heuristic dependence of such ascriptions on the very model of language.

The bearing of these difficulties on central-state materialism (Armstrong [1968]) is straightforward. By central-state materialism, Armstrong means essentially the doctrine that "mental states are identified with physical states of the organism that has the mind, in particular, with states of the brain or central nervous system". (Armstrong [1968], it may be noted, fails to distinguish correctly the claims of functional materialism and eliminative materialism; consequently, he holds that the doctrine is supported not only by Feigl and Smart but also by Putnam and Feyerabend.) Against Smart [1962] and Place [1956], Armstrong declares that he wishes to "defend a central-state account of *all* the mental concepts", whereas these earlier theorists held a behavioristic theory of intentions and the like. Nevertheless, quite apart from functionalist considerations, Armstrong is forced into an impasse in considering the reductive identity of beliefs "with neurophysiological states of the brain". Thus, his theory [1973] leads him to hold that, "Given a belief-state, Bap, we can say that it is also the belief-state Baq if, and only if, 'p' and 'q' are simply different notational expressions of the same organization of Ideas in the one belief-state". But this makes the identity of belief-states depend on the identity of Ideas (that is, adjusting Geach's theory [1957], " 'exercises' of concepts") and of concepts themselves; but we have already seen that the ascription of concepts depends on linguistic intensions or the heuristic description of mental states — under the control of a theory of a given creature's rationality, which cannot be reduced to an account of the central states of the *parts* of such a creature. Armstrong goes on to say, "Perhaps all would agree that the state of affairs Ba(Fb & Gb) is the very same state of affairs as Ba(Gb & Fb). But what of, say, Ba(if p, then q) and Ba(if-q, then-p)? Have we two beliefs here, or only one? Presumably, we would have to look to the future theoretical identification or correlations of neurophysiology to settle such questions with any show of decisiveness." But there are no causal correlations between neural processes *and* beliefs except where the beliefs in question *are already characterized in terms of the speech-act model* (that is, by reference to sentient agents), and there are no independent causal regularities involving Ideas or concepts. This shows, unmistakably, the sense in which, instead of identifying neural processes and mental states by means of some relevant empirical correlations, we cannot but *assign* the intentional content of mental states to neural processes (if we wish) on the basis of correlations between such processes and such states *as already intentionally characterized*. We cannot, in other words, eliminate reference to the sentient states *of* sentient organisms or persons.

Much the same sort of difficulty that confronts the identity of mental states and brain states (Armstrong; Smart [1962]) confronts the alternative theory that holds that states of consciousness are, as a matter of fact, states of information-processing of a certain complexity. The theory is not as such a materialistic theory but is compatible with materialism insofar as information-processing systems are embodied in, or embodied exclusively in, material systems (Sayre [1969]; Sayre and Crosson [1968]; Sayre [1965]). The difficulty can be identified by considering several remarks of Kenneth Sayre's [1969]: "Although presumably the brain remains capable of rudimentary forms of patterned response when the subject is unconscious, I have maintained only that patterned sensory responses of a high level of complexity are instances of consciousness ... Consciousness involves the discrimination of different forms of objects, and ... to discriminate different forms of objects is to issue patterned neural responses to peripheral stimulation ... 'Consciousness' is a 'state word', indicating the presence of one or another conscious response on the part of the behaving organism. It should be clear that by 'conscious response' I mean a form of response of the nervous system to its sensory inputs and not a form of consciously performed overt behavior." If, on the information-processing theory, the relevant processing were accomplished by the *organism* or *person* or *machine*, then the theory would not as such facilitate a reductive program; for then, the very ascription of consciousness would require the admission of entities (like organisms or persons) *whose* consciousness might be explained by reference to — but would not as such be identified with — whatever processes obtained in *parts of its* body or in parts of some surrogate physical system. Sayre, it should be noted, admits that information-processing ("patterned responses") may obtain *in the brain* though the *subject be unconscious*. If so, then either consciousness is not information-processing though it may entail it; or else information-processing that is consciousness does not obtain in the brain (or in any other part of the nervous system) though it may entail information-processing, of a suitably complex sort, in the brain or nervous system. Correspondingly (as has already been remarked), if a mental state is ascribed to an organism or a person (or a machine, if the extension be permitted), then it could not coherently be identified with whatever state may obtain in any part of that organism's or person's (or machine's) body or physical system. For example, if we speak of an organism's or a person's *thinking that p* or *desiring q*, there is no coherent sense in which a thought or desire may be a property of any part of a mere body or of any process ascribed to any part of the body — except, perhaps, elliptically, in the sense in which what is *ascribed* to the organism or person directly (in virtue of a theory of that organism's characteristic behavior) is thereupon *assigned*, for purposes of explanatory convenience, to the parts or processes of parts of *that* organism's or person's body. Thus, knowing that *S* (an organism or person) fears *r*, we may say that the "seat" of emotion or the "controlling center" of emotion is in the hypothalamus. It is not simply a question of cross-category constraints (Cornman [1968a]), which make it impossible to translate sentences about mental events by sentences about physical events or to ascribe to physical systems attributes ascribable to entities said to "have minds". It is rather that we simply have no theory that shows the sense in which what may be ascribed to sentient organisms or persons could be identical with whatever may be ascribed to the parts or processes of parts of physical systems, in which such organisms or persons are embodied or realized. Alternatively put, the maneuver required would at best demonstrate that persons or organisms and their attributes were nothing but bodies and their attributes — the thesis of physicalism (T. Nagel [1965]). But even this thesis reduces *whole persons or organisms to whole bodies*. It does not attempt to construe attributes predicable of whole bodies or of whole physical systems as predicable of any of the parts of such systems.

The proper analogue of consciousness, here, is action. Actions are attributable to persons, organisms, perhaps machines (Sayre [1969]). Conceivably, on a viable, reductive theory, full-fledged actions (signing checks, searching for food, flipping a light switch, pumping water) could be construed in terms of the overt, molar "behavior" or overt bodily movements of bodies or physical systems of a certain appropriate complexity. Nevertheless, where nonsentient machines are involved, the ascription of relevant actions (sentiently informed actions) is either metaphoric, elliptical, or invalid. Matson rightly observes that "insentient devices cannot think" — the literal notion involves a contradiction in terms; "computers can't compute"; and counting "requires consciousness". It would be quite impossible to construe the actions of a person or organism in terms of changes, movements, processes — however detailed and complex — of the various interior parts of given bodies or physical systems. For one thing, in correctly ascribing actions, we normally have not the faintest idea of the detailed bodily changes that may be involved in the performance of a given action. For another, the performance of an action does not normally require a fixed set of particular (or even alternative particular) interior movements and processes or a fixed set of particular (or even alternative particular) overt bodily movements (Taylor [1964]). In this sense, action tends to be a polymorphous concept (Ryle [1949]; White [1967]). But more than this, actions, performed by creatures, persons, or machines may be said to have been accomplished through, or to have been dependent upon, or to have involved or required, these or those interior bodily changes or bodily processes or processes ascribable to these or those interior bodily events or states. Actions are molar ascriptions of some sort. That is, there is not the remotest plausibility in attempting to identify particular actions with anything at all that may be ascribed to parts of given bodies or parts of given physical systems. There is, in a word, a kind of adequation between entities of given sorts and attributes of given sorts that may be matched with them. It appears that the performance of actions and the manifesting of consciousness both are ascribable to entities only of a suitable complexity; and that *to be a part of* a physical system that either embodies such an entity or is (on a putatively viable thesis) identical with such an entity precludes the ascription of action or consciousness to the part in question — except, as on the information-processing model, metaphorically or elliptically. The brain cannot be conscious, though an organism is conscious because (in part) it has a brain. An arm cannot throw a ball, though a man may throw a ball with his arm. If the retina of the eye, the optic nerve, the brain stem, the cerebral cortex embody a cascade of information-processing channels, then *that* system cannot be conscious nor can its information-processing states be identical with states of consciousness, though an organism that is conscious (or even unconscious, for that matter) may be provided with sensory information through those channels.

The argument is apt to be misleading if it is assumed that the principal pivot on which criticism of the alternative forms of the identity theory or of reductive materialism rests is simply the complaint that what may be ascribed to a given whole may not be ascribed to a part. No, it may be frankly admitted that such a predicative shift may, in principle, be defended by reference to a theory that permits us to explain how it merely appeared that an ascription — suitable for a part of a system — could be predicated only of the system as a whole. When, however, we speak of intentional properties and of entities to which such properties may be ascribed, the whole/part shift may be challenged precisely because of the special features of discourse about such entities and such properties. Even this is not yet to say why it is logically impossible to defend such a shift, only that the theory supporting such a shift needs to be supplied, that none has as yet been convincingly supplied, and that the lacuna is often though not a serious one because the distinction of intentional and linguistic capacities is too lightly treated (Sellars [1963a]).

The general argument against the shift from whole to part runs as follows. Wherever informational properties are ascribed to a given system, that system must itself (i) be sentient, or (ii) be part of a sentient system, or (iii) be an instrument of a sentient system. Intentional properties *are* informational properties and, hence, fall under the constraint. We cannot, therefore, treat the intentional mental states of persons or of sentient organisms (or even of machines) as the properties of the non-sentient parts of such systems or of the non-sentient parts of the systems in which such (sentient) systems are embodied or realized: the literal ascription of intentional mental states requires a sentient subject.

A problem rather similar to Armstrong's may also be posed for Dennett's [1969] account. Dennett asks straightforwardly, "What, if anything, permits us to endow neural events with content?" He sees, rather along the lines already sketched, that ascriptions of mental states having intentional content are conceptually connected with a teleological model of an organism's life and capabilities and, in particular, following Taylor [1964], that "the question of the elimination of the teleological is intimately bound up with the question of the reducibility of the Intentional". He rightly observes that the teleological characterization of the conditions of existence of neural structures "is explicable in terms of the operations of natural selection – a process that can be given a non-teleological description"; and he concludes that this itself counts as "a claim in favor of elimination of the teleological". Since the phenomena of natural selection are initially introduced non-teleologically, it is a foregone conclusion that a teleological account of such phenomena can be eliminated; in precisely the same sense, a teleological characterization of geological equilibrium can be eliminated. The question remains whether we can reduce teleological and intentional characterizations for phenomena for which there is no antecedently available non-intentional or non-teleological alternative, in particular, where sentience and intelligence are ascribed. Dennett himself concedes that, in developing the evolutionary analogue, "no strict justification has been yet proposed for what must be the crux of any centralist theory: the ascription of content or meaning to particular central states of the brain", but he plainly believes that his extended treatment of evolution provides a basis for the justification. He claims, for instance, that "the principles of evolution" provide not only for the "causes" but also for the "reasons for being" of the particular structures that an animal develops through evolution. He concedes that "the *raison d'être* of a neural structure" is not one that the animal or person has, in any sense related to that in which, say, a bird picks up twigs in order to make a nest. Nor is it a *raison d'être* in the sense in which, say, "a can-opener's existence depends on the recognition of its *raison d'être* by its maker". No, "the cash value of saying that a neural structure exists for a reason is just this: were the necessary conditions for the survival of a particular animal and the environmental circumstances in general other than they are, such that the neural structure in question would not have the role in survival it has, the structure would not exist." But, precisely, that *is* to maintain that to assign a *raison d'être* to neural structures in terms of evolutionary theory (in effect, to explain the assignment of intentional content) is hardly more than to employ a *façon de parler* for handling what are actually non-intentional causal accounts.

There is no reason advanced for thinking that the intentional mental states of sentient creatures could be analyzed analogously. As noted earlier on, Dennett concedes that mental states are ascribed to creatures or persons and

not to brains, which suggests why the ascription of "content" or "significance" to neural events and neural states depends initially on the molar
characterization of the behavior and mental states of whole organisms — as
well as why the evolutionary analogue is inapt. In order to make the argument
compelling, Dennett would have to show precisely how to reduce the intentional mental states *that we ascribe to persons and sentient creatures*; for, in
such circumstances, we appear confronted with an emergent teleology (in
Feigl's sense of 'emergent' [1967]) and not merely an alternative *façon de
parler*.

Consider what Dennett has to say about a frog's visual discrimination: we
might, he says, be inclined to hold that "object reference [say, a fly] is
permissible after convergence of signals from both eyes, or from several sense
organs"; still, "the frog will commit itself to a behavioral response on the
basis of information from one eye alone ... Here the shift from a retinal
reference to an object reference must depend on what effect a signal has on
behavior." But then, "the question facing the centralist is what the *organism*
'takes the signal to mean'" [italics added], not causal relations between
afferent and efferent processes involving the brain. Nothing could be clearer,
then, than that Dennett believes that a centralist solution regarding the
ascription of intentional content to neural processes must first concede that
such ascriptions cannot but be initially subordinate to intentional characterizations of the behavior and mental states of the organisms in question. (The
frog example, it may be added, is indecisive in any case if the frog's visual
perception is characterized as it often is in terms of structural/functional
invariances that need not even involve ascriptions of intelligence or cognition
[Lettvin *et al.* (1959); Wooldridge (1963)].) Nevertheless, in his central
maneuver to overtake the problem favorably, Dennett abandons "the ordinary
personal level term 'aware' [and replaces it] by two terms that still take persons (or whole systems) as subjects, but [that] have sub-personal criteria":
thus, "(1) A is aware$_1$ that p at time t if and only if p is the content of the
input state of A's 'speech center' at time t"; and "(2) A is aware$_2$ that p at
time t if and only if p is the content of an internal event in A at time t that is
effective in directing current behavior". Animals are said to be aware$_2$ but
people are both aware$_1$ and aware$_2$ of things. The difficulty, however, is
obvious and ineliminable by *any* maneuver of the sort Dennett proposes; for
(1) and (2) *may* well state empirically necessary and sufficient conditions for
awareness$_1$ and awareness$_2$; but, if so, they cannot be said to supply "sub-
personal" *criteria* of awareness of either sort. The reason is quite straightforward: nothing could be construed as the *propositional content* of the

input of A's speech center or the *propositional content* of an internal event in A except on the basis of an assignment controlled by what intentional ascriptions are initially made of A, the creature or person involved. Such putative *"sub-*personal" criteria, therefore, are really elliptical versions of full-blown personal criteria; it is, in fact, only by reference to the latter, that A's "speech center" and the relevant "internal events" in A can even be specified. The conclusion is also a direct consequence of Dennett's own expressed views regarding the processing of information.

Given these considerations, it is safe to say (Feigl [1967]) that no one has yet succeeded in reducing discourse about persons and sentient creatures to non-intentional discourse about the physical events and states of such systems. Thus, it cannot yet be said, with Dennett, that "the personal story [the ordinary story of a person's mental activities] . . . has a relatively vulnerable and *impermanent* place [italics added] in our conceptual scheme, and could *in principle* [italics added] be rendered 'obsolete' if some day we [*sic*] ceased to *treat* anything (any mobile body or system or device) as an Intentional system – by reasoning with it, communicating with it, etc." There is, at the moment, not the slightest prospect of eliminating persons or the higher animals as emergent entities.

Nor, for related reasons, is there the slightest prospect of exhausting the putative functioning of persons at the molar level in terms of the "social" interaction among a set of sub-personal but cognitively endowed agents, homunculi: only if a computational model of the sort Fodor [1975] advances or some suitably powerful analogue obtained, could the prospect offer any advantage, for otherwise we should have to enlarge the context of "social" interaction to include molar persons *and* their own sub-personal homunculi – which, paradoxically, would reinstate what was to be reduced though not eliminated. Dennett [1975] has apparently come to favor the sub-personal replacement of molar persons rather than their elimination. But he provides no independent computational model. The maneuver is an obvious improvement on the earlier claim, but in a sense it falls victim to the same difficulties. Dennett rightly emphasizes that "the *subject* of that access (whatever it is) [in the sense of that of which I am conscious, the access of personal consciousness] that exhausts consciousness is the *person*, and not any of the person's parts". Personal access or the access of personal consciousness is, then, to be contrasted with "computational access" (the access of molecular sub-routines to the information of other such routines) as well as with "public access" (roughly, the computational access of a print-out sub-routine that provides for the possibility of personal access but is not equivalent to it). Functionally, then, molecular access to information is to be construed sub-personally. Dennett wishes "to construct a full-fledged 'I' out of sub-personal parts by exploiting the sub-personal notions of access already introduced". And he maintains, quite plausibly, that "sub-personal theories proceed by analyzing a person into an organization of sub-systems (organs, routines, nerves, faculties, components — even atoms) and attempting to explain the behavior of the whole person as the outcome of the interaction of these sub-systems". But the essential consideration is that the relevant intentional or informational characterization of the sub-routines is always *assigned* on the basis of the analysis of the functional or intentional states of the molar person. Unless we had a computational algorithm of some sort by means of which we could, from the *structural* description of the sub-routines, reconstruct or *generate* (either in the linguistic or in a suitably analogous nonlinguistic sense) the functional states of molar persons, Dennett's program must fail (cf. Gunderson [1971]). Contrary to Dennett's account, therefore, a sub-personal theory of persons constitutes a psychological theory only to the extent that it assigns the components of the psychological processes of molar persons to molecular processes.

It remains to take notice once again of the respect in which sentient creatures that are not persons may be seen as emergent entities, which, in effect, is to respond to a central puzzle in Strawson's account [1959]. Sentient creatures (which Strawson calls "persons") are, as we have seen, ascribed mental states in a way that depends on a heuristic use of linguistic utterances. They are not actually persons because they lack the mastery of a language; but neither are they merely physical bodies because the specification and explanation of their characteristic properties requires an intentional and teleological idiom parasitic on the intentional, rule-governed features of language itself, which properties appear to be irreducible (for some animals at least) to purely physical phenomena, in the sense emphasized by Lewis [1966], namely, that "physical phenomena have none but purely physical explanations". Nevertheless, since the model of language provides, however ineliminably for the purpose, no more than a heuristic device by which to articulate the nature of the intentional states of non-language-using creatures, we could conceivably eliminate such intentional discourse about animals *if* we agreed to deny that they were sentient and intelligent. We could treat them as mere physical bodies, in a way in which we could not with ourselves, but we should thereby have lost the most important part of our interest in them and it may well be that their obvious sentience precludes the maneuver. Consequently, we treat animals as entities that have emerged from mere physical bodies in such a way, biologically, that sentience and intelligence may be ascribed to them. Regardless of what may be said of persons, therefore, on the characterization of which their own characterization depends, sentient creatures may well be a kind of basic particular, as Strawson claims. They are distinct from physical bodies in that their essential attributes cannot be predicated of mere bodies; but they do not require a form of dualism – hence, are "primitive" in the sense Strawson emphasizes – because, on the assumption of their minimal rationality, selected physical phenomena within them and involving them serve as grounds for ascribing functional mental states to them and for construing their molar movements as or as constituting intentional behavior. In a way, therefore, linguistic ability provides the essential criterion for distinguishing physical bodies, sentient creatures, and persons: intentional properties are always, in principle, eliminable for physical bodies and ascribable to sentient creatures in a way that depends heuristically on the capacity to use language.

We are now ready to say what sentience or consciousness or cognition is. From a formal point of view, it is obvious that cognitive or cognitively informed states are states of systems, in which propositional messages are conveyed or discriminated. This much is conceded also by Dennett [1969]. But we are still obliged to distinguish satisfactorily between metaphoric or elliptical and literal ascriptions of consciousness. Otherwise, we should not be able quite to explain where Dennett goes wrong in saying: "Of course any machine that, like our perceiving machine, had a speech centre attached would be aware$_1$ of the content of the input to this speech centre, and this may seem to be an intolerable situation, but only if one clings to the folklore that has accrued to the ordinary word 'aware'." Now, Fodor [1975] rightly criticizes Hubert Dreyfus [1972] for arguing against the possibility of machine models for human linguistic capacities on the grounds that machines could not use linguistic rules in the open-textured way that human linguistic rules apparently operate – for instance, that the applicaton of such rules may leave truth values indeterminate for the use of particular predicates. Nevertheless, Fodor seems to have missed the full gist of Dreyfus's argument, which is to the effect (i) that "human beings do not seem to themselves or to observers to be following strict rules" or to be following rules at all – certainly not in any sense in which rules are accessible to a digital computer; and (ii) that the simulation of cognitive processes is notably successful only for certain kinds of thinking (for instance involving "recursive application of all the available transformations to all the situations that occur" [Minsky (1968a)] or for fractions of certain kinds of thinking where convergence of results but not necessarily of the "heuristics" of problem-solving (Newell, Shaw, and Simon [1963]) are considered). The rejection of (i) leads to the thesis of artificial intelligence, and the search beyond [(ii)]) for the heuristics of problem-solving (that is, programs, unlike algorithmic programs, that, however successful, do not involve an exhaustive strategy for arriving at solutions) leads to the artificial simulation of intelligence (Minsky [1968b]; Feigenbaum and Feldman [1963]; Arbib [1972]). Clearly, the two ventures converge. If, therefore, machines were to resemble human beings in that respect in which sentience were ascribed to the latter, they too could be said to be sentient.

Now, if we consider sentience or consciousness as a theoretical concern – waiving for the present the intrusiveness of our own introspective abilities – the schematism provided in the following observations may help to identify the conditions under which we are normally prepared to ascribe sentience to an organism. For after all (*contra* Strawson [1959]), sentience and intelligence do not serve to distinguish persons from languageless animals. However tentative may be our view of the discovery of the laws of nature, of *nomic universals* (cf. Smart [1963]; E. Nagel [1961]), the notion of a natural law stresses invariant properties in virtue of which things behave in accord with putative laws. Even Karl Popper [1972c], who stresses the conjectural or hypothetical character of so-called "universal laws of nature", concedes a search for a kind of ("modified") essentialism: "our laws or our theories must be *universal*, that is to say, must make assertions about the world – about all spatio-temporal regions of the world . . . our theories make assertions about structural or relational properties of the world; and . . . the properties described by an explanatory theory must be, in some sense or other, deeper than those to be explained."

Charles Taylor [1964] contends, however, that "human behavior, or for that matter the behavior of animals or even living organisms in general, [may well be] in some way fundamentally different from the processes in nature which are studied by the natural sciences" (cf. Ayala and Dobzhansky [1974]). He therefore introduces the notion of a teleological explanation, where, briefly, "to offer a teleological explanation of some event or class of events, e.g., the behavior of some being, is, then, to account for it by laws in terms of which an event's occurring is held to be dependent on that event's being required for some end". Such laws, Taylor thinks, "can be verified or falsified, and, if true, . . . can be used to predict and control the phenomena like any others". Teleological laws differ from the usual laws of physical nature in that they cannot satisfy the condition that the terms linked in a relevent law cannot be not only "identifiable separately from each other . . .

but also ... identified separately from *any* law in which [either] term may figure". Teleological laws, therefore, cannot meet the usual Humean constraints. This particular claim may well be disputed, for it is not clear that Taylor has demonstrated that causal factors qualified in putatively goal-directed or functional terms cannot be specified independently of other causal elements (cf. Davidson [1963]); in fact, it is not clear that what he calls teleological explanation is not, rather, a specialized version of otherwise straightforward causal laws (Woodfield[1976]) or is not such that a non-teleological explanation will always and necessarily be able to replace it (Noble [1966–67]).

However, on Taylor's account, teleological laws may well involve invariances as strict as those of the usual laws of physical nature. Perhaps a fair illustration of this aspect of Taylor's account is provided by the views of the French entomologist J. H. Fabre [1923]. For, Fabre apparently believed that instinct, as a sort of innate life plan, accounted for animal behavior by invariantly and specifically leading toward the goals of individual and species preservation. A Fabrean animal world might be said not to justify the ascription of sentience or cognition – any more than Taylor's general formula – precisely because the regularities postulated are thought not to involve discrimination of the sort associated with the exercise of sentience. Taylor's formula, it will be noted, quite clearly omits any reference to sentience. In fact, Taylor expressly contrasts, later in his account, an "ordinary teleological system" and an "intentional system": "In an ordinary teleological system with goal G, B will occur in the condition where B is required for G; (let us call this condition 'T'). But in an 'intentional system' with goal G, T is not sufficient for B. In this latter case, however, B will occur when T is *seen* to hold by the 'system' (in the absence of deterring factors), for otherwise we could not ascribe goal G to it. In other words, the condition of an action occurring is that it be believed to be adequate to the goal, and not simply that it is in fact adequate. And the two may not go together. The situation as it really is may differ from the situation under its intentional description for the agent, that is, the intentional description may not in fact hold of it."

The point of the distinction is extremely important for our present concern. It is conceivable that a biological system be goal-directed in a sense suitable for teleological explanation, without it being the case that the system be sentient. It is also conceivable (E. Nagel [1961]; Ruse [1973]) that certain putatively goal-directed phenomena be explainable in non-teleological terms. But Taylor's emphasis on intentional systems actually moves away from considerations of lawlike regularities of any sort. As Taylor says, to use the notion of an action, we must be able "to identify the 'direction' of an action, i.e., what kind of action it is, independently of its antecedent condition or the laws by which it is explained. It must be the case that to make an action attribution is to make a statement about this event itself, that is, not one the verification for which lies in laws or regularities which this event instances." Here, Taylor stresses that we ascribe a distinctive "nature" to events that count as actions: "the notion of an action as directed behavior involves that of an intentional description." He adds that the notion of an action is inseparable from the "notion of a center of responsibility" — which corresponds to the model of minimal rationality we had earlier adduced. The trouble is that, although Taylor admirably details what is *entailed* by ascriptions of consciousness or intentionality, he says nothing directly about the conditions *under which* we should ascribe consciousness. Thus he says, characteristically, that "the claim that animate organisms are purposive can . . . be interpreted as the claim that their behavior, or some range of it, can only be accounted for as action". Furthermore, his well-known criticism of early behaviorism (Hull [1973], [1943]; Skinner [1953]) in terms of the unavoidability of *teleological* explanations is not as such responsive to the question of consciousness; for, on his own view, there may well be teleological but non-sentient systems.

Consider, therefore, that, for a teleological system, *biological universals* rather than merely nomic universals may obtain. The point of the contrast is this. Nomic universals relate invariantly the structural or determinate physical properties of physical systems; but biological universals relate functional, abstract, or goal-oriented features of a physically realized system, or relate in functionally or informationally uniform ways structurally variable attributes and relations. Where physicalistic reduction obtains, biological universals (and their analogues in realized Turing machines) can always be replaced by nomic universals. Provisionally, where, in a biological system, reductionism is either not yet adequate on the evidence or, conceivably, not adequate in principle (cf. Grene [1974]), we note that a system "responds" to structurally different stimuli as if they were functionally similar. Circadian rhythms in plants, for example, where sentience does not obtain, may be offered as a reasonable specimen. If so, then, sentience requires that biological universals be mediated by the relevant activation of sensory sub-systems within the organism itself. How inconclusive this consideration actually is by itself is clear both from the obviously circular nature of general accounts of the causal theory of perception (cf. Grice [1961]; Pitcher [1971]; Margolis [1972a]) and from the nature of detailed cases. For example, Jean-Claude Ruwet [1972] cites an observation of von Uexküll's: "A mated female tick, sightless, but having a diffuse light sense in the skin, orients itself toward sunlight, climbing high up on a perch to lie in wait. It remains there as long as necessary, until it is alerted to the passage of a mammal by perceiving butyric acid emanating from the mammal's cutaneous secretions. Then, the tick lets itself drop and, with a little luck, comes in contact with its host. The impact induces the tick to move about on the surface of the mammal. When the tick finally encounters a hairless area of skin having a higher temperature, it stops there and begins to suck blood." Here, what one feels is that the phenomenon is not, though it involves the activation of relevant senses, cognitively perceptual. The reason, roughly, is that the creature does not, in context, show a sufficient capacity for perceptually learned responses, that the responses are essentially too invariant (Tinbergen [1969]; Lorenz [1970]; Stenhouse [1973]). That sensory systems are activated encourages us to employ an information-processing model, but the idiom appears here to be more metaphorical than literal.

The distinction required is in fact much more delicate. Niko Tinbergen [1969] provides innumerable episodes in which "an innate releasing mechanism" accounts for the perceptually informed behavior of creatures, in which — precisely because they are notably capable of perceptual learning of a certain complexity and flexibility — we are inclined to treat the innately released behavior as entailing cognition or consciousness. For instance, he says: "Now a male stickleback often moves in a very special way. When encountering another male near the boundary of its territory (which is where most of the fighting takes place) it adopts a posture with the head pointed downward, holding itself in a very peculiar vertical position. Now it can easily be shown that a dummy will evoke a much more vigorous attack when it is presented in this 'threatening' position than when shown in a normal position. The fighting response of a male stickleback, therefore, is not only released by a red male, but also by the special movements (posturing) of a male. The response, therefore, is dependent on a combination of these two sign stimuli." On the other hand, Tinbergen himself resists construing 'instinctive activity' or 'instinctive act' as either exclusively "highly variable and adaptive in relation to a goal" or "entirely rigid" or "fixed". He holds rather that "the lower levels [of instinctive behavior] give rise to increasingly simple and more stereotyped movements, until at the level of the consummatory act we have to do with an entirely rigid component, the fixed pattern, and a more or less variable component, the taxis [the orienting mechanism], the variability of which, however, is entirely dependent on changes in the outer world. This seems to settle the controversy; the consummatory act is rigid, the higher patterns are purposive and adaptive. The dispute about whether 'instinctive behavior' is rigid or adaptive has been founded on the implicit and entirely wrong assumption that there is only one type of instinctive activity." Clearly, on Tinbergen's view, some form of perceptual discrimination — conceivably, perceptual learning — may be involved in instinctual behavior; hence, the ascription of consciousness depends very much on the virtuosity of the taxis and a given creature's capacity to learn behavior that deviates from fixed consummatory acts. David Stenhouse [1973], therefore, presses the possibility (following Lorenz [1965]) of "an innate or instinctive 'capacity or propensity to learn'." "In instinctive patterns which incorporate learned components", he maintains, "it is clear that if the final 'innate plus learned' configuration of behavior is to be adaptive the specific learnings within it must have been guided and directed so that they do in fact contribute (in the majority of cases anyway) to the final adaptiveness . . . guidance toward the appropriate learnings must be, in some sense of the word, 'innate'. It need not be argued that this 'guidance' should be determinative and rigid. It will not be an argument against its existence, that maladaptive learnings do on occasion occur."

Konrad Lorenz [1970], however, offers a particularly telling instance that can hardly be denied the status of perceptual sentience: "one of the few things which the young birds really learn from the adult birds in cases where the young remain with the parents for some time after fledging is *path-conditioning.* These conditioned pathways are so rigidly followed by jackdaws that one could almost speak of 'runways'. They are just as rigidly transmitted (or, more exactly, passed on as a tradition) from one generation to the next. This was very obvious when my colony of tame jackdaws had met with a mishap and I subsequently set some young birds together with the only surviving bird, an old female, in order to provide the germ of a new free-living jackdaw colony. The young jackdaws, twenty-nine of which were introduced to the adult female one-by-one in the course of two years, took over the conditioned pathways of the surviving adult so exactly that (to name one example) they still avoid those parts of the garden where our tom-cat used to hunt. The cat is long since dead and the juvenile birds have never seen him themselves. In view of the great part played by path-conditioning in birds which cannot be regarded as migratory and which are in any case occupying their breeding territory, it is not surprising that similar conditions operate along the migratory pathways followed by the birds when migrating by day in family groups. The 'knowledge' of the path to be followed is not innate; it is passed on as a tradition. Young Greylag geese, for example, will not usually migrate if there is no leader acquainted with the migratory route. In these birds, the only apparently instinctive factor is the general drive to fly large distances. They do not possess an accompanying inherited drive to hold to a particular direction, so that in hand-reared individuals the autumnal phase of migratory restlessness only results in unsystematic and non-directional wandering within a fairly small radius." Here, the pattern is obviously learned; the relative invariances are linked to goal-directed behavior; the determinately variable flight patterns are pertinently uniform in a functional sense; and the behavior is relevantly mediated by the activation of the senses.

The notion of functionally uniform sensory discrimination linked to individual and species survival or to the developed and learned interests of organisms (even in the face of physically anomalous elements) is strongly emphasized in accounts of the perception of humans and of animals (Gibson [1966]; Neisser [1967]; Bruner, Goodnow, and Austin [1956]). Donald Griffin [1976] for instance reports that bats appear to rely on a "cognitive map" or "spatial memory": in spite of their remarkable technique of echolocation, "when flying through thoroughly familiar surroundings, many bats seem to rely heavily on spatial memory", he says. "Although orientation sounds continue to be emitted in an apparently normal manner, the bats collide with newly placed obstacles and turn back from the former location of objects that have suddenly been removed." Ulric Neisser, who favors the thesis that perceptual constancies "operate *before* recognition, to make recognition possible", concedes that this "is not an invariable principle". It seems not unreasonable to theorize that there must be both non-epistemic sensory constancies to facilitate perception and that the biologically organized and learned interests of cognitively competent creatures affect perceptual constancy. Stated another way, there is good evidence that perceptual discrimination among both humans and animals depends on biologically favored similarities and that our own linguistically formulated distinctions must rest on these. This is a thesis that Quine [1970], [1960] has favored (though it is otherwise incompatible with his well-known insistence on the non-correlativity of word and sentence (cf. Margolis [1973b]). The important point, however, is that to perceive something in a cognitively relevant way is to be able, in some sense, to subsume what is perceived under a concept for which indefinitely many things, structurally variable, will also fall; and, secondly, that the way in which we construe things perceptually is very probably controlled, minimally, by certain ways in which fundamental perceptual arrays are biologically favored as yielding similarity. This must be part of the import of the fact that some creatures are instinctually so ordered that, without pre-cluding learning (baby chicks that peck for food pellets on hatching), they appear to be cognitively competent to sort things as similar in ways that favor survival; that human beings learn language and the first application of language to the perceivable things of the world from a prelinguistic basis at least partially analogous to that of creatures whose perceptual competence is organized instinctually and by imprinting; that although no *formulated* conceptual scheme can fail to be revisable (with ingenuity), the apparent unity of subsuming diverse things under common terms — the famous pro-blem of universals (cf. Aaron [1967]; Wolterstorff [1970]) — would be an utterly arbitrary arrangement, impossible to master from the vantage of non-linguistic skills, without (in Kantian terms) what may be called the constitutive function of a (biologically organized) imagination; and that perception itself appears to be a complex autonomous process of constructing a stable percep-tual field from at least a combination of subcognitive perceptual information (for instance, varying retinal images) and a hierarchically ordered (relatively) species-invariant (cognitive) detection of key features or patterns of any perceptual array (Lettvin *et al.* [1959]; Neisser [1967]; Gibson [1966]).

We may, therefore, postulate a biological basis that provides for the gradual emergence of all the forms of perceptual cognition: from the sensory but not cognitively significant responsiveness of lower organisms to (biologically) functional universals (cf. Best [1972]), through the intermediary capacity of cognitively qualified creatures in which perceptual learning is minimal, to the higher intermediary capacity of cognitively qualified creatures that depend increasingly on perceptual learning without achieving a language, to human infants that learn to master linguistically specified similarities on the strength of some prelinguistic perceptual competence, to linguistically trained persons capable of *introducing* symbolic distinctions with respect to which things are thereupon perceived to be similar. Again, in Kantian terms, the regulative function of linguistically specified concepts must (*contra* Goodman [1970]) depend, for biological reasons, on *some* prior constitutively functioning concepts (or concept-like regularities) by which the *non*-propositional objects of perception (and imagination) are cognitively discriminated. P. F. Strawson [1970] has put the (Kantian) point perspicuously: "There would be no question of counting any transient perception as a perception of an enduring and distinct object unless we were prepared or ready to count some different perceptions as perceptions of one and the same enduring and distinct object. The thought of *other* actual or possible perceptions as related in this way to the *present* perception has thus a peculiarly intimate relation to our counting or taking — to our ability to count or take — this present perception as the perception of such an object ... the past perceptions are *alive* in the present perception, which is not just a matter of an external, causal relation." The lion that tracks the eland must, if perceptual cognition be ascribed at all, be in a state functionally analogous to that of ourselves manipulating linguistic categories. Among biological universals, then, instinctual patterns for instance, cognitively emergent similarities may gradually be marked; and linguistic universals begin at least in tandem with prelinguistic perceptual and behavioral uniformities (Paivio [1971]; Stenhouse [1973]).

PART THREE

SENTIENCE AND CULTURE

CHAPTER 11

PSYCHOPHYSICAL INTERACTION

The normal consequence of defending the reality of consciousness, sentience, cognition is to confirm the causal role of mental states. And the admission of conscious, sentient, intelligent entities normally entails that the observable molar movements of such entities are, in some essential way, psychologically informed, that is, informed by particular *mental* states — and thereby construed as behavior. Such states are, at the very least, introduced to explain the apparently purposive congruence of sets of otherwise random or purposeless movements in accord with the functional requirements of minimal rationality, or, assuming the particular needs, wants, interests, perceptual capacities of particular kinds of creatures, with the coherence requirements of that particular network (Rundle [1972]). In short, the assumption that a system is *purposive* is simply the assumption that the functional properties of the system are informed by (Woodfield [1976]), and that it is causally affected by, its mental states — where, the ascription of mental states (to languageless creatures) presupposes a (heuristically formed) model of the species-typical rationality of such a creature. *If* 'good' is construed in such a way that the functioning of the parts of the system are said to be good only insofar as they contribute to the determinate goals *assigned* by our model of rationality or by analogous models applied to nonsentient systems, then we are not bound (*contra* Woodfield), in admitting purposiveness or "natural function", to defend the view "that a biological end of an organism is essentially a state or activity that is intrinsically good for the organism" (cf. Margolis [1975a], [1977h]). The "biological end" may be merely determinable; alternatively, it may signify a plausible way in which the functioning of an organism may be construed, not *the* end that it has in some essential way. Among persons — that is, entities possessing language — the general prudential ordering of life is given a variably determinate form by intervening doctrinal and ideological commitments (Margolis [1976], [1975b]); among sentient but languageless systems, apart from species survival, the interpretation of prudential interests is modelled on the human; and among nonsentient systems, plants for instance or the nonsentient subsystems of sentient systems, analogous arguments are, frankly, metaphorically developed. The intentionality of purposive systems is naturally facilitated by the assumption of sentience; the intentionality of nonsentient functional systems assigned an internal goal ('X does A in order to do F') inevitably obscures the difference between *how*, on an explanatory theory, a system functions typically or statistically and what *the* function of the system is supposed to be (cf. Wright [1976] ; Woodfield; Sorabji [1964]). These considerations bear also on the tenability of behaviorism and of epiphenomalism. For behaviorism is concerned with the conceptual connection alleged to hold between sentience and behavior; and epiphenomenalism, with the causal relationship between the *qualia* of direct experience and behavior or other psychological phenomena. An ulterior question, to which we shall return, concerns the tenability of psychophysical causality itself.

There are, of course, many forms of behaviorism. The most extreme and the most naive is attributable to J. B. Watson [1924], as in the claim that "We use the term *stimulus* in psychology as it is used in physiology", or as in the remark [1948], "I believe we can write a psychology . . . and never use the terms consciousness, mental states, mind, content, introspectively verifiable, imagery, and the like . . . It can be done in terms of stimulus and response . . .". Essentially the same reductive tendency appears in B. F. Skinner [1953], [1964]. The guiding assumption of this so-called radical behaviorism is apparently that mental concepts are meaningless or eliminable. Feigl [1967] holds that the denial of "the existence of raw feels", the *qualia* of direct experience (Meehl and Sellars [1956]), is "absurdly false". He takes notice, also, of methodological behaviorism, the thesis that "the subject matter of scientific and experimental psychology can be nothing but behavior", and logical behaviorism, which defines raw feels "in $physical_1$ observation terms" (where, by '$physical_1$', is meant the property of "a conceptual system anchored in sensory observation and designed for increasingly comprehensive and coherent explanations of the intersubjectively confirmable facts of observation"). Thus understood, it is argumentative whether so-called logical behaviorism must be confined to behavior in the sense posited by methodological behaviorism itself. Not only are mind/body and mental/functional identity theories open to substantial challenge, but Feigl himself maintains that "an adequate and plausible construal of mentalistic concepts by explicit definition on the basis of purely *behavioral* concepts" is simply not forthcoming: "mind is not identifiable with behavior" and "to maintain that planning, deliberation, preference, choice, volition, pleasure, pain, displeasure, love, hatred, attention, vigilance, enthusiasm, grief, indignation, expectations, remembrances, hopes, wishes, etc. are not among the causal factors which determine human behavior, is to fly in the face of the commonest of evidence, or else to deviate in a strange and unjustifiable way from the ordinary use of language".

The elimination of mental concepts, then, includes the elimination both of "raw feels" and of intentional mental states. Radical behaviorism, it may be anticipated, fails to the extent both that "raw feels" cannot be eliminated and that purposive behavior cannot be adequately characterized non-intentionally. But the full import of these constraints is hardly clear.

The variations of behaviorism invite us to consider a large number of possible distinctions. A few are decisive. First of all, Watson's interpretation of 'stimulus' and 'response' entails that sentience can be reduced to mere physiological processes — *a fortiori*, that sentient organisms and persons are merely complex physical bodies. Where behavior is not construed merely as a complex set of responses in Watson's sense but is construed rather as cognitively informed (Tolman [1932]), it becomes conceptually impossible to avoid assuming a model of purposiveness or minimal rationality in terms of which the "molar responses" of an organism to its "stimuli" (as opposed to the "molecular" details Watson favored — the terms are Tolman's) may be specified: 'stimulus' and 'response' must themselves be construed, in such a context, in sentient or cognitively pertinent ways. What needs to be emphasized is that *if* behavior is construed in terms of structural/functional invariances or as programmed in the manner of automata or as falling below the threshold of consciousness, or if construing bodily movements teleologically is a metaphor or a *façon de parler*, or if actions or behavior may be explained in terms of physiological laws alone, then there will be no need to introduce purposive activity, that is, activity entailing an awareness of and striving after intentional goals, "on the same order as [our awareness of] our immediate experience" (McDougall [1934]), or else sentience can, with equal (and equally vacuous) facility, be extended to automata (cf. Suppes [1969a]; Summerhoff [1974]). Otherwise, it is impossible to identify all mental states with behavior or behavioral dispositions, and it is impossible even to specify the central cases of (cognitively informed) behavior except in terms of a relevant set of postulated central mental states (Scriven [1956]). For one thing, mental states need not always be manifested in actual behavior or in behavioral dispositions (however they may be supposed to be detected): we are always, therefore, confronted with the empirical possibility of "minimal skepticism", that is, that there may be no observable behavioral evidence sufficient to confirm an actual and determinate mental state — for instance, as in suddenly remembering one's father or in having a mental image of one's father. In this regard, Jerry Fodor [1968] usefully defines behaviorism as committed to construing the following proposition (*P*) as a necessary truth:

"for each mental predicate that can be employed in a psychological explanation, there must be at least one description of behavior to which it bears a
logical connection" ('logical connection' may be construed in as weak a way
as one wants, as for instance, in not entailing either a necessary or sufficient
condition; hence, an entire range of alternative forms of behaviorism may be
generated). The rejection of behaviorism, as in construing mental states as the
causes of behavior (cf. Armstrong [1968]), at once entails "minimal skepticism" (and what Fodor terms "mentalism" — the denial of "necessarily *P*"
— a thesis to be distinguished from that of dualism).

Another consideration is this. Although observable stimuli and responses
must be of a physical nature or at least physically realized, the concepts of
stimulus and response are functionally defined and may, therefore, take an
indefinite variety of particular physical forms: without an empirically satisfactory invariance thesis, there is no way, except in terms of purposiveness
and cognition, to characterize behavior one way or another (Taylor [1964];
Ryle [1949]; White [1967]). *Assuming* the limitations of a digital computer
because of the nature of the task to be performed, W. I. Matson [1976] holds
for instance that "there is no standard tiger shape, considering all the angles
and distances from which a tiger may be seen and the postures it may be in.
There is no template, nor set of them, that we can store in the computer with
instructions that anything matching one of these is to be considered a tiger."
The pattern recognition problem affects animals as well as persons. So
behaviorism must be supplemented at the very least by the admission of
mental states, regardless of what theory we may adopt about their analysis
(Armstrong [1968]). Also, the complexity of our initial assumptions regarding
the coherence of wants, beliefs, perceptions and the like or of rule-following
capacities depends entirely on the functional or purposive characterization of
the range of behavior to be described and explained. In the nature of the case,
linguistic behavior is the most advanced and the most variable with respect to
its possible manifestations. The untenability of a behavioristic theory of
language, therefore, may be expected to reveal most perspicuously the
ineliminability of intentional mental states *vis-à-vis* the cognitively informed
behavior of higher animals and human beings. Still, (*contra* Chomsky [1959],
[1966], [1972]), the defeat of a behavioristic theory of language ought not
to be construed as the defeat of empiricism with respect to language.

The best-known behaviorist theory of language is W. V. Quine's [1960],
though Skinner's [1957] appeared somewhat earlier. Quine claims that "The
recovery of a man's current language from his currently observed responses is
the task of the linguist who, *unaided by an interpreter*, is out to penetrate

and translate a language hitherto unknown. All the objective data he has to go on are the forces that he sees impinging on the native's *surfaces* and the observable behavior, vocal and otherwise, of the native" [italics added]. On Quine's view, the learning of languages that are bilingually accessible and the infant's learning of his first language are fundamentally like the field linguist's learning a utterly alien language, and the latter case requires a strictly behavioristic account. But if the learning of a first language is *sui generis* (*contra* Goodman [1967]) and if learning an alien language (having a first) is (for that reason) not significantly unlike learning a second language for which there are competent bilinguals, then the principal conceptual issue concerns whether we are driven to a behavioristic account in talking in general about the learning of second languages, whether behaviorism is itself intrinsically viable, and what may be the bearing of the probable inadequacy of behaviorism to explain first-language learning, on our theorizing about the learning of a second.

The critical issues are (i) that Quine's behavioristic account of language actually generates and must generate conceptual puzzles that it cannot itself coherently admit and, therefore, cannot possibly solve; and (ii) that behaviorism is demonstrably inadequate when applied to linguistic behavior. The conjunction of these two findings obviates the need for Quine's well-known skepticism regarding the understanding and translation of language – in particular, undermines his theories of the indeterminacy of radical translation and the inscrutability of reference.

Consider the principle of the indeterminacy of translation. Briefly put, Quine's thesis is this: "manuals for translating one language into another can be set up in divergent ways all compatible with the totality of speech dispositions, yet incompatible with one another". But *if* the presumed indeterminacy of translation holds in the face of *no detectable behavioral discrepancy* for a given range of non-verbal stimulations, on the basis of which the field linguist is expected to set up his translation manual, then it is obvious that, *even for Quine*, the linguistically relevant divergences presuppose that linguists (the field linguist among them) cannot coherently be restricted to nothing but behavioristically admissible data. For, if they were thus restricted, what Quine calls an indeterminacy could not even arise or be recognized: sentences would or would not be equivalent on behavioristic grounds, and that would be that. Semantic differences among sentences occupy a place in a theory of mind analogous to that of mental states; consequently, the failure of Quine's theory is analogous to the failure of a behavioral reduction of mental states. To admit that two sentences may differ in semantic import though their use in speech behavior need not be detectably different is tantamount to denying the adequacy of extensional (or behavioral) criteria of such import.

To admit the question of indeterminacy is, implicitly, to admit the inadequacy of a behavioristic theory of language, and to hold to the adequacy of the latter is to preclude the question. Quine cannot have it both ways. On the other hand, although the question seems entirely eligible, there is, if we are not confined to behaviorism, no reason to suppose it cannot be fairly met in a way that obviates skepticism. For, if we suppose that linguistic non-equivalences are detectable even though not correlated with behavioral differences, merely to be able to fix such differences seems to go a long way toward the denial of indeterminacy. Certainly, it precludes radical indeterminacy and obliges us to construe given indeterminacies as relatively benign empirical problems for which our inductive evidence may still be inadequate. Empirical ignorance is simply not a conceptual issue of the order of importance of that of radical indeterminacy of translation.

The alleged inscrutability of reference fares no better and is, indeed, a somewhat specialized application of the principle just considered. For, on Quine's view, behaviorism pretty well gives us a fair manual of translation for *a certain range of sentences* having, as he puts it, relatively firm, direct "links" with non-verbal stimulation, but it breaks down utterly when we come to specifying the words of the native's vocabulary, in particular, the terms that designate the things he refers to. The passage in which Quine advances this thesis is deservedly famous. He imagines the field linguist studying his alien language and, noting the "stimulus synonymy" (that is, the behavioristically contrived correspondence) of the "occasion sentences" 'Gavagai' and 'Rabbit' (sentences purportedly "called forth" on the occasion of an appropriate sensory stimulation, possibly, as we would say, either when a rabbit or a counterfeit rabbit is visually present), he speculates: "Who knows but what the objects to which this term [that is, 'gavagai'] applies are not rabbits after all, but mere stages, or brief temporal segments, of rabbits? In either event the stimulus situations that prompt assent to 'Gavagai' would be the same as 'Rabbit'. Or perhaps the objects to which 'gavagai' applies are all and sundry undetached parts of rabbits; again the stimulus meaning would register no difference. When from the sameness of stimulus meanings of 'Gavagai' and 'Rabbit' the linguist leaps to the conclusion that a gavagai is a whole enduring rabbit, he is just taking for granted that the native is enough like us to have a brief general term for rabbits and no brief general term for rabbit stages or parts ... The distinction between concrete and abstract object, as well as that between general and singular term is independent of stimulus meaning ...

Synonymy of 'Gavagai' and 'Rabbit' as sentences turns on considerations of prompted assent; not so synonymy of them as terms." This thesis turns out to be as incoherent as the first (behavioristically construed) and, in fact, it may be shown to be incoherent even if we do not confine ourselves to a behavioristic theory of language.

The counterargument is relatively straightforward. For, we must suppose, in studying the native speaker behaviorally (but not committing ourselves to an exclusively behavioristic theory of language), that the sensory stimulations to which the native appropriately responds by performing some bit of verbal behavior *can actually be fixed*. That's all there's to it: if the stimulations can be fixed, then we have at the very least a fair approximation of some range of the speaker's *terms* and not merely a jungle manual matching unanalyzed *sentences*. The importance of this conclusion ought not to be underestimated, for the specification of a speaker's terms are conceptually linked to our theory of (our model of rationality linking) the range of wants, beliefs, perceptual capacities ascribable to him, in virtue of which what these designate may be detailed. Consider, for one thing, that the behavioral approach must suppose that the speaker's *verbal responses*, "prompted" (as Quine explicitly insists) by certain surface stimulations, must be discriminated in some cognitively relevant way by the speaker. If they are not, then there is no sense in which the native is affirming anything about the perceivable order of things: the stimulation cannot then be said to *prompt* his response; he cannot be said to *assent* to any query about anything; and there remains no sense in which his utterance may then be relevantly construed (on the hypothesis) as a *sentence* having some determinate meaning. Nevertheless, when Quine discusses "the native's assent to 'Gavagai?'" he offers two entirely divergent observations regarding stimulation. His point is that what prompts the native's assent are "stimulations and not rabbits", because, after all, we must allow for counterfeit rabbits, variations in angle, lighting, and the like which might make a difference. Perfectly reasonable. When, however, he begins to generalize about stimulation, he says that "a visual stimulation is perhaps best identified, for present purposes, with the pattern of *chromatic irradiation of the eye*" [italics added] – which, in effect, returns us to Watson. But *that* would mean that stimulations are to be specified in ways that are *not* cognitively accessible to the speaker the dilemma is clear: if the stimulations are cognitively accessible and, proceeding behaviorally, we can fix them, then we do have some grasp of the native speaker's *terms* (*because* we have some grasp of his interests and perceptual abilities and the like) and the radical inscrutability of reference becomes untenable; and if we hold to the thesis and/or construe stimulations in a *non*-cognitive sense, we shall not be able to speak even of the stimulus-meaning of the native's *sentences*. The same conclusion follows if we admit, with Quine, that we can fix the native speaker's *assent* and *dissent*; for, there is no way to determine these unless we construe the relevant stimulations in a way that is cognitively accessible to the speaker. Again, the same conclusion follows if we suppose, with Quine, that we are interested in the stimulations that "prompt" or "elicit" the native's verbal responses, not irrelevancies or discountable errors or the like.

It may well be that semantical and syntactical differences of considerable importance obtain among different languages and that our terms are not matched one for one with those of other cultures. But this is, once again, a relatively benign, empirical matter, given intra- and interlinguistic communication. There is no room for the radical inscrutability of reference: the very notion of understanding the native speaker's *sentences*, within limits, entails some grasp of his *terms*. 'Sentence' and 'term' are indissolubly linked distinctions. The ulterior question of the possible range of divergence among the terms of the entire family of human languages is an important and independent issue. But we may, even at this point, venture that an adequate theory of perception, of physiological processes, of work and behavior, cannot but set considerable constraints on alternative conceptual networks and, ultimately, on alternative ontologies. (This has already been adumbrated by the concept of "biological universals".) To admit the correlativity of words and sentences *and* a theory of language that relies on, or is even restricted to, behavioral data cannot fail to set minimal but significant constraints on conceptual systems and ontologies. But to admit *that* is, in effect, to draw a conclusion from Quine's own way of proceeding that is diametrically opposed to some of his most favored doctrines.

Another line of inquiry leads to the conclusion that behaviorism as such is untenable not only as far as linguistic phenomena are concerned but also when applied to mental and behavioral phenomena in general. For reasons of economy, we may confine our attention to the context of language, but relevant parallels will not be difficult to imagine. The key, once again, is conveniently provided by Quine's reflections: "We may [define] the *affirmative stimulus meaning* of a sentence [S] such as 'Gavagai', for a given speaker, as the class of all the stimulations (hence evolving ocular irradiation patterns between properly timed blindfoldings) that would prompt his assent." But, Quine asks, "What now of that strong conditional, the 'would' in our definition of stimulus meaning?": "Its use here is no worse than its use when we explain '*x* is soluble in water' meaning that *x* would dissolve if it were in water. What the strong conditional defines is a disposition, in this case a disposition to assent to or dissent from S when variously stimulated. The disposition may be presumed to be some subtle structural condition, like an allergy and like solubility . . .". Speaking thus, Quine quite correctly prefers a behaviorism that can admit central states of the organism, reference to which alone makes the explanation of *dispositions* possible; in this respect, rightly, he does not confine himself to the behaviorism espoused by Skinner [1953], [1957]. Nevertheless, he construes those central states solely in physical or causal terms that preclude *rules*, rulelike habits, intentional considerations, and the like, whatever is most distinctive about language and mind. Quine himself, it should be said, nowhere attempts to demonstrate the adequacy of a physicalist reduction of language or mind. In any case, in the absence of a successful reductive argument, the concept of a verbal disposition can hardly be freed from such considerations as *of norms of appropriate and inappropriate utterance and of the intention to conform to norms* (cf. Grice [1957]). Counterpart non-verbal dispositions linked to some suitable model of rationality will, of course, have to be similarly analyzed (as we have already seen in ascribing sentient states to animals). The breach of linguistic regularities is hardly physically impossible and may be analyzed in terms of inadvertence, error, misunderstanding, misinformation, ambiguous clues, and the like, whereas nothing remotely similar obtains with the causal or nomic regularities involved in allergies and solubility.

What this means is that the very notions of *stimulus* and *response*, in the behavioral setting, as opposed to the notions of temporally correlated *physical events*, presuppose central states of a sentient organism characterized in terms of purposes, drives, interests, habits, conformity with rules and norms, cognitive capacities, and the like — in short, presuppose mental states congruent with the constraints of minimal rationality. Stimuli and responses are not identified in terms of their merely physical properties but rather in terms of a governing theory of the intentionally significant dispositions of a given organism. An experimental rat seeking food, searches and eventually, on the basis of *perceptual discriminations* and *adjustments* in his behavior, *finds* his pellets. For cognitive agents, actions are relatively polymorphous as far as physical manifestation is concerned (Ryle [1949] ; White [1967]) and whatever laws may govern cognitively informed behavior must, as such, be construed in intentional terms (Taylor [1964]). Variable physical occurrences may be identified as, or as the "realization" of, the same stimulus or response — think of perceptual invariances under altered conditions of lighting, perspective, and the like (Gibson [1966]) — when suitably interpreted in accord

with the appropriate rulelike or intentional formula; and the relevant interpretation entails reference to categories that do not allow for directly predicating such properties of bare physical objects in a way that permits the required
reduction (Lewis [1966]). Physical events may be construed as emergent
actions or as embodying actions; neural states can only be *assigned* the intentional content of the mental states with which they are linked. Similarly,
sounds produced by alien natives may be construed as embodying speech.

In short, there is a functional condition, introduced by way of a theory of
human or animal behavior, in terms of which alone physical data may be
construed as *behaviorally* significant. Hence, it is quite impossible, on Quine's
hypothesis, for the field linguist to study the verbal behavior of alien speakers
without an initial theory about the grammar and vocabulary of the natives'
language or about the bearing of a deeper theory of the characteristic form of
life of the species studied upon the possible range of alternative languages —
that may well be adjusted on the basis of empirical findings. What Quine calls
the linguist's "analytical hypotheses" — *his* own "prior linguistic habits" by
means of which he translates the native's sentences, finding terms for what he
takes to be the native's terms — must, contrary to what Quine explicitly says,
operate from the very start of his study of the native's verbal behavior (cf.
Hirsch [1977]). Quine insists that the translations are "unverifiable" and
that that they "proceed without mishap must not be taken as pragmatic
evidence of good lexicography for mishap is impossible". But this conclusion
is simply the result of Quine's insistence on the linguist's confinement to
behavioral cues and surface stimulations and to his failure to concede the
implications of behavioral studies as such. The admission that the translations
provided are unverifiable in principle is simply incoherent in the very context
of basing translation on observable *verbal behavior*.

The truth, then, is that a field linguist must study an alien language in a
way that presupposes a theory precluding a radical behavioristic interpretation
of his own enterprise. He will subscribe, however informally, to what may be
called an ontological view of the difference between speech and physical
sound, or of action and movement, corresponding to differences already
noted between persons, sentient creatures, and physical bodies. This will
entail, as far as his empirical inquiry is concerned, assumptions about the
grammar of natural languages (doubtless confirmed by noting the relative
convergence of known languages and the testimony of bilinguals) and about
the categories governing reference and predication that his native speakers are
likely to have adopted (doubtless confirmed by a detailed knowledge of their
physiology, their perceptual and manual abilities or orientation, their wants,

interests, intentions and the like affecting whatever culturally prominent work or behavior may be ascribed to them). Under these circumstances, it seems most unreasonable to characterize the prospects of empirical inquiry into the semantic features of a language in radically skeptical terms. Also, if the foregoing be conceded, then, precisely because of the conceptually parasitic (heuristic) nature of ascriptions of mental states in non-verbal contexts, studies of the behavior of animals cannot but be derivatively informed by a reasoned adjustment of the very anthropomorphic categories in accord with which the purposive behavior of human beings is described and explained.

Radical behaviorism, then, is indefensible and inadequate on at least two counts: first, because it requires and cannot supplant the admission of central (intentionally qualified) mental states — not themselves reducible behavioristically — in order, precisely, to construe bodily movements as cognitively informed behavior; second, because the admission of cognitively accessible mental states entails the admission of the *qualia* or "raw feels" (Feigl [1967]) of direct experience. The admission of the *qualia* of sentience generates its own puzzles, several of which are distinctly tangential to our principal concern. These, the prospect of a purely phenomenal language of science and the provision of a public language regarding private mental states are troublesome only if the first is thought to be quite favorable or adequate and the second, impossible or unnecessary. As it happens, no phenomenal idiom of subjective experiential reports can be free from a conceptual dependence on a perceptual idiom addressed to publicly discriminable objects (cf. Carnap [1953], [1949]; Sellars [1963b]); and, although mentalistic terms cannot be analyzed in behavioral terms, nevertheless we cannot escape relying on behavioral and other public "criteria" (having a logical force normally weaker than that of either necessary or sufficient conditions), on which the learning of mentalistic terms initially depends and on the satisfaction of which intelligible and empirically supportable predications of mental states depend (Wittgenstein [1963]; Malcolm [1954]; Fodor [1968]). Apart from the so-called Wittgensteinianism of Norman Malcolm, first-person reports of immediate experience are normally admitted, certainly by phenomenalists (Carnap [1928]) and even by radical materialists (Smart [1962]; cf. Cornman [1968a]). Furthermore, Norman Malcolm's thesis is ultimately untenable, as may be seen from the following consideration. Malcolm [1954] summarizes (not necessarily canonically [Geach (1957)]) Wittgenstein's notion of what is involved in apparently referring to (private) sensations thus: "Wittgenstein asks the question 'How do words *refer* to sensations?' transforms it into the question 'How does a human being learn the meaning of the names of sensations?' and gives this answer: 'Words are connected with the primitive, the natural expressions of the sensation and used in their place. A child has hurt himself and he cries; and then the adults talk to him and *teach* him [italics added] exclamations and, later, sentences. They teach the child new pain behavior' (*Philosophical Investigations*, 244). Wittgenstein must be talking about how it is that a human being learns to refer with words to his *own* sensations — about how he *learns* [italics added] to use 'I am in pain'; not about how he learns to use 'He is in pain.' What Wittgenstein is saying is indeed radically different from the notion that I learn what 'I am in pain' means by fixing my attention on a 'certain' sensation and calling it 'pain'. But is he saying that what I do instead is to fix my attention on my *expressions* of pain and call them 'pain'? Is he saying that the word 'pain' means crying? 'On the contrary: the verbal expression of pain replaces crying and does not describe it' (244). My words for sensations are used *in place of* the behavior that is the natural expression of the sensations; they do not *refer* to it." This justly famous passage fails, however, to explain how it is possible to *teach* a child to use words to *replace* natural expressions *of* pain, when such expressions are not identical with pain and when their occurrence does not entail the occurrence of pain or the occurrence of pain, their occurrence. If a child learns to make the replacement, then there would seem to be no coherent way in which to admit the achievement except by admitting that one can refer to one's own pain and report its occurrence. The matter is even clearer in the instance of mental images for which there is no remotely relevant (image) behavior (Margolis [1966a]).

What remains troublesome is the threat of epiphenomenalism. By epiphenomenalism, we may understand (Feigl [1967]) "the hypothesis of a one-one correlation of Ψ's to (some, not all) $\emptyset$'s, with determinism (or as much of it as allowed for by modern physics) holding for the $\emptyset$-series, and of course the 'dangling' nomological relations connecting the Ψ's with the $\emptyset$'s". Epiphenomenalism "has generally been considered objectionable", Feigl adds, "because it denies the causal efficacy of raw feels; and because it introduces peculiar lawlike relations between cerebral events and mental events. These correlation laws are utterly different from any other laws of (physical$_2$) science [bearing on the reduction of biological phenomena] in that, first, they are nomological 'danglers', i.e., relations which connect intersubjectively confirmable events with events which *ex hypothesi* are in principle not intersubjectively and independently confirmable . . . And second, these correlation laws would, unlike other correlation laws in the natural sciences be (again *ex hypothesi*) absolutely underivable from the premises of even the most inclusive and enriched set of postulates of any future theoretical physics or biology." Epiphenomenalism, in this sense, is a thesis somethat more restricted than the view attributable to T. A. Huxley [1893], in accord with which even "volition, which is a state of consciousness . . . has not the slightest community of nature with matter in motion". But this itself gives us a clue to the most reasonable account.

We need not save mental and physical interactionism by way of a dualism of energy (Shope [1971]), by construing (McDougall [1934]) psychic energy and activity as "no less causally efficacious" than physical energy and activity — though fundamentally of a different nature (*horme*) (cf. Boden [1972]). For one thing, states of consciousness are functionally ascribed to sentient creatures or persons in such a way that their physical states, to which the intentional content of mental states may be assigned, may enter into physical$_1$ interactions (that is, [Feigl (1967)], "processes which can be described [and possibly explained or predicted] in the concepts of a language with an intersubjective observation basis"). Secondly, if mentalistic descriptions of private experience are, in principle, introduced in and controlled by public discourse, then the very intelligibility of private reference entails, however informal the connection, a physical$_1$ language. Even these considerations force some qualification of the objection against "nomological danglers", at least as Feigl has formulated it. But more than this, "raw feels", of whatever range they may be thought to be (Meehl and Sellars [1956]), are no more than the phenomenal *content* of direct experience, whatever is privately claimed to be (in the first person) the experienced quality of experience: in this sense (*contra* Feigl) no causal role need be assigned to "raw feels" as such, since, for conceptual reasons, they cannot be detached from states of consciousness (. . . having or feeling such felt qualities) which *do* enter into causal relations — as functional states (events, processes) emergently linked to particular physical states (events, processes). Otherwise, the term equivocally signifies *the very states of experiencing qualia* that do enter into causal interactions. Hence, epiphenomenalism may be eliminated in the sense that there is no causal efficacy of "raw feels" to deny. To speak of sentient information below the threshold of consciousness is not yet to speak of "raw feels". Such information may, by way of construing physical states and processes cybernetically, enter into causal relations; but epiphenomenalism is irrelevant there. Above the threshold of consciousness, *being in the state of being directly aware of* . . . pains, images, "appeared-to" phenomena (Chisholm [1957]) and the like may well enter into causal relations; but again, epiphenomenalism is irrelevant there. In short, such states are simply central mental states: if intentional, their content must be assigned to associated physical states; if "raw feels", they are not as such, being intransitive (*contra* Armstrong [1962]), *perceptually* accessible. The *qualia* of direct experience are benign, then, with respect to empirical science, not because they are "nomological danglers" but because they enter into descriptive discourse only as the intransitive accusatives (Margolis [1973a]) of verbs of sentience and awareness; that is, they "exist" only insofar as they are "felt". But feeling a pain or "having" a mental image — not pains or mental images *tout court* — *does* enter into causal relations.

The issue is a strenuous one and invites a trimmer summary. Consider, then, that Descartes does not satisfactorily sort the different kinds of mental phenomena. Certainly, states like those of belief and desire are quite different from states like those of (having) pain or images. The first are intentional states that, in Brentano's [1973] sense, are "directed upon" an object, are such that they may be assigned propositional content. Pain is more troublesome precisely because it is not intentional in the same sense. Brentano himself was much exercised by the difference, and he takes care to distinguish "between pain in the sense in which the term describes the apparent condition of a part of the body [which is a physical condition], and the feeling of pain which is connected with the concomitant sensation [which is a mental condition]". The important consideration is this. Intentionally qualified mental states, with the exception of awareness, need not be (occurrently) conscious states: one may well believe or desire something without being aware of it; here, it is only intentionality that distinguishes the mental and the merely physical. But though sensations and images lack intentionality in the sense of belief and desire, they are normally not admissible except in the context of awareness (which undoubtedly explains the foundationalist penchant for claiming the indubitability of direct experience (cf. Chisholm [1966]; Margolis [1977i]; Lehrer [1973]). Hence, sensations and images are always embedded in mental states or events that, for their part, *do* exhibit intentionality in at least the sense (not quite canonically rendered, in Brentano's terms) (i) that what is discriminated may be rendered propositionally ("that there is a pain in my left upper molar") and (ii) that the mode of sentience involved is an intransitive mode (that is, that discriminating pain is not a form of perception [*contra* Pitcher (1970)], that "pain exists only in being felt"). Both sorts of mental states, therefore, exhibit properties that mark what is meant by the privacy of mental states — which is neither to confirm indubitability (*contra* Baier [1962]) nor to deny public information about such states. Now then, intentionally qualified mental states are, in effect, states in which abstract, functional properties are "realized" (in Putnam's sense [1960]) in some determinate physical form (to admit that angels may have beliefs is merely to admit that functionalism is not materialism). Such states are ascribed to suitably selected entities (sentient creatures, persons) in virtue of a theory of the species-typical life of such entities — *relative to which*, evidence regarding the molar movements of the systems in question is construed as behaviorally significant and, therefore, as signifying the presence of particular intentional states. Hence, on a theory, functional properties are assigned to suitably selected physical states: the resulting systems are (in Feigl's sense [1967]) emergent. On the other hand, sensations and images, suitably embedded in cognitive states, preserve both the "raw feels" (the phenomenal qualities marked in first-person direct experience) and the functional (propositional) import of one's being aware of such states. Hence, the complex mental state, the state of being aware of one's sensations or images, must be "realized" in the same way in which the simpler intentional states are; undoubtedly, also, there may well be other physical (*a fortiori*, non-propositional) differences to be noted in the way in which sensations are realized as opposed to the way in which beliefs are realized. Sensations (and beliefs) are private in the proprietary sense and in the phenomenal sense of first-person awareness; they are publicly accessible in the sense that behavioral evidence regarding their onset and occurrence are available. In the case of sensations (and images), "minimal skepticism" (Fodor [1968]) concerns the occurrence of the relevant phen--mena but also the correct phenomenal characterization of what is felt or "had" (*contra* Stevens [1935]; cf. Savage [1970]); in the case of beliefs and similar mental states, it concerns also the correct intentional object (the intensional or propositional characterization of that object) of the state in question. On this view, epiphenomenalism simply confuses the content of intentional states with those states themselves or fails to observe that such phenomena as sensations and images occur only embedded in cognitively or consciously qualified states regarding which the same (epiphenomenalist) error obtains. And radical behaviorism simply fails to notice that 'behavior', in the sense relevant for psychology, signifies that the molar movements of a system are both intentionally informed and produced by particular mental states. Thus, a hand movement constitutes (or "embodies") a signal and is produced by particular beliefs, desires, intentions and the like.

Causal interaction between mental states and physical states is, of course, impressively varied. A man decides to utter a greeting to another and his mouth and throat somehow are appropriately set into motion in accord with his intention; or, in understanding and favoring another's sexual advances, certain autonomic processes – sweating, blood flow, hearbeat – will be instantly altered; or, influenced by and conforming to a particular hypnotic suggestion, one will, under seemingly anomalous conditions, stand motionless on one foot and have a sensory-like experience as of smelling roses. The most extraordinary and illuminating commonplaces of psychophysical interaction and control concern, not merely such exotic disciplines as those of the yoga and Zen masters (Wallace and Benson [1972]) but also and even more impressively, the testable and untrained competence of ordinary people to alter deliberately, though indirectly and without involving the voluntary skeletal musculature, bodily conditions known to be controlled autonomically; or else, phenomena involving rather simple training in the control of autonomic processes (so-called biofeedback) (DiCara [1970]; N. Miller [1969]; Nowlis and Kamiya [1970]; Shapiro, Tursky, and Schwartz [1970]). Thus, on the instruction to increase one's heartbeat, one can set oneself to imagine that one has been running strenuously (*not*, usually, "willing" one's heartbeat to increase) and the heartbeat will increase; or, on the instruction to reduce the temperature of the forehead, one can imagine an icepack on one's forehead and thereby lower the surface temperature within a desired interval. There is no plausible explanation of such phenomena that does not admit that intentional mental states involving imagination may trigger and modify biological invariances governing behavior, autonomic processes, and perception that are closely linked to the conditions of species-survival of the human animal and, possibly, the higher mammals as well (cf. Kolers and Eden [1968]; Richardson [1969]; Ohwaki and Kihara [1953]; Perky [1910]; Haber and Haber [1964]; Sperling [1960]; Gibson [1966]; Neisser [1967]; Dement *et al.* [1970]; Siegel and West [1975]). The concession bears nicely on the causal explanation of weakness of will (*akrasia*).

But *can* there be psychophysical laws?

The most intriguing negative view of the question has been advanced by Donald Davidson [1970], since Davidson is prepared to argue both that mental events play a causal role and that mental events are identical with physical events. The triad appears inconsistent; Davidson attempts to demonstrate that it is not. Reductionists like Paul Feyerabend [1963b] of course, noting precisely that the identity thesis entails the causal efficacy of mental events and the formulability of psychophysical laws, favors the elimination of mental events altogether – assuming "that the only entities existing in the world are atoms, aggregates of atoms and that the only properties and relations are the properties of, and the relations between such aggregates" – and the correspondingly radical retranslation of relevant sentences. The issue is clearly strategic, because it links in a dialectically focussed way the alternatives of several kinds of reductive materialism, dualistic interactionism, and the possible viability of nonreductive materialism. The eliminative materialist, wishing to avoid the identity thesis and psychophysical laws, rejects mental phenomena as real, preferring to construe the idiom of mental discourse as a certain picturesque vestige. Clearly, the force of this maneuver rests with an appraisal of the adequacy of a replacement idiom of the physicalistic sort. In particular, it rests with a systematic replacement for talk of sentience, intentional action, and speech and thought (cf. Cornman [1968a], [1968b]). Herbert Feigl [1967] concedes, with his usual candor, that, though still holding to identity and therefore (in a weak sense) to interactionism, he now believes himself to have been mistaken in admitting psychophysical laws: in the " 'finished' scientific conception of the world . . . there would be no need for the phenomenal terms – just as there would be no need for typically biological or physiological concepts"; his own former disposition to allow nomological danglers as "innocuous" was simply mistaken. Feigl reports himself now to be somewhat more in sympathy with J. J. C. Smart than with Feyerabend. In this respect, Feigl's view is perhaps even more sanguine than Davidson's, since Davidson says nothing about the working details of actually replacing the idiom of the mental. Still, there is a puzzle to be faced. In Feigl's latest account, it would appear that interactionism is itself a "category mistake", because it involves "mixing phenomenal and physical language" in the causal context; whereas, in Davidson's view, the causal interaction of the mental and physical is openly and fully conceded – it is only the formulation of psychophysical laws that is rejected. We have already accommodated Feigl's difficulty in resolving the problem of epiphenomenalism. We may reasonably reject a full-blooded dualistic account; there seem to be no promising grounds on which to support, empirically, the co-presence of a distinct, nonmaterial substance. But if, by "dualism", one merely means to concede the causal interaction of the mental and the physical or the formulability of psychophysical laws, without a Cartesian interpretation, then the concessions of Davidson and the later Feigl – not to mention those of the earlier Feigl and what the eliminative materialists believe to be the import of the identity thesis – lend some force to the position.

To enter nonreductive materialism in the lists is a little more complicated. The nonreductive materialist is committed (i) to the real occurrence of mental and psychological phenomena, (ii) to the untenability of Cartesian dualism, and (iii) to the inadequacy of the identity thesis. By (i), his position differs from Feyerabend's; and by (iii), his position differs from Davidson's and Feigl's. If he accepts (iv) the interaction of mental and physical phenomena, say, with Davidson, then he still faces the question of whether psychophysical laws are formulable. He may reject (iv), but then it would appear that he *must* hold a position very much like Feigl's earlier position except (a most important matter) for his rejection of (iii), the identity thesis. The difference would then be that the nonreductive materialist would hold a sort of double-aspect (or epiphenomenalist) theory (much like the earlier Feigl), in which the mental aspect, however, precludes causal interaction. But, if he accepts (iv), the nonreductive materialist would, like Davidson – and unlike the later Feigl – face the prospect of an inconsistent triad. Alternatively put, the threat of inconsistency does *not* depend on adopting the identity thesis; it depends on admitting the reality of mental phenomena *and* causal interaction. So the relative force of the identity theorist's position and the nonreductive materialist's regarding psychophysical laws depends on the alternative possibilities for interpreting the relationship between causal contexts and contexts of causal explanation. They do not depend on the tenability of the identity thesis, which, in any case, is merely advocated, hardly independently defended, by Davidson.

The interesting form of the question with which we began, then, is this: Assuming psychophysical interaction, can there be psychophysical laws? The options are all controlled by the admissibility of a principle (or, possibly, analogues of the principle) that Davidson himself assumes. He calls it "the Principle of the Nomological Character of Causality": that "where there is causality, there must be a law: events related as cause and effect fall under strict deterministic laws". It should be noted that the two explicative clauses need not be taken as equivalent: the first asserts only that causality falls under laws; the second, that causal laws are strict deterministic laws. In a footnote to the remark, Davidson concedes that his own argument does not require "that the laws be deterministic", that he will relax the condition in the sequel. Hence, there is no reason to deny, in the context of Davidson's argument – or even more generally – that causal laws can be probabilistic in form (cf. Hempel [1965], [1966]).

On this condition, the options are as follows: (a) the admission of psychophysical interaction entails that there are psychophysical laws; (b) since causal contexts and contexts of causal explanation are of logically different sorts and since causal explanations function by subsuming individual events under causal laws, it does not follow that psychophysical interaction entails that there are psychophysical laws; and (c) since causal laws have the distinctive logical properties that they do, it is impossible, even admitting psychophysical interaction, that there are psychophysical laws. Davidson's purpose is to show both that his original triad is consistent (selecting in effect the (b)-option) and that there are no psychophysical laws (selecting in effect the (c)-option). The counterargument requires at least defeating (c); a stronger argument would defeat (b) as well. If it could be provided, then, a materialist would be obliged either to reject psychophysical interaction (say, by the strategies of Feyerabend or the later Feigl) or to admit psychophysical laws, regardless of whether he was initially an identity theorist or a nonreductive materialist. The advantage of putting the argument in this way is simply that the pressures on any reductive materialism that concedes (i) (the real occurrence of mental and psychological phenomena) and (iv) (the interaction of mental and physical phenomena) are extremely great once (v) the irreducibility of the intentional and of the intensional (even under a variety of interpretations) is conceded (cf. Sellars [1963a]). For if the mental and the psychological are essentially characterized in intentional and intensional terms (admitting the great variety of relevant phenomena, not claiming that they can be characterized under a single and all-comprehensive interpretation of intentionality, and not attempting here to provide a satisfactory account of the intentional) (cf. Cornman [1962]), there would seem to be *no* sufficiently potent version of materialism that could sustain the identity thesis.

So, if option (a) obtains (that the admission of psychophysical interaction entails that there are psychophysical laws) and if (v) be admitted (the irreducibility of intentionality), then a materialist must be a nonreductive materialist – in at the least the sense of not being (A) an eliminative materialist (like Feyerabend or Richard Rorty [1965], and of not being (B) an identity theorist (like Smart [1962] or Davidson). The nonreducibility of the intentional would also exclude the kind of explanatory reductionism advocated by Feigl himself, that is, (C) the adequacy of a "physical$_2$" system of explanatory concepts – in which "the type of concepts and laws which suffice in principle for the explanation and prediction of inorganic processes" can be satisfactorily extended to "the phenomena of organic life". The strategy is as important as the argument, here. It is an essential part of Davidson's account that the admission of (i) and (iv) (the reality and causal efficacy of mental phenomena) do not preclude reductionism of either the (B) or (C) sort (the identity thesis or explanatory reductionism). On Davidson's view and on the view of a great many other theorists who favor reductionism, it is only if (C) is untenable (whether or not [(B)] is supported) that the most serious blow to reductionistic programs will have been struck. But if (i) and (iv) *and* (v) be admitted (the irreducibility of the intentional), then (C) will have been defeated, psychophysical laws would have to be admitted *if* explanation obtained at all, and we would in effect be committed to what had earlier been characterized as attribute dualism — that is, to the nonreducibility of the intentional to the nonintentional. In short, we would be committed to a thoroughly non-reductionistic form of materialism.

The pivotal issue deserves to be made more explicit, even if we avoid here, for the sake of the dialectical aspect of the argument, attempting to formulate the nature of intentionality in an adequate way. Feigl [1967] provides the clue; for he admits that "*intentional* (in Brentano's sense) features [are] irreducible to a physicalistic description . . . though this does not seem to me a serious flaw in physicalism". *If* intentional features are irreducible, then *if* they do not qualify events in any way essential to their causal function (mental or psychological events) or do not relevantly qualify whatever it is that serves to explain events in a causal way (as by psychophysical laws), then their admission is, clearly, as Feigl says, not "a serious flaw in physicalism". But *if* option (a) obtains (so that causal interaction entails psychophysical laws), then the irreducibility of intentionality is absolutely decisive. Hence, the convergence, despite important differences, between Feigl's and Davidson's programs. For Feigl, after the Postscript to his *Essay*, wishes by the identity theory and a physical$_2$ language to replace the mental and the psychological in both causal and explanatory contexts; and for Davidson, the admission of the causal efficacy of the mental does not disturb reductionism since, holding to options (b) and (c), there are no psychophysical laws. In effect, for David-son, mental events causally interact with physical events *because mental events are physical events*. The position is rather close to that of Smart, whom Davidson cites somewhat favorably, except that Smart (be believes), as well as David Lewis [1966], fails to distinguish between particular events and kinds of events. The distinction is required in order to maintain that the original triad is consistent, that is, in particular, that some mental events enter into causal relations, that causality is nomological, and that there are no psycho-physical laws: the nomological character of causality is intended to accommodate particular events that, *qua* physical, enter into causal contexts; whereas psychophysical laws would require a nomic connection between *kinds* of mental and kinds of physical events — which Davidson resists.

The alternative strategies are now reasonably clear, and we can turn to Davidson's particular argument. With respect to psychophysical laws, Davidson offers four possibilities, viz. *nomological monism* (say, the positions of Smart, Feigl, Feyerabend); *nomological dualism* (say, parallelism, epiphenomalism); *anomalous dualism* (which Davidson believes Cartesianism illustrates, but perhaps occasionalism would illustrate better);and finally, *anomalous monism* (which, he says, "classifies the position I wish to occupy"). Davidson characterizes anomalous monism as a position that "resembles materialism in its claim that all events are physical, but rejects the thesis, usually considered essential to materialism, that mental phenomena can be given purely physical explanations". Interestingly, then, Davidson takes the rejection of psychophysical laws to be sufficient to disallow the term "reductionism", though the support of psychophysical identities is itself normally taken as a form of reductionism.

Here, both Davidson's argument and the counterargument depend on admitting the extensionality of (psychophysical) identity and of (psychophysical) causal contexts. The two theses are, in fact, linked in his account. Thus he says: "The demonstration of identity follows easily. Suppose *m*, a mental event, caused *p*, a physical event; then under some description *m* and *p* instantiate a strict law. This law can only be physical, according to [its having been shown that the mental does not . . . constitute a closed system]. But if *m* falls under a physical law, it has a physical description; which is to say it is a physical event. An analogous argument works when a physical event causes a mental event. So every mental event that is causally related to a physical event is a physical event." Mental events, taken distributively, enter into causal relations; but since causality is nomological, they can do so only because they are identical with physical events; only a physical system constitutes an appropriately closed system exhibiting such laws. We know, therefore, that some mental events (at least) are identical with particular physical events, though we may not know with which ones: the "anomalism of the Mental" arises because "there are no strict laws at all on the basis of which we can predict and explain mental phenomena". In fact, Davidson says quite explicitly: "Causality and identity are relations between individual events no matter how described. But laws are linguistic; and so events can instantiate laws, and hence be explained or predicted in the light of laws, only as those events are described in one or another way. The principle of causal interaction deals with events in extension and is therefore blind to the mental-physical dichotomy. The principle of the anomalism of the mental concerns events described as mental, for events are mental only as described".

This is admirably clear. But is it defensible? It seems not, for an extremely simple reason. Whatever the peculiarities of the idiom regarding the mental, *the idiom is sufficiently successful in individuating mental events so that such events can be identified extensionally*. Davidson's identity thesis makes this clear, and his causal thesis makes this clear. That is, both identity and causal contexts behave extensionally *and* mental events, designated as such, may, veridically, have predicated of them their being identical with given physical events and their having caused or having been caused by given physical events. But if this much is granted, then there cannot be any *linguistic* difficulty regarding the mental idiom that would disqualify psychophysical laws. It may well be *empirically* difficult to formulate psychophysical laws — though there is reason to think, for example, that psychopharmacological laws are not impossible (cf. Valzelli [1973]). Davidson concedes that *any* mental event that enters into causal relations may, as such, be extensionally identified and is identical with some particular physical event, even if we are unable to identify that physical event with which it is identical. Hence, whatever they are, the peculiarities of the mental idiom cannot be such as to defeat our specifying *kinds* of events that enter into causal relations: if they did, there would be no basis on which we should ever know that a particular mental event entered into a causal relation with a physical event. If we have a set of mental events that are known to have entered into causal relations with physical events, what is to prevent us from theorizing about the kinds of properties those events exhibit in virtue of which they instantiate causal laws? Certainly not the language of the mental itself — for it was the use of that very language that facilitated our detection of particular psychophysical relations. Certainly not the (putative) truth that the mental cannot form a closed system — for the psychophysical relations detected presuppose, if they presuppose anything at all, that the joint domain of the mental and the physical forms a closed system. The only possibility open to Davidson rests with the logical peculiarities of explanations in the domain of the mental. And in fact, that is precisely what he depends upon.

There are two foci in Davidson's argument. One has already been cited, that is, that causal laws are "linguistic", are specified only in explanatory contexts, and that events are said to instantiate laws (are explained or predicted in the light of laws) only under a favorable description. Explanatory contexts behave non-extensionally (cf. Davidson [1963], [1969b]). But since this is uniformly true for both physical and mental phenomena, it cannot be that the mere intensionality of explanatory contexts accounts for the inadmissibility of psychophysical laws: physical laws would have to be precluded as well. Furthermore, even though causal laws are linguistic, we must suppose that valid laws are congruent with the actual regularities that hold among events of just the kinds of which the laws provide a perspicuous formulation. At the very least, this means that the psychophysical regularities exhibited by a set of mental and physical events admitted to enter, as particulars, into causal relations lend some evidence in support of psychophysical laws. More weakly put, whatever reason we have for construing psychophysical generalizations as not lawlike in nature, we cannot argue to that conclusion either from the actual occurrence of causal events of the psychophysical sort or from the conceptual features of causal laws. As Davidson puts the matter: "The thesis is . . . that the mental is nomologically irreducible: there may be *true* general statements relating the mental and the physical, statements that have the logical form of a law; but they are not *lawlike* (in a strong sense to be described). If by absurdly remote chance we were to stumble on a non-stochastic true psychophysical generalization, we would have no reason to believe it more than roughly true." The question remains, why should it not be the case that some psychophysical generalizations are lawlike — are at least of the form of probabilistic laws; and why should it not be the case that *some* psychophysical generalizations can be refined to the point that they yield such laws?

Here, the second focus of the argument appears. For, Davidson is prepared to hold that "there are generalizations whose positive instances give us reason to believe the generalization itself can be improved by adding further provisons and conditions stated in the same general vocabulary as the original generalization". Such generalizations he terms *homonomic*, instantiated by physical laws. The apparent laws of mental phenomena are all, he thinks, *heteronomic*: they are "generalizations which when instantiated . . . give us reason to believe there is a precise law at work, but one that can be stated only by shifting to a different vocabulary". The trouble is that we have as yet no clear way in which to decide whether psychophysical generalizations are homonomic or heteronomic, as far as psychophysical laws are concerned. The reason is simply that the *vocabulary* of the initial generalizations is *already* psychophysical. Two cases arise. First of all, *if* there are psychophysical laws, then psychophysical generalizations are homonomic. Secondly, *if* there are physical laws by which to explain psychophysical generalizations, then, admitting the identity thesis, it is logically possible that the relevant lawlike formulations may be cast as well in psychophysical terms — again, homonomic. Hence, the burden of Davidson's argument rests with what he means when he says that the relevant law "can be stated *only* by shifting to a different [that is, a purely physical] vocabulary".

Apparently, on Davidson's view, "There are no strict psychophysical laws because of the disparate commitments of the mental and physical schemes"; in particular, "the attribution of mental phenomena must be responsible to the background of reasons, beliefs, and intentions of the individual". Davidson insists, therefore, that "there is a categorial difference between the mental and the physical". But if this were intended strictly, then Davidson would be unable to explain how it is that *some* mental events at least (he is prepared to favor the view that all mental events) enter into causal relations with other (physical) events. The "categorial difference" does not, on the thesis, preclude identity and causal claims; hence, it *may* not, for all we know, preclude psychophysical laws either. Or, if it excludes psychophysical laws, then *how* can it accommodate identity and causal claims? There is no clear answer.

But there is a clue. Davidson wishes to argue that the specification of particular beliefs, desires and the like is controlled by "the constitutive ideal of rationality"; and that that ideal must be an "evolving" one, subject to the drift of accumulating evidence. Fair enough. But is this not also true of physical theory, in spite of the fact that physical phenomena are not specified in terms of an ideal of rationality? Certainly, the characteristic Quinean emphasis in Davidson's account on testing theories *en bloc*, on pragmatic adjustment, on indeterminacy of translation, forces the point. On the other hand, *if* what he wishes to stress is that, for particular cases, the role of rationality is such that we cannot individuate mental events extensionally — because, relative to rationality, there are always alternative designations of mental events within given causal contexts, where we cannot say whether particular designations identify the same or different mental events (cf. Armstrong [1973]) — then Davidson cannot maintain, as he obviously intends, that particular mental events enter into causal relations and are identical with particular physical events. Either, therefore, emphasis on the evolving nature of our theories of the mental is too strong, in that physical theories are similarly affected; or else emphasis on the indeterminacy of intentional contexts is too strong, in that identity and causality would be precluded as well as psychophysical laws. The fact that we are "typically interested" in explanations of mental events in terms of purposiveness, "in a conceptual framework removed from the direct reach of physical law by describing both cause and effect, reason and action, as aspects of a portrait of a human agent", seems true but irrelevant. The reason is simply that, on Davidson's own thesis, mental events *do* enter into causal relations and *are* capable of being identified with particular physical events. There is, therefore, a fundamental dilemma confronting Davidson's account: either, admitting mental causality, Davidson must admit the possibility of psychophysical laws; or denying psychophysical laws, he must deny mental causality. But that there are psychophysical causal interactions seems extremely difficult to deny. As Davidson himself says, "if someone sank the

Bismarck, then various mental events such as perceivings, notings, calculations, judgments, decisions, intentional actions and changes of belief played a causal role in the sinking of the *Bismarck*". It is difficult to improve on the reasonableness of this admission.

Our conclusion then must be that there are psychophysical laws: the possibility of psychophysical laws cannot be denied; empirical evidence supports the formulation of psychophysical laws; but, granting the irreducibility of the intentional, psychophysical laws cannot be nomic universals. Davidson is right in a sense, then, when he says that there are no psychophysical laws. For he means to emphasize that would-be psychophysical laws cannot be nomic universals *and* that genuine laws are nomic universals. But if the identity thesis is denied and the irreducibility of the intentional admitted, then to hold that mental events enter into causal relations is, effectively, to deny that the laws by which mental events are to be explained *are* nomic universals. Hence, there is as yet no reason to deny psychophysical laws. Alternatively, if identity is affirmed and laws are taken as nomic universals, then Davidson cannot have shown that psychophysical laws cannot be nomic universals. (We shall return to the full import of these concessions later.)

There remains a further thread to be caught up. For, as we have seen, admitting psychophysical interaction, (iv) precludes eliminative materialism but not the identity thesis. In fact, (iv), particularly in the form that Davidson advocates, does not preclude explanatory reductionism of the sort Feigl favors, that is, the explanatory adequacy of a physical$_2$ vocabulary. It is really only if (v) is established (that is, the irreducibility of intentionality) or some suitable analogue, that the admission of (iv) and, now, the entailed conclusion that there are psychophysical laws *may* force us to adopt a form of nonreductive materialism. We have already seen that Feigl concedes the irreducibility of the intentional, which is also admitted (or insisted on) by others (Sellars [1964]; Körner [1966]). But Feigl takes this irreducibility to be not "a serious flaw in physicalism". The question is, why? Here (as we have already seen), Feigl appeals to Sellars' argument that the "irreducibility is on a par with (if not a special case of) the irreducibility of logical categories to psychological or physiological ones". Hence, *if* the irreducibility of the intentional is conceded, and *if* (as has been argued) it is not the intentionality merely of language that is at stake but rather the intentionality of the *linguistic ability or mastery of human persons*, then the only viable form of materialism must be of a nonreductive sort. Conceding (iv) and (v), therefore, leads directly to nonreductive materialism. Consequently, if (i) there are real mental and psychological phenomena, and if (iv) mental and physical phenomena interact, then there are psychophysical laws; and if (v) the intentional is irreducible (characterizes the very nature of human persons and of the higher animals at least), then only a form of nonreductive materialism can be a viable form of materialism.

CHAPTER 12

THE NATURE AND IDENTITY OF CULTURAL ENTITIES

To characterize persons as cultural entities is to subsume at least a portion of psychological theory under the theory of culture. This breeds complications both because the nature of other sentient creatures and a large part of the sentient nature of man, an animal with a distinctive biological endowment, are not to be explained in cultural terms and because much that counts as cultural phenomena befalls entities that are not themselves endowed with minds. The intersection of the psychological and the cultural serves as well to focus our attention on the possible continuities and discontinuities between the natural sciences and what are variously called the behavioral or social or human sciences. That is, it challenges the assumption of the unity of science (Neurath *et al.* [1955]). It challenges it in two ways at one stroke: admitting the distinction of persons and other cultural entities, admitting the irreducibility of the intentional (Sellars [1963a]), entails that the methodology appropriate to physics and its allied sciences are inadequate for the explanation of the phenomena in question; *a fortiori*, it entails the untenability of physicalism.

Now, cultural entities have a peculiar and distinctive ontology. Persons obviously count as the principal kind of cultural entity, since it is by the activity of persons that words and sentences, works of art, artifacts, and machines are produced — the other principal kinds of cultural entities. Special problems attach to the admission of collective entities (such as nations) or of actions (conventional or symbolic or linguistic actions), but they do not affect the generalizations intended.

A convenient way of understanding certain of the ontological puzzles that cultural entities generate is afforded by attending to the central inconsistency of P. F. Strawson's [1959] well-known account of "descriptive metaphysics". Strawson holds that "we can make it clear to each other what or which particular things our discourse is about because we can fit together each other's reports and stories into a single picture of the world; and the framework of that picture is a unitary spatio-temporal framework, of one temporal and three spatial dimensions". In accord with this picture, Strawson inquires as to whether there is "any one distinguishable class or category of particulars such that, as things are, it would not be possible to make all the identifying references which we do make to particulars of other classes, unless we make identifying references to particulars of that class, whereas it would be possible to make all the identifying references we do make to particulars of that class without making identifying reference to particulars of other classes". Such particulars, in effect, constitute the framework within which the identification and reindentification of particulars are achieved. Strawson's answer is that "only those [things] satisfy these requirements which are, or possess, material bodies — in a broad sense of the expression". The solution at this point, because of the hedging in the phrase "are, or possess, material bodies", is open to both reductive and nonreductive materialism. Strawson himself opts for a nonreductive materialism because he holds that both persons and physical bodies are basic particulars. On Strawson's view, physical bodies cannot count as the proper parts of persons, since, on that view, persons could not be basic particulars; and persons cannot count as physical bodies, since, on the hypothesis, they are distinct entities with distinct kinds of attributes. In fact, on Strawson's view, "M-predicates" (designating material or physical attributes) are ascribable to both physical bodies and persons; but "P-predicates" (designating states of consciousness) are ascribable only to persons. The latter, as he says, are "of a certain unique type": "the concept of a person is to be understood as the concept of a type of entity such that *both* predicates ascribing states of consciousness *and* predicates ascribing corporeal characteristics, a physical situation &c. are equally applicable to an individual entity of that type". It is clear, from Strawson's reflections on the identification and reidentification of places and the identification and reidentification of things, that he is committed to holding that each particular thing occupies one place at a time (cf. Quinton [1973]): this is, in fact, the motivating insight of his entire scheme of descriptive metaphysics. But it is obvious that, on his own view, persons and physical bodies *can occupy the very same place*, in spite of the fact (i) that they are not identical with one another, (ii) that they are entities of quite different kinds, and (iii) that neither is a proper part of the other. There appears to be no way of reconciling these internal features of Strawson's account; furthermore, the inconsistency does not depend on an adequate theory of persons — as we have seen, Strawsonian persons are actually sentient animals. Hence, *if* Strawson is right about physical bodies *and* sentient creatures being basic particulars, we have already exhibited the untenability of a familiar assumption made by nearly all schemes for the identification of particulars within a materialist ontology. Hence, it may reasonably be maintained that persons, true persons, entities capable of language, also count as basic particulars. Whatever arguments support the irreducibility of sentient creatures must support the irreducibility of persons, since persons, uniquely, are capable of speech acts, a heuristic model of which accounts for the distinction of sentient creatures themselves. They must, therefore, just as sentient creatures must, bear a relation to their bodies different from that of both identity and composition. In the case of sentient creatures, as we have already seen, all that is required is that the emergent intentional properties (including, in a suitably embedded way, the elements of sensation and of images) be functionally "realized" (in Putnam's sense [1960]) in some physical or structural system. The peculiarity of cultural entities, including persons, argues, however, that an utterly different relationship be conceded. In any case, it is fair to suppose that nonreductive materialists will have to admit that two particulars (of certain kinds) can occupy the same place. This explains in part the appeal of reductionism, but it is hardly a reason for flinching.

Strawson is clearly committed — in holding that "persons, having corporeal characteristics, perceptibly occupying space and time, can be distinguished and identified, as other items having a material place in the spatio-temporal framework can be distinguished and identified [and] they can, of course be reidentified" — that each person has one and only one body. But he offers no evidence for the claim. He actually softens his thesis in an important respect when he maintains: "I am not denying that we might, in unusual circumstances, be prepared to speak of two persons alternately sharing a body, or of persons changing bodies &c. But none of these admissions counts against the thesis that the primary concept is that of a type of entity, a person, such that a person necessarily has corporeal attributes as well as other kinds of attributes." The point to notice is that the theory of the *nature* of a person does not in the least entail the necessary or sufficient or necessary and sufficient conditions for the individuation and reindentification of persons — here, also, Strawson is obviously thinking of persons proper. Strawson does *not* concede here that there may be two persons "occupying" the same body simultaneously: he only concedes that two persons may "alternately" share a body or change bodies. But *if* persons are basic particulars, then it is hard to see (or at any rate the explanation is lacking about) how two persons could share a body or exchange bodies; alternatively, if they could, then it is hard to see why it would be impossible for multiple persons to share one and the same body. Clearly, the reductive view that persons simply are bodies (Williams [1970]) would have to be rejected, since at the very least there cannot be more than one physical body occupying a given place (except where one is a proper part of another or shares a proper part of another). But *if* Strawson

228 SENTIENCE AND CULTURE

concedes that it is coherent to admit that two persons may alternately share the same body, then he is obviously committed to the view (a) that bodily identity is *not* a necessary or sufficient condition of personal identity, and (b) that personal identity *can* be managed on grounds other than those of occupying a certain spatio-temporal place. But if that is so, then there is no conceptual reason for denying the possibility that more than one person can share one and the same body. Of course, none of these reflections need be construed as favoring Strawson's apparent relapse into dualism, in considering the intelligibility of disembodied existence (cf. Penelhum [1970]; Price [1965]).

We may hold in abeyance the provisional finding that the *identity* of persons does not depend on the identity of bodies, even though, rejecting dualism and espousing materialism, the *nature* of persons is such (agreeing with Strawson) that persons "have" bodies (which can be independently reidentified). There is a venerable tradition beginning with John Locke (despite Locke's notorious difficulties in appealing to memory as a criterion of personal identity) that personal identity does not depend upon or does not always depend upon bodily identity (cf. Quinton [1962]; Shoemaker [1959]; Grice [1941]; Parfit [1971]; Perry [1975]). But we may come back to our speculations on this issue when we have considered some more fundamental features of the nature of persons and of other cultural entities. For, it is extraordinary how few philosophers concerned with the problem of personal identity have bothered to say anything of the nature of persons, on the apparent assumption that a full-fledged theory could not be expected to alter our initial intuitions about numerical identity.

Here, we must remember that persons have been defined as beings essentially capable of using language, of performing speech acts (Austin [1962]; Searle [1969]). The general empiricist theory of language acquisition advanced earlier on entails that persons are essentially culturally emergent entities, since, on the thesis, it is only by being a member of a language-using community that one can learn a natural language – and since language itself, *a fortiori*, linguistic ability, is physicalistically irreducible. Furthermore, again on empiricist grounds (but also even on rationalist grounds), the learning of a language presupposes a sentient capacity to discriminate the physical marks or sounds or the like by means of which words and sentences are somehow conveyed or communicated. So a person is a sentient, culturally emergent being capable of using language.

The most characteristic activities of persons include reporting one's mental states, organizing or sustaining social groupings in terms of formulated objectives or rationalizations, inventing or making or doing things to serve interests to which one's society's explicable norms would apply, and discoursing with one another. The central role of language is obvious. But also, various other items that emerge in a cultural setting — artifacts, works of art, sentences, machines, possibly also actions and institutions and organized groups — clearly depend on the initiative of persons. This is not to advocate a social contract theory of any sort, merely to emphasize that the executive energy of a culture rests with the efforts of individual persons, whether acting singly or in concert, whether by deliberate choice or by induced habit or ideology.

We are liable not to notice, therefore, that, regarding what persons do or produce, a measure of tolerance obtains as to how we should characterize the objects yielded by human activity. For example, we may say that a word or sentence is an entity, a particular of a distinctive sort. But if we say so, we are bound to notice that words and sentences can hardly be identified with the marks or sounds by which they are conveyed. For one thing, words and sentences, in and only in a suitably selected cultural context, are recognizably such or even function as such. For another, words and sentences "have" meanings or are inherently meaningful. For a third, their being meaningful is a functional property of some sort, determined in accord with the rulelike regularities of a language and even of the distinctive rulelike regularities of an enveloping culture that are explicitly not those of linguistic phenomena. For a fourth, there are no formulably determinate physical constraints regarding which determinate marks or sounds alone could serve as the "medium" for a particular word or sentence. There is no algorithm for generating all and only those physical marks or sounds that can serve, in a cultural context, to convey a string of words or a set of sentences. The alarming complexity of speculating about what sort of thing a word or sentence is, therefore, encourages the view that language is itself to be understood as no more than a distinct way of functioning which physical sounds and marks (a kind of inscriptionalism) (cf. Goodman [1966]; Scheffler [1963]) sometimes serve. In itself, this is a possible way of speaking, though it is misleading or noticeably incomplete, for the sounds and marks assigned their appropriate function must be interpreted as such by persons, who cannot, as we have seen (*contra* Sellars [1963a]) be similarly construed as physical bodies or even sentient creatures merely assigned a certain "additional" (linguistic) role. Linguistic ability is too essential to the nature of persons; and, as the characteristic agents of speech, we could hardly deny that we are distinctive entities of some sort — if there are any entities at all.

Of course, there is a fair sense in which whatever can be discriminated in the world may be the subject of some predication: in that sense, whatever is actual may be treated as an entity. But to say this — as has already been suggested, in noting the problem of making distinct predications of pains and of experiences of pain — is simply to say that reference and predication (and quantification) are merely grammatical activities and do not as such (*contra* Quine [1953]; cf. Alston [1958]) entail any ontic commitment. But if this is so, then inscriptionalism, whatever may be assumed to be its contribution to nominalism, entails a distinction between the natural order of physical marks and the cultural order of linguistic functions somehow conveyed by those marks. Insofar as inscriptionalism cannot produce a physicalistic reduction of persons, in virtue of which words and sentences are discriminated as such, no conceptual disadvantage accrues in treating words and sentences as entities of a distinct kind, that is, as the subjects of some discourse. But if so, then since words and sentences exist only in a cultural context, in which alone their functional properties may be discerned, *under circumstances in which they cannot be identified as particular words and sentences by reference to any fixed set of physical marks*, they are bound to generate problems of identity peculiar to themselves and to similar cultural entities. It should be noted that, on the inscriptionalist view, an impossible condition is imposed on the set of sentences of any natural language, viz. (Scheffler): "two sentence-inscriptions represent the same sentence if and only if they are *replicas* of each other (i.e., are spelled exactly alike), have similar language affiliation (i.e., both are French, both Italian, etc.), and lack indicator terms (i.e., term-inscriptions which are replicas, though one appears in one of the sentence-inscriptions with one denotation, and another appears in the other sentence-inscription with differing denotation)"; the most recent refinement of such constraints, proposed by Nelson Goodman [1968] leads to inevitable anomalies regarding natural languages and their notations (cf. Margolis [1970]). No formulable rule *can* be given by which to set constraints on the admissible range of physical marks that may count as instances of the same sentence in a natural language; and the constraints on belonging to the same language and having the same denotation depend on intentional considerations that appear to be extensionally irreducible. In any event, *if* we choose to treat words and sentences as entities, or works of art, or persons, we shall have to concede the ontological complexities that result from their exhibiting the peculiar properties that they do. Also, it is not farfetched to think that, thus construed, the principal kinds of cultural entities should exhibit an essentially similar ontology, in spite of the fact that some "have" minds and some are merely produced or created by those entities that do have minds.

Let us, therefore, sort these features without initially introducing persons. The detour will not take us far afield, will in fact confirm the important respect in which the problem of relating physical nature and culture may be seen as an analogue of the mind/body problem. Our principal findings will be the following: (i) that cultural entities are tokens-of-a-type, which is to say, particulars (tokens) that instantiate abstract particulars (types); and (ii) that cultural entities are embodied in physical entities, with which they are not identical. If so, then cultural entities — notably, persons — have rather unusual ontological properties; for nowhere else do we find particulars instantiated by other particulars, and the relationship of embodiment is distinctive of the cultural domain. In fact, it is because cultural entities are tokens-of-a-type that they exhibit the relationship of embodiment.

Consider, then, for example, Jack Glickman's [1976] remark, reflecting on a variety of culturally significant creations: "Particulars are made, types created." The remark is a strategic one, but it is either false or misleading. Glickman offers as an instance of the distinction he has in mind, the following: "If the chef created a new soup, he created a new kind of soup, a new recipe; he may not have made the soup [that is, some particular pot of soup]." *If*, by 'kind', Glickman means to signify a universal of some sort, then, since universals are not created (or destroyed), it could not be the case that the chef "created" a new soup, a new kind of soup (cf. Wolterstorff [1975]; Margolis [1977b]). It must be the case that the chef, *in* making a particular (new) soup, created in some sense (to use Glickman's idiom) a kind of soup; otherwise, of course, that the chef created a new (kind of) soup may be evidenced by his having formulated a relevant recipe (which locution, in its own turn, shows the same ambiguity between type and token).

What is important, here, may not meet the eye at once. If he can be said to create (to invent) a (new kind of) soup, and if universals cannot be created or destroyed, then, in creating a kind of soup, a chef must be creating something other than a universal. The odd thing is that a kind of soup thus created is thought to be individuated among related creations; hence, it appears to be a particular of some sort. But also, *a kind* of soup must be an abstract entity if it is a particular at all. Hence, although it may be possible to admit abstract particulars in principle (cf. Goodman [1966]), it is difficult to concede that what the chef created *is* an abstract particular *if* one may be said to have *tasted* what the chef created. The analogy with art (and also with words and sentences and persons) is plain. If Picasso had only created a new *kind* of painting, in painting *Les Demoiselles d'Avignon*, he could not have done so *by using oils*; and if persons were abstract entities, then they could not age or bathe.

There is only one solution *if* we mean to speak in this way. It must be possible to instantiate particulars (of a certain kind or of certain kinds) as well as to instantiate universals or properties. The term 'type' — in all contexts in which the type/token ambiguity arises — that is, all and only cultural contexts, signifies abstract particulars of a kind that can themselves be instantiated. Thus, printings properly pulled from Dürer's etching plate for *Melancholia I* are instances of *that* etching; but *bona fide* instances of *Melancholia I* need not have all their relevant physical properties in common, since later printings and printings that follow a touching up of the plate or printings that are themselves touched up may be genuine instances of *Melancholia I* and still differ markedly from one another — at least to the sensitive eye. The same is clearly true of words and sentences. Also, a forgery of a Dürer may not be relevantly distinguishable from a genuine Dürer (cf. Goodman [1968]; Margolis [1977j]) in terms of its perceivable properties, and a parrot may produce a sound that, uttered by a human in a relevant cultural context, would convey a word. Such entities as works of art and words, therefore, are identifiable as such only in the inten*t*ional context of a culture and only relative to certain inten*s*ional distinctions of what is admissible and inadmissible. So to think of types as particulars (of a distinctive kind) accommodates the fact that we individuate works of art in unusual ways — performances of the same (piece of) music, printings of the same etching, copies of the same novel — and that works of art may be created and destroyed. The same is true of language itself: we speak of different instances of *the same particular word*; and at least some human languages have surely been lost. If, further, we grant that, in creating a new soup, a chef stirred the ingredients in his pot and that, in creating a new kind of painting, in painting *Les Demoiselles*, Picasso applied paint to canvas, we see that it is at least normally the case that one does not create a new kind of soup or a new kind of painting without (in Glickman's words) making a particular soup or a particular painting. In general, then, when an artist *creates* a new kind of art, he *makes* a particular instance (or token) of a particular type. He cannot create the universals that are newly instantiated by what he has created, since universals cannot be created. He can create a new type-particular but he can do so only by making a token-particular of that type. Hence, there are actually no types of art that are not instantiated by some token-instances or for which we lack a notation (not the work itself) by reference to which (as in the performing arts) admissible token-instances of the particular type-work may be generated (cf. Margolis [1977c]).

The reason for this strengthened conclusion has already been given. When an artist creates his work using the materials of his craft, the work he produces must have some perceptible physical properties at least; but it could not have such properties if the work were merely an abstract particular (or, of course, a universal) (*contra* Wolterstorff [1975]; cf. Wollheim [1968]). Hence, wherever an artist produces his work directly, even a new kind of work, he cannot be producing an abstract particular; he could only be producing a particular token having certain physical properties that instantiated the abstract type that he is creating; also, he need not have made, in creating his work, the entire set of tokens of the *particular* work he has created. With the chef's soup and drama (and often even with etchings) the point is quite clear. Alternatively put, to credit an artist with having created a new *type* of art – a particular art-type – we must (normally) be thus crediting him in virtue of the particular (token) work he has made or of the notation (he has deposited) for generating tokens of the work. In wood sculpture, it may be admitted, the particular piece an artist makes is normally the unique instance or token of his work; in bronzes, it is more usually true that, as shown by Rodin's peculiarly industrious methods, there are several or numerous tokens of the very same (type) sculpture. (Among persons, we normally admit only unique tokens; but the concept of clone persons or of reincarnation is not incoherent.) Hence, though we may credit the artist with having created the type, the type does not exist except instantiated in its proper tokens. We may, by a kind of courtesy, say that an artist who has produced the cast for a set of bronzes has created an artwork-type; but the fact is: (i) he has *made* a particular cast, and (ii) the cast he has made is not the work *created*. Similar considerations apply to an artist's preparing a musical notation for the sonata he has created: (i) the artist makes a token instance of a type notation; and (ii) all admissible instances of his sonata are so identified by reference to the notation. The result is that, insofar as he creates a type, an artist must make a token. A chef's assistant may actually make the first pot of soup – of the soup the chef has created, but the actual soup exists only when the pot is made. Credit to the chef in virtue of his recipe is partly an assurance that his authorship is to be acknowledged in each and every pot of soup that is properly an instance of his creation, whether he makes it or not; and it is partly a device for individuating proper token instances of particular type objects. But only the token instances *of* a type actually exist, and interest in the type is given point only in virtue of one's interest in actual or possible tokens – as in actual or contemplated performances of a particular sonata.

Here, a second ontological oddity must be conceded. For consider that a particular printing of Dürer's *Melancholia I* has the property of being a particular token of *Melancholia I* (the artwork-type), but the physical paper and physical print do not, on any familiar view, have the property of being a token of a type. Similarly, the particular printed word 'the' is a token of the type word THE, but the physical marks that convey the token word do not, on any familiar view, constitute as such tokens of any type. Only subjects having *such* intentional properties as that of "being created" or of "having meaning" or "symbolic import" or the like can have the property of being a token of a type (cf. Peirce [1939]). In short, only objects that exist as culturally emergent entities can have the property. A token and the physical "medium" by which it is conveyed or through which it actually exists must, therefore, exhibit a distinctive relationship. We may call that relationship "embodiment", understanding by the term a relationship that holds at least between physical bodies and entities that exist only in a cultural setting but that cannot actually exist except *via* a physical body of some sort. Clearly, the relationship can avoid ontic dualism and accommodate cultural emergence if and only if (a) cultural entities cannot exist independently of physical entities; and (b) cultural entities cannot be physicalistically reduced. In this sense, the notion of embodiment promises a solution to Strawson's dilemma about basic particulars, since it is quite possible that persons be basic particulars at the same time they satisfy conditions (a) and (b).

The meaning of 'embodiment' has already been given. But the necessary and sufficient conditions for one particular's being embodied in another may be stated more explicitly then before: (i) two particulars thus related are not identical; (ii) the existence of the embodied particular presupposes the existence of the embodying particular; (iii) the embodied particular possesses some (at least) of the properties of the embodying particular; (iv) the embodied particular possesses properties that the embodying particular does not possess; (v) the embodied particular possesses properties of a kind that the embodying particular cannot possess; (vi) the individuation of the embodied particular presupposes the existence of some embodying particular, (vii) the embodying particular is not a proper part of the embodied particular. On a theory, for instance a theory about the nature of a work of art, a particular physical object will be taken to embody a particular object of another kind in such a way that a certain systematic relationship will hold between them. Thus, for instance, a sculptor will be said to make a particular sculpture by cutting a block of marble: Michelangelo's *Pietà* will (emergently) exhibit certain of the physical properties of the marble and certain representational and purposive properties as well; it will also have the property of being a unique token of the creation *Pietà*. The reason for theorizing thus is, quite simply, that works of art are the products of culturally informed labor and that physical objects are not. So seen, they must possess properties that physical objects, *qua* physical objects, do not and cannot possess, properties exploiting traditions, institutions, doctrines, rules, and the like.

So the dependencies of the two ontological traits mentioned are quite different. There are no types that are separable from tokens because there are no tokens except tokens-of-a-type. The very process for individuating tokens entails individuating types, that is, entails individuating different sets of particulars as the alternative tokens of this or that particular type. Tokens-of-a-type, then, have properties that physical objects lack; but possessing physical properties themselves, they cannot exist except embodied in some physical body. This is simply another way of saying that token objects are culturally emergent entities; that is, that exhibiting the distinctive properties they do and being the kind of entity that can exhibit such properties do not depend on the presence of any substance other than what may be ascribed to purely physical objects. Tokens are distinguished therefore solely by certain abstract functional or intentional properties realized in determinate physical ways.

We are claiming, then, that entities like persons, works of art, words and sentences are both physically embodied and culturally emergent. Embodiment serves jointly to facilitate an account of the individuation and identity of cultural entities and to advance a coherent nonreductive materialism; and emergence facilitates an account of the propriety of admitting the existence of particular cultural entities and constitutes resistance to reductionism. By 'emergence', we understand Feigl's [1967] sense of the term in the context in which he usefully distinguishes between 'physical$_1$' terms and 'physical$_2$' terms: "*If* . . . there is genuine emergence," Feigl says, "i.e., logical underivability, in the domains of organic, mental, and/or social phenomena, then the scope of 'physical$_2$' terms is clearly narrower than that of 'physical$_1$' theoretical terms." "By 'physical$_1$ terms'", Feigl says, "I mean *all* (empirical) terms whose specification of meaning essentially involves logical (necessary or, more usually, probabilistic) connections with the intersubjective observation language itself . . . By 'physical$_2$' I mean the kind of theoretical concepts (and statements) which are sufficient for the *explanation*, i.e., the deductive or probabilistic derivation, of the observation statements regarding the inorganic (lifeless) domain of nature." Clearly, to construe persons as culturally embodied entities entails, on Feigl's usage (though not on his own view), construing them as emergent entities as well.

We should perhaps note, briefly, other distinctions regarding the notion of emergence. For example, Mario Bunge [1977] holds that "an emergent thing (or just *emergent*) is one possessing properties that none of its components possesses". On Bunge's account, then, embodied entities are emergents. But on his view, "emergence is relative", since, for example, "the ability to think is an emergent property of the primate brain relative to its component neurons, but it is a resultant property of the primate because it is possessed by one of the latter's components, namely its brain". The example is not entirely happy, though the distinction is useful, since thinking is, on any usual view, a property of a creature or person or agent and not a property of any part of such a creature. (We have already considered the matter.) But Bunge wishes to support a number of distinct postulates, viz.: "Postulate 1. Some of the properties of every system are emergent"; "Postulate 2. Every emergent property of a system can be explained in terms of properties of its components and of the couplings amongst these"; "Postulate 3. Every thing belongs to some level or other"; "Postulate 4. Every complex thing belonging to a given level has self-assembled from things of the preceding level." Effectively, this is to resist reductionism in the precise sense that explanatory theories regarding the mental must involve "suitably enriching [lower-level theories] with new assumptions and data" — at the same time that the mental does not distinguish a distinct level since "the mind is not a thing composed of lower level things ... but a collection of functions of neuron assemblies". The trouble with Bunge's thesis is that, if the embodiment claim be admitted, then it is not clear how (or it is false that) Postulate 4 can accommodate the emergence of cultural phenomena; hence it is equally unclear how (or false that) Postulate 2 can hold. In any case, Feigl's conception of emergence ('emergence$_F$') essentially is defined in terms of the denial of reductive explanation; and Bunge's ('emergence$_B$') is defined in terms of the properties of wholes and of parts, though it also entails the denial of reductive explanation. Our own notion of emergence ('emergence$_M$') favors Feigl's conception, and is compatible with Bunge's to the extent that Postulates 2 and 4 are not conceded. But it is distinctive since it is addressed to the (emergent) existence of entities that can be specified only in certain intensional contexts. Hence, contrary to Postulate 4, persons (but not minds) *are* things that are not "self-assembled from things of the preceding level"; and contrary to Postulate 2, their distinctive (cultural) properties cannot be explained "in terms of properties of [their] components and of the couplings amongst these", however enriched by assumptions regarding things formed *in accord with* Postulate 4. If, then, we should specify the distinction of 'emergence$_M$' it should be this:

that the explanation of phenomena that are emergent$_M$ cannot be explained by theories that are not enriched with assumptions regarding embodied phenomena, where embodied phenomena are emergent$_F$ but are not emergent$_B$; they are not emergent$_B$, once again, because (i) they are not *composed* of the parts of some lower level things (for any theory of plural levels); and (ii) their properties are not explainable by reference to theories concerning things that are composed of the parts of lower level things.

By 'cultural', then, is meant the property of any system in virtue of which certain entities emerge and exist in it, a system in which *both* persons *and* what they characteristically produce or do as persons exist or once existed or occurred. A cultural system is a system of tokens-of-types. Such a system is at once rule-governed, in that what is typically produced is intelligible only in terms of rulelike regularities, and rule-following, in that persons are essentially capable of using language, of intentionally acting in accord with rules which they understand and are able to violate. But all discourse about rule-governed and rule-following phenomena and, in a fair sense, the phenomena themselves are intensional. Consider only that rulelike regularities provide for the distinction between such paired categories as "appropriate"/"inappropriate", "legitimate"/"illegitimate", "admissible"/"inadmissible", "correct"/"incorrect", "right"/"wrong", "good"/"bad", "beautiful"/"ugly", "legal"/"illegal", "meaningful"/"meaningless", and a host of others. Now, nothing can be ascribed such attributes, except under a relevant description, a description in accord with the postulated criteria by which, precisely, those attributes are rightly ascribed. But the intensional is at once essentially linguistic and cultural: only a creature capable of construing something *under one description rather than another* could possibly be said to understand the nature of a rule and to follow it intentionally. Furthermore, if reference (cf. Donnellan [1966]), if semantic ambiguity (cf. Ziff [1965]), if the inseparability of the surface and deep structure of language and the ineliminable bearing on meaning of background information and factual beliefs and presuppositions (cf. Lakoff [1971a]); Bennett [1976]), if the opacity of belief contexts and the like (cf. Margolis [1977e]) cannot be denied or overtaken by some extensionalist canon, then the inherent informality – the improvisational and incompletely formalizable aspect of cultural rules – begins to dawn on us, and with that, the profound sense in which human persons cannot be physicalistically reduced.

It is in this sense that the cultural is said to concern the "significant", and it is in this sense that rule-following behavior either is incipiently linguistic or presupposes linguistic ability. It is easy to see that reasons may arise, particularly with respect to complex, socially learned behavior among animals — not unlike the chimpanzee's learning of language — for which we might wish to concede that rule-following sequences obtain that are not yet fully linguistically informed. In all such cases, we also wonder whether we could train such animals to "speak". Some have even speculated that "free-ranging chimpanzees are already using a linguistic system [that] reflects a difference in species endowment, the two species [man and ape] having a syntax that encodes distinctly different kinds of information, which can be traced to differences in life conditions" (McNeill [1972]); but one suspects that that particular maneuver is intended to facilitate the rationalist theory of language acquisition. Also, the "language" of the bees may be discounted here, not because bees fail to communicate, but because their "language" is genetically fixed, not rule-governed at all, not intensional in character, not culturally emergent (Frisch [1955]; Frisch [1967]). Yet, it must be admitted that, even among the honeybees, lacking as we do a full account of what explains the variable import of a particular dance, given the changing circumstances of a hive's fortunes, we are inclined to fall back to thinking in terms of intensionally distinguished messages associated with what appear to be the same dance (cf. Griffin [1976]). Nevertheless, the evidence strongly supports the thesis that, however variable the apparent import of the dance, however genuine the capacity of bees to learn (cf. Gould [1975]), the bee language is an entirely extensional language reducible in principle to purely lawlike regularities. A few remarks of von Frisch's [1967] make this perfectly clear: "With increasing distance to the goal the dance tempo slows down; the number of circuits per unit time decreases; the duration of the individual circuits increases. The dance tempo indicates the distance of the goal. This regularity can be followed out to a range of 11 km. Different colonies may diverge somewhat in their tempo of dancing. During a single dance the dance tempo of an individual bee is not identical for all circuits; it varies about a mean value striven for. With different bees individual differences in the dance tempo are seen. Newcomers to the feeding place dance relatively rapidly; with increasing age since the first flight the dance tempo customarily becomes somewhat slower. Observations over a period of several days' flight to the same place suggest a decrease in the scatter of the indication of distance, as a result of greater experience. External factors may influence the dance tempo. (*a*) Dancing is somewhat more rapid when environmental temperature is high than when it is low. But the increase is so slight that as a rule it is demonstrable only statistically . . . (*b*) A headwind on the way to the feeding place acts like an increase in the distance: the dance tempo grows slower. A tailwind on the way to the goal speeds up the tempo of dancing." Yet, more tantalizingly, Konrad Lorenz [1970] deliberately speaks of the "traditional" routes that jackdaws favor in flight. Roughly what this means is that the communication skills of languageless animals are, actually, proto-linguistic or proto-cultural or else that the communicated habits of such animals begin to approximate the rulelike regularities of human societies.

Our principal concern, however, is with persons. If they are construed as culturally emergent entities in the manner sketched, then they exhibit the following peculiarities with regard to numerical identity: (i) being embodied in but not composed of physical bodies, persons can occupy one and the same place with their embodying bodies; (ii) though normally instantiated in a unique token, persons are tokens-of-a-type, hence may be multiply instantiated (as in the familiar claims of reincarnation and newer speculations about clone persons); (iii) in that their nature is essentially distinguished by their linguistic ability, persons are, however individuated and identified, marked as persons only in virtue of certain abstract functional properties; (iv) in that they are physically embodied, their existence depends on the existence of some embodying entity, the identity and nature of which neither constitute a sufficient condition of the *existence* of a person nor, on any obvious grounds, a necessary condition for the *identity* of a person; (v) if persons are marked by the coherent functioning of sentient states and linguistic abilities, then it is not impossible that multiple persons may simultaneously occupy the same body. In short, *if* particular persons, embodied in *some* body (suitably capable of sustaining the functional attributes of sentience and linguistic ability), may be identified in terms of some distinctive pattern of the functioning of sentient states and linguistic abilities, then bodily identity may be *a necessary condition for identifying a person* without being *a necessary condition of personal identity itself*.

This explains, for instance, the lack of force in Bernard Williams's [1957] contention that "bodily identity is always a necessary condition of personal identity where 'bodily identity' includes the notion of spatio-temporal continuity". For the essential consideration of Williams' argument depends on the seeming anomaly of admitting that two distinct persons might well undergo the same changes in virtue of which where one (on the argument) is supposed to be identical with some previously existing person, the other would also have to be thought to be identical with that person. On Williams' story, Charles, undergoing a "radical change of character", wakes up claiming "to remember witnessing certain events and doing certain actions" that appear to fit uniquely the "life-history of . . . Guy Fawkes". Williams argues (quite correctly) that "it is logically impossible that two different men should (correctly) remember being the man who did A or saw E; but it is not logically impossible that two different persons should *claim* to remember being this man ... ". He draws the conclusion from this "that we are not forced to accept the description of Charles's condition as his being identical with Guy Fawkes". But neither are we, so far forth, obliged to deny that Charles is identical with Guy Fawkes. Williams then offers a consideration in virtue of which "we should not be justified in accepting this [the favorable] description": "If it is logically possible that Charles should undergo the changes described, then it is logically possible that some other man should simultaneously undergo the same changes; e.g., that both Charles and his brother Robert should be found in this condition ... They cannot both be Guy Fawkes; if they were, Guy Fawkes would be in two places at once, which is absurd. Moreover, if they were both identical with Guy Fawkes, they would be identical with each other, which is also absurd ... We might instead say that one of them was identical with Guy Fawkes, and that the other was just like him; but this would be an utterly vacuous maneuver, since there would be *ex hypothesi* no principle determining which description was to apply to which."

Now, it is entirely possible, on the theory that persons (as cultural entities) are tokens-of-a-type, that both Charles and Robert, though different token-persons, may, on the hypothesis, be tokens of the same type-person – in fact, tokens of the same type-person of which Guy Fawkes was also a token. Just as we say that two different prints of Dürer's *Melancholia I* are the same (type) *etching*, so we may say that Charles and Robert and Guy Fawkes are the same (type) *persons*. So far, there is no incoherence. But then, if, on the evidence, Charles and Robert both remember "being the man who did A or saw E", then they must be different tokens of the same (type) person. Where reincarnation is assumed to obtain uniquely if it obtains at all, there will be no incoherence in claiming that Charles is one and the same token-person as Guy Fawkes. All that will be needed is a suitable causal connection linking the unique histories of Fawkes and Charles, so that "each" represents the same token at a different stage in a single career (as in aging or the like) and so that, as tokens-of-the-same-type, each represents a person-phase of the career of a unique token-person. So Williams is simply mistaken in concluding that the conditions of his story are incoherent.

He draws, however, a particularly ambiguous conclusion: "it is a necessary condition of making the supposed identification on non-bodily grounds that at some stage identifications should be made on bodily grounds. Hence any claim that bodily considerations can be absolutely omitted from the criteria of personal identity must fail ...". On the view here proposed, "bodily considerations" do bear on the criteria of personal identity because they provide the necessary conditions on which the *existence* of a person depends. But they do not and need not provide *criteria* of personal identity in the sense that a suitable congruity or incongruity in the set of intentional mental states ascribed to *some* person embodied *in a particular body* may justify our inferring that the person thus embodied is one and the same, or different from, a (type) person embodied in another body. Recall once again that token instances of the same type-etching are thought to be the same etching, may exist simultaneously, may "reincarnate" the etching at different times, and may exhibit noticeably different physical properties. Whatever can be said of etchings in this regard can be said of persons, though what distinguishes the same etching (normally, production from a common plate under authorized conditions) and what distinguishes a person (a distinctive network of beliefs and memories and actions and the like) are bound to be quite different. If, on some theory, a human clone could be provided with the distinguishing pattern of mental states thought to mark a particular person, then, in spite of the further divergences in thought and behavior of the original and the clone, it would be perfectly coherent to treat each as alternative tokens of the same type-person. The ultimate question here is an empirical one, probably tied more closely to technology than to the claims of reincarnation. Still, we have provided a conceptual scheme for such eventualities, that appear to be ruled out by Williams' account. It is easy to see that the usual puzzles of brain transplants and split-brain phenomena are open to a related resolution (cf. Gazzaniga [1970] ; Puccetti [1973]). If for instance memories are redundantly "stored" in different parts of both hemispheres of the brain (Rose [1972]), then it is quite conceivable that tokens of the same person should be produced (cf. Vesey [1974]).

The issue that is crucial, however, in speaking of personal identity is that there are two different elements to be reconciled in any viable theory: (a) what it is that constitutes the distinctive functional network of a particular person, and (b) what the conditions are under which some particular realization of such a network can be assigned to an actual person. In order to speak of a particular person, one must identity some particular body in which the putative person is embodied: in this sense, personal identity depends on identifying a body in which a person is embodied. But if what distinguishes a person is a certain distinctively organized network of intentional states, then, once that network is instantiated in a particular token embodied in a particular body, there is no need to restrict the identity of the person to that particular embodiment. No one has ever shown for instance that the interpretation of the phenomena of multiple personality (cf. Prince [1903] ; Thigpen [1957]) or of split-brain phenomena cannot coherently be construed in terms of plural persons occupying the same body; but that concession alone shows that reference to an embodying body fixes the possibility of identifying a person but not the criteria of its identity (*contra* Shoemaker [1959]). To say this much, however, is emphatically not to say that it is possible to speak of persons without invoking criteria of personal identity (*contra* Parfit [1971]).

Cultural entities are identified extensionally, then, because their being identified is necessarily linked to the identification of some body (in which they are putatively embodied); but their being identified as the kind of entity they are rests on whatever is taken to be the individuating functional or intentional properties of the entity involved. For example, the identification of tokens of the same etching depends on the condition and authorized use of the printing plate and the defensibility of viewing the somewhat different designs of particular prints as alternative tokens of the type-design intended. Such a procedure is obviously coherent and does not in the least rule out the instantiation of *kinds* of physical properties. Similarly, with persons, *if* one thought that there was a formulable program for the distinctive states of mind of a particular person — rather in the way in which there could be a program for a particular machine — then it would be impossible to deny that there could be plural tokens of the same person. In effect, the argument here advanced exploits the possibility without admitting that there is any finite-state machine program that can be applied to the lives of human persons and even without denying that kinds of physical properties might well be thought essential to different token instantiations of the same person. So the resolution of the problem of personal identity rests in a curious way on an identification-schema that holds for all cultural entities whether they have minds or do not.

Beyond this, the distinctions provided suggest a continuum of emerging changes from the inanimate to the personal and its bearing on the unity of science. Schematically, that may be marked by the following shifts: from nomic universals to probabilistic laws, from the non-teleological to the teleological, from the functional to the intentional, from the intentional to the intensional. The salient features of certain of these shifts are yet to be considered.

CHAPTER 13

ACTION AND IDEOLOGY

If we attend to the larger social implications of the nonreductive theory of persons that has been advanced, it will be readily seen (i) that persons are not natural entities, though, embodied as they are in physical bodies, they exhibit natural properties as well as culturally emergent properties; and (ii) that persons need not be individuated and identified in the same way in which their bodies are individuated and identified, though their identification depends on the identifiability of some body or other. Two consequences follow at once: (a) that alternative but otherwise coherent criteria for the individuation and identity of persons will bear substantively on the defensibility of ascriptions of personal responsibility in moral and related contexts (cf. Parfit [1971]; T. Nagel [1970]; Williams [1976]); and (b) that there cannot be any merely natural norms of conduct and life that could defensibily be taken to be an objective and adequate guide for the behavior of all human persons (cf. Margolis [1975b]). Still, persons have been characterized as entities essentially capable of following rules, in particular, linguistic rules, and, because of that, capable of self-reference and deliberate and responsible behavior. Even with languageless but sentient creatures, we found that the ascription of mental states and actions depended on a heuristic use of a linguistic model in tandem with an appropriate theory of the purposive life of the species in question. That theory, suited as much to human persons as to languageless animals, entailed that a certain characteristic coherence or rational connection obtains within and among the various occasions on which intentions, perceptions, desires, beliefs, and actions are called into play. The relevant model of coherence sets a number of distinct constraints on particular ascriptions: for one thing, there can be no basis for ascribing the usual mental states without some evidence, on some occasions, of relevant behavior (cf. Wittgenstein [1963]); for another, the ascription of distinct mental states and of distinct instances of sentiently informed behavior is controlled by the same model, so there can be no (sentiently informed) behavior without the admission of independent mental states (cf. Armstrong [1968]); for a third, a minimal model of rationality must provide for cognitive, conative, affective, and active elements, no matter how variable or attenuated their instantiation may be (cf. Rundle [1972]; Kenny [1963]); and for a fourth, particular ascriptions of mental states must conform to certain minimal conceptual requirements (cf. Meiland [1970]). Regarding the last constraint, for instance, one cannot be said to intend to do what one believes to be impossible, one cannot intend to do what one believes is already accomplished, one cannot be said to have beliefs that are invariably or even predominantly contrary to one's desires or overt behavior. The conceptual connections governing ascriptions of mental states and action are simply too close. But in addition to these very general constraints, some species-typical model of the coherent ordering of given kinds of perceptual abilities, affective dispositions, concepts, and the like must, on empirical grounds, be assigned to each kind of creature to which particular ascriptions are made. As it happens, that model is characteristically prudential — accommodating the *passage* of creatures through the stages of sentient but largely instinctual, intelligent and improvisational, and linguistically informed behavior in the sense that all sentient species are seen as minimally rational in favoring, typically at least, the preservation of life, the reduction of pain, the security of goods or territory, self-defense and the defense of offspring, the provision of food and shelter, gratification of sexual desire, and the like. So, not only must there be a certain congruence among the perceptions, desires, intentions, and actions of a creature; that congruence must be deployed in a detailed manner over a lifetime in such a way that the species-typical prudential interests of that creature will be exhibited. This is simply another way of making the critical concession that sentience is itself an evolutionary development favoring individual and species survival (cf. Piaget [1971]; Stenhouse [1974]; Skolimowski [1974]).

It is on the human level that the inadequacy of a purely prudential model of conduct becomes clear, because (i) the prudential interests assigned are entirely determinable without being determinate (e.g., how long and in what way and under what conditions ought life to be preserved?); (ii) prudential interests facilitate higher-order interests that take precedence over them and may even entail waiving them without a loss of rationality (e.g., the pursuit of some ideal or self-sacrifice or suicide); (iii) the determinate form of favored prudential interests need not, and, under certain circumstances doubtless will not, accord with species-typical or merely statistical regularities (e.g., the conviction that, under increasingly persistent pollution, the expected life-span of the average individual ought still to be increased); (iv) doctrinal and ideological quarrels about favored norms of life are characteristically compatible with determinable prudential interests (notably, species survival) though not with one another (e.g., utilitarian and anti-utilitarian disputes about justice and punishment); (v) it is thought to be an open question, relative to the justification of behavior, whether one ought to gratify particular desires as such or particular prudential concerns as such (e.g., whether or not one should favor a fair distribution of goods even at the risk of some personal prudential disadvantage). But the principal reason that human persons cannot be supposed to be adequately guided by merely prudential concerns is simply that, as culturally emergent entities, they are capable of deliberately changing the conditions under which they survive, hence, of changing what they themselves regard as acceptable determinately prudential constraints. This is the reason that all evolutionary and putatively utilitarian ethical systems are either utterly indefensible or cryptic versions of ulterior (and doctrinally favored) normative preferences (cf. Flew [1967]; Williams [1973a]). What they draw attention to is the difficulty and even the impossibility of constructing an exclusively valid account of the normative direction of human behavior.

Persons, then, are in a sense not natural entities: they exist only in cultural contexts and are identifiable as such only by reference to their mastery of language and of whatever further abilities presuppose such mastery (cf. Popper [1972a], [1972b]; Jarvie [1972]). Among those "further abilities" is, precisely, the ability to change the interests and direction of human activity for reasons of contingent and variable doctrinal conviction. This is an extraordinary and unique capacity, imposing a distinctive burden on explanatory models — both in the sense of requiring the admission of linguistically informed causal forces and the admission of explanations of a sort logically different from causal explanations. (We shall return to the issue.) But to the extent that this is conceded, the prospects of the so-called unity of science (Neurath *et al.* [1955]) are rather less than dim; and the distinction between the so-called social or historical or psychological sciences and the natural sciences, between *Geisteswissenschaften* and *Naturwissenschaften* (Dilthey [1961]), is well-founded though without entailing the admission of privileged cognitive faculties like that of empathy (Dilthey; Winch [1958]; cf. Jarvie [1970]) or of peculiar "historical laws" like the Hegelian or the Marxist (cf. Popper [1957]). Nevertheless, not unreasonably, empathy may signify the logical distinction of attending to intentional phenomena in culturally relevant contexts (cf. Gadamer [1976]), and historical laws may signify, for human persons endowed with their characteristic interests, the purposive order of intensionally significant phenomena (cf. Habermas [1971]; Bernstein [1976]; Timpanaro [1975]). There need be no conceptual scandals involved, not even the loss of the unity of science, only the defeat of the reductionism of the unity of science movement.

What is required is a theory that reconciles freedom and causality within the framework both of biological evolution and of cultural emergence. For freedom is essentially the capacity of linguistically competent beings (though it has an obvious behavioral analogue among the higher mammals), but it must — as the learning of a first language confirms — depend on prelinguistic capacities of a distinctively inventive sort. Also, beings that are capable of freedom — persons — are, as we have already seen, physically embodied; hence, their characteristic powers — in effect, their freedom — must inform the order of purely physical causes in a distinctive way (cf. Popper [1972d]).

That there is a distinctive prelinguistic factor facilitating the even greater plasticity of linguistically endowed creatures is strongly supported by the inquiries of the ethologists. Konrad Lorenz [1965] stresses, on the basis of extensive comparative studies, that "truly 'new' learned movements . . . can evidently be developed only by very few animals". The suggestive import of the observation is that "new" behavior can appear only where a certain deficiency or "gap" in instinctual behavioral accommodation obtains. As David Stenhouse [1973] explains: "One way in which this could occur would be if the genetic 'code' for the behavior came to be deficient at the appropriate place. It is quite unnecessary to postulate a simple one-to-one relationship between genes on the one hand and behavioral elements on the other, and that a gene must be 'missing' before a new learned element of behavior can be substituted for a previously instinctive one. The real situation is likely to be both more complex and more subtle than this, with the 'deficiency' occurring perhaps as a pleiotropic effect of genetic interaction. Nevertheless the simple model does represent what is causally required: the absence of whatever genetic and/or epigenetic configuration previously determined the behavioral element now to be missed out. Thus the opportunity to learn something new is in this frame of reference directly dependent upon a prior genetic or developmental change. It is, in fact, an evolutionary change." Stenhouse postulates a "P-factor", a " 'gap-creating' mechanism to permit the develop-ment of intelligence, that is, a capacity to control behavior that is "super-ordinate to instinct, hence also to learning", in effect, "the capacity for the control and direction of instinct and therefore also of learning". The novelty and promise of the view lies essentially with the concession of learning at levels that fall within the range of complex instinctual mechanisms. And the peculiarity of the mechanism postulated, which accounts for the remarkably accelerated rate with which "phenotypic (behavioral) innovation can occur" as contrasted with "the slow processes of genetic change", is that it must have "multiplied" the adaptive value of learning. Lorenz provides the coordinate clue, speculating about the higher primates and the cetacians: "Dissociated, or to be more exact, unassociated muscle contractions are at the beck and call of the pyramidal system and can, therefore, be directly and independently activated by our will. They are the raw material which motor learning strings, like beads on a thread, into a sequence and welds them into one skilled movement ... The possible explanation [of cetacean skills] which I venture to suggest is that the ancestors of the whales were, at the time they began to revert to aquatic life, carnivora with comparatively highly developed brains and were endowed with a fair portion of voluntary movement. When, consequently, a selection pressure was brought to bear on the development of motor patterns that were entirely new to a terrestrial animal, some of it, instead of creating new phylogenetically adapted fixed motor patterns, caused a higher development of voluntary movements which ... could be turned to any purpose, including efficient swimming techniques. This would account for the fact that aquatic mammals, for example otters, sea lions, and whales, are able to produce such an amazing multiformity of newly created and elegant, skilled movements in their 'play'." Similarly, the un-learning of established habits, Stenhouse argues, must presuppose the P-factor, since otherwise, without the compensating plasticity and the requisite motivation, the reversal would be discouraged by the effects of behaving thus (cf. Bittermann [1965]). Stenhouse concludes: "it is possible to perform a 'voluntary' action only so long as one cannot perform an involuntary one. This 'not performing' is the peculiar function of the P-factor of evolutionary intelligence."

Linguistic behavior, both by gesture and utterance, may reasonably be supposed to depend on the P-factor and on just such "unassociated muscle contractions" that account for the emergence of intelligence itself. Stenhouse briefly suggests as much, though in conceding the species-specific capacity involved, he links the thesis, without argument, with Chomsky's nativism (Chomsky [1967]). The point at issue is simply that "a species-specific capacity for language" is not, as such, a species-specific innate linguistic capacity. It is precisely on the basis of exploring that equivocation that we were led to the thesis that human persons are physically embodied but culturally emergent entities; hence, that they are not natural entities in the sense that their characteristic behavior cannot be entirely explained without admitting causal factors that are themselves linguistically informed. This is the relatively powerful consequence of admitting (Sellars [1963a]) the irreducibility of the intentional *and* (*contra* Sellars) the irreducibility of human linguistic abilities. There can, then, be no "natural norms" governing human conduct. Not only is classification in *Homo sapiens* intrinsically inadequate to provide the norms appropriate to culturally emergent (human) persons, but mere classification as a human animal does not presuppose any molar function, in the broadly Aristotelian sense (*contra* Hampshire [1961] and Vendler [1967]), in virtue of which any natural or essential excellence may be ascribed to man (Margolis [1966b], [1971b]). Mere resemblance to standard or admissible instances suffices. In fact, on the evidence of physical anthropology (Dart [1955], [1959]; Leakey [1935]; Clark [1957], [1962]), there is good reason to believe that the full development of the neocortex postdates the appearance of an incipient culture among proto-hominid creatures from which *Homo sapiens* probably evolved. And so, even speculations about the "restoration" of a natural ecological balance (Commoner [1971]) are meaningless — though the notion of ecological balance is not — in that human beings never existed without a language, never existed in a physical setting devoid of cultural transformation, and, therefore, never existed without some set of culturally developed norms that their rules, institutions, practices, and traditions convey. Even the norms of medicine are affected (cf. Margolis [1976]).

It is, however, because they are intensional, because whatever falls under a rule does so under selected descriptions, that rules as such are not logically reducible to natural laws. Only if there were a completely extensional *replacement* for all intensional distinctions (or at least for the most salient or "important" ones) (cf. Quine [1960]), or if there were a program suited for a finite automaton (a Turing machine with a finite tape) that could be provided for the discrimination of any set of intensional distinctions (cf. Putnam [1960]), could reference to rules be replaced by reference to laws — for the range covered. So there may well be a sense in which machines can follow rules (cf. Putnam [1964]). But to say this is not *yet* to say that the needed conditions can be fulfilled with respect to the life of human persons. There is *no* way to show that these reductive conditions are logically impossible, but we have already considered both conceptual and empirical difficulties that show no prospect of being overtaken. Hilary Putnam [1964], therefore, misleads us somewhat when he remarks: "can a robot have a sensation? Well, it can have a 'sensation'. That is, it can be a 'model' for *any* psychological theory [italics added] that is true of human beings. If it is a 'model' for such a theory, then when it is in the internal state that corresponds to or 'realizes' the psychological predicate 'has the visual sensation of red', it will act as a human would act (depending also on what other 'psychological' predicates apply)." Putnam is obviously — in fact, trivially — correct in what he says: *if* a man and a robot are "psychologically isomorphic", then "the behavior of the two *species* is most simply and revealingly analyzed, at the psychological level (in abstraction from the details of the internal physical structure), in

terms of the same 'psychological states' and the same hypothetical para-
meters". The problem precisely, is to *show* in what way the actual functional
organization (linguistic abilities and linguistically informed abilities) of human
beings can be provided by a machine analogue (cf. Dreyfus [1972]). Doubtless, if such an undertaking could be fulfilled, it would entail substantial
revisions in the meaning of 'consciousness', 'freedom', and related terms. But
without the actual empirical achievement, our distinctions pretty well stand
as before. It is, in fact because, as things stand, a rule specifies what constitutes
conformity to, and deviation from, a norm, with respect to which a set of
things may be appraised, and because creatures that can understand the nature
of a rule and follow rules must, for conceptual reasons, be capable of deliberately conforming to, deviating from, and instituting (new) rules (Lewis
[1969] ; Shwayder [1965]) that human beings are said to exhibit the capacity
of free choice and free action. So the interesting thing is that the admission of
persons as cultural entities entails the capacity to act of one's own volition —
freely.

Clearly, then, the admission of human freedom cannot be incompatible
with the causal order of things, either in the sense that free actions are contra-
causal, as C. A. Campbell [1951] seems to have supposed, or in the sense that
free actions cannot be explained at all in causal terms, as A. I. Melden [1961]
and R. S. Peters [1958] seem to have supposed. The reason is that the actions
of persons, as cultural phenomena (not merely free action: think of compul-
sive action), are, like the persons to which they are ascribed, embodied
phenomena. The physical events in which they are embodied must be subject
at least to purely physical laws, though, on the thesis, *purely* physical laws
cannot explain the causal efficacy of sentiently or linguistically informed
action. To speak of freedom and choice, then, is to characterize acts adverbially, as in saying, "He struck him deliberately", "He married of his own free
will". So speaking, we mean to say that the act in question was done in a way
that depends on appraising relevant aspects of one's conforming to rules,
institutions, traditions, practices, formulated alternatives, and the like, without precluding causal connections regarding the embodying physical events
or the causal efficacy of culturally informed actions. All that needs to the
precluded are those *particular* causal influences like compulsion or physical
force that are themselves incompatible with ascriptions of having acted freely,
deliberately, intentionally, and the like; also, of course, the denial of so-called
hard determinism — the thesis that the extension of the actual and the possible
are the same (Margolis [1966b]). To have acted freely, for instance, may be
to have acted with due deliberation, to have intended to commit the act in

question for reasons that bear on the satisfaction of one's wants or desires or objectives, in accord with a network of standing beliefs and interests and without the act's having been caused by drugs, hypnosis, force, inadvertence, uncontrollable impulses, or the like. In this sense, freedom is a mixed category admitting both lawlike and rulelike considerations and both purely physical causes and intentionally informed causes. One's having the intention to act in a certain way, that is, one's being in such a state of intending, may be admitted as a cause of an act in question (cf. *The Human Agent* [1968]; Whiteley [1973]; Binkley *et al.* [1971]; Brand [1970]). The denial (Melden [1961]; Taylor [1964]) confuses the *concept* of an intention, which can only be defined in terms of the concept of an action, with an *actual* intention, which is an intentional mental state contingently connected with actions that it may partially cause (Davidson [1963]). One may intend to do A and actually not act; and one may intend to do A and actually do B, which one's intention partially causes. Otherwise, causal connections involving mental states would have to be said to be merely conceptual rather than contingent connections, since 'The cause of A causes A' could not then be construed as affirming a contingent connection.

What *is* true about discourse regarding the actions of persons is that where linguistically informed mental states are specified as causes, such causes can be identified only in cultural contexts, relative to stable institutions or habits or practices that are in principle open to historical change; consequently, they can never enter into nomic universals but (at best) only into statistical laws (Hempel [1965]). The upshot is that intentionally qualified causes that are not reducible to physical causes set logical constraints on the scope of laws ranging over the relevant social or behavioral sciences. It is, for instance, always possible that the "laws" of the economic market change with significant changes in the stable expectations, interests, and habits of human communities; notably, Keynsian economics, regardless of its adequacy, is premissed on the present and future "expectations" of an economic community (Keynes [1936]) — hence, on factors subject to culturally informed transformations. This is to say nothing, of course, of whatever distinctions may obtain among so-called historical explanations; but it does serve to insure (*contra* Davidson [1963]) that explanations by reasons is not a "species of causal explanation", even if it is the case that what serves as a reason may also serve as a cause.

That conclusion follows at once on noting that reasons for actions are formulable only relative to some rule, institution, tradition, practice, habit or the like and never relative to a causal law (unless dependently, once the reason advanced is required to be a reason "had" as well, that is, a causally efficacious reason). Since actions are intentionally specified with respect to appropriate schemata of rationality, reasons are ascribable to actions only in intensional contexts, only under preferred descriptions. Consequently, if one and the same action may be alternatively described (Davidson [1963]; Anscombe [1957]), then the reason for committing a particular act can only obtain for that act under some description; but causal contexts, though not contexts of causal explanation (indeed, not any contexts of explanation), behave extensionally (Davidson [1967a]; Margolis [1973a]). Thus, if *flipping the light switch*, *turning on the light*, *illuminating the room*, and *alerting the prowler* are alternative descriptions of one and the same action, then one's intention to illuminate the room may well have *caused* the action, where such claims behave extensionally; even though the *reason* one has for flipping the light switch, namely, wanting to illuminate the room, cannot have been a reason for (inadvertently) alerting the prowler.

So a reason "had" (in the causally relevant sense) can be a cause of some action, however the action is described or identified, but it cannot be the "reason" for that action except relative to an appropriate description. There is, therefore, an equivocation on one's "having a reason" relative to two entirely different kinds of explanatory patterns. Causal explanations involving reasons "had" *presuppose* a theory or model of purposive life, in terms of which particular ascriptions may be defensibly made of given agents; but the explanation is not as such purposive in itself. It is not purposive for the simple reason that *if* a cause can be assigned to an action under a given description (congruent with some model of the rational ordering of belief, desire, intention, and the like), then, assuming the extensionality of causal contexts, the cause will be operative for the action in question under any co-designative description (where a new description need not conform with the actual intentional states ascribed to the agent). On the other hand, explanations by reasons (by reasons "had") are, precisely, accounts of (or of at least a part of) the rational coherence or purposiveness of given acts. Once, on the model of rationality, an agent may be said to have a reason for acting (relative to some act identified under a relevant description), the reason had may be treated as the cause or part of the cause for the act produced (regardless of how it is then described or identified). Nevertheless, to explain in the causal sense is to suppose (it is claimed) that the putative causes for the singular event explained fall under suitable covering laws even if we are ignorant of those laws (Davidson [1963]). But to explain in the sense of providing reasons is to show, on a certain model of rationality, without reference to such laws, that the action performed by the agent, where the act *is viewed in an intentional sense by the agent, that is, under a certain description*, conforms to the conditions of purposiveness or rationality. To insist on the distinction is not to deny that the reasons an agent has for what he does may not also serve as the cause or part of the cause of what he does. But it is also not to confuse two distinct kinds of explanatory endeavors. Failure to note the distinction mars the competing view (Goldman [1970]) attacking the "identity thesis" (that one and the same action may be identified under different descriptions), by failing to distinguish satisfactorily between one and the same act's being identified under different definite descriptions and different acts. The competing view construes acts as uniquely individuated with respect to one kind or another: "act-tokens" are said to be "tokens of only one property each", where "an act-type is simply an act-property, a property such as mowing one's lawn, writing a letter, or giving a lecture". But then, obviously, by admitting polyadic qualifications of actions, an infinite number of distinct acts is "generated" in generating any act at all, where 'generate' ranges over, but is not restricted to, causal processes.

There is this much to be said for the alternative theory: the individuation of acts and actions is conventional and intentionally linked to prevailing rules and institutions. But against it, it may be said that the conventions provide for the reidentification of acts under alternative descriptions as well. The motivation for the alternative theory, moreover, rests on a fundamental mistake (Margolis [1975d]), namely, the confusion of causal contexts and contexts of causal explanation. It is to avoid anomalies of the following sort that the "identity thesis" is rejected (Goldman): if, say, John's *pulling the trigger* and *John's killing Smith* are said to be one and the same action under alternative descriptions, then why is it that if it is true that "John's act of pulling the trigger . . . caused the event in question, i.e., . . . caused the gun to fire", "it would be extremely odd to say that John's killing Smith caused the gun to go off". The answer is elementary: it would be odd to say so because so saying would not serve to explain why the gun went off; it would *not* be odd in the sense that the action in question (however described or identified) was *not* the cause or part of the cause of the gun's going off (*it was the cause*). But disarming the puzzle disables the theory. This is not to deny that some events may be non-causally "generated" by others, for instance, that "If my sister had not given birth at *t*, I would not have been an uncle at *t*" (Kim [1973]) — which in effect shows the weakness of attempting to explain "causal dependency in terms of counterfactual dependence". But it goes no distance at all toward showing that every "act-type is simply an act-property, a property such as mowing one's lawn, running, writing a letter, or giving a lecture" *and* that "act-tokens . . . are *tokens* of only one property each" (Goldman; cf. Kim [1969]). There is no reason to suppose that every act-token is identified in terms of and only in terms of its essential property: the notion goes entirely contrary to ordinary practices of reference and predication — and defeats the requirements of polyadic predication. Goldman's contention is that the anomalies of causal relations are such as to *require* the rejection of the (so-called) identity theory. In the example given (regarding John's killing Smith), he concludes therefore that *John's pulling the trigger* and *John's killing Smith* are not identical because they do not have the same properties in common, namely, the property of causing the gun to go off. But of course, "they" do have the property. The irony is that Goldman's attempted "act-essentialism" is predicated on avoiding "the unattractive consequence of committing us to the view that causation is somehow *language-dependent*" — the alleged consequence of adhering to the identity theory. But as we see, the need for the maneuver is itself just the result of confusing causal contexts and contexts of causal explanation.

The quarrel yields an ulterior finding as well. For, if the individuation of acts and actions depends on prevailing rulelike conventions and institutions, then the characterization of what a man does by way of performing actions may well be open to radically different views both with regard to the "proper" nature of what he does and with regard to how many distinct acts he has performed. The proper clue, here, is found in the law: if a man swings his fist in a way that describes an arc making final contact with the point of the chin of another, then, depending on legal conventions, he may be charged with two or five or ten acts — for instance, striking an officer, causing a public disturbance, committing an assault, resisting an arrest, and so on. Individuation, here, is congruent neither with psychological states nor with causal lines and their distinct physical consequences (*contra* Davidson [1970]). This conforms nicely with the intensional nature of reasons. It may be argued (Danto [1963], [1973]) that such "mediated" actions always presuppose a "basic" action in order to avoid the regress, that if "I must do something else *through* which the first thing is done, then nothing could be done at all". But this does not insure that such basic actions can always be uniquely specified (cf. Brand [1968]; Stoutland [1968]) and it does not justifiably exclude omissions from counting as distinct acts, for which, *ex hypothesi*, no basic actions can be provided (D'Arcy [1973]).

In particular, it is always possible to specify an act by a description that elides terms antecedently provided for an act and its consequence. The implications for history, morality, and the law are obvious. Eric D'Arcy

[1963] has offered the strongest resistence to this view, holding that "Certain kinds of act are of such significance that the terms which denote them may not, special contexts apart, be elided into terms which (a) denote their consequences, and (b) conceal, or even fail to reveal the nature of the act itself." Examples that D'Arcy offers include "acts of killing, maiming, slandering, torturing, deceiving, or seriously offending another person; betraying or deserting a friend or an ally; breaking a contract or a promise or a confidence; stealing or destroying or spoiling something which the owner, or the community, looks on as precious; sacrificing or endangering one's own happiness, good name, health, or property". But his thesis can be maintained only if there are inviolable and essential norms appropriate to human nature. Notably, if there were determinate prudential norms somehow required by human nature, then D'Arcy's thesis could be sustained. But we have already explored the limitations of that proposal. Also, as has been argued, man's nature (as person) is specifiable only in terms of his cultural emergence; and in that sense, no "natural" function or excellence can be assigned him. The upshot is that D'Arcy's constraints, no matter how humane, can only (though he would deny this) mirror his own moral convictions as to what may be the limits of elision beyond which the description of particular acts "may not" proceed.

On reflection, it will be seen that there is a sensible emphasis in D'Arcy's claim, namely, that, for both sentient creatures and persons, certain prudential interests may be putatively assigned, as of perserving life, avoiding pain, insuring security, and the like, which conform rather closely to what D'Arcy seems to intend by the phrase 'such significance'. But these interests are merely putative, determinable, statistically prevalent, presumptively rational — not essential in the sense that rejecting or ignoring or altering or obscuring such distinctions in particular descriptions may be said to go contrary to human nature (Margolis [1971b]). One has only to think of the possibility of rational suicide, rational sacrifice, the rational pursuit of war, and the like, as well as the ease with which the forbidden elisions will be countenanced in different societies subscribing to relevantly different ethical categories, to appreciate the tendentiousness of D'Arcy's thesis.

Nevertheless, it is because human persons are rule-following creatures that they are capable of free action; and it is because they are capable of free action that they are said to be "responsible" agents. So the "forensic" theory of persons (in Locke's general sense, the sense in which a person is a thing to which responsibilities are assigned; cf. Sellars [1963a]) follows as a consequence of construing persons as culturally emergent entities — viewed in the normally minimal respect of presupposing the prudential interests of the members of a human society (cf. Margolis [1975b]). But it is a sense that pre-supposes rather than assigns the status of persons. Also, there may well be necessary formal constraints on moral and related disputes and on the charac-terization of human actions — coherence and consistency, for instance, or universalizability taken as a linguistic rule (Hare [1952] ; Margolis [1971b]); and, dialectical constraints bearing on the elimination of arbitrariness, insis-tence on relevance, congruence with neutral facts, and the like; and even provisional but substantive constraints as of presupposing (as we have just acknowledged) the prudential interests of others. But these latter may, in principle, be overridden at particular points by assuming a suitable system of norms and values and, in any case, they are determinable only and can be fixed only by constraints of the sort D'Arcy wishes to support. In short, the individuation and characterization of human acts is informed by, and corres-ponds to, some articulated ideology — in which the minimal and provisional constraints sketched are accommodated to some extent but in which, also, such constraints are supplemented by a theory of the rights, duties, obliga-tions, ideals, happiness, and well-being of an entire community. In this sense, 'ideology' is a term of art. The point of importance, however, is that the sufficient conditions for determining the "correctness" of descriptions of action, in preparation for appraisals of a significant variety — moral, legal, medical, historical, and the like — cannot but be controlled by an ideology for which, on the thesis, there is no prospect of objective confirmation or escape (*contra* Habermas [1971], [1975] ; Bell [1960]). In this sense, judg-ments of the validity and invalidity of moral, legal, historical, and related claims behave asymmetrically as far as objectivity is concerned. For, a parti-cular claim may be shown to be invalid, objectively, in having violated mini-mal constraints of consistency, conformity with neutral facts, and avoidance of arbitrariness; but, for alternative ideologies meeting *such* constraints, all serious disputes about the "significance" (to use D'Arcy's term) of what has occurred will remain unresolvable except from the vantage of one partisan ideology or another. A minimal skepticism, here, is unavoidable (Weber [1946], [1949]). Human history, to take the paradigm, cannot in principle, be ideologically neutral; to admit this much (*contra* Zinn [1970]) is not even to be able to formulate a doctrine devoted to "fundamental humanistic interests [*sic*] above any particular class, party, nation, ideology — which . . . we should consciously serve". If "ideology is the conversion of ideas into social levers" (Bell), particularly where normative considerations bearing on conduct and aspiration are involved, then there can be no escape from ideology; also, given that human persons are culturally emergent entities, there

can be no escape from some form of relativism at least (cf. Lukes [1974]).
An ideology may in fact be regarded as a schema for the determinate manage-
ment of the prudential values of an entire society — normally, implicit in
some large part of the behavior of its members (cf. Margolis [1976]).

In fact, given the realistic necessity for ideologies, that is, the need for the
members of some organized society to be able to act spontaneously and
appropriately in improvisational ways with respect to one another, and given
that persons are culturally emergent beings, there is no prospect of escaping
relativism (*contra* Keat and Urry [1975]; cf. Margolis [1976]). There is also
no need to embrace the apparent incoherencies of radical relativism (cf.
Feyerabend [1975]). One cannot coherently relativize the concepts of truth,
meaningfulness, and consistency, however one may relativize the criteria for
particular ascriptions: for example, truth cannot be adequately defined within
the context of a particular language ('true-in-L') without implicitly providing
trans-linguistic grounds for comparing the conventions of particular languages
(cf. Tarski [1956]); one cannot hold that conceptual systems are radically
different from our own if their features can be identified (cf. Black [1962]).
But beyond such constraints, particularly with regard to valuational considerations, a robust or moderate relativism is entirely defensible. The seemingly
easy refutation of relativism rests on the assumption that the relativist must
assign incompatible truth-values to one and the same judgments. Grant only
that a relativistic set of judgments lacks truth-values (true and false) or takes
values other than those of truth and falsity, the required defense lies at hand.
It is of course possible to hold that judgments are relativized in the sense that
every validating "principle" is said to subtend its own sector of judgments
and that no two principles have intersecting sectors (cf. Harman [1975]).
But, although this is a possible strategy, it is quite uninteresting, since what
we want is a relativism that admits some range of competing claims, claims
for which there are at least minimal grounds justifying the joint applicability
of competing principles. Relativism in this sense entails the following constraints: (i) the rejection of skepticism and universalism (that is, the doctrine
that there is one and only one principle for validating a range of judgments in
question); (ii) the provision that relativized judgments take values other than
those of truth and falsity (for example, plausibility or reasonableness) and
include incongruent judgments (that is, judgments that, on a model of truth
and falsity, would be incompatible); (iii) the rejection of cognitivism (that is,
the rejection of the view that, for the properties ascribed in the judgments in
question (notably, interpretive and valuational judgments [cf. Margolis
(1977k), (1971b)]), we possess a matching cognitive faculty the normal

exercise of which enables us to make veridical discriminations regarding their presence or absence (entailed by [(ii)] [cf. Margolis (1975a)]); (iv) the admission of the joint relevance of competing principles in validating the ascriptions or appraisals in question (entailed by [(ii)]); (v) the admission that relativistic sets of judgments presuppose some range of non-relativistic judgments, or that relativistic judgments are dependent on there being some viable range of non-relativistic judgments (entailed by [(i)]); (vi) the admission that a set of judgments is relativistic if their validation is determined by considerations bearing on the individual sensibilities of anyone who relevantly judges — including, prominently, sensibilities formed by adherence to some prevailing ideology. Given the coherence of these conditions *and* given the culturally emergent nature of persons, it is difficult to see how some form of relativism with respect to norms of conduct and the interpretation of behavior and of cultural production can possibly be avoided.

   To admit sentience and intentional behavior, then, is to suppose a model of rationality suitable for particular species. And to admit linguistically informed sentience is to suppose a capacity for freedom and for favoring doctrinally skewed conceptions of coherent and purposeful behavior. Reasons explain in an intensional way intensionally qualified actions; and since the having of such reasons may serve as the cause of one's actions, causal explanations at the cultural level cannot be freed from the shifting currents of historical conviction and ideology. The results are (i) that the causal regularities of the cultural disciplines are not merely probabilistic but also only contextually operative — so long that is as a given society exhibits certain habits and convictions rather than others; and (ii) that alternative, non-converging interpretations or redescriptions of behavior in intensional terms merely reflect the relativized but systematic convictions of different observers. The admission of culture, therefore, entails the repudiation of reductionism. There is no reason to suppose that the physical phenomena in which seemingly lawlike cultural phenomena are embodied exhibit as such a corresponding lawlike relationship — though subsets of such phenomena will instantiate relevant physical laws (cf. Fodor [1975]). But the relativization of cultural explanation affects as well the appraisal of the conduct of persons, for these enterprises are not logically independent of one another. Certainly (*contra* Wilson [1975]), there is no clear sense in which the distinctions to which human beings respond on the cultural level can be (*ever*) either entirely or even principally formulated in terms of genetic factors or the like. To say (with Wilson) that "a genetically accurate and hence completely fair code of ethics must also wait" for the development of an adequate science (sociobiology)

— perhaps within a hundred years — is simply to miss the distinction of the cultural disciplines.

What these reflections demonstrate, apart from the severity of certain claims (for instance, that there is no objectively confirmable morality though there are objective grounds for disconfirming particular moral judgments), is simply that it appears impossible to develop an adequate theory of minds and persons without consequences for a ramified theory of human values; and, that one's theory of minds and persons cannot escape being informed by one's antecedent convictions regarding the objectivity and neutrality of findings within the behavioral and historical sciences, the law, medicine, politics, economics, the arts, and morality. The development of these issues is not our present concern — only the clear sense of their connection with the theory of persons. Nevertheless, the requirements of coherence, or intelligibility, under conditions of diachronic conceptual change or of synchronic relativism, appear to include the following. It is, at any point in time, impossible to admit alternatives to the beliefs one favors in any domain without admitting the coordinate intelligibility of such alternatives within a single order of meaningful discourse (*contra* Feyerabend [1975]); without admitting that formal constraints on shifts affecting analytic/synthetic distinctions cannot fail to preserve conditions of consistency and noncontradiction that are not subject to comparable revision (*contra* Quine [1953b]); without admitting that truth claims are, because of the requirements of intelligibility, ultimately trans-linguistic (exceeding Tarski [1965]); without admitting that there must be a comprehensive schema for the identification and reidentification of whatever there is (accepting Strawson's intent [1959] but not his doctrine). Historical change, therefore, provides the framework within which seemingly incommensurable theories are viewed as the alternative projections of an understanding mind (cf. Lakatos and Musgrave [1970]); and otherwise incompatible ideologies, the alternative possibilities of commitment of a mind capable of more distinctions than those of truth and falsity (cf. Feyerabend [1975]).

Finally, if we cannot confirm empirically either physicalism or the functionalist thesis that a finite automaton could simulate at the molecular level a human being's competence to act in intentional ways, then it cannot be the case that the prediction and explanation of human behavior falls under the conventional covering-law model (*contra* Hempel [1962]; Davidson [1963], [1970]; Armstrong [1968]; Dennett [1969]). Also, it becomes misleading to construe the behavioral, social, and cultural sciences as aiming at the prediction and explanation of behavior *tout court*: *that* formulation actually favors one or another version of reductionism and fails to draw attention to the distinction of a commonsense psychology lacking nomic universals at the level of intentional behavior. If we attend to what has just been noted regarding the institutional life of human societies, the appeal to explanatory reasons, the pervasiveness of ideology, the irresistibility of relativism — in a word, the intensional dimension of human behavior — then it must be seen that the relevant sciences aim at predicting and explaining what may be called *reasoned behavior*. By this, is meant: (i) the mere identification of human actions as such already invokes "covering" institutions rather than covering laws; (ii) relevant institutions play a causal role insofar as they form, inform, groom, influence, habituate a population so that its members tend to act in functionally (intentionally) appropriate ways in virtue of having internalized the model of reasoning favored by those institutions; (iii) normally, the characterization of a human agent's behavior as an action of this or that sort entails the prediction that that agent's beliefs, intentions, desires, and the like conform to the functional model of reasoning favored by the relevant institutions; (iv) the institutions themselves, *a fortiori* the determinate forms of reasoning favored by culturally distinct populations, are subject to historical change and replacement. These conditions confirm the sense in which causal explanation in the behavioral disciplines essentially depends on intentional distinctions drawn from the (*non*-causal) model of explanation by reasons. There is, therefore, no such thing as the prediction of mere behavior: to predict how a human being will behave (under conditions already qualified in institutionally relevant ways) is to predict how that human being will match reasoning and action, where the congruence predicted as well as the very characterization of the behavior in question are thought to be due to prevailing institutions and ideologies. From this point of view, both the statistical generalizations of social psychology, however often obvious, and the anecdotal explanations of realistic fiction and the case study (cf. Goffman [1957]) serve to confirm the operative force of the motivational factors that obtain in this society or that. We may say that explanation in the behavioral sciences invokes statistical laws rather than nomic universals. But even that way of speaking is misleading because it suggests a mere methodological weakness relative to the objectives of the covering-law model. The truth is that the "laws" of the cultural domain are institutions and practices governing embodied phenomena, the embodying medium of which *is* subject to whatever laws obtain at the physical and biological levels.

Perhaps this is a good sign in itself of the promise of a theory, since it restores one's sense of the unity of personal life — if not of science; for it sets our speculations in a context of sufficient breadth and flexibility that no aspect of our concern with human existence need be slighted — at the same time, admittedly, that it disqualifies, for cause, particular doctrines.

There is a deeper consideration that we should not altogether neglect before drawing the account to a close, a consideration bearing jointly on the famous problem of the compatibility of freedom and determinism and on the distinctive model of explanation here sketched. For *if* the covering-law model is taken to signify that individual causes are, as causes, subsumable under nomic universals (cf. Hempel [1965]) and *if* to be subsumable under nomic universals signifies that antecedent sufficient conditions for producing a certain effect may be specified, then determinism of the covering-law sort as applied to human action would be incompatible with human freedom and choice. If, that is, agreeing with Anthony Kenny's [1975] application of Hume's distinctions, freedom may be said to entail both "liberty of sponta- neity" (that is, "we are free in doing something if and only if we do it because we want it") and "liberty of indifference" (that is, "we are free in doing some- thing if and only if it is in our power not to do it"), then actions cannot both be determined and free. We may move to support "compatibilism" in a variety of ways: (a) by denying that nomic universals have the status assigned; (b) by restricting freedom to "liberty of spontaneity"; (c) by admitting that causal laws may be of the form of statistical generalizations rather than nomic universals (Hempel [1965] ; Salmon [1975]); (d) by denying that the explana- tion of free actions is a form of causal explanation; and (e) by denying that, even though nomic universals are exceptionless there is no basis for supposing that there is a complete set of such universals covering every item of every kind subject to such laws. Kenny favors (d) because he is persuaded that causal explanation presupposes nomic universals in the strong sense suggested; and he favors (e) because he recognizes that he must make provision for "different phenomena" following "identical antecedent conditions". As he puts it: "It is surely true to say that if someone has the ability and oppor- tunity to do X at *t*, and does his best to do X at *t*, then he will (normally) do X at *t*. What makes the difference between such an ascription of personal power and the ascription of natural power is that the principle just enun- ciated, unlike 'if you set a match to it it will burn' is some kind of logical or conceptual truth and not a causal generalization linking two independent states of affairs." "Wants", Kenny insists, "are not circumstances . . . The locus of wanting is precisely this gap between circumstances and action, the gap left by the unpredictability of action from circumstance. To say that an action is the result of a want, or is an exercise of a personal power, does not say anything about determinism; but it does say something about determinism by external factors. Personal powers are powers to do things when you want to . . . ."

Of alternative strategies, we may say this. (a) is too strong, in the sense that it does not force the problem of compatibilism. (b) is too weak in the sense that freedom of action seems to entail "liberty of indifference". (c) we may leave for a moment. (d) seems preposterous in the sense that free action depends in a causal way on the culturally distinct practices in which we are trained and groomed (cf. Pears [1967a]; Davidson [1963]). And (e) fails as yet to show, if (d) is denied, that nomic universals do not obtain for just the kinds of actions that we call free actions.

Now, it is also insufficient to adopt alternative (c), since to hold that explanations under statistical laws exhibit a different logical form from that of "nomological-deductive" explanations (Hempel [1965]; Salmon [1975]) does not in itself settle the question whether nomic universals are presupposed wherever nomological regularities of the statistical sort obtain. "Some people", Wesley Salmon observes, "maintain, often on *a priori* grounds, that A is homogeneous (not merely practically or epistemically homogeneous) for B only if all A's are B or no A's are B; such people are determinists. They hold that causal factors always determine which A's are B and which A's are not B; these causal factors can, in principle, be discovered and used to construct a place selection for making a statistically relevant partition of A. I do not believe in this particular form of determinism. It seems to me that there are cases in which A is a homogeneous reference class for B even though not all A's are B." Salmon means by a "homogeneous reference class for B", a class for which "every property that determines a place selection is statistically irrelevant to B in A", that is, a class for which "there is no way, even in principle, to effect a statistically relevant partition without already knowing which elements have the attribute in question and which do not". The notion of a "place selection", borrowed from von Mises [1957], is the notion of a "selection of a partial sequence [from a reference class] in such a way that we decide whether an element should or should not be included without making use of the attribute of the element". Thus for instance, in drawing variously colored balls from an urn, every kth draw where k is prime provides a place selection but every draw of a red ball would not do so. In effect, "each member of a homogeneous reference class is a random member".

Salmon's provisions, however, are made "epistemically" (relative to our information even if we suspect that our reference class is not homogeneous) or "practically" (under the circumstance of not being able to obtain decisive

information about initial conditions affecting the homogeneity of our reference class). Salmon's important thesis is that the homogeneity of A for B
does not entail determinism and that determinism itself "cannot be settled *a
priori*". Still, Salmon merely expresses his faith that determinism does not
obtain: in the sense assigned, it threatens to remain incompatible with freedom. On the other hand, in admitting statistical explanation and in resisting
the *a priori* presumption that, whatever the state of our knowledge, individual
causal events are in principle subsumable under nomic universals, we provide
at least for the possibility that freedom and determinism are compatible, without however providing the requisite explanatory model. The only promising
maneuver requires a defense of (e).

Here, precisely, is where the concept of a "covering institution" is helpful.
For it provides: (i) a setting in which only statistical laws could obtain; and
(ii) a distinctive explanatory model in which causal factors are themselves
intentionally informed in accord with the model of explanation by reasons.
To explain human behavior of the culturally emergent sort is to explain the
performance of actions (specified, in accord with given institutions, under
appropriate descriptions) done for reasons suitably congruent with the institutions in question. The critical feature of such explanation is simply that the
very institutions in accord with which individuals are effectively trained or
groomed are themselves subject to causal influence and change within an
historical culture. Covering institutions, therefore, cannot be or yield nomic
universals. Another way of putting the point is this: the admission of cultural
emergence entails either ontic dualism or (e). The first alternative we have
already rejected; the second is clear in the sense that if the entire range of
physical phenomena were, in principle, explainable in terms of nomic universals, emergence could not but be illusory (if not dualistic). So we cannot
show that determinism does not hold full sway. But the failure to formulate
a complete determinism reveals the sense in which freedom is compatible
with a causal order in which some deterministic conditions obtain.

The logical peculiarities of the explanatory model sketched have hardly
been explored. In the context of our present inquiry, however, only its eligibility needs to be made clear. For on the admission of cultural emergence,
compatibilism is insured.

REFERENCES

Aaron, R. I. [1967], *The Theory of Universals* (Oxford: Clarendon).

Alston, W. P. [1958], "Ontological Commitment", *Philosophical Studies*, 9.

Anscombe, G. E. M. [1957], *Intention* (Oxford: Basil Blackwell).

Anscombe, G. E. M. [1963], "The Intentionality of Sensation: A Grammatical Feature", in R. J. Butler (ed.), *Analytical Philosophy*, Second Series (Oxford: Basil Blackwell).

Arbib, Michael [1972], *The Metaphorical Brain* (New York: Wiley-Interscience).

Armstrong, D. M. [1962], *Bodily Sensations* (London: Routledge and Kegan Paul).

Armstrong, D. M. [1968], *A Materialist Theory of the Mind* (London: Routledge and Kegan Paul).

Armstrong, D. M. [1973], *Belief, Truth and Knowledge* (Cambridge: Cambridge University Press).

Ashby, W. Ross [1956], *An Introduction to Cybernetics* (London: Chapman and Hall).

Austin, J. L. [1962], *How to Do Things with Words* (Oxford: Clarendon).

Ayala, F. J. and T. Dobzhansky (eds.) [1974], *Studies in the Philosophy of Biology* (Berkeley and Los Angeles: University of California Press).

Ayer, A. J. [1940], *The Foundations of Empirical Knowledge* (London: Macmillan).

Bach, Emmon [1968], "Nouns and Noun Phrases", in E. Bach and R. T. Harms (eds.), *Universals in Linguistic Theory* (New York: Rinehart and Winston).

Baier, Kurt [1962], "Smart on Sensations", *Austr. J. Philosophy*, 40.

Bell, Daniel [1960], *The End of Ideology* (New York: Free Press).

Bennett, Jonathan [1964], *Rationality* (London: Routledge and Kegan Paul).

Bennett, Jonathan [1976], *Linguistic Behavior* (Cambridge: Cambridge University Press).

Bergmann, Gustav [1962], "Purpose, Function, Scientific Explanation", *Acta Sociologica*, 5.

Bernstein, Richard [1968], "The Challenge of Scientific Materialism", *Int. Philoso. Quart.*, 8.

Bernstein, Richard [1976], *The Restructuring of Social and Political Theory* (New York: Harcourt Brace Jovanovich).

Best, Jay Boyd [1972], "The Evolution and Organization of Sentient Biological Behavior Systems", in A. D. Breck and W. Yourgrau (eds.), *Biology, History, and Natural Philosophy* (New York: Plenum).

Binkley, Robert *et al.* (eds.) [1971], *Agent, Action, and Reason* (Toronto: University of Toronto Press).

Bittermann, M. E. [1960], "Toward a Comparative Psychology of Learning", *American Psychologist*, 15.

Black, Max [1962], "Linguistic Relativity", in *Models and Metaphors* (Ithaca: Cornell University Press).

Black, Max [1968], *The Labyrinth of Language* (New York: Praeger).

Bloomfield, Leonard [1933], *Language* (New York: Holt, Rinehart, and Winston).

Boden, Margaret A. [1972], *Purposive Explanation in Psychology* (Cambridge: Cambridge University Press).

Bogen, J. E. [1969a], "The Other Side of the Brain I: Dysgraphia and Dyscopia following Cerebral Commissurotomy", *Bull. Los Angeles Neurol. Soc.*, 34.

Bogen, J. E. [1969b], "The Other Side of the Brain II: An Appositional Mind", *Bull. Los Angeles Neurol. Soc.*, 34.

Bogen, J. E. and Bogen, G. M. [1969], "The Other Side of the Brain III: The Corpus Callosum and Creativity", *Bull. Los Angeles Neurol. Soc.*, 34.

Bogen, J. E., DeZure, R., Tenhouten, W. D. and Marsh, J. F. [1972], "The Other Side of the Brain IV: The A/P Ratio", *Bull. Los Angeles Neurol. Soc.*, 37.

Boring, E. G. [1963], *The Physical Dimensions of Consciousness* (New York: Dover).

Brand, Miles [1968], "Danto on Basic Actions", *Nous* 2.

Brand, Miles (ed.) [1970], *The Nature of Human Action* (Glenview, Ill.: Scott, Foresman).

Brandt, Richard and Kim, Jaegwon [1967], "The Logic of the Identity Theory", *J. Philos.*, 64.

Brentano, Franz [1973], "The Distinction between Mental and Physical Phenomena" (1874), ed. Oskar Kraus; Eng. edition ed. Linda L. McAlister *Psychology from an Empirical Standpoint*, (London: Routledge and Kegan Paul).

Broad, C. D. [1925], *Mind and Its Place in Nature* (London: Routledge and Kegan Paul).

Brodbeck, May [1963], "Meaning and Action", *Philosophy of Science*, 30.

Brodbeck, May [1966], "Mental and Physical: Identity versus Sameness", in P. K. Feyerabend and G, Maxwell (eds.), *Mind, Matter, and Method* (Minneapolis: University of Minnesota Press).

Brown, Roger [1956], "Language and Categories", in Jerome S. Bruner, Jacqueline J. Goodnow, and George A. Austin (eds.), *A Study of Thinking* (New York: John Wiley).

Brown, Roger [1970], "The First Sentences of Child and Chimpanzee", in *Psycholinguistics: Selected Papers* (New York: Free Press).

Brown, Roger [1973], *A First Language* (Cambridge: Harvard University Press).

Bruner, Jerome, Goodnow, Jacqueline J. and Austin, George A. (eds.) [1956], *A Study of Thinking* (New York: John Wiley).

Bunge, Mario [1977], "Emergence and the Mind", *Neuroscience*, forthcoming.

Campbell, C. A. [1951], "Is 'Free Will' a Pseudo Problem?", *Mind* 60.

Campbell, Keith [1970], *Body and Mind* (Garden City: Anchor Books).

Carnap, Rudolf [1949], "Logical Foundations of the Unity of Science" (1938), in Herbert Feigl and Wilfrid Sellars (eds.), *Readings in Philosophical Analysis* (New York: Appleton-Century-Crofts).

Carnap, Rudolf [1953], "Testability and Meanings" (1936–37), in Herbert Feigl and May Brodbeck (eds.), *Readings in the Philosophy of Science* (New York: Appleton-Century-Crofts).

Carnap, Rudolf [1967], *The Logical Structure of the World* (1928), trans. Rolf A. George (Berkeley: University of California Press).

Cartwright, Richard [1971], "Identity and Substitutivity", in Milton Munitz (ed.), *Identity and Individuation* (New York: New York University Press).

Cassinari, Valentino and Pagni, Carlo A. [1969], *Central Pain: A Neurosurgical Survey* (Cambridge: Harvard University Press).

Chihara, C. S., and Fodor, J. A. [1965], "Operationalism and Ordinary Language: A

Critique of Wittgenstein", *American Philosophical Quarterly*, 2.

Chisholm, Roderick M. [1955–56], "Sentences about Believing", *Proc. Aristotelian Soc.*, 56; revised in Sellars and Chisholm [1958].

Chisholm, Roderick M. [1957], *Perceiving* (Ithaca: Cornell University Press).

Chisholm, Roderick M. [1966], *Theory of Knowledge* (Englewood Cliffs: Prentice-Hall).

Chisholm, Roderick M. [1967], "On Some Psychological Concepts and the 'Logic' of Intentionality", in Hector-Neri Castañeda (comp.), *Intentionality, Minds, and Perception* (Detroit: Wayne State University Press).

Chisholm, Roderick M. [1973], "A Defense of Leibniz's Law", unpublished manuscript.

Chomsky, Noam [1959]. Review of B. F. Skinner, *Verbal Behavior, Language* 35.

Chomsky, Noam [1965], *Aspects of the Theory of Syntax* (Cambridge: M.I.T. Press).

Chomsky, Noam [1966], *Cartesian Linguistics* (New York: Harper and Row).

Chomsky, Noam [1967], "Recent Contributions to the Theory of Innate Ideas", *Synthese* 17.

Chomsky, Noam [1972], *Language and Mind*, revised (New York: Harcourt, Brace).

Chomsky, Noam and Halle, Morris [1968], *The Sound Pattern of English* (New York: Harper and Row).

Clark, W. E. LeGros [1957], *The Fossil Evidence for Human Evolution* (Chicago: University of Chicago Press).

Clark, W. E. LeGros [1962], *History of the Primates* (London: British Museum).

Close, Daryl [1976], "The Ascription of Beliefs to Animals", (Ann Arbor: University Microfilms).

Commoner, Barry [1971], *The Closing Circle* (New York: Knopf).

Cornman, James [1962], "The Identity of Mind and Body", *J. Philos.* 59.

Cornman, James [1966], *Metaphysics, Reference and Language* (New Haven: Yale University Press).

Cornman, James [1968a], "On the Elimination of 'Sensations' and Sensations", *Rev. Metaphysics* 22.

Cornman, James [1968b], "Mental Terms, Theoretical Terms, and Materialism", *Philosophy of Science* 34.

Cornman, James [1971], *Materialism and Sensations* (New Haven: Yale University Press).

Crosson, Frederick J., and Sayre, Kenneth M. (eds.) [1967], *Philosophy and Cybernetics* (Notre Dame: University of Notre Dame Press).

Danto, Arthur C. [1963], "What We Can Do", *J. Philos.* 60.

Danto, Arthur C. [1973], *Analytical Philosophy of Action* (Cambridge: Cambridge University Press).

D'Arcy, Eric [1963], *Human Acts* (Oxford, Clarendon).

Dart, Raymond A. [1955], "Cultural Status of the South African Man-apes", *Annual Report of the Smithsonian Institute* (Washington: Government Printing Office).

Dart, Raymond A. [1959], *Adventures with the Missing Link* (New York: Harper).

Davidson, Donald [1963], "Actions, Reasons, and Causes", *J. Philos.* 60.

Davidson, Donald [1967a], "Causal Relations", *J. Philos.* 64.

Davidson, Donald [1967b], "Truth and Meaning", *Synthese* 17.

Davidson, Donald [1969a], "How is Weakness of Will Possible?", in Joel Feinberg (ed.), *Moral Concepts* (Oxford: Oxford University Press).

Davidson, Donald [1969b], "The Individuation of Events", in Nicholas Rescher (ed.),

Essays in Honor of Carl G. Hempel (Dordrecht: Reidel).

Davidson, Donald [1970], "Events as Particulars", *Nous* 4.

Davidson, Donald [1970], "Mental Events", in Lawrence Foster and J. M. Swanson (ed.), *Experience & Theory* (Amherst: University of Massachusetts Press).

Davidson, Donald [1975], "Thought and Talk", in Sam Guttenplan (ed.), *Mind and Language* (New York: Oxford University Press).

Dement, W. C. *et al.* [1970], "Hallucinations and Dreaming", in D. Hamburg (ed.), *Perception and Its Disorders* (Baltimore: Williams and Wilkins).

Dennett, Daniel [1969], *Content and Consciousness* (London: Routledge and Kegan Paul).

Dennett, Daniel [1975], "Toward a Cognitive Theory of Consciousness", in C. Wade Savage (ed.), *Minnesota Studies in the Philosophy of Science*, Vol. 9 (Minneapolis: University of Minnesota Press, forthcoming).

Dennett, Daniel [1976], "Why You Can't Make a Computer That Feels Pain", *Synthese*, forthcoming.

Derwing, Bruce L. [1973], *Transformational Grammar as a Theory of Language Acquisition* (Cambridge: Cambridge University Press).

Descartes, René [1931], *Meditations on First Philosophy*, in *The Philosophical Works of Descartes*, 2 vols., trans. Elizabeth S. Haldane and G. R. T. Ross (Cambridge: Cambridge University Press).

DiCara, Leo V. [1970], "Learning in the Autonomic Nervous System", *Scientific American*, 122.

Dilthey, Whilhelm [1961], *Meaning in History: Dilthey's Thought on History and Society*, trans. and ed. H. P. Rickman (London: Allen & Unwin).

Donnellan, Keith S. [1966], "Reference and Definite Descriptions", *Philos. Rev.* 75.

Dretske, Fred I. [1969], *Seeing and Knowing* (Chicago: University of Chicago Press).

Dretske, Fred I. [1976], "Knowledge and Information", presented at the Oberlin College Philosophy Colloquium (1976).

Dreyfus, Hubert L. [1972], *What Computers Can't Do* (New York: Harper and Row).

Eccles, John C. [1965], "Conscious Experience and Memory", in J. C. Eccles (ed.), *Brain and Conscious Experience* (New York: Springer-Verlag).

Eccles, John C. [1970], *Facing Reality* (New York: Springer-Verlag).

Englehardt, H. Tristram, Jr. [1973], *Mind-Body: A Categorial Relation* (The Hague: Martinus H. Nijhoff).

Estes W. K. *et al.* [1954], *Modern Learning Theory* (New York: Appleton-Century-Crofts).

Fabre, J. H. [1923], *Souvenirs Entomologiques*, 80th ed. (Paris: Librarie Delagrave).

Feigenbaum, Edward A. and Feldman, Julian (eds.) [1963], *Computers and Thought* (New York: McGraw-Hill).

Feigl, Herbert [1967], *The 'Mental' and the 'Physical': The Essay and a Postscript* (Minneapolis: University of Minnesota Press).

Feigl, Herbert and Scriven, Michael (eds.) [1956], *Minnesota Studies in the Philosophy of Science*, Vol. 1 (Minneapolis: University of Minnesota Press).

Fessard, A. [1961, "The Role of Neuronal Networks in Sensory Communication with the Brain", in W. A. Rosenblith (ed.), *Sensory Communication* (New York: Wiley).

Feyerabend, P. K. [1962], "Explanation, Reduction, and Empiricism", in Herbert Feigl *et al.* (eds.), *Minnesota Studies in the Philosophy of Science*, Vol. 3 (Minneapolis:

University of Minnesota Press).

Feyerabend, P. K. [1963a], "Mental Events and the Brain", *J. Philos.* 60.

Feyerabend, P. K. [1963b], "Materialism and the Mind-Body Problem", *Rev. Metaphys.* 17.

Feyerabend, P. K. [1975], *Against Method* (London: NCB).

Flew, A. G. N. [1967], *Evolutionary Ethics* (London: Macmillan).

Fodor, Jerry A. [1968], *Psychological Explanation* (New York: Random House).

Fodor, Jerry A. [1975], *The Language of Thought* (New York: Crowell).

Frankfort, Harry [1971], "Freedom of the Will and the Concept of a Person", *J. Philos.* 68.

Frege, G. [1960], "On Sense and Reference", in Peter Geach and Max Black (eds.), *Translations from the Philosophical Writings of Gottlob Frege*, (Oxford: Basil Blackwell).

Frisch, K. von [1955], *The Dancing Bees*, trans. Dora Ilse (New York: Harcourt, Brace).

Frisch, K. von [1967], *The Dance Language and Orientation of Bees*, trans. Leigh E. Chadwick (Cambridge: Harvard University Press).

Gadamer, Hans-Georg [1976], *Philosophical Hermeneutics*, trans. David E. Linge (Berkeley and Los Angeles: University of California Press).

Gardner, Beatrice T., and Gardner, R. Allen [1971], "Two-way Communication with an Infant Chimpanzee", in Allan M. Schrier and Fred Stollnitz (eds.), *Behavior of Nonhuman Primates*, Vol. 4 (New York: Academic Press).

Gardner, R. A., and Gardner, Beatrice T. [1969], "Teaching Sign Language to a Chimpanzee", *Science* 165.

Gazzaniga, Michael [1970], *The Bisected Brain* (New York: Appleton-Century-Crofts).

Geach, P. T. [1957], *Mental Acts* (London: Routledge and Kegan Paul).

Geschwind, N. [1965], "Disconnection Syndromes in Animal and Man", *Brain* 88.

Gibson, A. R., Filbey, R. A. and Gazzaniga, M. S. [1970], "Hemispheric Differences as Reflected by Reaction Time", *Federation Proceedings* 29.

Gibson, J. J. [1966], *The Senses Considered as Perceptual Systems* (Boston: Houghton Mifflin).

Glickman, Jack [1976], "Creativity in the Arts", in Lars Aagaard-Mogensen (ed.), *Culture and Art* (Atlantic Highlands: Humanities Press).

Goffman, Erving [1957]. *The Presentation of Self in Everyday Life* (Garden City: Doubleday).

Goldman, Alvin [1970], *A Theory of Human Action* (Englewood Cliffs: Prentice-Hall).

Goodman, Nelson [1966], *The Structure of Appearance*, revised (Indianapolis: Bobbs-Merrill).

Goodman, Nelson [1967], "The Epistemological Argument", *Synthese* 17.

Goodman, Nelson [1968], *Languages of Art* (Indianapolis: Bobbs-Merrill).

Goodman, Nelson [1970], "Seven Strictures on Similarity", in Lawrence Foster and J. W. Swanson (eds.), *Experience & Theory* (Amherst: University of Massachusetts Press).

Gould, J. L. [1974], "Honey Bee Communication: Misdirection of Recruits by Foragers with Covered Ocelli", *Nature* 252.

Gould, J. L. [1975], "Honey Bee Communication: The Dance-language Controversy", *Science* 189.

Grene, Marjorie [1974], *The Understanding of Nature: Essays in the Philosophy of*

Biology (Dordrecht: D. Reidel).

Grice, H. P. [1941], "Personal Identity", *Mind* 50.

Grice, H. P. [1957], "Meaning", *Philos. Rev.* 66.

Grice, H. P. [1961], "The Causal Theory of Perception", *Proc. Aristotelian Soc.* 35, Suppl.

Griffin, Donald R. [1976], *The Question of Animal Awareness* (New York: Rockefeller University Press).

Gunderson, Keith [1971], *Mentality and Machines* (Garden City: Doubleday).

Haber, R. N. and Haber, R. B. [1964], "Eidetic Imagery I: Frequency", *Perceptual and Motor Skills* 19.

Habermas, Jürgen [1971], *Knowledge and Human Interests*, trans. Jeremy J. Shapiro (Boston: Beacon Press).

Habermas, Jürgen [1975], *Legitimation Crisis*, trans. Thomas McCarthy (Boston: Beacon Press).

Hacking, Ian [1975], *Why Does Language Matter to Philosophy?* (Cambridge: Cambridge University Press).

Hampshire, Stuart [1961], *Thought and Action* (London: Chatto and Windus).

Hanson, N. R. [1963], "The Dematerialization of Matter", in Ernin MacMullin (ed.), *The Concept of Matter* (Notre Dame: University of Notre Dame Press).

Hare, R. H. [1952], *The Language of Morals* (Oxford: Clarendon).

Hare, R. H. [1963], *Freedom and Reason* (Oxford: Clarendon).

Harman, Gilbert [1973], *Thought* (Princeton: Princeton University Press).

Harman, Gilbert [1975], "Moral Relativism Defended", *Philos. Rev.* 84.

Hartnack, Justus [1972], "On Thinking", *Mind* 81.

Hebb, D. O. [1974], "What Psychology is About", *Am. Psychol.* 29.

Hempel, Carl G. [1962], "Explanation in Science and in History", in R. G. Colodny (ed.), *Frontiers of Science and Philosophy* (Pittsburgh: University of Pittsburgh).

Hempel, Carl G. [1965], *Aspects of Scientific Explanation, and Other Essays in the Philosophy of Science* (New York: Free Press).

Hempel, Carl G. [1966], *Philosophy of Natural Science* (Englewood Cliffs: Prentice-Hall).

Hintikka, Jaakko [1962], *Knowledge and Belief* (Ithaca: Cornell University Press).

Hirsch, Eli [1977], *The Persistence of Objects* (Philadelphia: Philosophical Monographs).

Hull, C. L. [1937], "Mind, Mechanism and Adaptive Behavior", *Psychol. Rev.* 44.

Human Agent, The. Royal Institute of Philosophy Lectures, Vol. 1, 1966/7 [1968] (London: Macmillan).

Huxley, T. H. [1893], "On the Hypothesis that Animals are Automata", in *Method and Results* (London: Macmillan).

Hydén, H. [1967], "Biochemical Changes Accompanying Learning", in Gardner C. Quarton *et. al.* (eds.), *The Neurosciences* (New York: The Rockefeller University Press).

Jacob, François [1974], *The Logic of Life*, trans. Betty E. Spillman (New York: Pantheon).

Jakobson, R. [1961], "Linguistics and Communication Theory", in R. Jakobson (ed.), *Structure of Language and Its Mathematical Aspects. Proceedings of Symposia in Applied Mathematics*, Vol. 12 (Providence: American Mathematical Society).

Jarrard, Leonard E. (ed.) [1971], *Cognitive Processes of Nonhuman Primates* (New

York: Academic Press).

Jarvie, I. C. [1970], "Understanding and Explanation in Sociology and Social Anthropology", in Robert Borger and Frank Cioffi (eds.), *Explanation in the Behavioral Sciences* (Cambridge: Cambridge University Press).

Jarvie, I. C. [1972], *Concepts and Society* (London: Routledge and Kegan Paul).

Jones, O. R. [1975], "Can One Believe What One Knows?", *Philos. Rev.* 84.

Katz, Jerrold [1964], "Mentalism in Linguistics", *Language* 40.

Keat, Russell and Urry, John [1975], *Social Theory as Science* (London: Routledge and Kegan Paul).

Kempson, Ruth M. [1975], *Presupposition and the Delimination of Semantics* (Cambridge: Cambridge University Press).

Kenny, Anthony [1963], *Action, Emotion and Will* (London: Routledge and Kegan Paul).

Kenny, Anthony [1975], *Will, Freedom and Power* (Oxford: Basil Blackwell).

Kenny, A. J. P. [Anthony] [1973], "The Origin of Language", in A. J. P. Kenny *et al. The Development of Mind* (Edinburgh: Edinburgh University Press).

Keynes, John Maynard [1936], *The General Theory of Employment, Interest, and Money* (New York: Harcourt, Brace).

Kim, Jaegwon [1966], "On the Psycho-physical Identity Theory", *Am. Philos. Quar.* 3.

Kim, Jaegwon [1969], "Events and Their Descriptions", in Nicholas Rescher *et al.* (eds.), *Essays in Honor of Carl G. Hempel* (Dordrecht: D. Reidel).

Kim, Jaegwon [1973], "Causes and Counterfactuals", *J. Philos.* 70.

Kolers, Paul A. and Eden, Murray (eds.) [1968], *Recognizing Patterns* (Cambridge: MIT).

Körner, Stephen [1966], *Experience and Theory* (London: Routledge and Kegan Paul).

Kuhn, Thomas S. [1970], *The Structure of Scientific Revolutions* (Chicago: University of Chicago Press).

Lakatos, Imre and Musgrave, Alan [1970], *Criticism and the Growth of Knowledge* (Cambridge: Cambridge University Press).

Lakoff, George [1971a], "Presuppositions and Relative Well-formedness", in Danny D. Steinberg and Leon A. Jakobovits (eds.), *Semantics* (Cambridge: Cambridge University Press).

Lakoff, George [1971b], "On Generative Semantics", in Danny D. Steinberg and Leon A. Jakobovits (eds.), *Semantics* (Cambridge: Cambridge University Press).

Langer, Susanne K. [1972], *Mind: An Essay on Human Feeling*, Vol. 2 (Baltimore: Johns Hopkins Press).

Lashley, K. S. [1923], "The Behavioristic Interpretation of Consciousness", *Psychol. Rev.* 30.

Lashley, K. S. [1950], "In Search of the Engram", in *Symposium of the Society for Experimental Biology*, No. 4 (Cambridge: Cambridge University Press).

Leakey, Louis S. B. [1935], *Adam's Ancestors* (New York: Longmans, Green).

Lehrer, Keith [1973], "Skepticism and Conceptual Change", in Roderick M. Chisholm and Robert J. Swartz (eds.), *Empirical Knowledge* (Englewood Cliffs: Prentice-Hall).

Lehrer, Keith [1974], *Knowledge* (Oxford: Clarendon).

Lettvin, J. Y., *et al.* [1959], "What the Frog's Eye Tells the Frog's Brain", *Proc. Inst. Radio Eng.* 47.

Lévi-Strauss, Claude [1963], *Structural Anthropology* [1958], trans. Claire Jacobson and Brooks Grundfest Schoepf (New York: Basic Books).

Levy, J., Trevarthen, C. and Sperry, R. W. [1972], "Perception of Bilateral Chimeric Figures Following Hemispheric Deconnection", *Brain* 95.

Lewis, David K. [1966], "An Argument for the Identity Theory", *J. Philos.* 63.

Lewis, David K. [1969], *Convention* (Cambridge: Harvard University Press).

Lilly, John Cunningham [1967], *The Mind of the Dolphin* (New York: Doubleday).

Locke, John [1894], *An Essay Concerning Human Understanding*, (ed.) A. C. Fraser (Oxford: Oxford University Press).

Lorenz, Konrad [1965], *Evolution and Modification of Behavior* (Chicago: University of Chicago).

Lorenz, Konrad [1970], *Studies in Animal and Human Behavior*, 2 vols. trans. Robert Martin (Cambridge: Cambridge University Press).

Lorenz, Konrad [1971], "Part and Parcel in Animal and Human Society" [1950], in Konrad Lorenz, *Studies in Animal and Human Behavior*, trans. Robert Martin, Vol. 2 (Cambridge: Harvard University Press).

Lukes, Steven [1974], "Relativism: Cognitive and Moral", *Proc. Aristotelian Soc.* 48.

Luria, S. E. [1973], *Life: The Unfinished Experiment* (New York: Charles Scribner's Sons).

Mackay, Donald M. [1969], *Information, Mechanism and Meaning* (Cambridge: MIT).

Malcolm, Norman [1954], "Wittgenstein's Philosophical Investigations", *Philos. Rev.* 63.

Malcolm, Norman [1973], "Thoughtless Brutes", *Proc. Add. Am. Philos. Assoc.* 46, (1972–73).

Margolis, Joseph [1962], "Fourteen Points on the Senses and Their Objects", *Theoria* 28.

Margolis, Joseph [1966a], "After-images and Pain", *Philosophy* 41.

Margolis, Joseph [1966b], *Psychotherapy and Morality* (New York: Random House).

Margolis, Joseph [1970a], "Notes on Feyerabend and Hanson", in Michael Radner and Stephen Winokur (eds.) *Minnesota Studies in the Philosophy of Science*, Vol 4 (Minneapolis: University of Minnesota Press).

Margolis, Joseph [1970b], "Numerical Identity and Reference in the Arts", *Brit. J. Aesthetics* 10.

Margolis, Joseph [1971a], "Difficulties for Mind-Body Identity Theories", in Milton Munitz (ed.) *Identity and Individuation* (New York: New York University Press).

Margolis, Joseph [1971b], *Values and Conduct* (Oxford: Clarendon).

Margolis, Joseph [1972a], Review of George Pitcher, *A Theory of Perception, Metaphilosophy* 30.

Margolis, Joseph [1972b], Review of Fred Dretske, *Seeing and Knowing, Metaphilosophy* 3.

Margolis, Joseph [1972c], "The Problem of Justified Belief", *Philos. Studies* 23.

Margolis, Joseph [1973a], *Knowledge and Existence* (New York: Oxford University Press).

Margolis, Joseph [1973b], "Behaviorism and Alien Languages", *Philosophia* 3.

Margolis, Joseph [1973c], "Mastering a Natural Language: Rationalists vs. Empiricists", *Diogenes* 84.

Margolis, Joseph [1975a], "Moral Cognitivism", *Ethics* 85.

Margolis, Joseph [1975b], *Negativities. The Limits of Life* (Columbus: Charles Merrill).

Margolis, Joseph [1975c], "Puccetti on Brains, Minds, and Persons", *Philosophy of Science* 42.

Margolis, Joseph [1975d], Review of Alvin Goldman, *A Theory of Human Action*, *Metaphilosophy*.

Margolis, Joseph [1976], "The Concept of Disease", *J. Med. Philos.* 1.

Margolis, Joseph [1977a], "The Axiom of Existence: Reductio and Absurdum", *S. J. Philos.* 15.

Margolis, Joseph [1977b], *Art and Philosophy* (Atlantic Highlands: Humanities Press).

Margolis, Joseph [1977c], "The Ontological Peculiarity of Works of Art", *J. Aesthetics and Art Christicism* 36.

Margolis, Joseph [1977d], "Pain and Perception", *Studi Internazionale di Filosofia* 8.

Margolis, Joseph [1977e), "The Stubborn Opacity of Belief Contexts", *Theoria* 43.

Margolis, Joseph [1977f], "Problems Regarding the Ascription of Knowledge", *The Personalist* 63.

Margolis, Joseph [1977g], "Knowledge and Belief: Facts and Propositions", *Grazer Philosophische Studien* 2.

Margolis, Joseph [1977h], "G. E. Moore and Intuitionism", *Ethics* 87.

Margolis, Joesph [1977i], "Skepticism, Foundationalism, and Pragmatism", *Am. Philos. Quart.* 14.

Margolis, Joseph [1977j], "Aesthetic Appreciation and the Imperceptible", *Brit. J. Aesthetics* 16.

Margolis, Joseph [1977k], "Robust Relativism", *J. Aesthetics and Art Criticism* 35.

Massey, J. L. [1967], "Information, Machines, and Men", in Frederick J. Crosson and Kenneth M. Sayre (eds.), *Philosophy and Cybernetics* (Notre Dame: University of Notre Dame Press).

Matson, Wallace I. [1976], *Sentience* (Berkeley and Los Angeles: University of California Press).

McCawley, James D. [1971a], "Where Do Noun Phrases Come From?", revised in Danny D. Steinberg and Leon A. Jakobovits (eds.) *Semantics* (Cambridge: Cambridge University Press).

McCawley, James D. [1971b], "Meaning and the Description of Languages", in Jay F. Rosenberg and Charles Travis (eds.) *Readings in the Philosophy of Language* (Englewood Cliffs: Prentice-Hall).

McDougall, William [1934], *The Frontiers of Psychology* (London: Cambridge University Press).

McNeill, David [1970], *The Acquisition of Language* (New York: Harper and Row).

McNeill, David [1971], "Are There Specifically Linguistic Universals?", in Danny D. Steinberg and Leon A. Jakobovits (eds.), *Semantics* (Cambridge: Cambridge University Press).

McNeill, David [1972], "Some Signs of Language", unpublished manuscripts, CIBA conference on competence in infancy, London, England.

Meehl, P. E., and Sellars, Wilfrid [1956], "The Concept of Emergence", in Herbert Feigl and Michael Scriven (eds.), *Minnesota Studies in the Philosophy of Science*, Vol. 1 (Minneapolis: University of Minnesota Press).

Meiland, Jack W. [1970], *The Nature of Intention* (London: Methuen).

Melden, A. I. [1961], *Free Action* (London: Routledge and Kegan Paul).

Melzack, Roland [1973], *The Puzzle of Pain* (New York: Basic Books).

Miller, George A. [1970], "Four Philosophical Problems of Psycholinguists", *Philosophy of Science* 37.

Miller, Neal E. [1969], "Learning of Visceral and Glandular Responses", *Science* 163.
Minsky, Marvin [1968a], "Descriptive Languages and Problem Solving", in Marvin Minsky (ed.), *Semantic Information Processing* (Cambridge: MIT).
Minsky, Marvin [1968b], *Semantic Information Processing* (Cambridge: MIT).
Monod, Jacques [1971], *Chance and Necessity*, trans. Austryn Wainhouse (New York: Knopf).
Mountcastle, V. A. [1965], "The Neural Replication of Sensory Events in the Somatic Afferent System", in J. C. Eccles (ed.), *Brain and Conscious Experience* (New York: Springer-Verlag).
Nagel, Ernest [1961], *The Structure of Science* (New York: Harcourt, Brace and World).
Nagel, Thomas [1965], "Physicalism", *Philos. Rev.* 74.
Nagel, Thomas [1969], "Linguistics and Epistemology", in Sidney Hook (ed.), *Language and Philosophy* (New York: New York University Press).
Nagel, Thomas [1970], *The Possibility of Altruism* (New York: Oxford University Press).
Nagel, Thomas [1971], "Brain Bisection and the Unity of Consciousness", *Synthese* 22.
Nagel, Thomas [1974], "What is it like to be a bat?", *Philos. Rev.* 83.
Neisser, Ulric [1967], *Cognitive Psychology* (Englewood Cliffs: Prentice-Hall).
Neurath, Otto *et al.* (eds.) [1955], *International Encyclopedia of Unified Science*, Vols. 1–2 (Chicago: University of Chicago Press).
Newell, Allen, Shaw, J. C. and Simon, H. A. [1963], "Empirical Explorations with the Logic Theory Machine: A Case Study in Heuristics", in Edward A. Feigenbaum and Julian Feldman (eds.), *Computers and Thought* (New York: McGraw-Hill).
Noble, D. [1966–67], "Charles Taylor on Teleological Explanation", *Analysis* 27.
Nowlis, David P., and Kamiya, J. [1970], "The Control of Electroencephalographic Alpha Rhythms through Auditory Feedback and the Associated Mental Activity", *Psychophysiology* 6.
Ohwaki, Y. and Kihara, T. [1953], "A New Research on the So-called 'Bocci Image' ", *Tohoku Psychologica Folia* 8.
Oppenheim, Paul and Hilary Putnam [1958], "Unity of Science as a Working Hypothesis", in Herbert Feigl *et al.* (eds.), *Minnesota Studies in the Philosophy of Science*, Vol. 2 (Minneapolis: University of Minnesota).
Paivio, Allan [1971], *Imagery and Verbal Processes* (New York: Holt, Rinehart and Winston).
Parfit, Derek [1971], "Personal Identity", *Philos. Rev.* 80.
Pears, D. F. [1967a], "Are Reasons for Acting Causes?", in Avrum Stroll (ed.), *Epistemology* (New York: Harper and Row).
Pears, D. F. [1967b], *Bertrand Russell and the British Tradition in Philosophy* (London: Fontana).
[Peirce, Charles Sanders] [1939], *Collected Papers of Charles Sanders Peirce*, edit. Charles Hartshorne and Paul Weiss (Cambridge: Harvard University Press), Vol. 4.
Penelhum, Terence [1970], *Survival and Disembodied Existence* (London: Routledge and Kegan Paul).
Penfield, Wilder [1965], "Speech, Perception and the Uncommitted Cortex", in J. C. Eccles (ed.), *Brain and Conscious Experience* (New York: Springer-Verlag).
Perky, C. W. [1910], "An Experimental Study of Imagination", *Am. J. Psychol.* 21.
Perry, John [1975], "Personal Identity, Memory and the Problem of Circularity", in

John Perry (ed.), *Personal Identity* (Berkeley and Los Angeles: University of California Press).

Peters, R. S. [1958], *The Concept of Motivation* (London: Routledge and Kegan Paul).

Piaget, Jean [1923], *Le language et la pensée chezl'enfant* (Neuchâtel-Paris: Delachaux and Niestlé).

Piaget, Jean [1926], *Judgment and Reasoning in the Child* (1924), trans. M. Warden (New York: Harcourt, Brace and World).

Piaget, Jean [1970], *Structuralism*, trans. Chinanah Maschler (New York: Basic Books).

Piaget, Jean [1971], *Biology and Knowledge*, trans. Beatrix Walsh (Chicago: University of Chicago Press).

Pitcher, George [1970], "Pain Perception", *Philos. Rev.* 79.

Pitcher, George [1971], *A Theory of Perception* (Princeton: Princeton University Press).

Place, U. T. [1956], "Is Consciousness a Brain Process?", *Brit. J. Psychology* 47.

Polten, Eric [1973], *Critique of the Psycho-Physical Identity Theory* (The Hague: Mouton).

Popper, Karl [1957], *The Poverty of Historicism* (London: Routledge and Kegan Paul).

Popper, Karl [1972a], "Epistemology without a Knowing Subject", in *Objective Knowledge* (Oxford: Clarendon).

Popper, Karl [1972b], "On the Theory of the Objective Mind", in *Objective Knowledge* (Oxford: Clarendon).

Popper, Karl [1972c], "The Aim of Science", in *Objective Knowledge* (Oxford: Clarendon).

Popper, Karl [1972d], "Of Clouds and Clocks", in *Objective Knowledge* (Oxford: Clarendon).

Premack, David [1971], "On the Assessment of Language Competence in the Chimpanzee", in Allan M. Schrier and Fres Stollnitz (eds.), *Behavior of Nonhuman Primates*, Vol. 4 (New York: Academic Press).

Price, H. H. [1965], "Survival and the Idea of 'Another World' ", in J. R. Smythies (ed.) *Brain and Mind* (London: Routledge and Kegan Paul).

Prince, Morton [1903], *The Dissociation of a Personality* (New York: Longmans, Green).

Puccetti, Roland [1973], "Brain Bisection and Personal Identity", *Brit. J. Philos. Sc.* 24.

Putnam, Hilary [1960], "Minds and Machines", in Sidney Hook (ed.), *Dimensions of Mind* (New York: New York University).

Putnam, Hilary [1961], "Some Issues in the Theory of Grammar", *Structure of Language and its Mathematical Aspects. Proceedings of Symposia in Applied Mathematics*, 7 (Providence: American Mathematical Society).

Putnam, Hilary [1964], "Robots: Machines or Artificially Created Life?", *J. Philos.* 61.

Putnam, Hilary [1965], "How not to talk about meaning", in Robert S. Cohen and Marx W. Wartofsky (eds.), *Boston Studies in the Philosophy of Science*, Vol. 2 (New York: Humanities Press).

Putnam, Hilary [1967a], "The Nature of Mental States", in W. H. Capitan and D. D. Merrill (eds.), *Art, Mind, and Religion* (Pittsburgh: University of Pittsburgh Press).

Putman, Hilary [1967b], "The 'Innateness Hypothesis' and Explanatory Models in Linguistics", *Syntheses* 17.

Quine, V. W. [1953], "On What There Is", in *From a Logical Point of View* (Cambridge: Harvard University Press).

Quine, V. W. [1957], "The Scope and Language of Science", *Brit. J. Philos. Sci.* 8.

Quine, V. W. [1960], *Word and Object* (Cambridge: MIT Press).

Quine, V. W. [1966], "On Mental Entities", in *The Ways of Paradox and Other Essays* (New York: Random House).

Quine, V. W. [1970], "Grades of Theoreticity", in Lawrence Foster and J. W. Swanson (eds.), *Experience & Theory* (Amherst: University of Massachusetts Press).

Quine, V. W. [1974], *The Roots of Reference* (LaSalle, Ill.: Open Court).

Quinton, Anthony [1962], "The Soul", *J. Philos.* 59.

Quinton, Anthony [1973], *The Nature of Things* (London: Routledge and Kegan Paul).

Rescher, Nicholas [1973], *The Coherence Theory of Truth* (Oxford: Clarendon).

Richardson, Alan [1969], *Mental Imagery* (New York: Springer).

Rorty, Richard [1965], "Mind-Body Identity, Privacy, and Categories", *Rev. Metaphys.* 19.

Rorty, Richard [1970], "In Defense of Eliminative Materialism", *Rev. Metaphys.* 24.

Rose, Steven [1972], *The Conscious Brain* (London: Weidenfeld and Nicolson).

Rosenthal, David [1977], "Keeping Matter in Mind", unpublished paper presented at a philosophy colloquium, University of Pennsylvania.

Rundle, Bede [1972], *Perception, Sensation and Verification* (Oxford: Clarendon).

Ruse, Michael [1973], *The Philosophy of Biology* (London: Hutchinson).

Russell, Bertrand [1905], "On Denoting", *Mind* 14.

Russell, Bertrand [1918], "The Relation of Sense-Data to Physics", in *Mysticism and Logic* (London: Longman, Green).

Russell, Bertrand [1956], "Knowledge by Acquaintance and Knowledge by Description", in *Mysticism and Logic* (London: Allen and Unwin).

Russell, Bertrand [1966], "On the Nature of Truth and Falsity", in *Philosophical Essays* (New York: Simon and Schuster).

Ruwet, Jean-Claude [1972], *Introduction to Ethology*, trans. Joyce Diamanti (New York: International Universities Press).

Ryle, Gilbert [1949], *The Concept of Mind* (London: Hutchinson).

Salmon, Wesley [1975], "Statistical Explanation", in Wesley Salmon, *Statistical Explanation and Statistical Relevance* (Pittsburgh: University of Pittsburgh Press).

Sauerbruch, Ferdinand, and Wenke, Hans [1963], *Pain: Its Meaning and Significance*, trans. E. Fitzgerald (London: Allen and Unwin).

Saul, R. E., and R. W. Sperry [1968], "Absence of Commissurotomy Symptoms with Agenesis of the Corpus Callosum", *Neurology* 18.

Savage, C. Wade [1970], *The Measurement of Sensation* (Berkeley and Los Angeles: University of California Press).

Sayre, Kenneth M. [1965], *Recognition: A Study in the Philosophy of Artificial Intelligence* (Notre Dame: University of Notre Dame Press).

Sayre, Kenneth M. [1969], *Consciousness: A Philosophic Study of Minds and Machines* (New York: Random House).

Sayre, Kenneth and Crosson, Frederick J. (eds.) [1968], *The Modeling of Mind. Computers and Intelligence* (Notre Dame: Notre Dame University Press).

Scheffler, Israel [1963], *The Anatomy of Inquiry* (New York: Knopf).

Schrier, Allan M. and Stollnitz, Fred (eds.) [1971], *Behavior of Non-human Primates; Modern Research Trends*, Vol. 4 (New York: Academic Press).

Schwayder, David [1965], *The Stratification of Behavior* (New York: Humanities Press).

Scriven, Michael [1956], "A Study of Radical Behaviorism", in Herbert Feigl and

Michael Scriven (eds.), *Minnesota Studies in the Philosophy of Science*, Vol. 1 (Minneapolis: University of Minnesota Press).

Searle, John [1969], *Speech Acts* (Cambridge: Cambridge University Press).

Sellars, Wilfrid [1963a], "Philosophy and the Scientific Image of Man", in *Science, Perception, and Reality* (London: Routledge and Kegan Paul).

Sellars, Wilfrid [1963b], "Empiricism and the Philosophy of Mind", in *Science, Perception, and Reality* (London: Routledge & Kegan Paul).

Sellars, Wilfrid [1964], "Notes on Intentionality", *J. Philos.* 61.

Sellars, Wilfrid [1965], "The Identity Approach to the Mind-Body Problem", *Rev. Metaphys.* 18.

Sellars, Wilfrid and Chisholm, Roderick M. [1958], "Intentionality and the Mental", in Herbert Feigl and Michael Scriven (eds.), *Minnesota Studies in the Philosophy of Science*, Vol. 2 (Minneapolis: University of Minnesota).

Shaffer, Jerome [1961], "Could Mental States be Brain Processes?", *J. Philos.* 59.

Shaffer, Jerome [1966], "Persons and Their Bodies", *Philos. Rev.* 25.

Shannon, C. E., and Weaver, W. [1949], *Mathematical Theory of Communication* (Urbana: Yniversity of Illinois Press).

Shapiro, David, Tursky, Bernard and Schwartz, Gary E. [1970], "Differentiation of Heart Rate and Systolic Blood Pressure in Man by Operant Conditioning", *Psychosomatic Medicine* 32.

Sherrington, C. S. [1906], *Integrative Action of the Nervous System* (New Haven: Yale University Press).

Sherrington, C. S. [1951], *Man on his Nature* (Cambridge: Cambridge University Press).

Shoemaker, Sydney [1959], "Personal Identity and Memory", *J. Philos.* 66.

Shoemaker, Sydney [1963], *Self-Knowledge and Self-Identity* (Ithaca: Cornell University Press).

Shope, Robert K. [1971], "Physical and Psychic Energy", *Philosophy of Science* 58.

Sibley, F. N. [1971], "Analysing Seeing (1)", in F. N. Sibley (ed.), *Perception; A Philosophical Symposium* (London: Methuen).

Siegel, R. K. and West, L. J. (eds.) [1975], *Hallucinations; Behavior, Experience, and Theory* (New York: John Wiley).

Simon, Michael A. [1971], *The Matter of Life; Philosophical Problems of Biology* (New Haven: Yale University Press).

Skinner, B. F. [1953], *Science and Human Behavior* (New York: Macmillan).

Skinner, B. F. [1957], *Verbal Behavior* (New York: Appleton-Century-Crofts).

Skinner, B. F. [1964], "Behaviorism at Fifty", in T. W. Wann (ed.), *Behaviorism and Phenomenology: Contrasting Bases for Modern Psychology* (Chicago: University of Chicago Press).

Skolimowski, Henryk [1974], "Problems of Rationality in Biology", in Francisco Jose Ayala and Theodosius Dobzhansky (eds.), *Studies in the Philosophy of Biology; Reduction and Related Problems* (Berkeley and Los Angeles: University of San Francisco: University of California).

Smart, J. J. C. [1962], "Sensations and Brain Processes", revised in V. C. Chappell (ed.), *The Philosophy of Mind* (Englewood Cliffs: Prentice-Hall).

Smart, J. J. C. [1963], *Philosophy and Scientific Realism* (London: Routledge and Kegan Paul).

Solomon, Robert C. [1974], "Freud's Neurological Theory of Mind", in Richard

Wollheim (ed.), *Freud; A Collection of Critical Essays* (Garden City: Anchor Books).

Sommerhoff, Gerd [1974], *Logic of the Living Brain* (London: John Wiley).

Sorabji, R. [1964], "Function", *Philos. Quart.* 14.

Sperling, G. [1960], "The Information Available in Brief Visual Presentations", *Psychological Monographs* 74.

Sperry, R. W. [1966], "Brain Bisection and Consciousness", in J. C. Eccles (ed.), *Brain and Conscious Experience* (New York: Springer-Verlag).

Sperry, R. W. [1968], "Hemisphere Deconnection and Unity of Conscious Awareness," *Am. Psychologist* 23.

Sperry, R. W. [1969], "A Modified Concept of Consciousness", *Psychol. Rev.* 76.

Spicker, Stuart F. (ed.) [1970], *The Philosophy of the Body* (Chicago: Quadrangle Books).

Stalker, Frank [1976], *Deep Structure* (Philadelphia: Philosophical Monographs).

Steiner, George [1975], *After Babel* (New York: Oxford University Press).

Stenhouse, David [1973], *The Evolution of Intelligence* (London: George Allen and Unwin).

Sternbach, Richard A. [1968], *Pain, A Psychophysiological Analysis* (New York: Academic Press).

Stevens, S. S. [1935], "The Operational Definition of Psychological Concepts", *Psychol. Rev.* 42.

Stoutland, Frederick [1968], "Basic Actions and Causality", *J. Philos.* 65.

Strawson, P. F. [1950], "On Referring", *Mind* 59.

Strawson, P. F. [1959], *Individuals* (London: Methuen).

Strawson, P. F. [1966], *The Bounds of Sense* (London: Methuen).

Strawson, P. F. [1970], "Imagination and Perception", in Lawrence Foster and J. W. Swanson (eds.), *Experience & Theory* (Amherst: University of Massachusetts Press).

Suppes, Patrick [1969a], "Stimulus-Response Theory of Finite Automata", *J. Math. Psychol.* 6.

Sweet, W. H. [1959], "Pain", in John Field *et al.* (eds.), *Handbook of Physiology*, Sec. 1, Vol. 1 (Washington: American Physiological Society).

Tarski, Alfred [1944], "The Semantic Conception of Truth", *Philos. Phenomenol. Res.* 4.

Tarski, Afred [1956], "The Concept of Truth in Formalized Languages", in *Logic, Semantics, Metamathematics*, trans. J. H. Woodger (Oxford: Clarendon).

Taylor, Charles [1964], *The Explanation of Behavior* (London: Routledge and Kegan Paul).

Thigpen, Corbett H. [1957], *Three Faces of Eve* (New York: McGraw-Hill).

Timpanaro, Sebastiano [1975], *On Materialism*, trans. Lawrence Garner (London: NLB).

Tinbergen, N. [1969], *The Study of Instinct* (London: Oxford University Press).

Tolman, E. C. [1932], *Purposive Behavior in Animals and Man* (New York: Appleton-Century-Crofts).

Trigg, Robert [1970], *Pain and Emotion* (Oxford: Clarendon Press).

Turbayne, Colin Murray [1969], "Visual Language from the Verbal Model", *Journal of Typographic Research*, 3.

Turbayne, Colin Murray [1972], "Metaphors for the Mind", in Richard Rudner and Israel Scheffler (eds.), *Language and Art. Essays in Honor of Nelson Goodman* (Indianapolis: Bobbs-Merrill).

Turing, A. M. [1950], "Computing Machinery and Intelligence", *Mind* 59.
Valzelli, Luigi [1973], *Psychopharmacology* (New York: Spectrum).
Vendler, Zeno [1967], *Linguistics in Philosophy* (Ithaca: Cornell University Press).
Vendler, Zeno [1972], *Res Cogitans* (Ithaca: Cornell University Press).
Vesey, G. N. A. [Godfrey] (ed.) [1964], *Body and Mind* (London: Allen and Unwin).
Vesey, G. N. A. [Godfrey] [1965], *The Embodied Mind* (London: Allen and Unwin).
Vesey, Godfrey [1974], *Personal Identity; A Philosophical Analysis* (Ithaca: Cornell University Press).
Vol'kenshtein, Mikhail V. [1970], *Molecules and Life; An Introduction to Molecular Biology*, trans. Serge N. Timasheff (New York: Plenum).
von Mises, Richard [1957], *Probability, Statistics and Truth*, 2nd English ed. (London: George Allen and Unwin).
Vygotsky, L. S. [1962], *Thought and Language*, trans. Eugenia and Hanfmann and Gertrude Vakar (Cambridge: MIT).
Wallace, Robert K., and Benson, Herbert [1972], "The Physiology of Medication", *Scientific American*. 226.
Watson, J. B. [1924], *Psychology from the Standpoint of a Behaviorist* (London: J. P. Lippincott).
Watson, J. B. [1948], "Psychology as the Behaviorist Views It" (1913), in Wayne Dennis (ed.), *Readings in the History of Psychology* (New York: Appleton-Century-Crofts).
Watson, James D. [1970], *Molecular Biology of the Gene*, 2nd ed. (New York: Benjamin).
[Weber, Max] [1946], *From Max Weber: Essays in Sociology*, trans. H. H. Gerth and C. Wright Mills (New York: Oxford University Press).
[Weber, Max] [1949], *On the Methodology of the Social Sciences*, trans. and ed. E. A. Shils and H. A. Finch (Glencoe, Free Press).
White, Alan R. [1967], *The Philosophy of Mind* (New York: Random House).
White, J. C. and Sweet, W. H. [1955], *Pain. Its Mechanisms and Neurosurgical Control* (Springfield: Charles Thomas).
Whiteley, C. H. [1973], *Mind in Action* (London: Oxford University Press).
Wiggins, David [1967], *Identity and Spatio-Temporal Continuity* (Oxford: Basil Blackwell).
Williams, B. A. O. [Bernard] [1957], "Personal Identity and Individuation", *Proc. Aristotelian Soc.* 57.
Williams, B. A. O. [Bernard] [1970], "Are Persons Bodies?", in Stuart F. Spicker (ed.), *The Philosophy of the Body* (New York: Quadrangle).
Williams, B. A. O. [Bernard] [1973a], "A Critique of Utilitarianism", in J. J. C. Smart and Bernard Williams, *Utilitarianism for and Against* (Cambridge: Cambridge University Press).
Williams, B. A. O. [Bernard] [1973b], *Problems of the Self* (Cambridge: Cambridge University Press).
Williams, B. A. O. [Bernard] [1976], "Persons, Character and Morality", in Amélie Oksenberg Rorty (ed.), *The Identities of Persons* (Berkeley and Los Angeles: University of California).
Wilson, Edward O. [1975], *Sociobiology: The New Synthesis* (Cambridge: Harvard University Press).
Winch, Peter [1958], *The Idea of a Social Science* (London: Routledge and Kegan Paul).
Wisdom, John [1952], *Other Minds* (Oxford: Basil Blackwell).

Wittgenstein, Ludwig [1963], *Philosophical Investigations*, 2nd ed., trans. G. E. M. Anscombe (London: Basil Blackwell).
Wollheim, Richard [1968], *Art and Its Objects* (New York: Harper).
Wolterstorff, Nicholas [1970], *Universals* (Chicago: University of Chicago Press).
Wolterstorff, Nicholas [1975], "Toward an Ontology of Art Works", *Nous* 9.
Woodfield, Andrew [1976], *Teleology* (Cambridge: Cambridge University Press).
Woolridge, Dean E. [1963], *The Machinery of the Brain* (New York: McGraw-Hill).
Wright, Larry [1976], *Teleological Explanations* (San Francisco and Los Angeles: University of Chicago Press).
Ziff, Paul [1965], "What An Adequate Grammar Couldn't Do", *Foundations of Language* 1.
Zinn, Howard [1970], *The Politics of History* (Boston: Beacon Press).

GENERAL INDEX

"ability of intention" (Kenny) 164
act-essentialism (Goldman) 253
actions
  and bodily movements 182, 249
  and consciousness 182
  and covering institutions 259
  and responsibility 191
  as intentional 252
  as molar ascriptions 182
  characterization of 254, 259
  D'Arcy on 253, 255
  embodied 249
  Goldman on 252-253
  individuation of 252, 253
  intentional context of 251
  of persons 249
  polyadic qualification of 252
  reasons for 250
  Taylor on 191
Active/passive transformation 154-155,
    157
acts
  adverbial qualification of 249
  and consequences 253-254
  and freedom 249
  individuation of 252, 253
act-tokens (Goldman) 252, 253
act-types (Goldman) 252
agenesis 79
akrasia 166
analytic/synthetic 258
"analytical hypotheses" (Quine) 208
animal beliefs 131, 151-158, 159, 161

animal concepts 151, 157, 161, 178
animal psychology 146, 150, 156
animals
  and acquisition of language 102-103,
    121, 122, 124, 149
  and cognition 130, 140
  and convention T 148-149
  and inference 153
  and thoughts 147, 148, 149
  Armstrong on 155
  as emergent 187
  as sentient 146
  beliefs of 130-131, 135-136
  capable of perceptual cognition 123,
    131, 134-135, 147, 150, 153, 164, 165
  capable or not capable of thought
    (belief) 120, 121, 131, 147, 148, 149,
    150, 164
  Davidson on 131, 147
  Geach on 165
  heuristic ascriptions regarding 123, 161
  Kenny on 164, 165
  lacking and not lacking concepts 134,
    151, 161, 178
  lacking language 147, 148, 150, 151,
    153, 156, 157, 158, 161, 243
  Malcolm on 147
  Sibley on 155-156, 168
  Vendler on 163-164
  volitional and intellectual capacities of
    164
    See Fido
anomolous monism (Davidson) 219

Anscombe, G. E. M. 66
aphasias 96
Arbib, Michael 133
Aristotle 166
Armstrong, D. M. 31, 50, 144-145, 155,
    159, 160, 161, 167, 176-177, 178-
    180
artificial intelligence 189
attributes
    emergent 7
    functional 50
    logical 63
    mental 63
    Smart on 5
automata 146, 201, 258
autonomic processes 214
aware₁ (Dennett) 185, 188
aware₂ (Dennett) 185
awareness 176, 177, 201, 212
Axiom of Existence (Searle) 6

"basic" actions (Danto) 253
basic particulars (Strawson) 8, 24, 83,
    226, 227
bats 194
behavior, explanation of 258-259
behavioral sciences and statistical laws
    259
behaviorally significant 208
behaviorism 23, 99, 136, 191, 200, 203,
    207
    and "raw feels" 201
    Feigl on 200
    Fodor on 201-202
    logical 200
    methodological 200
    of Skinner 200, 207
    radical 200, 209, 213
    Watson on 200
belief, capacity for
    Davidson on 147
    Kenny on 164
    Malcolm on 147
    Sibley on 155, 156
    Vendler on 163-164
belief contexts 37, 50, 153, 157, 159

See intentional contexts
beliefs
    and cognitive agents 133, 134
    and language 147, 148, 153, 155, 160,
        161, 163, 164, 173
    and logical equivalence 152
    and oratio obliqua 156
    and rationality 156, 160, 177, 178, 188
    ascription of 168
    as psychological states 153, 166
    as real 130, 131, 135, 136
    fictive theory of 130, 131
    heuristic theory of 130, 131
    intensional complexities of 126, 153,
        155, 157, 158, 159
    intentional (propositional) content of
        144, 150, 159, 160, 167
    of languageless animals 153-156, 157,
        158, 159, 160
    of the linguistically competent 152,
        158, 160, 161
    propositional structure of 130, 154, 159,
        162
    Quine on 157
    See animals
Bell, Daniel 255
Bergmann, Gustav 32
Berkeley, George 31, 33, 118
bilinguals 203
biofeedback 214
"biological universals" (Margolis)
    149, 191, 195, 196, 206
Bloomfield, Leonard 114
'body' 28, 29, 30
Bogen, J. E. 94
brain transplants 241
Brentano, Franz 13, 14, 30, 74, 144,
    212, 218
Brodbeck, May 32
Brown, Roger 121, 124
Bunge, Mario 236
Butler, Joseph 16

Campbell, C. A. 249
Cartesian automaton 146
Cartesian insight 129

category mistake (Ryle) 41, 44
causal contexts, extensionality of 251
causal explanation of intentional behavior 250, 251, 259
causal laws 216, 218, 220, 221, 260
causalgic pain 67
causality and freedom 245, 249, 260
causes, intentionally qualified 247, 250
central-state materialism (Armstrong) 179-180
cetacians 246, 247
Charles/Guy Fawkes case (Williams) 86-87, 88, 239-240
chicks 195
chimpanzees 103, 121, 124, 149, 238
Chisholm, Roderick M. 15, 17, 23
Chomsky, Noam 9, 17, 18, 19, 72, 98-100, 102-103, 104, 106-107, 108-110, 112-115, 116, 117, 119, 120, 121, 124, 136, 139, 163, 247
circadian rhythm 191
clone persons 233, 239
co-designative terms 36, 157, 251
cognitive agents (systems) 133, 207
  and access to information 132, 133, 134, 207
  and beliefs 130-131, 132, 133, 134, 136
  and capacity for intentional states 133
  using language 140
"cognitive map" (Griffin) 194
cognitive psychology 142
cognitive states (cognition) 71, 199
  and machines 71
commissurotomy (brain-bisection) 89, 91-92, 95, 96
  Puccetti on 90-92
  Sperry on 91
compatibilism 260, 261, 262
composition 3, 4, 8, 41
compulsion 249
computational model 138, 141, 142-143, 186
concepts 126, 134, 138, 139
  and Platonic paradox 146
  Armstrong on 144, 155, 161, 178-

179, 180
  as heuristic entities 161, 162
  biological basis of 195
  causal theory of 179
  Fodor on 138, 139-140
  Geach on 144, 165
  learning 138-139
  Piaget on 140
  Sibley on 155-156
conceptual capacity 139-140
conduct, prudential model of 244
consciousness 169, 173, 174, 175, 180, 182, 186, 188, 189, 191, 199
  and action 182
  Armstrong on 176-177
  as theoretical 189
  Dennett on 186, 188
  materialistic interpretation of 4
  Matson on 175
  Sayre on 180-181
contextual reference 101
convention T (Tarski) 147, 148, 149
Cornman, James 41-42, 45, 49-50
couvade 67
"covering" institutions, distinct from covering laws 259, 262
covering-law explanation 174, 251, 258, 259, 260
cross-category identities 41, 44, 54, 56, 57, 60, 67
  and Leibniz's law 41-42, 44, 52
  Cornman on 41-42, 49
  Fodor on 63
  Smart on 41
culture
  and functional properties 21
  and neocortex 248
  and persons 245
  and reductionism 257
  and rules 20-21
  intentionality of 21
'cultural' 237
cultural emergence, and freedom 246
cultural entities, 7, 8, 20-21
  existence conditions of 234
  extensionally identified 242

individuation of 234
irreducibility of 234
ontology of 225, 226, 230, 235
variety of 229, 237
cultural explanation relativized 257
cultural phenomena (systems)
  and intensional distinctions 8
  and linguistic ability 237
  and psychological phenomena 225
  as emergent 8
  as rule-following 237
  as rulelike 237
  causal explanation of 22
  not endowed with minds 225

D'Arcy, Eric 253-255
David (Michelangelo) 7
Davidson, Donald 131, 141, 147, 148-149, 214-223
Demoiselles d'Avignon, Les (Picasso) 231, 232
Dennett, Daniel 50, 132, 143-144, 145, 159, 183-188
Descartes, René 17, 19, 20, 51, 60, 77, 108, 121, 212
descriptive metaphysics (Strawson) 225, 226
determinism 260, 261, 262
  hard 249
deterministic laws 216
disembodied existence 228
dissociative personality 92, 96
dolphins 103, 149
Dretske, Fred I. 133, 144
Dreyfus, Hubert L. 188
dualism 4, 5, 6, 7, 24, 28, 31, 33, 72, 74, 82, 175, 215, 228
  and functional states 72
  attribute 58, 60
  Cartesian 51, 58, 60, 62, 72, 89, 175
  of energy 211
  ontic 32, 58, 60
  Polten on 61
  semantic theories regarding 60, 61
  three sorts of 60-63

Eccles, John C. 60, 75, 76, 77
ecological balance 248
"egocentric speech" (Piaget) 127
eliminative materialism 32, 47, 48, 49, 58, 83, 97
  and first-person reports 47-48, 49
  Cornman on 49
  Feyerabend on 45, 46-47
  Rorty on 45, 47-49
embodied entities 7, 20, 25, 234, 235, 239, 241
embodiment 3, 8, 22, 23-25, 234, 235, 259
  and Strawson's theory of persons 24
  conditions of 234
emergence 7, 8
  Bunge on 236
  Feigl on 235, 236
  emergence$_B$ 236, 237
  emergence$_F$ 236, 237
  emergence$_M$ 236, 237
emergent entities 23, 26, 236
  Bunge on 236
  See cultural entities
emergentist materialism 9, 58
empathy 245
engram 76
epiphenomenalism 72, 73, 74, 175, 200, 210-211, 213, 215
  Feigl on 210
  Huxley on 211
etching 232
ethical systems 245
events 252
events and states 43-44, 52, 53, 54, 56, 57
experience, Lewis on 73-74
explanation by reasons 251
explanations, "nomological-deductive" (Hempel) 261
explanatory contexts, intensionality of 220
extensionalist canon 237

Fabre, J. H. 190
Feigl, Herbert 13, 15, 16, 17, 18, 20,

21, 23, 42, 52, 177, 178, 179, 185, 200, 210-211, 213, 215, 216, 217, 218, 223, 235, 236
feral children 105
Feyerabend, P. K. 45-48, 179, 214, 215, 217, 218
fiat (Kenny) 166
Fido 134-136, 147, 151-155, 156-158, 177
first-person reports (reporting role) 47-49, 63, 64, 69, 72, 209
  Malcolm on 210
  Wittgenstein on 210
Fodor, Jerry A. 63-65, 68, 72, 74, 137-143, 186, 188, 201-202
forgery 232
Frankenstein Axiom (Matson) 171-172, 173
freedom
  and causality 245, 249, 260
  and determinism 249-250, 260
  and linguistically competent beings 246
  as a mixed category 250
  Campbell on 249
  Kenny on 260
  Meldon on 249
  Peters on 249
Frege, G. 61
Freud, Sigmund 12, 13
  Solomon on 12-13
Frisch, K. von 238
frog 188
functional entities 26
  See cultural entities
functional (logical) states 4, 63-65, 68, 71, 72, 73, 74, 75, 76, 172
  and cognitive states 69, 71
  and dualism 72
  and first-person reports 72
  and machines 63, 77
  and pains 65, 66, 67, 68, 69, 71
  Fodor on 64
functional materialism 72
functional properties 21, 25, 42, 171, 172, 173, 174, 213

Galileo 47
Gardner, Beatrice T. 121, 122
Gardner, R. A. 121, 122
'Gavagai' (Quine) 204-205, 206
Geach, P. T. 123, 144, 160, 161, 162-163, 164, 165, 166, 180
Geistewissenschaften and Naturwissenschaften 245
generative semantics 117
Gibson, J. J. 94, 168
Glickman, Jack 231-232
God
  as man's artificer 109
  Berkeley's 33
Gödel's proof 10
Goldbach's conjecture 111
Goldman, Alvin 252-153
'good' 199
Goodman, Nelson 119, 120, 121, 123, 230
grammatically deviant sentences 101
  Lakoff on 104
Greylag geese 194
Griffin, Donald R. 194

Hare, R. H. 166
'have' 54, 55, 56
having (possessing) mental and physical states 52-56, 57
  Nagel on 52, 54, 55
heteronomic (Davidson) 221
heuristic ascriptions 123, 123, 125, 126, 149, 161
heuristic entities 161, 162, 167
heuristic model 123, 126, 129, 139, 146, 155-156, 160, 161, 169, 173, 187, 199, 227
historical laws 245
history 255
Hobbes, Thomas 5, 31
holophrastic period (McNeill) 110
Homo sapiens 247, 248
"homogeneous reference class" (Salmon) 261
homonomic (Davidson) 221
honeybees 150, 238-239

von Frisch on 238-239
horme (McDougall) 211
Hume, David 100, 259
Huxley, T. H. 211
Hydén, H. 76

idealism 31, 33, 82
Ideas (Geach) 144, 160, 163, 165, 166,
    180
  Armstrong on 144
identity 34-35
  and assignment of intentional content
      38-39, 42, 50, 51, 160
  and kinds of "entities" 29, 31, 34,
      39-40, 42-44
  and Leibniz's law 36, 38
  and linguistic contexts 35-36
  contingent 34
  of attributes 57
  self- 34, 35
  strict 45
  theoretical 65, 69, 76
identity theory 10, 12, 13, 19, 34-35,
    37, 39, 41, 42, 43, 56, 57, 65, 72,
    76, 97, 171, 172, 175, 180, 183,
    200, 219
  and cross-category identities 41-42, 56,
      57
  and eliminative materialism 45
  and kinds of entities 39-40
  and one-one correspondence 42, 49
  and sortals 40
  Cornman on 41-42
  "disappearance form" of 45
  Feyerabend on 45-47
  Fodor on 68
  Matson on 171, 172
  Rorty on 45
  "translation form" of 95
identification and reidentification 226,
    240-241
identifying references 226
"identity thesis" (Goldman) 252, 253
ideological commitments 199, 244
ideology 255, 256, 257, 258, 259

Bell on 255
imagination 195
incorrigibility 49
indeterminacy of translation (Quine)
    203-204, 222
indubitability 212
information 129, 133, 168, 169, 175,
    178
  and functional properties 175
  and sentience 175
  ascription of 183
  at the sub-cognitive level 132-133, 137
  Dennett on 132-133, 178
  Dretske on 133
  processing of 181, 182, 183
  propositionally specified 132, 133
innate ideas (grammar) 100, 106, 118, 121,
    163
"innate releasing mechanism" (Tinbergen)
    192
innate rules 106-107, 109, 112, 113
innatism 109
inscriptionalism (Goodman) 229, 210
  Scheffler on 230
inscrutability of reference (Quine) 204,
    205
instinct
  Lorenz on 246
  Stenhouse on 246
instinctive activity (act) 192, 193
  and learning 193, 194, 246
institutions 259
integrons (Jacob) 116
intensionality (intensional distinctions) 8,
    16
  and explanatory contexts 220
  and language 16, 18, 162
  and linguistic ability 161-162
  and mental phenomena 76, 77, 126
  and persons 16
  and referential opacity 157
  not applying to languageless animals
      153-154, 155, 157, 158
  paradoxes of 126
intentional contexts, opacity of 37, 50,

251
intentional idiom 150
intentionality (intentional attributes,
    states)
  and cognitive agents 133, 183
  and consciousness 212, 213
  and language 14, 16, 17, 18, 20, 237
  and logical behaviorism 23
  and mental phenomena 30, 126
  and persons 15
  and rules 21
  and sentient organisms (sentience) 15,
    21, 183
  and scientific image 15
  and teleological model 184, 190
  Armstrong on 144-145
  assigned to neural states 38-39
  assigned to the sub-personal 187
  Brentano on 13, 14, 30, 74, 144, 212,
    218
  Chisholm on 15, 17, 23
  Dennett on 184
  Feigl on 14, 16, 17, 223
  irreducibility of 14, 15, 17, 18, 217-
    218, 223, 225, 247
  Körner on 15, 17
  of science 15
  Sellars on 14, 15-16, 17, 23, 24, 25
  Taylor on 190
intentions (intentional states) 250
  and persons 15-16
  as functional states 65
  causal role of 259
interaction of mind and body 60
internal representation 106, 124, 135,
    136, 137, 138, 140, 141, 142,
    160, 173
  Fodor on 137-143
'invariances', various sense of 114
'is', various senses of 3-4

jackdaws 193, 239
Jacob, François 116
justice 244

Kempson, Ruth M. 104-105
Kenny, Anthony 164-166, 260
Keynsian economics 250
kinds 231, 232
Körner, Stephan 15, 17

Lakoff, George 104
language(s)
  acquisition of 9, 97, 98, 108
  actual 1-5
  artificial 103-104
  as cultural 97, 105-106
  as "species specific" 100, 103
  behavioristic theories of 99, 202-208
  cognitive or conceptual constraints on
    111, 113-114
  functionally characterized 106
  Goodman on 119
  irreducibility of 14-15, 16, 17, 20
  Kantian constraints on 103
  of bees 238
  Quine on 202-208
  See language acquisition
language acquisition
  and animals 102-103, 121, 122, 124
  and second-language model 119, 120,
    124, 126, 163
  and "taking on of culture" 124-125
  Brown on 121, 124-125
  Chomsky on 97-100, 102, 103, 104,
    106, 108, 109, 113, 114, 118,
    120, 121
  empiricist theory of 98, 99, 100, 102,
    105, 106, 107, 108, 109, 118,
    120, 121, 123, 228
  Gardners on 121
  Goodman on 119, 121, 123
  Lenneberg on 121
  McNeill on 111, 120
  Putnam on 100
  rationalist theory of 98-101, 102-104,
    105, 106, 107, 108, 112, 114,
    118, 120, 123, 149
  Turbayne on 118, 121, 123
  Vendler on 120

See Washoe
Law of Transferable Epithets (Fodor) 37
lawlike regularities 106, 108, 112
learning
  Lorenz on 246, 247
  Stenhouse on 246, 247
Leibniz, Gottfried 21, 100, 108
Leibniz's law 36, 37, 38, 40, 41, 43,
  44, 52
Lenneberg, Eric 121
Lewis, David K. 73-74, 75, 76, 176, 187,
  218
"liberty of indifference" (Hume) 260, 261
"liberty of spontanity" (Hume) 260
linguistic ability 101-102, 107, 247
  and intentionality 14, 16, 17, 18, 20
  and reductionism 6, 14-15
linguistic competence (Chomsky) 101,
  105, 107
linguistic model 132, 148, 150, 156, 158,
  159, 165, 173, 187
linguistic universals 17-18, 104, 106,
  109, 110, 111, 112, 113, 120,
  173
  and exceptions 105
  as idealizations 109
  as innate 106-107, 109
  as rulelike 112
  Chomsky on 106, 110, 112, 113
  McNeill on 111-112
linguistics and cognitive psychology 115
Locke, John 16, 31, 87, 100, 108, 228,
  254
Lorenz, Konrad 193, 239, 246

M- and P-predicates (Strawson) 51, 83,
  84, 85
machines
  and knowledge 70, 71
  and language 107, 108, 109
  and persons 172
  and rules 109
Malcolm, Norman 147, 209
Malebranche, Nicolas 33
many-many correlations 9, 42, 68
  See one-one correspondence

Martians 103
material bodies 226-228
  Strawson on 226-228
"materialese" (Feyerabend) 46, 47
materialism
  and dualism 5
  as physicialism 5
  attribute 5, 6, 9
  eliminative 108, 215
  emergentist 9, 58
  functional 1, 5, 72, 76
  nonreductive 215, 217, 223, 224, 226,
    227, 235
  ontic 5, 6
  reductive 20, 22, 49, 81, 83, 108, 215
  Strawson on 226
  strong thesis of 4-5
  theories characterized as 3, 4, 19, 30,
    32-33
  See eliminative materialism
Matson, Wallace I. 171-173, 175, 182, 202
McNeill, David 111-112, 120
meaning
  as functional property 229
  Kempson on 105
medicine 248
Melancholia I (Dürer) 232, 234, 240
Melden, A. I. 249
Melzack, Ronald 66-67
memories 241
"Mental" (Geach) 162
mental acts (Geach) 165
"Mental" and the "Physical", The (Feigl)
  14
mental phenomena (states, attributes)
  146, 154, 159, 160, 173, 179,
  180, 181
  and action 244
  and behavior 199, 200-201, 244
  and behaviorism 200-202
  and conceptual ability 244
  and purposive system 199
  and rationality 177
  Armstrong on 176-177, 178-180
  ascriptions of 243, 244
  Brentano on 13, 30

causal role of 199, 200, 214, 215, 216, 217, 218, 219, 220, 222
characterized functionally 65, 68, 173
Davidson on 214-223
Dennet on 184
Descartes on 30
distinguished from physical phenomena (states, attributes) 13, 30, 32, 37-38, 63, 68
Feigl on 200
Fodor on 68
Geach on 176
intensionality of 126, 173
reality of 162
mentalism 202
methodology of physical sciences 225
'mind' 28, 30
minds 9, 34
Freud on 12
(infant), preset for language 98, 101, 103, 107, 109, 111, 114, 114
plural 91, 94
minimal skepticism 201, 255
modes of thinking, Bogen on 94
molar responses (Tolman) 201
monism and materialism 31, 32-33, 48, 172
Monod, Jacques 116
moths 168-169
multiple personality 242
music 232

Nagel, Thomas 52-55
nativism 139, 141, 247
natural languages 17, 98, 101, 102, 103, 105, 106, 108, 109
acquisition of 98
and chimpanzees 103
and convention 148-149
and Leibniz's law 36
as cultural achievements 105-106
Chomsky on 17, 98-100, 102-103, 106-109
"preset for" 103, 104, 107
Tarski on 141
Neisser, Ulric 194

neural events (states), Dennett on 193-195
nociceptors 67
nomic universals 250, 259, 260, 262
nominalism 230
nominalization 43
nomological danglers (Feigl) 20, 210, 211
nonsentient biological systems 174, 199
nonsentient subsystems 199
norms 247, 248, 254
numerical properties 62

observation language
as theory-laden 47
Feyerabend and Putnam on 46-47
one-one (one-many) correspondence 42, 77, 173
and machine programs 42
Cornman on 42, 49
Feigl on 42
Fodor on 74
ontic commitment 6, 29, 57, 230
ontic monism 172
ontological economy 32
oratio obliqua 123, 125
oratio recta 156, 162-163
Geach on 163
Original Word Game (Brown) 124-125

P- and M-predicates (Strawson) 51, 83, 84, 85, 226
P-factor (Stenhouse) 246
pains
and affect or aversion 66-67
and dualism 28
and functional states 65, 66, 67
and ordinary English 28-29
and the identity theory 50
Anscombe on 66
as "entities" 28-29
as lacking an intentional nature 50, 66
Brentano on 212
description of 54, 67
Feyerabend on 46

location of 66
Malcolm on 210
Melzack on 66-67
perceptual model of 67-68, 69, 212
phenomenal quality of 66
Pitcher on 67
Wittgenstein on 210
  See sensations (bodily)
parallelism 42, 73
parrot 232
particulars 225-226, 227, 230, 231, 232,
    233, 234
pattern recognition 202
Penfield, Wilder 60
perception
  and animal beliefs 134-136
  and belief 121
  and information 169, 195
  and *oratio obliqua* 125
  and propositional content 122, 123
  and "raw feels" 212
  and sensation 68-69
  and "symbol systems" 119, 122
  behavioral account of 61
  biological emergence of 195
  cognitive 146-147
  epistemic sense of 147
  linguistic model of 128
  Lorenz on 193
  Neisser on 194
  non-epistemic 167-168, 169
  Sibley on 155
  Strawson on 195-196
  transitivity of 69-70
  Turbayne on 118-119
perceptual verbs 66, 69-70, 147
personal identity
  and bodily identity 228, 239
  and memory 228
  criteria and conditions of 85-85, 88-
    89, 228
  Locke on 228
  questions of 241, 242
  Williams on 85-87, 88-89, 239-241
persons

activities of 225, 228-229
alternately occupying one body 227
and belief states 130
and bodies 11, 12, 50, 51, 82, 87-88,
    90, 226, 227, 228
and commissurotomy 89, 91, 92
and functional properties 21, 25, 115,
    225, 228
and intentionality 15, 17, 19
and linguistic ability 9, 16, 19-20, 97,
    228, 229, 243
and machines 172
and physicalism 50-51
and plural minds 91, 92
and responsibility 243, 254
and sentient organisms 7, 8, 11, 13,
    15, 18, 19-20, 44, 82, 85
and sub-personal homunculi 186-187
and works of art 20
as bodies 227, 229
as cognitive agents 129
as cultural(ly emergent entities) 9, 19,
    22, 23, 25
as embodied entities 19, 24, 99, 239,
    246
as or as not natural 17
as rule-following 20, 23, 249
as tokens-of-a-type 239
capable of freedom 246, 249
Dennett on 186-187
Descartes on 51
distinguished from other cultural
    entities 225
existence of 239
Feigl on 14, 15
forensic theory of 16, 254
identity of 239, 243
irreducibility of 15-16
Locke on 16
nature and individuation of 227, 243
non-human 19
nonreductive theory of 243
not natural entities 243, 245
plural, and one body 89-90, 91, 94
Puccetti on 90-96

reporting role of 23
Sellars on 15-17, 22, 81-82
Solomon on 12
Strawson on 7, 11, 24, 25, 51, 82-85,
     89, 96, 97, 187-188, 226-228
Williams on 11, 82, 84-90, 96, 239-
     241
Peters, R. S. 249
phantom limb 66
"physical" (Feigl) 14
"physical$_1$" (Feigl) 200, 235
"physical$_2$" (Feigl) 14, 22, 210, 217,
     223, 235
physical explanation
    Chomsky on 17-18
    Feigl on 14
physical location 38, 52, 53, 66, 226,
     227
    Strawson on 226-227
physical medium 234
physical replica 171
physical states (events), extensional
     treatment of 159
physicalism 14, 44, 50-52, 53-56, 57,
     58, 81, 145, 159, 225, 258
    Feigl on 14, 218, 223
    Nagel on 52-55
Piaget, Jean 123, 140
Pietà (Michelangelo) 234, 235
Pitcher, George 67
Place, U. T. 179
plants 199
Plato 138
Platonism 106, 115
Plato's myth of recollection 138
Polten, Eric 61, 62
Popper, Karl 189
post-traumatic pain 67
PR (Lakoff) 104
practical reasoning 165-166
    Kenny on 166
predicates
    and law of transferable epithets 37
    and qualification of sensations 28-29
    Smart on 5
predication 230, 253, 259

pre-established Harmony (Leibniz) 33
Premack, David 121
preying mantis 168
principle of sufficient reason (Leibniz) 108
Principle of the Nomological Character
     of Causality (Davidson) 216
problem of other minds 34
propositions (propositional content) 131,
     148, 151, 159, 162, 167, 185, 186
    and information 132
    and non-cognitive systems 132, 133,
     134-135
    assigned to mental states 131-132
    assigned to neural processes 140, 193-
     195
    at the sub-cognitive level 132-133, 135
    heuristically ascribed 123, 125
    linguistically modelled 123, 130, 132,
     148
    Vendler on 162, 167
prudential interests 199, 244, 245, 254,
     256
psychogenic pain 67
psychophysical laws 73, 214, 216, 217,
     218, 219, 220, 223, 224
    Davidson on 214, 216, 217, 220,
     221, 222
psychophysical interaction (causality)
     32, 175, 213, 214, 216, 220, 221
    Davidson on 214, 215, 216, 217, 218,
     219, 222
    Feigl on 215
Puccetti, Roland 90-96
punishment 244
purposive order (system) 199, 245
Putnam, Hilary 47, 63, 65, 68-72, 75,
     100, 179, 213, 227, 248
pyramidal system 247

qualia 200, 209, 211, 212
Quine, W. V. 6, 8, 37, 99, 157, 194,
     202-208
quantification 230

rationalism (Chomsky) 98-101
  distinguished from empiricism 108
rationality
  and ascriptions of mental states 177,
    178, 188
  chimpanzees' 124
  infant 110
  minimal 199
  model of 156, 160, 169, 243, 251,
    257, 173
  species-typical 199
"raw feels" (Feigl; Meehl and Sellars)
    201, 209, 210, 211, 212, 213
"reasoned behavior" 259
reasons 250
  as causes 250
  having 250, 251
  intensional nature of 253, 257
  relative to rules, institutions 250
reductionism 6, 7, 10, 20, 145, 146,
    150, 175, 183, 217, 245, 257, 259
  and linguistic ability 6, 14-15, 16, 18
reference
  and "entities" 31, 56-57
  and identification 226
  as ontically neutral 31
  as purely grammatical 29, 31
  intentional features of 142, 237
  opaque 37, 157
  Polten on 61-62
reincarnation 233, 239
relativism 256, 259
  constraints on 256-257
  robust 256
replicas (Scheffler) 230
RNA 75-76
robots 248
  Putnam on 248
rules (rule-governed phenomena) 21-22
  and freedom 249
  as intensional 115, 248
  and linguistic universals 17, 106, 107,
    108
  and persons 20
  and societal life 115

contrasted with natural laws 248
  Dreyfus on 188
  Fodor on 188
  machines and 248
Ruwet, Jean-Claude 191
Ryle, Gilbert 32, 175

Salmon, Wesley 261-262
Saul, R. E. 95
Sayre, Kenneth M. 180-181
Scheffler, Israel 230
schizophrenia 92, 96
sciences, natural and human 225
scientific image (Sellars) 15, 17
Scientific Project (Freud) 12
sculpture 233
Searle, John 6
seeing-eye dog 164
self-sacrifice 244
Sellars, Wilfrid 6, 14, 15, 17, 20, 21,
    22-23, 24, 25, 81-82, 85, 172, 223
semantic ambiguity 237
semantic conception of truth (Tarski)
    141
sensations (bodily) 28, 48-49, 66
  Putnam on 248-249
  See pains
sensory perception, verbs of 69-70
sentience 173, 175, 176, 177, 199
  as evolutionary development 244
  Feigl on 177
  Matson on 171-172
sentient organisms (systems)
  and intentionality 15, 17
  and persons 7, 8, 11, 13, 15, 17, 19-
    20, 44, 82, 85, 97, 189
Sherrington, C. S. 60, 95
Shoemaker, Sydney 88, 90
Sibley, F. N. 155-156, 168
similarity, biologically favored 194-195,
    196
skepticism 156
Skinner, B. F. 99, 150, 200, 202
Smart, J. J. C. 6, 31, 32, 41, 60-61, 64,
    75, 179, 215, 217, 218

social sciences
  and explanation of behavior 258
  contrasted with natural sciences 245
sociobiology 257
solipsism 85
Solomon, Robert C. 12-13
sortals 40, 43
speech acts 228
speech and thought 121, 122
  Davidson on 131, 147
  Kenny on 164, 165
  Malcolm on 147
  Sibley on 155-156, 168
  Vendler on 120, 121, 125, 163-164
  Vygotsky on 125, 127-129
Sperry, R. W. 60, 89-90, 91, 95
Spinoza, Baruch 32
split-brain phenomena 9, 92, 96, 241
states and events 43-44, 52, 53, 54, 56, 57
statistical laws 250, 259, 261
  Salmon on 261-262
Stenhouse, David 193, 246-247
Stern, William 125
stimulus meaning (Quine) 204, 206
'stimulus' (stimulus) and 'response' (response) 200, 201, 202
stimulus synonymy (Quine) 204
Strawson, P. F. 7, 8, 11, 12, 13, 24-25, 51, 82-85, 88, 89, 96, 97, 187-188, 195, 225-228
Strawsonian persons 226-227
structural/functional invariances 201
structural properties 171, 172
subaltern particulars (Margolis) 44, 57
sub-personal routines 187
suicide 244

tabula rasa (Locke) 100
Tantsprache (Frisch) 150
Tarski, Alfred 141, 148
taxis 192
Taylor, Charles 184, 189-191
teleological explanation 174
teleological idiom 187

teleology (teleological features) 146, 150, 169, 184
  not presupposing a linguistic model 150
  of nonsentient biological systems 174
teleonomy (Monod) 117
theoretical entities 63, 68
  Fodor on 63-64
thermometer 133, 134
thermostat 134
thinking, distinguished from thoughts 147
thought
  and animals 147
  and language 147, 148-149
  and oratio obliqua 125
  and speech 121, 122, 162
  as intentional 143
  as propositional 120, 123
  contrasted with sensation 146
  Davidson on 147
  Dennett on 143-144
  Descartes on 77
  Geach on 161, 162, 163
  heuristic representation of 123
  linguistic model of 128
  Vendler on 120, 121, 125, 162, 163
  Vygotsky on 125, 127-129
Tic douloureux 67
Tinbergen, N. 192-193
token-of-a-type 231, 235, 237, 239, 240
tokens 231, 232, 233, 234, 235, 242
Tolman, E. C. 116, 201
"topic-neutral" (Smart) 60-61, 75
transcommissural exchange (Puccetti) 93
truth claims (truth values) 256, 258
truth, theory of 147
Turbayne, Colin Murray 118-119, 120, 121, 123
Turing machine (program) 62-63, 64, 71, 108, 159, 160, 167, 173, 248
  Putnam on 63, 71
  structural states of 63
type/token distinction 232
types 231, 232, 234, 235, 242, 244
  Glickman on 231, 232

unity of science 18, 20, 22, 33, 150,
    225, 245
universalizability 255
universals 195, 231, 233

Vendler, Zeno 120, 121, 123, 125, 162-
    163, 167
verbal behavior 208
verbal disposition 107
von Mises, Richard 261
von Uexküll, Jakob 192
Vygotsky, L. S. 125, 127-129

wants 260-261
Washoe 122, 124, 140

weakness of will *(akrasia)* 166
whole/part shift 183
Wiggens, David 88, 90
William of Ockham 162
Williams, B. A. O. [Bernard] 11, 12, 82,
    84, 85-90, 96, 239-241
Wittgenstein, Ludwig 172, 209-210
words 229, 230, 232, 234
works of art 20, 26, 232, 235

yoga 214

ZR (Geach) 165
Zen masters 214

INDEX OF REFERENCES

Aaron, R. I.
  [1967] 195
Alston, W. P.
  [1958] 29, 230
Anscombe, G. E. M.
  [1963] 66
  [1957] 175, 251
Arbib, Michael
  [1972] 132, 189
Armstrong, D. M.
  [1962] 67, 70, 212
  [1968] 31, 155, 159, 168, 176, 179, 202, 243, 258
  [1973] 50, 77, 123, 126, 144, 146, 150, 160, 161, 167, 173, 178, 180, 222
Ashby, W. Ross
  [1956] 133
Austin, J. L.
  [1962] 228
Ayala, F. J. and Dobzhansky, T.
  [1974] 189
Ayer, A. J.
  [1940] 29

Bach, Emmon
  [1968] 109
Baier, Kurt
  [1962] 28, 212
Bell, Daniel
  [1960] 255
Bennett, Jonathan
  [1964] 130

[1976] 104, 237
Bergmann, Gustav
  [1962] 32
Bernstein, Richard
  [1968] 48
  [1976] 245
Best, Jay Boyd
  [1972] 195
Binkley, Robert et al.
  [1971] 250
Bitterman, M. E.
  [1965] 247
Black, Max
  [1962] 256
  [1968] 150
Bloomfield, Leonard
  [1933] 114
Boden, Margaret A.
  [1962] 211
Bogen, J. E.
  [1969a] 90, 94
  [1969b] 90, 94
Bogen, J. E. and Bogen, G. M.
  [1969] 90
Bogen, J. E. and DeZure, R., Tenhouten, W. D. and March, J. F.
  [1972] 90
Boring, E. G.
  [1963] 175
Brand, Miles
  [1968] 253
  [1970] 250
Brandt, Richard and Kim, Jaegwon

[1967] 38
Brentano, Franz
   [1973] 13, 30, 37, 74, 212
Broad, C. D.
   [1925] 32, 175
Brodbeck, May
   [1963] 32, 72
   [1966] 32, 72, 175
Brown, Roger
   [1956] 124
   [1970] 121
   [1973] 124
Bruner, Jerome, Goodnow, Jacqueline
   J., and Austin, George
   [1956] 194
Bunge, Mario
   [1977] 236

Campbell, C. A.
   [1951] 249
Campbell, Keith
   [1970] 175
Carnap, Rudolf
   [1928] 209
   [1949] 209
   [1953] 209
Cartwright, Richard
   [1971] 36
Cassinari, Valentino and Pagni, Carlo A.
   [1969] 50
Chihara, C. S. and Fodor, J. A.
   [1965] 69
Chisholm Roderick M.
   [1955-56] 24
   [1957] 37, 211
   [1966] 37, 49, 69, 70, 71, 123, 147,
      175, 212
   [1967] 16
   [1973] 36
Chomsky, Noam
   [1959] 24, 99, 202
   [1965] 98, 100, 102
   [1966] 98, 100, 106, 202
   [1967] 247
   [1972] 9, 17, 72, 98, 99, 101, 103,
      106, 113, 119, 120, 150, 173, 202

Chomsky, Noam and Halle, Morris
   [1968] 102, 112, 113, 120
Clark, W. E.
   [1957] 248
   [1962] 248
Close, Daryl
   [1976] 154
Commoner, Barry
   [1971] 248
Cornman, James
   [1962] 32, 41, 45, 217
   [1966] 50
   [1968a] 23, 38, 48, 54, 69, 173, 181,
      209, 215
   [1968b] 48, 215
   [1971] 28, 49
Crosson, Frederick J. and Sayre, Kenneth
   [1967] 133

Danto, Arthur C.
   [1963] 253
   [1973] 253
D'Arcy, Eric
   [1963] 253, 254
Dart, Raymond A.
   [1955] 248
Davidson, Donald
   [1963] 190, 220, 250, 251, 258, 261
   [1967a] 251
   [1967b] 29, 105, 141
   [1969a] 166
   [1969b] 29, 220
   [1970] 43, 214, 253, 258
   [1975] 131, 147
Dement, W. C. et al.
   [1970] 214
Dennett, Daniel
   [1969] 39, 50, 66, 126, 130, 143, 150,
      159, 160, 167, 177, 178, 183, 258
   [1975] 186
   [1976] 132
Derwing, Bruce L.
   [1973] 108
Descartes, René
   [1931] 77
DiCara, Leo W.

[1970] 24
Dilthey, Wilhelm
    [1961] 245
Donnellan, Keith S.
    [1966] 62, 142, 237
Dretske, Fred I.
    [1969] 147, 152, 168
    [1976] 133
Dreyfus, Hubert L.
    [1972] 188, 249

Eccles, John C.
    [1965] 56, 75
    [1970] 51, 60, 75
Engelhardt, H. Tristam, Jr.
    [1973] 51
Estes, W. K. *et al.*
    [1954] 150

Fabre, J. H.
    [1923] 190
Feigenbaum, Edward A. and Feldman,
    Julian
    [1963] 189
Feigl, Herbert
    [1967] 15, 41, 42, 51, 52, 69, 72, 173,
        176, 185, 186, 200, 209, 210, 211,
        213, 215, 218, 235
Feigl, Herbert and Scriven, Michael
    [1956] 23
Fessard, A.
    [1961] 75
Feyerabend, P. K.
    [1962] 46
    [1963a] 45, 83
    [1963b] 45, 62, 83, 214
    [1975] 3, 46, 256, 258
Flew, A. G. N.
    [1967] 245
Fodor, Jerry A.
    [1968] 4, 21, 23, 37, 52, 63,
        68, 74, 136, 146, 159, 171,
        201, 209, 213
    [1975] 77, 124, 136, 137, 160,
        167, 173, 186, 188, 257

Frankfort, Harry
    [1971] 66
Frege, G.
    [1960] 61
Frisch, K. von
    [1955] 238
    [1967] 150, 238

Gadamer, Hans-Georg
    [1976] 245
Gardner, Beatrice T. and Gardner,
    R. A.
    [1971] 106, 121
Gardner, R. A. and Gardner,
    Beatrice T.
    [1969] 102
Gazzaniga, Michael
    [1970] 91, 241
Geach, P. T.
    [1957] 77, 123, 144, 160, 162,
        165, 180, 209
Geschwind, N. (1965) 91
Gibson, J. J.
    [1966] 94, 130, 168, 194, 195,
        207, 214
Glickman, Jack
    [1976] 231
Goffman, Erving
    [1957] 259
Goldman, Alvin
    [1970] 252, 253
Goodman, Nelson
    [1966] 4, 229, 231
    [1967] 100, 119, 203
    [1968] 119, 230, 232
    [1970] 195
Gould, J. L.
    [1974] 150
    [1975] 150, 238
Grene, Marjorie
    [1974] 191
Grice, H. P.
    [1941] 228
    [1957] 104, 207
    [1961] 191

Griffin, Donald R.
  [1976] 150, 194, 238
Gunderson, Keith
  [1971] 187

Haber, R. N. and Haber, R. B.
  [1964] 214
Habermas, Jürgen
  [1971] 245, 255
  [1975] 255
Hacking, Ian
  [1975] 105
Hampshire, Stuart
  [1961] 248
Hanson, N. R.
  [1963] 4
Hare, R. H.
  [1952] 166, 255
  [1963] 166
Harman, Gilbert
  [1973] 152
  [1975] 256
Hartnack, Justus
  [1972] 147
Hebb, D. O.
  [1974] 175
Hempel, Carl G.
  [1962] 258
  [1965] 216, 250, 260, 261
  [1966] 216
Hintikka, Jaakko
  [1962] 152
Hirsch, Eli
  [1977] 40, 208
Hull, C. L.
  [1943] 191
  [1973] 191
Human Agent, The
  [1968] 250
Huxley, T. H.
  [1893] 211
Hydén, H.
  [1964] 75

Jacob, François
  [1974] 116

Jakobson, R.
  [1961] 108
Jarrard, Leonard E.
  [1971] 150
Jarvie, I. C.
  [1970] 245
  [1972] 245
Jones, O. R.
  [1975] 162

Katz, Jerrold
  [1964] 106
Keat, Russell and Urry, John
  [1975] 256
Kempson, Ruth M.
  [1975] 104
Kenny, Anthony (A. J. P.)
  [1963] 29, 166, 243
  [1973] 150
  [1975] 164, 165, 260
Keynes, John Maynard
  [1936] 250
Kim, Jaegwon
  [1966] 38
  [1969] 253
  [1973] 252
Kolers, Paul A. and Eden, Murray
  [1968] 214
Körner, Stephen
  [1966] 15, 175, 223
Kuhn, Thomas, S.
  [1970] 3, 46

Lakatos, Imre and Musgrave, Alan
  [1970] 46, 258
Lakoff, George
  [1971a] 104, 237
  [1971b] 104, 117
Langer, Susanne K.
  [1972] 150
Lashley, K. S.
  [1923] 175
  [1950] 76
Leakey, Louis S. B.
  [1935] 248
Lehrer, Keith

[1973] 212
[1974] 71
Lettvin, J. Y. *et al.*
 [1959] 185, 195
Lévi-Strauss, Claude
 [1933] 116
Levy, J., Trevarthen, C. and Sperry R. W.
 [1972] 91
Lewis, David K.
 [1966] 73, 75, 115, 176, 187, 208, 218
 [1969] 20, 115, 249
Lilly, John Cunningham
 [1967] 103, 149
Locke, John
 [1894] 16
Lorenz, Konrad
 [1965] 193, 246
 [1970] 192, 193, 239
 [1971] 112
Lukes, Steven
 [1974] 256
Luria, S. E.
 [1973] 170

Mackay, Donald M.
 [1969] 33, 146
Malcolm, Norman
 [1954] 175, 209
 [1973] 121, 147, 164
Margolis, Joseph
 [1962] 71
 [1966a] 210
 [1966b] 248, 249
 [1970a] 47
 [1970b] 230
 [1971a] 57
 [1971b] 248, 254, 255, 256
 [1972a] 191
 [1972b] 147
 [1972c] 152
 [1973a] 29, 44, 48, 69, 70, 71, 146,
  153, 212, 251
 [1973b] 23, 99, 194
 [1973c] 18
 [1975a] 199, 257

[1975b] 199, 243, 255
[1975c] 90
[1975d] 252
[1976] 174, 199, 248, 256
[1977a] 6, 29
[1977b] 21, 231
[1977c] 20, 21, 233
[1977d] 67
[1977e] 37, 153, 237
[1977f] 162
[1977g] 162
[1977h] 199
[1977i] 212
[1977j] 232
[1977k] 256
Massey, J. L.
 [1967] 133
Matson, Wallace I.
 [1976] 171, 202
McCawley, James D.
 [1971a] 104, 117
 [1971b] 117
McDougall, William
 [1932] 201
 [1934] 211
McNeill, David
 [1970] 110, 120
 [1971] 111
 [1972] 238
Meehl, P. E. and Sellars, Wilfrid
 [1956] 22, 200, 211
Meiland, Jack W.
 [1970] 244
Melden, A. I.
 [1961] 249, 250
Melzack, Ronald
 [1973] 50, 66, 67
Miller, George A.
 [1970] 99
Miller, Neal E.
 [1969] 214
Minsky, Marvin
 [1968a] 188
 [1968b] 189
Monod, Jacques

[1971] 116
Mountcastle, V. A.
[1965] 75

Nagel, Ernest
[1961] 5, 174, 189, 190
Nagel, Thomas
[1965] 40, 50, 52, 182
[1969] 107
[1970] 243
[1971] 90, 92
[1974] 131, 156
Neisser, Ulric
[1967] 194, 195, 214
Neurath, Otto *et al.*
[1955] 18, 20, 150, 225, 245
Newell, Allen, Shaw, J. C. and Simon,
    H. A.
[1963] 189
Noble, D.
[1966] 190
Nowlis, David P. and Kamiya, J.
[1970] 214

Ohwaki, Y. and Kihara, T.
[1953] 214
Oppenheim, Paul and Putnam, Hilary
[1958] 65

Paivio, Allan
[1971] 196
Parfit, Derek
[1971] 42, 96, 228, 242, 243
Pears, D. F.
[1967a] 261
[1967b] 160
Peirce, Charles Sanders
[1939] 234
Penelhum, Terence
[1970] 12, 228
Penfield, Wilder
[1965] 60
Perky, C. W.
[1910] 214
Perry, John
[1975] 228

Peters, R. S.
[1958] 249
Piaget, Jean
[1923] 127
[1926] 127
[1970] 140
[1971] 244
Pitcher, George
[1970] 67, 69, 70, 212
[1971] 130, 147, 191
Place, U. T.
[1956] 65, 179
Polten, Eric
[1973] 51, 58, 60, 62
Popper, Karl
[1957] 245
[1972a] 245
[1972b] 245
[1972c] 189
[1972d] 246
Premack, David
[1971] 103, 121
Price, H. H.
[1965] 228
Prince, Morton
[1903] 242
Puccetti, Roland
[1973] 90, 241
Putnam, Hilary
[1960] 4, 5, 21, 62, 107, 114, 159,
    160, 167, 171, 172, 213, 227, 248
[1961] 101
[1964] 248
[1965] 46
[1967a] 42, 69, 72, 75, 76
[1967b] 99, 100

Quine, V. W.
[1953] 6, 58, 230, 258
[1957] 62
[1960] 4, 6, 8, 29, 36, 37, 99, 141,
    153, 194, 202, 248
[1966] 48
[1969] 157
[1970] 194
[1974] 99

Quinton, Anthony
[1962] 228
[1973] 226

Rescher, Nicholas
[1973] 148
Richardson, Alan
[1969] 214
Rorty, Richard
[1965] 28, 31, 37, 45, 217
[1970] 3, 47
Rose, Steven
[1972] 241
Rosenthal, David
[1977] 49
Rundle, Bede
[1972] 177, 199, 243
Ruse, Michael
[1973] 174, 190
Russell, Bertrand
[1905] 105
[1918] 29
[1956] 160
[1966] 160
Ruwet, Jean-Claude
[1972] 191
Ryle, Gilbert
[1949] 6, 32, 41, 175, 182, 202, 207

Salmon, Wesley
[1975] 260, 261
Sauerbruch, Ferdinand and Wenke, Hans
[1963] 67
Saul, R. E. and Sperry, R. W.
[1968] 95
Savage, C. Wade
[1970] 213
Sayre, Kenneth M.
[1965] 180
[1969] 180
Sayre, Kenneth M. and Crosson,
    Frederick J.
[1968] 180
Scheffler, Israel
[1963] 229

Schrier, Allan M. and Stolnitz, Fred
[1971] 150
Schwayder, David
[1965] 20, 115, 249
Scriven, Michael
[1956] 201
Searle, John
[1969] 6, 29, 104, 228
Sellars, Wilfrid
[1963a] 4, 6, 15, 29, 51, 81, 98,
    110, 144, 160, 171, 173, 183, 217,
    225, 229, 247, 254
[1963b] 48, 209
[1964] 14, 223
[1965] 14
Sellars, Wilfrid and Chisholm, Roderick M.
[1958] 23
Shaffer, Jerome
[1961] 41
[1966] 51
Shannon, C. E. and Weaver, W.
[1949] 133
Shapiro, David, Tursky, Bernard and
    Schwartz, Gary E.
[1970] 214
Sherrington, C. S.
[1906] 95
[1951] 60
Shoemaker, Sydney
[1959] 228, 242
[1963] 88
Shope, Robert K.
[1971] 211
Sibley, F. N.
[1971] 70, 146, 147, 155, 168
Siegel, R. K. and West, L. J.
[1975] 214
Simon, Michael A.
[1971] 170
Skinner, B. F.
[1953] 191, 200, 207
[1957] 99, 202, 207
[1964] 200
Skolimowski, Henry
[1974] 244

Smart, J. J. C.
  [1962] 5, 21, 31, 35, 41, 52, 60, 62,
    75, 175, 179, 180, 209, 217
  [1963] 32, 58, 114, 189
Solomon, Robert C.
  [1974] 12
Sommerhoff, Gerd
  [1974] 201
Sorabji, R.
  [1964] 200
Sperling, G.
  [1960] 214
Sperry, R. W.
  [1966] 89
  [1968] 89, 91
  [1969] 60
Spicker, Stuart F.
  [1970] 32, 51
Stalker, Frank
  [1976] 104
Steiner, George
  [1975] 109
Stenhouse, David
  [1973] 192, 193, 196, 244, 246
Sternbach, Richard A.
  [1968] 67
Stevens, S. S.
  [1935] 213
Stoutland, Frederick
  [1968] 253
Strawson, P. F.
  [1950] 105
  [1959] 7, 8, 11, 24, 25, 32, 40, 43, 51,
    83, 96, 97, 129, 187, 225, 258
  [1966] 114
  [1970] 195
Suppes, Patrick
  [1969] 201
Sweet, W. H.
  [1959] 67, 69

Tarski, Alfred
  [1944] 148
  [1956] 141, 147, 256
  [1965] 258

Taylor, Charles
  [1964] 5, 174, 182, 184, 189, 202, 207,
    250
Thigpen, Corbett H.
  [1957] 242
Timpanaro, Sebastiano
  [1975] 245
Tinbergen, N.
  [1969] 192
Tolman, E. C.
  [1932] 116, 201
Trigg, Robert
  [1970] 67
Turbayne, Colin Murray
  [1969] 118
  [1972] 118
Turing, A. M.
  [1950] 62

Valzelli, Luigi
  [1973] 220
Vendler, Zeno
  [1967] 248
  [1972] 120, 123, 131, 147, 156, 162
Vesey, G. N. A.
  [1964] 32
  [1974] 241
Vol'kenshtein, Mikhail V.
  [1970] 170
Von Mises, Richard
  [1957] 261
Vygotsky, L. S.
  [1962] 125

Wallace, Robert K. and Benson, Herbert
  [1972] 214
Watson, J. B.
  [1924] 200
  [1948] 200
Watson, James D.
  [1970] 170
Weber, Max
  [1946] 255
  [1949] 255
White, Alan R.

[1967] 182, 202, 207
White, J. C. and Sweet, W. H.
  [1955] 50
Whiteley, C. H.
  [1973] 250
Wiggens, David
  [1967] 19, 40, 58, 88
Williams, B. A. O. (Bernard)
  [1956-57] 86, 239
  [1970] 39, 50, 85, 88, 227
  [1973a] 245
  [1973b] 11, 82, 84, 85
  [1976] 243
Wilson, Edward O.
  [1975] 257
Winch, Peter
  [1958] 245
Wisdom, John
  [1952] 34

Wittgenstein, Ludwig
  [1963] 142, 150, 171, 175, 209, 243
Wollheim, Richard
  [1968] 233
Wolterstorff, Nicholas
  [1970] 195
  [1975] 231, 233
Woodfield, Andrew
  [1976] 174, 190, 199, 200
Wooldridge, Dean E.
  [1963] 185
Wright, Larry
  [1976] 200

Ziff, Paul
  [1965] 101, 237
Zinn, Howard
  [1970] 255

SYNTHESE LIBRARY

Monographs on Epistemology, Logic, Methodology,
Philosophy of Science, Sociology of Science and of Knowledge, and on the
Mathematical Methods of Social and Behavioral Sciences

Managing Editor:
JAAKKO HINTIKKA (Academy of Finland and Stanford University)

Editors:

ROBERT S. COHEN (Boston University)
DONALD DAVIDSON (University of Chicago)
GABRIËL NUCHELMANS (University of Leyden)
WESLEY C. SALMON (University of Arizona)

1. J. M. Bocheński, *A Precis of Mathematical Logic.* 1959, X + 100 pp.
2. P. L. Guiraud, *Problèmes et méthodes de la statistique linguistique.* 1960, VI + 146 pp.
3. Hans Freudenthal (ed.), *The Concept and the Role of the Model in Mathematics and Natural and Social Sciences, Proceedings of a Colloquium held at Utrecht, The Netherlands, January 1960.* 1961, VI + 194 pp.
4. Evert W. Beth, *Formal Methods. An Introduction to Symbolic Logic and the Study of Effective Operations in Arithmetic and Logic.* 1962, XIV + 170 pp.
5. B. H. Kazemier and D. Vuysje (eds.), *Logic and Language. Studies Dedicated to Professor Rudolf Carnap on the Occasion of His Seventieth Birthday.* 1962, VI + 256 pp.
6. Marx W. Wartofsky (ed.), *Proceedings of the Boston Colloquium for the Philosophy of Science, 1961-1962,* Boston Studies in the Philosophy of Science (ed. by Robert S. Cohen and Marx W. Wartofsky), Volume I. 1973, VIII + 212 pp.
7. A. A. Zinov'ev, *Philosophical Problems of Many-Valued Logic.* 1963, XIV + 155 pp.
8. Georges Gurvitch, *The Spectrum of Social Time.* 1964, XXVI + 152 pp.
9. Paul Lorenzen, *Formal Logic.* 1965, VIII + 123 pp.
10. Robert S. Cohen and Marx W. Wartofsky (eds.), *In Honor of Philipp Frank,* Boston Studies in the Philosophy of Science (ed. by Robert S. Cohen and Marx W. Wartofsky), Volume II. 1965, XXXIV + 475 pp.
11. Evert W. Beth, *Mathematical Thought. An Introduction to the Philosophy of Mathematics.* 1965, XII + 208 pp.
12. Evert W. Beth and Jean Piaget, *Mathematical Epistemology and Psychology.* 1966, XII + 326 pp.
13. Guido Küng, *Ontology and the Logistic Analysis of Language. An Enquiry into the Contemporary Views on Universals.* 1967, XI + 210 pp.
14. Robert S. Cohen and Marx W. Wartofsky (eds.), *Proceedings of the Boston Colloquium for the Philosophy of Science 1964-1966, in Memory of Norwood Russell Hanson,* Boston Studies in the Philosophy of Science (ed. by Robert S. Cohen and Marx W. Wartofsky), Volume III. 1967, XLIX + 489 pp.

15. C. D. Broad, *Induction, Probability, and Causation. Selected Papers*. 1968, XI + 296 pp.
16. Günther Patzig, *Aristotle's Theory of the Syllogism. A Logical-Philosophical Study of Book A of the Prior Analytics*. 1968, XVII + 215 pp.
17. Nicholas Rescher, *Topics in Philosophical Logic*. 1968, XIV + 347 pp.
18. Robert S. Cohen and Marx W. Wartofsky (eds.), *Proceedings of the Boston Colloquium for the Philosophy of Science 1966-1968*, Boston Studies in the Philosophy of Science (ed. by Robert S. Cohen and Marx W. Wartofsky), Volume IV. 1969, VIII + 537 pp.
19. Robert S. Cohen and Marx W. Wartofsky (eds.), *Proceedings of the Boston Colloquium for the Philosophy of Science 1966-1968*, Boston Studies in the Philosophy of Science (ed. by Robert S. Cohen and Marx W. Wartofsky), Volume V. 1969, VIII + 482 pp.
20. J.W. Davis, D. J. Hockney, and W. K. Wilson (eds.), *Philosophical Logic*. 1969, VIII + 277 pp.
21. D. Davidson and J. Hintikka (eds.), *Words and Objections: Essays on the Work of W. V. Quine*. 1969, VIII + 366 pp.
22. Patrick Suppes, *Studies in the Methodology and Foundations of Science. Selected Papers from 1911 to 1969*. 1969, XII + 473 pp.
23. Jaakko Hintikka, *Models for Modalities. Selected Essays*. 1969, IX + 220 pp.
24. Nicholas Rescher *et al.* (eds.), *Essays in Honor of Carl G. Hempel. A Tribute on the Occasion of His Sixty-Fifth Birthday*. 1969, VII + 272 pp.
25. P. V. Tavanec (ed.), *Problems of the Logic of Scientific Knowledge*. 1969, XII + 429 pp.
26. Marshall Swain (ed.), *Induction, Acceptance, and Rational Belief*. 1970, VII + 232 pp.
27. Robert S. Cohen and Raymond J. Seeger (eds.), *Ernst Mach: Physicist and Philosopher*, Boston Studies in the Philosophy of Science (ed. by Robert S. Cohen and Marx W. Wartofsky), Volume VI. 1970, VIII + 295 pp.
28. Jaakko Hintikka and Patrick Suppes, *Information and Inference*. 1970, X + 336 pp.
29. Karel Lambert, *Philosophical Problems in Logic. Some Recent Developments*. 1970, VII + 176 pp.
30. Rolf A. Eberle, *Nominalistic Systems*. 1970, IX + 217 pp.
31. Paul Weingartner and Gerhard Zecha (eds.), *Induction, Physics, and Ethics: Proceedings and Discussions of the 1968 Salzburg Colloquium in the Philosophy of Science*. 1970, X + 382 pp.
32. Evert W. Beth, *Aspects of Modern Logic*. 1970, XI + 176 pp.
33. Risto Hilpinen (ed.), *Deontic Logic: Introductory and Systematic Readings*. 1971, VII + 182 pp.
34. Jean-Louis Krivine, *Introduction to Axiomatic Set Theory*. 1971, VII + 98 pp.
35. Joseph D. Sneed, *The Logical Structure of Mathematical Physics*. 1971, XV + 311 pp.
36. Carl R. Kordig, *The Justification of Scientific Change*. 1971, XIV + 119 pp.
37. Milič Čapek, *Bergson and Modern Physics*, Boston Studies in the Philosophy of Science (ed. by Robert S. Cohen and Marx W. Wartofsky), Volume VII. 1971, XV + 414 pp.

38. Norwood Russell Hanson, *What I Do Not Believe, and Other Essays* (ed. by Stephen Toulmin and Harry Woolf), 1971, XII + 390 pp.
39. Roger C. Buck and Robert S. Cohen (eds.), *PSA 1970. In Memory of Rudolf Carnap*, Boston Studies in the Philosophy of Science (ed. by Robert S. Cohen and Marx W. Wartofsky), Volume VIII. 1971, LXVI + 615 pp. Also available as paperback.
40. Donald Davidson and Gilbert Harman (eds.), *Semantics of Natural Language*. 1972, X + 769 pp. Also available as paperback.
41. Yehoshua Bar-Hillel (ed.), *Pragmatics of Natural Languages*. 1971, VII + 231 pp.
42. Sören Stenlund, *Combinators, λ-Terms and Proof Theory*. 1972, 184 pp.
43. Martin Strauss, *Modern Physics and Its Philosophy. Selected Papers in the Logic, History, and Philosophy of Science*. 1972, X + 297 pp.
44. Mario Bunge, *Method, Model and Matter*. 1973, VII + 196 pp.
45. Mario Bunge, *Philosophy of Physics*. 1973, IX + 248 pp.
46. A. A. Zinov'ev, *Foundations of the Logical Theory of Scientific Knowledge (Complex Logic)*, Boston Studies in the Philosophy of Science (ed. by Robert S. Cohen and Marx W. Wartofsky), Volume IX. Revised and enlarged English edition with an appendix, by G. A. Smirnov, E. A. Sidorenka, A. M. Fedina, and L. A. Bobrova. 1973, XXII + 301 pp. Also available as paperback.
47. Ladislav Tondl, *Scientific Procedures*, Boston Studies in the Philosophy of Science (ed. by Robert S. Cohen and Marx W. Wartofsky), Volume X. 1973, XII + 268 pp. Also available as paperback.
48. Norwood Russell Hanson, *Constellations and Conjectures* (ed. by Willard C. Humphreys, Jr.). 1973, X + 282 pp.
49. K. J. J. Hintikka, J. M. E. Moravcsik, and P. Suppes (eds.), *Approaches to Natural Language. Proceedings of the 1970 Stanford Workshop on Grammar and Semantics*. 1973, VIII + 526 pp. Also available as paperback.
50. Mario Bunge (ed.), *Exact Philosophy – Problems, Tools, and Goals*. 1973, X + 214 pp.
51. Radu J. Bogdan and Ilkka Niiniluoto (eds.), *Logic, Language, and Probability. A Selection of Papers Contributed to Sections IV, VI, and XI of the Fourth International Congress for Logic, Methodology, and Philosophy of Science, Bucharest, September 1971*. 1973, X + 323 pp.
52. Glenn Pearce and Patrick Maynard (eds.), *Conceptual Chance*. 1973, XII + 282 pp.
53. Ilkka Niiniluoto and Raimo Tuomela, *Theoretical Concepts and Hypothetico-Inductive Inference*. 1973, VII + 264 pp.
54. Roland Fraïssé, *Course of Mathematical Logic – Volume 1: Relation and Logical Formula*. 1973, XVI + 186 pp. Also available as paperback.
55. Adolf Grünbaum, *Philosophical Problems of Space and Time*. Second, enlarged edition, Boston Studies in the Philosophy of Science (ed. by Robert S. Cohen and Marx W. Wartofsky), Volume XII. 1973, XXIII + 884 pp. Also available as paperback.
56. Patrick Suppes (ed.), *Space, Time, and Geometry*. 1973, XI + 424 pp.
57. Hans Kelsen, *Essays in Legal and Moral Philosophy*, selected and introduced by Ota Weinberger. 1973, XXVIII + 300 pp.
58. R. J. Seeger and Robert S. Cohen (eds.), *Philosophical Foundations of Science. Proceedings of an AAAS Program, 1969*, Boston Studies in the Philosophy of

Science (ed. by Robert S. Cohen and Marx W. Wartofsky), Volume XI. 1974, X + 545 pp. Also available as paperback.

59. Robert S. Cohen and Marx W. Wartofsky (eds.), *Logical and Epistemological Studies in Contemporary Physics*, Boston Studies in the Philosophy of Science (ed. by Robert S. Cohen and Marx W. Wartofsky), Volume XIII. 1973, VIII + 462 pp. Also available as paperback.

60. Robert S. Cohen and Marx W. Wartofsky (eds.), *Methodological and Historical Essays in the Natural and Social Sciences. Proceedings of the Boston Colloquium for the Philosophy of Science, 1969-1972*, Boston Studies in the Philosophy of Science (ed. by Robert S. Cohen and Marx W. Wartofsky), Volume XIV. 1974, VIII + 405 pp. Also available as paperback.

61. Robert S. Cohen, J. J. Stachel and Marx W. Wartofsky (eds.), *For Dirk Struik. Scientific, Historical and Political Essays in Honor of Dirk J. Struik*, Boston Studies in the Philosophy of Science (ed. by Robert S. Cohen and Marx W. Wartofsky), Volume XV. 1974, XXVII + 652 pp. Also available as paperback.

62. Kazimierz Ajdukiewicz, *Pragmatic Logic*, transl. from the Polish by Olgierd Wojtasiewicz. 1974, XV + 460 pp.

63. Sören Stenlund (ed.), *Logical Theory and Semantic Analysis. Essays Dedicated to Stig Kanger on His Fiftieth Birthday*. 1974, V + 217 pp.

64. Kenneth F. Schaffner and Robert S. Cohen (eds.), *Proceedings of the 1972 Biennial Meeting, Philosophy of Science Association*, Boston Studies in the Philosophy of Science (ed. by Robert S. Cohen and Marx W. Wartofsky), Volume XX. 1974, IX + 444 pp. Also available as paperback.

65. Henry E. Kyburg, Jr., *The Logical Foundations of Statistical Inference*. 1974, IX + 421 pp.

66. Marjorie Grene, *The Understanding of Nature: Essays in the Philosophy of Biology*, Boston Studies in the Philosophy of Science (ed. by Robert S. Cohen and Marx W. Wartofsky), Volume XXIII. 1974, XII + 360 pp. Also available as paperback.

67. Jan M. Broekman, *Structuralism: Moscow, Prague, Paris*. 1974, IX + 117 pp.

68. Norman Geschwind, *Selected Papers on Language and the Brain*, Boston Studies in the Philosophy of Science (ed. by Robert S. Cohen and Marx W. Wartofsky), Volume XVI. 1974, XII + 549 pp. Also available as paperback.

69. Roland Fraïssé, *Course of Mathematical Logic* – Volume 2: *Model Theory*. 1974, XIX + 192 pp.

70. Andrzej Grzegorczyk, *An Outline of Mathematical Logic. Fundamental Results and Notions Explained with All Details*. 1974, X + 596 pp.

71. Franz von Kutschera, *Philosophy of Language*. 1975, VII + 305 pp.

72. Juha Manninen and Raimo Tuomela (eds.), *Essays on Explanation and Understanding. Studies in the Foundations of Humanities and Social Sciences*. 1976, VII + 440 pp.

73. Jaakko Hintikka (ed.), *Rudolf Carnap, Logical Empiricist. Materials and Perspectives*. 1975, LXVIII + 400 pp.

74. Milič Čapek (ed.), *The Concepts of Space and Time. Their Structure and Their Development*, Boston Studies in the Philosophy of Science (ed. by Robert S. Cohen and Marx W. Wartofsky), Volume XXII. 1976, LVI + 570 pp. Also available as paperback.

75. Jaakko Hintikka and Unto Remes, *The Method of Analysis. Its Geometrical Origin and Its General Significance*, Boston Studies in the Philosophy of Science (ed. by Robert S. Cohen and Marx W. Wartofsky), Volume XXV. 1974, XVIII + 144 pp. Also available as paperback.

76. John Emery Murdoch and Edith Dudley Sylla, *The Cultural Context of Medieval Learning. Proceedings of the First International Colloquium on Philosophy, Science, and Theology in the Middle Ages – September 1973*, Boston Studies in the Philosophy of Science (ed. by Robert S. Cohen and Marx W. Wartofsky), Volume XXVI. 1975, X + 566 pp. Also available as paperback.

77. Stefan Amsterdamski, *Between Experience and Metaphysics. Philosophical Problems of the Evolution of Science*, Boston Studies in the Philosophy of Science (ed. by Robert S. Cohen and Marx W. Wartofsky), Volume XXXV. 1975, XVIII + 193 pp. Also available as paperback.

78. Patrick Suppes (ed.), *Logic and Probability in Quantum Mechanics.* 1976, XV + 541 pp.

79. Hermann von Helmholtz: *Epistemological Writings. The Paul Hertz/Moritz Schlick Centenary Edition of 1921 with Notes and Commentary by the Editors.* (Newly translated by Malcolm F. Lowe. Edited with an Introduction and Bibliography, by Robert S. Cohen and Yehuda Elkana), Boston Studies in the Philosophy of Science (ed. by Robert S. Cohen and Marx W. Wartofsky), Volume XXXVII. 1977, XXXVIII+204 pp. Also available as paperback.

80. Joseph Agassi, *Science in Flux*, Boston Studies in the Philosophy of Science (ed. by Robert S. Cohen and Marx W. Wartofsky), Volume XXVIII. 1975, XXVI + 553 pp. Also available as paperback.

81. Sandra G. Harding (ed.), *Can Theories Be Refuted? Essays on the Duhem-Quine Thesis.* 1976, XXI + 318 pp. Also available as paperback.

82. Stefan Nowak, *Methodology of Sociological Research: General Problems.* 1977, XVIII + 504 pp.

83. Jean Piaget, Jean-Blaise Grize, Alina Szeminska, and Vinh Bang, *Epistemology and Psychology of Functions*, Studies in Genetic Epistemology, Volume XXIII. 1977, XIV+205 pp.

84. Marjorie Grene and Everett Mendelsohn (eds.), *Topics in the Philosophy of Biology*, Boston Studies in the Philosophy of Science (ed. by Robert S. Cohen and Marx W. Wartofsky), Volume XXVII. 1976, XIII + 454 pp. Also available as paperback.

85. E. Fischbein, *The Intuitive Sources of Probabilistic Thinking in Children.* 1975, XIII + 204 pp.

86. Ernest W. Adams, *The Logic of Conditionals. An Application of Probability to Deductive Logic.* 1975, XIII + 156 pp.

87. Marian Przełęcki and Ryszard Wójcicki (eds.), *Twenty-Five Years of Logical Methodology in Poland.* 1977, VIII + 803 pp.

88. J. Topolski, *The Methodology of History.* 1976, X + 673 pp.

89. A. Kasher (ed.), *Language in Focus: Foundations, Methods and Systems. Essays Dedicated to Yehoshua Bar-Hillel*, Boston Studies in the Philosophy of Science (ed. by Robert S. Cohen and Marx W. Wartofsky), Volume XLIII. 1976, XXVIII + 679 pp. Also available as paperback.

90. Jaakko Hintikka, *The Intentions of Intentionality and Other New Models for Modalities.* 1975, XVIII + 262 pp. Also available as paperback.

91. Wolfgang Stegmüller, *Collected Papers on Epistemology, Philosophy of Science and History of Philosophy*, 2 Volumes, 1977, XXVII + 525 pp.
92. Dov M. Gabbay, *Investigations in Modal and Tense Logics with Applications to Problems in Philosophy and Linguistics.* 1976, XI + 306 pp.
93. Radu J. Bogdan, *Local Induction.* 1976, XIV + 340 pp.
94. Stefan Nowak, *Understanding and Prediction: Essays in the Methodology of Social and Behavioral Theories.* 1976, XIX + 482 pp.
95. Peter Mittelstaedt, *Philosophical Problems of Modern Physics,* Boston Studies in the Philosophy of Science (ed. by Robert S. Cohen and Marx W. Wartofsky), Volume XVIII. 1976, X + 211 pp. Also available as paperback.
96. Gerald Holton and William Blanpied (eds.), *Science and Its Public: The Changing Relationship,* Boston Studies in the Philosophy of Science (ed. by Robert S. Cohen and Marx W. Wartofsky), Volume XXXIII. 1976, XXV + 289 pp. Also available as paperback.
97. Myles Brand and Douglas Walton (eds.), *Action Theory. Proceedings of the Winnipeg Conference on Human Action, Held at Winnipeg, Manitoba, Canada, 9-11 May 1975.* 1976, VI + 345 pp.
98. Risto Hilpinen, *Knowledge and Rational Belief.* 1978 (forthcoming).
99. R. S. Cohen, P. K. Feyerabend, and M. W. Wartofsky (eds.), *Essays in Memory of Imre Lakatos,* Boston Studies in the Philosophy of Science (ed. by Robert S. Cohen and Marx W. Wartofsky), Volume XXXIX. 1976, XI + 762 pp. Also available as paperback.
100. R. S. Cohen and J. J. Stachel (eds.), *Selected Papers of Léon Rosenfeld,* Boston Studies in the Philosophy of Science (ed. by Robert S. Cohen and Marx W. Wartofsky), Volume XXI. 1977, XXX + 927 pp.
101. R. S. Cohen, C. A. Hooker, A. C. Michalos, and J. W. van Evra (eds.), *PSA 1974: Proceedings of the 1974 Biennial Meeting of the Philosophy of Science Association,* Boston Studies in the Philosophy of Science (ed. by Robert S. Cohen and Marx W. Wartofsky), Volume XXXII. 1976, XIII + 734 pp. Also available as paperback.
102. Yehuda Fried and Joseph Agassi, *Paranoia: A Study in Diagnosis,* Boston Studies in the Philosophy of Science (ed. by Robert S. Cohen and Marx W. Wartofsky), Volume L. 1976, XV + 212 pp. Also available as paperback.
103. Marian Przełęcki, Klemens Szaniawski, and Ryszard Wójcicki (eds.), *Formal Methods in the Methodology of Empirical Sciences.* 1976, 455 pp.
104. John M. Vickers, *Belief and Probability.* 1976, VIII + 202 pp.
105. Kurt H. Wolff, *Surrender and Catch: Experience and Inquiry Today,* Boston Studies in the Philosophy of Science (ed. by Robert S. Cohen and Marx W. Wartofsky), Volume LI. 1976, XII + 410 pp. Also available as paperback.
106. Karel Kosík, *Dialectics of the Concrete,* Boston Studies in the Philosophy of Science (ed. by Robert S. Cohen and Marx W. Wartofsky), Volume LII. 1976, VIII + 158 pp. Also available as paperback.
107. Nelson Goodman, *The Structure of Appearance,* Boston Studies in the Philosophy of Science (ed. by Robert S. Cohen and Marx W. Wartofsky), Volume LIII. 1977, L + 285 pp.
108. Jerzy Giedymin (ed.), *Kazimierz Ajdukiewicz: The Scientific World-Perspective and Other Essays, 1931 - 1963.* 1978, LIII + 378 pp.

109. Robert L. Causey, *Unity of Science*. 1977, VIII+185 pp.
110. Richard E. Grandy, *Advanced Logic for Applications*. 1977, XIV + 168 pp.
111. Robert P. McArthur, *Tense Logic*. 1976, VII + 84 pp.
112. Lars Lindahl, *Position and Change: A Study in Law and Logic*. 1977, IX + 299 pp.
113. Raimo Tuomela, *Dispositions*. 1978, X + 450 pp.
114. Herbert A. Simon, *Models of Discovery and Other Topics in the Methods of Science*, Boston Studies in the Philosophy of Science (ed. by Robert S. Cohen and Marx W. Wartofsky), Volume LIV. 1977, XX + 456 pp. Also available as paperback.
115. Roger D. Rosenkrantz, *Inference, Method and Decision*. 1977, XVI + 262 pp. Also available as paperback.
116. Raimo Tuomela, *Human Action and Its Explanation. A Study on the Philosophical Foundations of Psychology*. 1977, XII + 426 pp.
117. Morris Lazerowitz, *The Language of Philosophy, Freud and Wittgenstein*, Boston Studies in the Philosophy of Science (ed. by Robert S. Cohen and Marx W. Wartofsky), Volume LV. 1977, XVI + 209 pp.
118. Tran Duc Thao, *Origins of Language and Consciousness*, Boston Studies in the Philosophy of Science (ed. by Robert S. Cohen and Marx. W. Wartofsky), Volume LVI. 1977 (forthcoming).
119. Jerzy Pelc, *Semiotics in Poland, 1894 - 1969*. 1977, XXVI + 504 pp.
120. Ingmar Pörn, *Action Theory and Social Science. Some Formal Models*. 1977, X + 129 pp.
121. Joseph Margolis, *Persons and Minds, The Prospects of Nonreductive Materialism*, Boston Studies in the Philosophy of Science (ed. by Robert S. Cohen and Marx W. Wartofsky), Volume LVII. 1977, XIV + 282 pp. Also available as paperback.

SYNTHESE HISTORICAL LIBRARY

Texts and Studies
in the History of Logic and Philosophy

Editors:

N. KRETZMANN (Cornell University)
G. NUCHELMANS (University of Leyden)
L. M. DE RIJK (University of Leyden)

1. M. T. Beonio-Brocchieri Fumagalli, *The Logic of Abelard*. Translated from the Italian. 1969, IX + 101 pp.
2. Gottfried Wilhelm Leibniz, *Philosophical Papers and Letters*. A selection translated and edited, with an introduction, by Leroy E. Loemker. 1969, XII + 736 pp.
3. Ernst Mally, *Logische Schriften*, ed. by Karl Wolf and Paul Weingartner. 1971, X + 340 pp.
4. Lewis White Beck (ed.), *Proceedings of the Third International Kant Congress*. 1972, XI + 718 pp.
5. Bernard Bolzano, *Theory of Science*, ed. by Jan Berg. 1973, XV + 398 pp.
6. J. M. E. Moravcsik (ed.), *Patterns in Plato's Thought. Papers Arising Out of the 1971 West Coast Greek Philosophy Conference*. 1973, VIII + 212 pp.
7. Nabil Shehaby, *The Propositional Logic of Avicenna: A Translation from al-Shifā: al-Qiyās*, with Introduction, Commentary and - Glossary. 1973, XIII + 296 pp.
8. Desmond Paul Henry, *Commentary on De Grammatico: The Historical-Logical Dimensions of a Dialogue of St. Anselm's*. 1974, IX + 345 pp.
9. John Corcoran, *Ancient Logic and Its Modern Interpretations*. 1974, X + 208 pp.
10. E. M. Barth, *The Logic of the Articles in Traditional Philosophy*. 1974, XXVII + 533 pp.
11. Jaakko Hintikka, *Knowledge and the Known. Historical Perspectives in Epistemology*. 1974, XII + 243 pp.
12. E. J. Ashworth, *Language and Logic in the Post-Medieval Period*. 1974, XIII + 304 pp.
13. Aristotle, *The Nicomachean Ethics*. Translated with Commentaries and Glossary by Hypocrates G. Apostle. 1975, XXI + 372 pp.
14. R. M. Dancy, *Sense and Contradiction: A Study in Aristotle*. 1975, XII + 184 pp.
15. Wilbur Richard Knorr, *The Evolution of the Euclidean Elements. A Study of the Theory of Incommensurable Magnitudes and Its Significance for Early Greek Geometry*. 1975, IX + 374 pp.
16. Augustine, *De Dialectica*. Translated with Introduction and Notes by B. Darrell Jackson. 1975, XI + 151 pp.